An Introduction to Executive Compensation

An
Introduction
to
Executive
Compensation

Steven Balsam

The Fox School of Business and Management
Temple University
Philadelphia, Pennsylvania 19122

ACADEMIC PRESS

An Elsevier Science Imprint

San Diego   San Francisco   New York   Boston   London   Sydney   Tokyo

Cover photo credit: © 2001 PhotoDisc, Inc.

This book is printed on acid-free paper. ∞

Academic Press
An Elsevier Science Imprint
525 B Street, Suite 1900, San Diego, California 92101-4495, USA
http://www.academicpress.com

Academic Press
32 Jamestown Road, London NW1 7BY, UK
http://www.academicpress.com

Library of Congress Catalog Card Number: 2002100067

International Standard Book Number: 0-12-077126-8

PRINTED IN THE UNITED STATES OF AMERICA
02   03   04   05   06   07   EB   9   8   7   6   5   4   3   2   1

To my loving wife Lori,
my wonderful daughter Gabby,
and in honor of my parents,
who dedicated their lives to raising me.

Contents

PART 1

An Introduction

1   *Introduction*

2   *Overview of the Compensation Package*

3 An Introduction to Designing the Executive Compensation Contract

PART II

The Components of the Compensation Package

4 Salary

5 *Bonuses: Short- and Long-Term*

6 *Stock Grants and Options*

7   *Deferred Compensation*

PART III

Related Issues

8 *Ownership of the Corporation*

9 *Corporate Governance*

PART IV

Considerations in Designing the Executive Compensation Package

10 Is Executive Compensation Really That High?

11 *The Effect of Corporate and Executive Characteristics on Designing an Optimal Compensation Contract*

12 *Designing a Compensation Contract*

PART V

Conclusion

13 *Recent Trends and Their Implications for the Future of Executive Compensation*

Acknowledgments

I would like to thank Laure Brasch and Donna Laansma for their invaluable research that helped me to prepare this book, as well as Debra Sinclair, Richard Gifford, and David Ryan for reading earlier versions of the manuscript. I would also like to thank the Fox School of Business, especially, Senior Associate Dean, Rajan Chandran, for their support in this endeavor. Finally, I would like to thank my wife Lori, who not only put up with me during the writing of the book, but who also contributed her time as a research assistant and editor.

PART I

An Introduction

CHAPTER 1

Introduction

I. INTRODUCTION AND OVERVIEW

Compensation paid to the top executives of publicly traded corporations is a polit-ically sensitive area, with critics claiming that amounts paid executives are too high (e.g., Crystal 1991), and corporations arguing they need to pay well to attract, retain, and motivate quality people (e.g., Kay 1998).[1] Opponents of current levels of executive pay, for example the AFL–CIO (Rose 1998), have resorted to publiciz-ing what they feel are excessive amounts via their Executive Pay Watch Internet Site (<http://www.aflcio.org/paywatch/index.htm> and introducing legislation in Congress (see Appendices 10.1, 10.2, and 10.3). Others have argued (e.g., Jensen and Murphy 1990b) that it's not how much you pay, but how you pay that matters. Regardless of your view, executive compensation, in particular that of the chief executive officer (CEO), is well followed in both academic journals and the popular press. For example, annual surveys of executive compensation are a fixture in most business publications and major newspapers, for example, *Forbes, Business Week, Fortune, The Wall Street Journal,* and *The Philadelphia Inquirer.*

Executive compensation is important. A well-designed compensation plan can reward both executives and shareholders, whereas a poorly designed one can waste corporate resources without motivating the executive. Research has shown that when the corporation is performing poorly, shareholder proposals on executive compensation are likely to be made (Thomas and Martin 1999). Other research shows that stock prices react positively to initiation or amendment of compensation plans (Morgan and Poulsen 2000; Brickley et al. 1985; Tehranian and Waegelein 1985), indicating that shareholders believe the plans will motivate executives to

---

[1]This controversy extends to not-for-profit institutions as well. In 1992 an uproar resulted from the disclosure that United Way of America President William Aramony had received an annual compensa-tion package worth $463,000. Even though Aramony resigned his position shortly after this disclosure, it was estimated that United Way collections would be down 10% in 1992 from the year earlier, with the implication that some, if not all of the drop was caused by the scandal (Stodghill et al. 1992).

increase shareholder value.[2] Executive compensation is also important because it affects compensation levels and composition throughout the organization (Gomez-Mejia 1994). It affects the level of compensation because lower management compensation is often a function of upper management compensation, and it affects the composition of their compensation package because the same goals may be applied as well. This book will examine the components of the compensation plan, identifying the effects and consequences of its various aspects, as well as discuss how to design an optimal plan for a set of circumstances.

Underlying the need for, and importance of, executive compensation plans is the separation of ownership from the control of the modern corporation (Berle and Means 1932; Jensen and Meckling 1976). Thus, the goal of the executive compensation plan is to align the interests of executives and stakeholders, commonly assumed to be shareholders. Issues to be discussed in this book include the components of the plan, the allocation of compensation among the components, the role of the individual components in motivating and retaining employees, and mitigating the owner–manager conflict. This discussion will draw upon the practitioner and academic literature as well as the popular press, including descriptive statistics and examples from well-known companies.

A basic assumption of this book, and of much of the academic literature, is that individuals are work averse, that is, they prefer to work as little and consume as much leisure as possible. One way, but not the only nor even the most efficient way, to overcome this tendency is with economic incentives. Without incentives, employees will slack off, providing the minimal effort necessary to retain their jobs. In fact, although this book focuses on the executive suite, much of the discussion is readily applicable to lower level employees. Much of corporate America already realizes this, as it continues to provide incentives such as commissions, bonuses, and stock options to more and more employees. Examples include paying salespeople by commission and authors with royalties. In the executive compensation arena, the current trend is stock options. Although stock options are a primary tool of compensation of high-technology corporations (e.g., Amazon.com, AOL, Dell, Intel, Microsoft), certain blue-chip corporations (e.g., Eli Lilly, Sunbeam, General Mills, Procter & Gamble, Du Pont, PepsiCo, Kimberly-Clark) grant stock options to every one of their employees. Further, the discussion also applies to profit and nonprofit organizations, although the latter need to be more creative (e.g., the Katz School of Business at the University of Pittsburgh).

Proper compensation is necessary to recruit and retain employees. If compensation is too low relative to the employee's best alternative opportunity, he or she will leave. Microsoft recently "increased base pay and stock options for most of its 30,000 employees," stating it was "an essential part of Microsoft staying competitive and

---

[2]An alternative view is that executives, who possess inside information, introduce or revise these plans when they believe the corporation is undervalued. Thus, the increased price reaction is a response to the information released, rather than the initiation or revision of the plan itself.

successful" (Bank 1999, p. B10). But how does one determine what is too low? Additionally, across-the-board pay raises may be insufficient to keep stellar performers and simply end up rewarding those who would have stayed otherwise, that is, those not valued by the marketplace.

II. OWNER–MANAGER CONFLICT: AGENCY THEORY

Understanding the executive compensation package and its role in the modern corporation requires a basic understanding of corporate governance, a topic that will be discussed in more detail in Chapter 9. In the modern, and sometimes not so modern, corporation, the ownership and management functions are separated. This separation can arise from two situations. In the first situation, there are individuals with preexisting businesses who either do not have the desire and/or skills required to manage the business. In the second, there are individuals with good ideas or products that may not have the funds necessary to bring those products to market and/or sustain themselves through the start-up period and thus must seek outside investors. Our capital markets, both public and private, allow these individuals to meet and transact business in a way favorable to both. Public capital markets include domestic and international stock and bond markets (for example, the New York and Tokyo Stock Exchanges). Private capital markets include venture capitalists, banks, friends, neighbors, and relatives. Given the freedom to contract, or not to contract, it is generally assumed that contracts are entered into only when both parties expect to profit.

This separation of the ownership and management functions can lead to conflicts. For example, although the owner(s) are concerned with the maximization of the value of their stake in the corporation, the executive(s) are concerned with the maximization of their well-being, which involves a trade-off between maximizing their wealth and minimizing their effort. At the extreme, owners bear the risk that executives will transfer the assets to themselves, which is to say, they will steal the assets. Although not a major risk in countries with well-developed legal systems, the risk does exist.[3] A more likely scenario is that executives, although not stealing the assets, may not manage them in a value-maximizing way. That is, they might pass up profitable investments because taking those investments would require increased effort on their part. They might also overconsume the perquisites of their position, for example, purchase a corporate jet rather than fly commercial airlines.

Academics refer to the costs arising from the separation of the ownership from the management of the corporation as *agency costs* (see Jensen and Meckling 1976). If these costs can be reduced, the gains can be shared between the owners and executives. Therefore, owners and executives have the incentive to minimize these costs.

[3]For an example of these problems in less developed nations see Leggett (2000).

The mechanisms for controlling the incentive conflicts arising from the separation of the ownership and control of the corporation include, but are not limited to, monitoring by large shareholders and the board of directors, equity ownership by executives, the market for corporate control, the managerial labor market, and compensation contracts that provide incentives to increase shareholder value. In publicly held corporations, shareholders elect a board of directors, which in turn has the power to hire and fire executives. They also have the responsibility of setting executive compensation, the topic of this book. The board may have a committee devoted to compensation issues, which is sometimes referred to as the compensation committee.

Monitoring by the board of directors has its limitations. For example, the board cannot review every decision the executive makes, and even if they could, they may lack the firm- or industry-specific expertise to evaluate those decisions.[4] Furthermore, given that most directors have limited investment in the corporations on whose board they sit, a director's incentives also may not be aligned with those of shareholders. The existence of a large shareholder, be it an individual or institution, can mitigate this problem as the large shareholder has both the incentives and the financial resources to monitor management.

Ownership by executives (discussed in more detail in Chapter 8) mitigates the incentive conflicts by aligning the interests of executives with those of shareholders. By making the executives shareholders in the corporation, they, like other shareholders, are interested in seeing the corporation's share price increase. Unfortunately, given that most executives have rather limited resources when compared to the market values of their employer, executives own rather small amounts of their employer. When the executive wealth constraint is combined with risk aversion, it may not be in the best interests of other shareholders for an executive to have a large amount of his or her wealth tied up in the corporation's stock (discussed in Chapter 8).

The market for corporate control, in theory, provides executives with incentives to increase shareholder value. If executives manage the corporation in a suboptimal way, the value of the corporation's shares will be low, and if a group of individuals or another corporation believes it could manage the corporation more efficiently, it has the incentive to purchase the corporation to obtain the increase in value from the improved management. If such a purchase were to occur, it is highly likely that the new owners would fire the executives it believed were managing the corporation suboptimally in the first place.

The managerial labor market, or market for a particular executive's services, mitigates the incentive conflicts by providing executives with the incentive to perform well, thereby increasing their market value, that is, their value to other potential employers. Unfortunately, some of the techniques used to retain executives,

---

[4]One reason the board cannot review every decision is the limited amount of time they have to spend on corporate matters, especially if the corporation is not their primary employer. For example, Silverman (2000b) reports that directors work an average of 173 hours annually.

such as noncompete agreements (discussed in Chapter 3), also reduce the incentives provided by the managerial labor market. That is, an executive with a noncompete agreement is contractually prohibited from working for some potential employers for a period of time after he or she leaves his or her current employer. Thus, that executive has less motivation to be concerned about his or her value to other employers.

The compensation package can also be used to align the interests of owners and executives. Properly designed, the compensation package can be a tool for mitigating the conflict between owners and executives. It does so by rewarding executives for taking actions that increase shareholder value. Owners (and directors) unfortunately have incomplete information about the actions of executives. Furthermore, they may not have the expertise to evaluate those actions, even if the actions are observable. Thus it is difficult to base compensation on actions alone. Rather, compensation is often tied to measures that are positively correlated with managerial effort, for example, accounting income or market share.

III. OTHER THEORIES EXPLAINING AND INFLUENCING EXECUTIVE COMPENSATION

Under agency theory, the compensation package is important because it is used to provide the proper incentives to executives, and hence, mitigate the conflict between owners and executives. Although the majority of this book, and many of the academic studies cited herein, are grounded in agency theory, other theories, both competing and complementary, exist to explain the composition and importance of the executive compensation package and will be (implicitly) drawn upon throughout the book. These theories include *class hegemony, efficiency wage, figurehead, human capital theory, marginal productivity, prospect, social comparison,* and *tournament theory.*

Class hegemony theory argues that executives share a common bond and that through boards composed primarily of CEOs, executives are able to pursue their own goals and interests (and not those of shareholders). In particular, Gomez-Mejia (1994) noted that "board input is primarily used to legitimize high executive pay, reflecting a shared commitment to protect the privileges and wealth of the managerial class," (p. 180). *Efficiency wage theory* (Prendergast 1999) suggests that executives are paid a premium to provide them with the incentive to exert effort to avoid being fired. This premium leads them to put forth effort, because of the consequences of being fired, that is, having to accept another position at a lower wage. In theory, this effort increases executive productivity and reduces turnover. Ungson and Steers (1984) argue that the CEO, unlike an operational manager, should not be paid based upon operating results, but rather for his or her role as leader or political figurehead (*figurehead theory*). As such, the CEO is both a symbol and representative of the corporation, representing the corporation at ceremonial events and political functions and managing interactions with owners, employees, government, and the general public. Under *human capital theory*, the value of the executive, and hence, his or her compensation, is based upon his or her accumulated knowledge and skills. Agarwal (1981, p. 39) explains the logic behind human capital theory:

> The amount of human capital a worker possesses influences his productivity, which in turn influences his earnings. The same general reason should hold for executives as well. Other things being equal, an executive with a greater amount of human capital would be better able to perform his job and thus be paid more.

Managerialism theory argues "that the separation of ownership and control in modern corporations gives top managers almost absolute power to use the firm to pursue their personal objectives" (Gomez-Mejia 1994, p. 179). They could then use this power to increase the level and reduce the risk of their compensation. Under *marginal productivity theory*, in equilibrium the executive should receive as compensation his or her value to the corporation. Gomez-Mejia (1994) defined this as the "observed performance of the firm minus what performance would be if the next best alternative executive was at the helm, plus the pay that would be necessary to acquire the latter's services" (p. 177). In contrast to agency theory, which assumes risk aversion, *prospect theory* focuses on the executive's loss aversion (Wiseman and Gomez-Mejia 1998). That is, in certain circumstances, for example, to avoid losses or missing goals or targets, the executive is actually willing to take risks. In contrast, the executive is unwilling to take risk once he or she has achieved his or her performance goals, as the benefit (to the executive) of increasing performance is more than offset by the possibility of falling below target. Under *social comparison theory*, board members use their own pay as a reference point when setting pay of executives (O'Reilly et al. 1988). Under *tournament theory* (Lazear and Rosen 1981; Rosen 1986), executive compensation is set to provide incentives, not to the executives themselves, but rather to their subordinates. The executive may in fact receive no incentives from the package, and he or she may be overpaid relative to his or her marginal product or value to the corporation. The incentive is for lower level executives to work hard, win the tournament, and be promoted to receive that higher level of compensation. Rosen (1986, p. 714) claimed, "Payments at the top have indirect effects of increasing productivity of competitors further down the ladder."

IV. EXTERNAL INFLUENCES ON THE COMPENSATION PACKAGE

A number of items external to the corporation and the executive influence both the amount and composition of the compensation package. For example, different components of the compensation package have different financial reporting treatments. That is, although items like salary and bonus reduce reported accounting income when earned by the executive, in most cases stock options do not reduce reporting accounting income. Given the desire of executives to report a higher level of income, this differential accounting treatment may cause them to design compensation packages that include more stock options, and less other compensation, than would otherwise be optimal.

Similarly, components of the compensation package are not treated equally for tax purposes. For example, Section 162(m) of the Internal Revenue Code limits the deductibility of compensation to the CEO and the next four highest paid executives to $1 million per individual, with an exception allowed if compensation is "performance based." Whereas salary can never be performance based, bonus plans can be modified to meet the exception, and in most cases, stock option plans are performance based by definition. Thus, the tax code provides incentives for corporations subject to this constraint to shift compensation from salary to bonus and stock option plans.

Finally, the political environment surrounding executive compensation has the potential to influence the level and composition of the compensation package because of the potential "political costs" that may be imposed upon the executive and the corporation. Narrowly defined, political costs are the costs imposed upon the executive and the corporation by the government's ability to tax and regulate. An example would be Section 162(m) of the Internal Revenue Code, which limited tax deductions, and hence, increased the after tax cost of executive compensation. Political costs also include actions taken by nongovernment regulators. For example, during the 1990s the Financial Accounting Standards Board (FASB) attempted to require corporations to recognize an expense for the stock options granted to employees, and did require corporations to recognize an expense for those options that are repriced. Broadly defined, political costs include the costs imposed upon the executive and the corporation by interested parties, which include, but are not limited to, politicians, regulators, unions, suppliers, and customers. These parties have made periodic accusations that executive compensation is excessive and unrelated to corporate performance. In theory, the pressure and costs imposed by these parties could reduce the level of executive compensation, and/or cause a shift from the components of compensation that are not based upon corporate performance (e.g., salaries and pensions) towards components of compensation that are based upon corporate performance (e.g., bonuses and stock options).

It is interesting to note that all three of these factors, that is, financial reporting, taxation, and political pressure, provide incentives for corporations to issue more stock options to their executives, which is exactly what has been observed in practice. This trend is documented in Chapter 2, and discussed throughout the book.

V. SOURCES OF DATA ON EXECUTIVE COMPENSATION

Data on executive compensation are contained in proxy statements mailed to shareholders and filed with the Securities and Exchange Commission (SEC). The SEC then makes these statements publicly available, both in their offices and on-line, via their Electronic Data Gathering, Analysis, and Retrieval system (EDGAR) at http://www.sec.gov/edaux. Section §229.402. Item 402, of SEC Regulation S-K (reproduced in Appendix 1.1) requires and governs the disclosures. It requires [see subsection (b)] disclosure of the following items of compensation for the CEO and the next four highest paid executives for the most recent 3-year period: salary, bonus, other annual compensation, restricted stock awards, (number of) securities underlying options and stock appreciation rights, long-term incentive plan payouts, and all other compensation. Additionally for options and stock appreciation rights granted during the previous fiscal year, the corporation must disclose the following [see subsection (c)] for the CEO and the next four highest paid executives: the number of securities underlying the grant, the percentage of options the grant represented relative to the total grants to all employees during the year, the exercise price, the expiration date, and the potential realizable value of the option assuming annual appreciation of 5 and 10% respectively, or alternatively the grant date value of the options calculated using an option-pricing model. In the proxy statement the compensation committee of the board of directors must also prepare a report [see subsection (k)], which discusses the corporation's compensation policies applicable to executive officers, the specific relationship of corporate performance to executive compensation, and the criteria upon which the CEO's pay was based. Finally, the corporation must present a graph [see subsection (l)] that shows how the returns to owning its common shares over the previous 5 years compared to the returns to owning a broad market index, and either a published industry or line-of-business index, peer issuer(s) selected in good faith, or issuer(s) with similar market capitalization(s).

This information is then compiled and disseminated in a number of ways. News organizations (e.g., *Forbes, Business Week, The Wall Street Journal, The Philadelphia Inquirer*) all publish annual surveys of executive compensation, in effect making the information freely available to the public in a more accessible form. Data intermediaries, such as Executive Compensation Advisory Services, compile and maintain databases of this information, which they then use to provide customized reports to clients. The database utilized in this book is Standard & Poors (S&P) ExecuComp, which contains information on executive compensation in the 1500 companies comprising the S&P 500, S&P MidCap 400, and S&P SmallCap 600 indices.

APPENDIX 1.1. ITEM 402 OF SEC REGULATION S-K

1. Executive Compensation.
   Reg. §229.402. Item 402

   (a) *General.*

   (1) *Treatment of Specific Types of Issuers.*

   (i) *Small Business Issuers.* A registrant that qualifies as "small business issuer," as defined by Item 10(a)(1) of Regulation S-B [17 CFR 228.10(a)(1)], will be deemed to comply with this item if it provides the information required by paragraph (b) (Summary Compensation Table), paragraphs (c)(1) and (c)(2)(i)-(v) (Option/SAR Grants Table), paragraph (d) (Aggregated Option/SAR Exercise and Fiscal Year-End Option/SAR Value Table), paragraph (e) (Long-Term Incentive Plan Awards Table), paragraph (g) (Compensation of Directors), paragraph (h) (Employment Contracts, Termination of Employment and Change in Control Arrangements) and paragraph (i)(1) and (2) (Report on Repricing of Options/SARs) of this item.

   (ii) *Foreign Private Issuers.* A foreign private issuer will be deemed to comply with this item if it provides the information required by Items 11 and 12 of Form 20-F [17 CFR 249.220f], with more detailed information provided if otherwise made publicly available.

   (2) *All Compensation Covered.* This item requires clear, concise and understandable disclosure of all plan and non-plan compensation awarded to, earned by, or paid to the named executive officers designated under paragraph (a)(3) of this item, and directors covered by paragraph (g) of this item by any person for all services rendered in all capacities to the registrant and its subsidiaries, unless otherwise specified in this item. Except as provided by paragraph (a)(5) of this item, all such compensation shall be reported pursuant to this item, even if also called for by another requirement, including transactions between the registrant and a third party where the primary purpose of the transaction is to furnish compensation to any such named executive officer or director. No item reported as compensation for one fiscal year need be reported as compensation for a subsequent fiscal year.

   (3) *Persons Covered.* Disclosure shall be provided pursuant to this item for each of the following (the "named executive officers"):

   (i) All individuals serving as the registrant's chief executive officer or acting in a similar capacity during the last completed fiscal year ("CEO"), regardless of compensation level;

(ii) The registrant's four most highly compensated executive officers other than the CEO who were serving as executive officers at the end of the last completed fiscal year; and

(iii) up to two additional individuals for whom disclosure would have been provided pursuant to paragraph (a)(3)(ii) of this item but for the fact that the individual was not serving as an executive officer of the registrant at the end of the last completed fiscal year.

1. *Instructions to Item 402(a)(3).*

   1. *Determination of Most Highly Compensated Executive Officers.* The determination as to which executive officers are most highly compensated shall be made by reference to total annual salary and bonus for the last completed fiscal year (as required to be disclosed pursuant to paragraph (b)(2)(iii)(A) and (B) of this item), but including the dollar value of salary or bonus amounts forgone pursuant to Instruction 3 to paragraph (b)(2)(iii)(A) and (B) of this item, *provided, however,* that no disclosure need be provided for any executive officer, other than the CEO, whose total annual salary and bonus, as so determined, does not exceed $100,000.

   2. *Inclusion of Executive Officer of Subsidiary.* It may be appropriate in certain circumstances for a registrant to include an executive officer of a subsidiary in the disclosure required by this item. *See* Rule 3b-7 under the Exchange Act [17 CFR 240.3b7].

   3. *Exclusion of Executive Officer due to Unusual or Overseas Compensation.* It may be appropriate in limited circumstances for a registrant not to include in the disclosure required by this item an individual, other than its CEO, who is one of the registrant's most highly compensated executive officers. Among the factors that should be considered in determining not to name an individual are: (a) the distribution or accrual of an unusually large amount of cash compensation (such as a bonus or commission) that is not part of a recurring arrangement and is unlikely to continue; and (b) the payment of amounts of cash compensation relating to overseas assignments that may be attributed predominantly to such assignments.

(4) *Information for Full Fiscal Year.* If the CEO served in that capacity during any part of a fiscal year with respect to which information is required, information should be provided as to all of his or her compensation for the full fiscal year. If a named executive officer (other than the CEO) served as an executive officer of the registrant (whether or not in the same position) during any part of a fiscal year with respect to which information is required, information shall be provided as to all compensation of that individual for the full fiscal year.

(5) *Transactions With Third Parties Reported under Item 404.* This item includes transactions between the registrant and a third party where the primary purpose of the transaction is to furnish compensation to a named executive officer. No information need be given in response to any paragraph of this item, other than paragraph (j), as to any such third-party transaction if the transaction has been reported in response to Item 404 of Regulation S-K (§229.404).

(6) *Omission of Table or Column.* A table or column may be omitted, if there has been no compensation awarded to, earned by or paid to any of the named executives required to be reported in that table or column in any fiscal year covered by that table.

(7) *Definitions.* For purposes of this item:

(i) The term *stock appreciation rights* ("SARs") refers to SARs payable in cash or stock, including SARs payable in cash or stock at the election of the registrant or a named executive officer.

(ii) The term *plan* includes, but is not limited to, the following: any plan, contract, authorization or arrangement, whether or not set forth in any formal documents, pursuant to which the following may be received: cash, stock, restricted stock or restricted stock units, phantom stock, stock options, SARs, stock options in tandem with SARs, warrants, convertible securities, performance units and performance shares, and similar instruments. A plan may be applicable to one person. Registrants may omit information regarding group life, health, hospitalization, medical reimbursement or relocation plans that do not discriminate in scope, terms or operation, in favor of executive officers or directors of the registrant and that are available generally to all salaried employees.

(iii) The term *long-term incentive plan* means any plan providing compensation intended to serve as incentive for performance to occur over a period longer than one fiscal year, whether such performance is measured by reference to financial performance of the registrant or an affiliate, the registrant's stock price, or any other measure, but excluding restricted stock, stock option and SAR plans.

(8) *Location of Specified Information.* The information required by paragraphs (i), (k) and (l) of this item need not be provided in any filings other than a registrant proxy or information statement relating to an annual meeting of security holders at which directors are to be elected (or special meeting or written consents in lieu of such meeting). Such information will not be deemed to be incorporated by reference into any filing under the Securities Act or the Exchange Act, except to the extent that the registrant specifically incorporates it by reference.

(9) *Liability for Specified Information.* The information required by paragraphs (k) and (l) of this item shall not be deemed to be "soliciting material" or to be "filed" with the Commission or subject to Regulations 14A or 14C [17 CFR 240.14a-1 *et seq.* or 240.14c-1 *et seq.*], other than as provided in this item, or to the liabilities of Section 18 of the Exchange Act [15 U.S.C. 78r], except to the extent that the registrant specifically requests that such information be treated as soliciting material or specifically incorporates it by reference into a filing under the Securities Act or the Exchange Act.

(b) *Summary Compensation Table.*

1. (1) *General.* The information specified in paragraph (b)(2) of this item, concerning the compensation of the named executive officers for each of the registrant's last three completed fiscal years, shall be provided in a Summary Compensation Table, in the tabular format specified below.

Summary Compensation Table

	Annual compensation				Long term compensation			
					Awards		Payouts	
(a) Name and principal position	(b) Year	(c) Salary ($)	(d) Bonus ($)	(e) Other annual compen- sation ($)	(f) Restricted stock award(s) ($)	(g) Securities underlying options/ SARs (#)	(h) LTIP payouts ($)	(i) All other compen- sation ($)
CEO	——							
	——							
	——							
A	——							
	——							
	——							
B	——							
	——							
	——							
C	——							
	——							
	——							
D	——							
	——							
	——							

(2) The Table shall include:

(i) The name and principal position of the executive officer (column (a));

(ii) Fiscal year covered (column (b));

(iii) Annual compensation (columns (c), (d) and (e)), including:

(A) The dollar value of base salary (cash and non-cash) earned by the named executive officer during the fiscal year covered (column (c));

(B) The dollar value of bonus (cash and non-cash) earned by the named executive officer during the fiscal year covered (column (d)); and

1. *Instructions to Item 402(b)(2)(iii)(A) and (B).*

1. Amounts deferred at the election of a named executive officer, whether pursuant to a plan established under Section 401(k) of the Internal Revenue Code [26 U.S.C. 401(k)], or otherwise, shall be included in the salary column (column (c)) or bonus column (column (d)), as appropriate, for the fiscal year in which earned. If the amount of salary or bonus earned in a given fiscal year is not calculable through the latest practicable date, that fact must be disclosed in a footnote and such amount must be disclosed in the subsequent fiscal year in the appropriate column for the fiscal year in which earned.

2. For stock or any other form of non-cash compensation, disclose the fair market value at the time the compensation is awarded, earned or paid.

3. Registrants need not include in the salary column (column (c)) or bonus column (column (d)) any amount of salary or bonus forgone at the election of a named executive officer pursuant to a registrant program under which stock, stock-based or other forms of non-cash compensation may be received by a named executive in lieu of a portion of annual compensation earned in a covered fiscal year. However, the receipt of any such form of non-cash compensation in lieu of salary or bonus earned for a covered fiscal year must be disclosed in the appropriate column of the Table corresponding to that fiscal year (i.e., restricted stock awards

(column (f)); options or SARs (column (g)); all other compensation (column (i)), or, if made pursuant to a long-term incentive plan and therefore not reportable at grant in the Summary Compensation Table, a footnote must be added to the salary or bonus column so disclosing and referring to the Long-Term Incentive Plan Table (required by paragraph (e) of this item) where the award is reported.

(C) The dollar value of other annual compensation not properly categorized as salary or bonus, as follows (column (e)):

(*1*) Perquisites and other personal benefits, securities or property, unless the aggregate amount of such compensation is the lesser of either $50,000 or 10% of the total of annual salary and bonus reported for the named executive officer in columns (c) and (d);

(*2*) Above-market or preferential earnings on restricted stock, options, SARs or deferred compensation paid during the fiscal year or payable during that period but deferred at the election of the named executive officer;

(*3*) Earnings on long-term incentive plan compensation paid during the fiscal year or payable during that period but deferred at the election of the named executive officer;

(*4*) Amounts reimbursed during the fiscal year for the payment of taxes; and

(*5*) The dollar value of the difference between the price paid by a named executive officer for any security of the registrant or its subsidiaries purchased from the registrant or its subsidiaries (through deferral of salary or bonus, or otherwise), and the fair market value of such security at the date of purchase, unless that discount is available generally, either to all security holders or to all salaried employees of the registrant.

1. *Instructions to Item 402(b)(2)(iii)(C).*

1. Each perquisite or other personal benefit exceeding 25% of the total perquisites and other personal benefits reported for a named executive officer must be identified by type and amount in a footnote or accompanying narrative discussion to column (e).

2. Perquisites and other personal benefits shall be valued on the basis of the aggregate incremental cost to the registrant and its subsidiaries.

3. Interest on deferred or long-term compensation is above-market only if the rate of interest exceeds 120% of the applicable federal long-term rate, with compounding (as prescribed under Section 1274(d) of the Internal Revenue Code, [26 U.S.C. 1274(d)]) at the rate that corresponds most closely to the rate under the registrant's plan at the time the interest rate or formula is set. In the event of a discretionary reset of the interest rate, the requisite calculation must be made on the basis of the interest rate at the time of such reset, rather than when originally established. Only the above-market portion of the interest must be included. If the applicable interest rates vary depending upon conditions such as a minimum period of continued service, the reported amount should be calculated assuming satisfaction of all conditions to receiving interest at the highest rate.

4. Dividends (and dividend equivalents) on restricted stock, options, SARs or deferred compensation denominated in stock ("deferred stock") are preferential only if earned at a rate higher than dividends on the registrant's common stock. Only the preferential portion of the dividends or equivalents must be included.

(iv) Long-term compensation (columns (f), (g) and (h)), including:

(A) The dollar value (net of any consideration paid by the named executive officer) of any award of restricted stock, including share units (calculated by multiplying the closing market price of the registrant's unrestricted stock on the date of grant by the number of shares awarded) (column (f));

(B) The sum of the number of securities underlying stock options granted (including options that subsequently have been transferred), with or without tandem SARs, and the number of freestanding SARs (column (g)); and

(C) The dollar value of all payouts pursuant to long-term incentive plans ("LTIPs") as defined in paragraph (a)(7)(iii) of this item (column (h)).

1. *Instructions to Item 402(b)(2)(iv).*

   1. Awards of restricted stock that are subject to performance-based conditions on vesting, in addition to lapse of time and/or continued service with the registrant or a subsidiary, may be reported as LTIP awards pursuant to paragraph (e) of this item instead of in column (f). If this approach is selected, once the restricted stock vests, it must be reported as an LTIP payout in column (h).

   2. The registrant shall, in a footnote to the Summary Compensation Table (appended to column (f), if included), disclose:

      a. The number and value of the aggregate restricted stock holdings at the end of the last completed fiscal year. The value shall be calculated in the manner specified in paragraph (b)(2)(iv)(A) of this item using the value of the registrant's shares at the end of the last completed fiscal year.

      b. For any restricted stock award reported in the Summary Compensation Table that will vest, in whole or in part, in under three years from the date of grant, the total number of shares awarded and the vesting schedule; and

      c. Whether dividends will be paid on the restricted stock reported in column (f).

   3. If at any time during the last completed fiscal year, the registrant has adjusted or amended the exercise price of stock options or freestanding SARs previously awarded to a named executive officer, whether through amendment, cancellation or replacement grants, or any other means ("repriced"), the registrant shall include the number of options or freestanding SARs so repriced as Stock Options/SARs granted and required to be reported in column (g).

   4. If any specified performance target, goal or condition to payout was waived with respect to any amount included in LTIP payouts reported in column (h), the registrant shall so state in a footnote to column (h).

(v) All other compensation for the covered fiscal year that the registrant could not properly report in any other column of the Summary Compensation Table (column (i)). Any compensation reported in this column for the last completed fiscal year shall be identified and quantified in a footnote. Such compensation shall include, but not be limited to:

(A) The amount paid, payable or accrued to any named executive officer pursuant to a plan or arrangement in connection with:

(*1*) The resignation, retirement or any other termination of such executive officer's employment with the registrant and its subsidiaries; or

(*2*) A change in control of the registrant or a change in the executive officer's responsibilities following such a change in control;

(B) The dollar value of above-market or preferential amounts earned on restricted stock, options, SARs or deferred compensation during the fiscal year, or calculated with respect to that period, except that if such amounts are paid during the period, or payable during the period but deferred at the election of a named executive officer, this information shall be reported as Other Annual Compensation in column (e). *See* Instructions 3 and 4 to paragraph 402(b)(2)(iii)(C) of this item;

(C) The dollar value of amounts earned on long-term incentive plan compensation during the fiscal year, or calculated with respect to that period, except that if such amounts are paid during that period, or payable during that period at the election of the named executive officer, this information shall be reported as Other Annual Compensation in column (e);

(D) Annual registrant contributions or other allocations to vested and unvested defined contribution plans; and

(E) The dollar value of any insurance premiums paid by, or on behalf of, the registrant during the covered fiscal year with respect to term life insurance for the benefit of a named executive officer, and, if there is any arrangement or understanding, whether formal or informal, that such executive officer has or will receive or be allocated an interest in any cash surrender value under the insurance policy, either

(*1*) The full dollar value of the remainder of the premiums paid by, or on behalf of, the registrant; or

(*2*) If the premiums will be refunded to the registrant on termination of the policy, the dollar value of the benefit to the executive officer of the remainder of the premium paid by, or on behalf of, the registrant during the fiscal year. The benefit shall be determined for the period, projected on an actuarial basis, between payment of the premium and the refund.

1. *Instructions to Item 402(b)(2)(v).*

    1. LTIP awards and amounts received on exercise of options and SARs need not be reported as All Other Compensation in column (i).

    2. Information relating to defined benefit and actuarial plans should not be reported pursuant to paragraph (b) of this item, but instead should be reported pursuant to paragraph (f) of this item.

    3. Where alternative methods of reporting are available under paragraph (b)(2)(v)(E) of this item, the same method should be used for each of the named executive officers. If the registrant chooses to change methods from one year to the next, that fact, and the reason therefor, should be disclosed in a footnote to column (i).

Instruction to Item 402(b). Information with respect to fiscal years prior to the last completed fiscal year will not be required if the registrant was not a reporting company pursuant to Section 13(a) or 15(d) of the Exchange Act at any time during that year, except that the registrant will be required to provide information for any such year if that information previously was required to be provided in response to a Commission filing requirement.

(c) *Option/SAR Grants Table.*

(1) The information specified in paragraph (c)(2) of this item, concerning individual grants of stock options (whether or not in tandem with SARs), and freestanding SARs (including options and SARs that subsequently have been transferred) made during the last completed fiscal year to each of the named executive officers shall be provided in the tabular format specified below:

Option/SAR Grants in Last Fiscal Year

		Individual grants			Potential realizable value at assumed annual rates of stock price appreciation for option term		Alternative to (f) and (g): grant date value
(a)	(b)	(c)	(d)	(e)	(f)	(g)	(h)
CEO							
A							
B							
C							
D							

(2) The Table shall include, with respect to each grant:

(i) The name of the executive officer (column (a));

(ii) The number of securities underlying options and SARs granted (column (b));

(iii) The percent the grant represents of total options and SARs granted to employees during the fiscal year (column (c));

(iv) The per-share exercise or base price of the options or SARs granted (column (d)). If such exercise or base price is less than the market price of the underlying security on the date of grant, a separate, adjoining column shall be added showing market price on the date of grant;

(v) The expiration date of the options or SARs (column (e)); and

(vi) Either (A) the potential realizable value of each grant of options or freestanding SARs or (B) the present value of each grant, as follows:

(A) The potential realizable value of each grant of options or freestanding SARs, assuming that the market price of the underlying security appreciates in value from the date of grant to the end of the option or SAR term, at the following annualized rates:

(*1*) 5% (column (f));

(*2*) 10% (column (g)); and

(*3*) If the exercise or base price was below the market price of the underlying security at the date of grant, provide an additional column labeled 0%, to show the value at grant-date market price; or

(B) The present value of the grant at the date of grant, under any option pricing model (alternative column (f)).

1. *Instructions to Item 402(c).*

1. If more than one grant of options and/or freestanding SARs was made to a named executive officer during the last completed fiscal year, a separate line should be used to provide disclosure of each such grant. However, multiple grants during a single fiscal year may be aggregated where each grant was made at the same exercise and/or base price and has the same expiration date, and the same performance vesting thresholds, if any. A single grant consisting of options and/or freestanding SARs shall be reported as separate grants with respect to each tranche with a different exercise and/or base price, performance vesting threshold, or expiration date.

2. Options or freestanding SARs granted in connection with an option repricing transaction shall be reported in this table. *See* Instruction 3 to paragraph (b)(2)(iv) of this item.

3. Any material term of the grant, including but not limited to the date of exercisability, the number of SARs, performance units or other instruments granted in tandem with options, a performance-based condition to exercisability, a reload feature, or a tax-reimbursement feature, shall be footnoted.

4. If the exercise or base price is adjustable over the term of any option or freestanding SAR in accordance with any prescribed standard or formula, including but not limited to an index or premium price provision, describe the following, either by footnote to column (c) or in narrative accompanying the Table: (a) the standard or formula; and (b) any constant assumption made by the registrant regarding any adjustment to the exercise price in calculating the potential option or SAR value.

5. If any provision of a grant (other than an antidilution provision) could cause the exercise price to be lowered, registrants must clearly and fully disclose these provisions and their potential consequences either by a footnote or accompanying textual narrative.

6. In determining the grant-date market or base price of the security underlying options or freestanding SARs, the registrant may use either the closing market price per share of the security, or any other formula prescribed for the security.

7. The potential realizable dollar value of a grant (columns (f) and (g)) shall be the product of: (a) the difference between: (i) the product of the per-share market price at the time of the grant and the sum of 1 plus the adjusted stock price appreciation rate (the assumed rate of appreciation compounded annually over the term of the option or SAR); and (ii) the per-share exercise price of the option or SAR; and (b) the number of securities underlying the grant at fiscal year-end.

8. Registrants may add one or more separate columns using the formula prescribed in Instruction 7 to paragraph (c) of this item, to reflect the following:

   a. the registrant's historic rate of appreciation over a period equivalent to the term of such options and/or SARs;

   b. 0% appreciation, where the exercise or base price was equal to or greater than the market price of the underlying securities on the date of grant; and

c. N% appreciation, the percentage appreciation by which the exercise or base price exceeded the market price at grant. Where the grant included multiple tranches with exercise or base prices exceeding the market price of the underlying security by varying degrees, include an additional column for each additional tranche.

9. Where the registrant chooses to use the grant-date valuation alternative specified in paragraph (c)(2)(vi)(B) of this item, the valuation shall be footnoted to describe the valuation method used. Where the registrant has used a variation of the Black–Scholes or binomial option pricing model, the description shall identify the use of such pricing model and describe the assumptions used relating to the expected volatility, risk-free rate of return, dividend yield and time of exercise. Any adjustments for non-transferability or risk of forfeiture also shall be disclosed. In the event another valuation method is used, the registrant is required to describe the methodology as well as any material assumptions.

(d) *Aggregated Option/SAR Exercises and Fiscal Year-End Option/SAR Value Table.*

(1) The information specified in paragraph (d)(2) of this item, concerning each exercise of stock options (or tandem SARs) and freestanding SARs during the last completed fiscal year by each of the named executive officers and the fiscal year-end value of unexercised options and SARs, shall be provided on an aggregated basis in the tabular format specified below:

Aggregated Option/SAR Exercises in Last Fiscal Year and FY-End Option/SAR Values

(a)	(b)	(c)	(d)	(e)
			Number of securities underlying unexercised options/SARs at FY-end (%)	Value of unexercised in-the-money options/SARs at FY-end ($)
Name	Shares acquired on exercise ($)	Value realized ($)	exercisable/ unexercisable	exercisable/ unexercisable
CEO				
A				
B				
C				
D				

(2) The table shall include:

(i) The name of the executive officer (column (a));

(ii) The number of shares received upon exercise, or, if no shares were received, the number of securities with respect to which the options or SARs were exercised (column (b));

(iii) The aggregate dollar value realized upon exercise (column (c));

(iv) The total number of securities underlying unexercised options and SARs held at the end of the last completed fiscal year, separately identifying the exercisable and unexercisable options and SARs (column (d)); and

(v) The aggregate dollar value of in-the-money, unexercised options and SARs held at the end of the fiscal year, separately identifying the exercisable and unexercisable options and SARs (column (e)).

1. *Instructions to Item 402(d)(2).*

   1. Options or freestanding SARs are in-the-money if the fair market value of the underlying securities exceeds the exercise or base price of the option or SAR. The dollar values in columns (c) and (e) are calculated by determining the difference between the fair market value of the securities underlying the options or SARs and the exercise or base price of the options or SARs at exercise or fiscal year-end, respectively.

   2. In calculating the dollar value realized upon exercise (column (c)), the value of any related payment or other consideration provided (or to be provided) by the registrant to or on behalf of a named executive officer, whether in payment of the exercise price or related taxes, shall not be included. Payments by the registrant in reimbursement of tax obligations incurred by a named executive officer are required to be disclosed in accordance with paragraph (b)(2)(iii)(C)(4) of this item.

(e) *Long-Term Incentive Plan ("LTIP") Awards Table.*

(1) The information specified in paragraph (e)(2) of this item, regarding each award made to a named executive officer in the last completed fiscal year under any LTIP, shall be provided in the tabular format specified below:

Long-Term Incentive Plans—Awards in Last Fiscal Year

			Estimated future payouts under non-stock price-based plans		
(a)	(b)	(c)	(d)	(e)	(f)
		Performance or other period until			
	Number of shares, units or other				
		maturation	Threshold	Target	Maximum
Name	rights (%)	or payout	($ or %)	($ or %)	($ or %)
CEO					
A					
B					
C					
D					

(2) The Table shall include:

(i) The name of the executive officer (column (a));

(ii) The number of shares, units or other rights awarded under any LTIP, and, if applicable, the number of shares underlying any such unit or right (column (b));

(iii) The performance or other time period until payout or maturation of the award (column (c)); and

(iv) For plans not based on stock price, the dollar value of the estimated payout, the number of shares to be awarded as the payout or a range of estimated payouts denominated in dollars or number of shares under the award (threshold, target and maximum amount) (columns (d) through (f)).

1. *Instructions to Item 402(e).*

   1. For purposes of this paragraph, the term "long-term incentive plan" or "LTIP" shall be defined in accordance with paragraph (a)(7)(iii) of this item.

   2. Describe in a footnote or in narrative text accompanying this table the material terms of any award, including a general description of the formula or criteria to be applied in determining the amounts payable. Registrants are not required to disclose any factor, criterion or performance-related or other condition to payout or maturation of a particular award that involves confidential commercial or business information, disclosure of which would adversely affect the registrant's competitive position.

3. Separate disclosure shall be provided in the Table for each award made to a named executive officer, accompanied by the information specified in Instruction 2 to this paragraph. If awards are made to a named executive officer during the fiscal year under more than one plan, identify the particular plan under which each such award was made.

4. For column (d), "threshold" refers to the minimum amount payable for a certain level of performance under the plan. For column (e), "target" refers to the amount payable if the specified performance target(s) are reached. For column (f), "maximum" refers to the maximum payout possible under the plan.

5. In column (e), registrants must provide a representative amount based on the previous fiscal year's performance if the target award is not determinable.

6. A tandem grant of two instruments, only one of which is pursuant to a LTIP, need be reported only in the table applicable to the other instrument. For example, an option granted in tandem with a performance share would be reported only as an option grant, with the tandem feature noted.

(f) *Defined Benefit or Actuarial Plan Disclosure.*

(1) *Pension Plan Table.*

(i) For any defined benefit or actuarial plan under which benefits are determined primarily by final compensation (or average final compensation) and years of service, provide a separate Pension Plan Table showing estimated annual benefits payable upon retirement (including amounts attributable to any defined benefit supplementary or excess pension award plans) in specified compensation and years of service classifications in the format specified below:

Pension Plan Table

Remuneration	Years of service				
	15	20	25	30	35
125,000					
150,000					
175,000					
200,000					
225,000					

(continues)

Pension Plan Table *(continued)*

Remuneration	Years of service				
	15	20	25	30	35
250,000					
300,000					
400,000					
450,000					
500,000					

(ii) Immediately following the Table, the registrant shall disclose:

(A) The compensation covered by the plan(s), including the relationship of such covered compensation to the annual compensation reported in the Summary Compensation Table required by paragraph (b)(2)(iii) of this item, and state the current compensation covered by the plan for any named executive officer whose covered compensation differs substantially (by more than 10%) from that set forth in the annual compensation columns of the Summary Compensation Table;

(B) The estimated credited years of service for each of the named executive officers; and

(C) A statement as to the basis upon which benefits are computed (e.g., straight-life annuity amounts), and whether or not the benefits listed in the Pension Plan Table are subject to any deduction for Social Security or other offset amounts.

(2) *Alternative Pension Plan Disclosure.* For any defined benefit or actuarial plan under which benefits are not determined primarily by final compensation (or average final compensation) and years of service, the registrant shall state in narrative form:

(i) The formula by which benefits are determined; and

(ii) The estimated annual benefits payable upon retirement at normal retirement age for each of the named executive officers.

1. *Instructions to Item 402(f).*

    1. *Pension Levels.* Compensation set forth in the Pension Plan Table pursuant to paragraph (f)(1)(i) of this item shall allow for reasonable increases in existing compensation levels; alternatively, registrants may present as the highest compensation level in the Pension Plan Table an amount equal to

120% of the amount of covered compensation of the most highly compensated individual named in the Summary Compensation Table required by paragraph (b)(2) of this item.

2. *Normal Retirement Age.* The term "normal retirement age" means normal retirement age as defined in a pension or similar plan or, if not defined therein, the earliest time at which a participant may retire without any benefit reduction due to age.

(g) *Compensation of Directors.*

(1) *Standard Arrangements.* Describe any standard arrangements, stating amounts, pursuant to which directors of the registrant are compensated for any services provided as a director, including any additional amounts payable for committee participation or special assignments.

(2) *Other Arrangements.* Describe any other arrangements pursuant to which any director of the registrant was compensated during the registrant's last completed fiscal year for any service provided as a director, stating the amount paid and the name of the director.

Instruction to Item 402(g)(2). The information required by paragraph (g)(2) of this item shall include any arrangement, including consulting contracts, entered into in consideration of the director's service on the board. The material terms of any such arrangement shall be included.

(h) *Employment Contracts and Termination of Employment and Change-in-Control Arrangements.* Describe the terms and conditions of each of the following contracts or arrangements:

(1) Any employment contract between the registrant and a named executive officer; and

(2) Any compensatory plan or arrangement, including payments to be received from the registrant, with respect to a named executive officer, if such plan or arrangement results or will result from the resignation, retirement or any other termination of such executive officer's employment with the registrant and its subsidiaries or from a change-in-control of the registrant or a change in the named executive officer's responsibilities following a change-in-control and the amount involved, including all periodic payments or installments, exceeds $100,000.

(i) *Report on Repricing of Options/SARs.*

(1) If at any time during the last completed fiscal year, the registrant, while a reporting company pursuant to Section 13(a) or 15(d) of the Exchange Act [15 U.S.C. 78m(a), 78o(d)], has adjusted or amended the exercise price of stock options or SARs previously awarded to any of the named executive officers, whether through amendment, cancellation

or replacement grants, or any other means ("repriced"), the registrant shall provide the information specified in paragraphs (i)(2) and (i)(3) of this item.

(2) The compensation committee (or other board committee performing equivalent functions or, in the absence of any such committee, the entire board of directors) shall explain in reasonable detail any such repricing of options and/or SARs held by a named executive officer in the last completed fiscal year, as well as the basis for each such repricing.

(3)   (i) The information specified in paragraph (i)(3)(*ii*) of this item, concerning all such repricings of options and SARs held by *any* executive officer during the last ten completed fiscal years, shall be provided in the tabular format specified below:

Ten-Year Option/SAR Repricings

(a)	(b)	(c)	(d)	(e)	(f)	(g)
Name	Date	Securities underlying options/SAR repriced or amended (%)	Market price of stock at time of repricing or amendment ($)	Exercise price at time of repricing or amendment ($)	New exercise price ($)	Length of original option term remaining at date of repricing or amendment

(ii) The Table shall include, with respect to each repricing:

(A) The name and position of the executive officer (column (a));

(B) The date of each repricing (column (b));

(C) The number of securities underlying replacement or amended options or SARs (column (c));

(D) The per-share market price of the underlying security at the time of repricing (column (d));

(E) The original exercise price or base price of the cancelled or amended option or SAR (column (e));

(F) The per-share exercise price or base price of the replacement option or SAR (column (f)); and

(G) The amount of time remaining before the replaced or amended option or SAR would have expired (column (g)).

Instructions to Item 402(i).

1. The required report shall be made over the name of each member of the registrant's compensation committee, or other board committee performing equivalent functions or, in the absence of any such committee, the entire board of directors.

2. A replacement grant is any grant of options or SARs reasonably related to any prior or potential option or SAR cancellation, whether by an exchange of existing options or SARs for options or SARs with new terms; the grant of new options or SARs in tandem with previously granted options or SARs that will operate to cancel the previously granted options or SARs upon exercise; repricing of previously granted options or SARs; or otherwise. If a corresponding original grant was canceled in a prior year, information about such grant nevertheless must be disclosed pursuant to this paragraph.

3. If the replacement grant is not made at the current market price, describe the terms of the grant in a footnote or accompanying textual narrative.

4. This paragraph shall not apply to any repricing occurring through the operation of:

a. a plan formula or mechanism that results in the periodic adjustment of the option or SAR exercise or base price;

b. a plan antidilution provision; or

c. a recapitalization or similar transaction equally affecting all holders of the class of securities underlying the options or SARs.

5. Information required by paragraph (i)(3) of this item shall not be provided for any repricings effected before the registrant became a reporting company pursuant to Section 13(a) or 15(d) of the Exchange Act.

(j) *Additional Information with Respect to Compensation Committee Interlocks and Insider Participation in Compensation Decisions.* Under the caption "Compensation Committee Interlocks and Insider Participation,"

(1) The registrant shall identify each person who served as a member of the compensation committee of the registrant's board of directors (or board committee performing equivalent functions) during the last completed fiscal year, indicating each committee member who:

(i) was, during the fiscal year, an officer or employee of the registrant or any of its subsidiaries;

(ii) was formerly an officer of the registrant or any of its subsidiaries; or

(iii) had any relationship requiring disclosure by the registrant under any paragraph of Item 404 of Regulation S-K (§229.404). In this event, the disclosure required by Item 404 shall accompany such identification.

(2) If the registrant has no compensation committee (or other board committee performing equivalent functions), the registrant shall identify each officer and employee of the registrant or any of its subsidiaries, and any former officer of the registrant or any of its subsidiaries, who, during the last completed fiscal year, participated in deliberations of the registrant's board of directors concerning executive officer compensation.

(3) The registrant shall describe any of the following relationships that existed during the last completed fiscal year:

> (i) an executive officer of the registrant served as a member of the compensation committee (or other board committee performing equivalent functions or, in the absence of any such committee, the entire board of directors) of another entity, one of whose executive officers served on the compensation committee (or other board committee performing equivalent functions or, in the absence of any such committee, the entire board of directors) of the registrant;

> (ii) an executive officer of the registrant served as a director of another entity, one of whose executive officers served on the compensation committee (or other board committee performing equivalent functions or, in the absence of any such committee, the entire board of directors) of the registrant; and

> (iii) an executive officer of the registrant served as a member of the compensation committee (or other board committee performing equivalent functions or, in the absence of any such committee, the entire board of directors) of another entity, one of whose executive officers served as a director of the registrant.

(3) Disclosure required under paragraph (j)(3) of this item regarding any compensation committee member or other director of the registrant who also served as an executive officer of another entity shall be accompanied by the disclosure called for by Item 404 (§229.404) with respect to that person.

1. *Instruction to Item 402(j)*. For purposes of this paragraph, the term "entity" shall not include an entity exempt from tax under Section 501(c)(3) of the Internal Revenue Code [26 U.S.C. 501(c)(3)].

(k) *Board Compensation Committee Report on Executive Compensation.*

> (1) Disclosure of the compensation committee's compensation policies applicable to the registrant's executive officers (including the named executive officers), including the specific relationship of corporate performance to executive compensation, is required with respect to compensation reported for the last completed fiscal year.

(2) Discussion is required of the compensation committee's bases for the CEO's compensation reported for the last completed fiscal year, including the factors and criteria upon which the CEO's compensation was based. The committee shall include a specific discussion of the relationship of the registrant's performance to the CEO's compensation for the last completed fiscal year, describing each measure of the registrant's performance, whether qualitative or quantitative, on which the CEO's compensation was based.

(3) The required disclosure shall be made over the name of each member of the registrant's compensation committee (or other board committee performing equivalent functions or, in the absence of any such committee, the entire board of directors). If the board of directors modified or rejected in any material way any action or recommendation by such committee with respect to such decisions in the last completed fiscal year, the disclosure must so indicate and explain the reasons for the board's actions, and be made over the names of all members of the board.

Instructions to Item 402(k).

1. Boilerplate language should be avoided in describing factors and criteria underlying awards or payments of executive compensation in the statement required.

2. Registrants are not required to disclose target levels with respect to specific quantitative or qualitative performance-related factors considered by the committee (or board), or any factors or criteria involving confidential commercial or business information, the disclosure of which would have an adverse effect on the registrant.

(*l*) *Performance Graph.*

(1) Provide a line graph comparing the yearly percentage change in the registrant's cumulative total shareholder return on a class of common stock registered under Section 12 of the Exchange Act (as measured by dividing (i) the sum of (A) the cumulative amount of dividends for the measurement period, assuming dividend reinvestment, and (B) the difference between the registrant's share price at the end and the beginning of the measurement period; by (ii) the share price at the beginning of the measurement period) with

(i) the cumulative total return of a broad equity market index assuming reinvestment of dividends, that includes companies whose equity securities are traded on the same exchange or NASDAQ market or are of comparable market capitalization; *provided, however,* that if the registrant is a company within the Standard & Poor's 500 Stock Index, the registrant must use that index; and

(ii) the cumulative total return, assuming reinvestment of dividends, of:

(A) a published industry or line-of-business index;

(B) peer issuer(s) selected in good faith. If the registrant does not select its peer issuer(s) on an industry or line-of-business basis, the registrant shall disclose the basis for its selection; or

(C) Issuer(s) with similar market capitalization(s), but only if the registrant does not use a published industry or line-of-business index and does not believe it can reasonably identify a peer group. If the registrant uses this alternative, the graph shall be accompanied by a statement of the reasons for this selection.

(2) For purposes of paragraph (*l*)(1) of this item, the term "measurement period" shall be the period beginning at the "measurement point" established by the market close on the last trading day before the beginning of the registrant's fifth preceding fiscal year, through and including the end of the registrant's last completed fiscal year. If the class of securities has been registered under section 12 of the Exchange Act for a shorter period of time, the period covered by the comparison may correspond to that time period.

(3) For purposes of paragraph (*l*)(1)(ii)(A) of this item, the term "published industry or line-of-business index" means any index that is prepared by a party other than the registrant or an affiliate and is accessible to the registrant's security holders; provided, however, that registrants may use an index prepared by the registrant or affiliate if such index is widely recognized and used.

(4) If the registrant selects a different index from an index used for the immediately preceding fiscal year, explain the reason(s) for this change and also compare the registrant's total return with that of both the newly selected index and the index used in the immediately preceding fiscal year.

Instructions to Item 402(l).

1. In preparing the required graphic comparisons, the registrant should:

a. use, to the extent feasible, comparable methods of presentation and assumptions for the total return calculations required by paragraph (*l*)(1) of this item; *provided, however,* that if the registrant constructs its own peer group index under paragraph (*l*)(1)(ii)(B), the same methodology must be used in calculating both the registrant's total return and that on the peer group index; and

b. assume the reinvestment of dividends into additional shares of the same class of equity securities at the frequency with which dividends are paid on such securities during the applicable fiscal year.

2. In constructing the graph:

(a) The closing price at the measurement point must be converted into a fixed investment, stated in dollars, in the registrant's stock (or in the stocks represented by a given index), with cumulative returns for each subsequent fiscal year measured as a change from that investment; and

(b) Each fiscal year should be plotted with points showing the cumulative total return as of that point. The value of the investment as of each point plotted on a given return line is the number of shares held at that point multiplied by the then-prevailing share price.

3. The registrant is required to present information for the registrant's last five fiscal years, and may choose to graph a longer period; but the measurement point, however, shall remain the same.

4. Registrants may include comparisons using performance measures in addition to total return, such as return on average common shareholders' equity, so long as the registrant's compensation committee (or other board committee performing equivalent functions or, in the absence of any such committee, the entire board of directors) describes the link between that measure and the level of executive compensation in the statement required by paragraph (k) of this Item.

5. If the registrant uses a peer issuer(s) comparison or comparison with issuer(s) with similar market capitalizations, the identity of those issuers must be disclosed and the returns of each component issuer of the group must be weighted according to the respective issuer's stock market capitalization at the beginning of each period for which a return is indicated.

CHAPTER 2

Overview of the Compensation Package

I. INTRODUCTION

This chapter will introduce the basic components of the compensation package, as well as provide some descriptive information about the usage of those components in executive compensation. By examining the components of these executive compensation packages, one can start to understand the importance of the total package and the implications in the hiring, motivation, and retention of executives.

II. COMPENSATION PACKAGE

The executive compensation package can, and most often does, contain many components. These components have differing affects on employee motivation and risk, as well as different costs for the corporation. A well-constructed compensation package must make trade-offs between these components to maximize the net benefit[1] to both the corporation and the executive. The major and most common components of compensation, which will be discussed in detail later in the book, are salary, bonus, stock options and stock grants, pensions, benefits, and perquisites. To start, I will define these components.

A. Salary

Salary is the fixed contractual amount of compensation that does not explicitly vary with performance. However, it can be affected by performance, as good

---

[1]Benefit less related costs.

performance can lead to higher salary in future periods. For example, the employment agreement between the Eastman Kodak Company and George M. C. Fisher, its Chief Executive Officer (CEO), entered into on October 27, 1993, explicitly states the following:[2]

> The Executive shall be paid an annualized Base Salary, payable in accordance with the regular payroll practices of the Company, of $2,000,000. The Base Salary shall be reviewed no less frequently than annually for increase in the discretion of the Board and its Executive Compensation and Development Committee.

B. Bonus

Bonus is a form of compensation that may be conditioned upon individual, group, or corporate performance. For most executives, bonus is both based upon group performance and is determined as part of a plan covering a larger group of employees. Thus, their individual employment contract may only specify their participation in the plan or a minimum bonus they are guaranteed. For example, the following passage from the contract of Lawrence A. Weinbach, CEO of the Unisys Corporation, dated September 23, 1997, specifies a minimum bonus (under the Executive Variable Compensation Plan or EVC) guaranteed regardless of performance, if he remains employed with the corporation:

> (b) For the 1997 EVC award year you will be guaranteed a minimum EVC payout equal to 100% of the base salary amounts paid to you in 1997, provided that you continue to be employed by the Corporation through the 1997 EVC payout date. For the 1998 and 1999 EVC award years, you will be guaranteed a minimum EVC payout equal to 100% of the base salary paid to you in each year, provided that you continue to be employed by the Corporation through the applicable EVC payout date for each of those years.

The performance conditions used to determine the bonus can be implicit or explicit, may be objective or subjective, and may be financial or nonfinancial. For example, for 2000 UAL modified their

> annual incentive program to include financial, operational, *customer satisfaction and employee satisfaction goals* [italics added], which will provide cash compensation opportunities that are aligned with the company's core objectives.[3]

In some cases bonuses can be based upon one factor, for example, net income or sales, whereas in other cases they can be based upon a combination of factors. In addition, bonuses can be based upon short-term or long-term measures.

[2]Two things should be noted. One, not all employees have written employment contracts. And two, even if not specified, the board, with the consent of the executive, could always enter into a new contract at a higher salary.

[3]UAL proxy statement filed with the Securities and Exchange Commission, March 23, 2000, p. 25.

C. Stock Options

Stock options allow their holder to purchase one or more shares of stock at a fixed "exercise" price over a fixed period of time. They have value if the corporation's share price is greater than the exercise price. Because the exercise price is normally set at the share price on the date of grant,[4] the ultimate value of the option depends upon the performance of a corporation's share price subsequent to the date of grant. That is, they can be extremely valuable when the share price rises dramatically, but can also expire worthless if the share price declines.[5] As with bonuses, in most cases the executive participates in a stock option plan along with other employees. Thus, the employment contract only specifies that the executive will participate in the plan and not the amount of the executives' grant. An exception to that rule is the employment agreement between the Walt Disney Company and Michael D. Eisner, its CEO, entered into on January 8, 1997, which states the following:

> 5. Stock Options
>
> (a) In connection with this Agreement Executive has been granted stock options on September 30, 1996, to purchase (i) 5,000,000 shares of Company common stock having an exercise price equal to the per share fair market value determined in accordance with the applicable provisions of the Company's 1995 Stock Incentive Plan (the "Plan") of Company common stock on September 30, 1996 (the "A Options") and (ii) 3,000,000 shares of Company common stock of which 1,000,000 shall have an exercise price equal to 125% of the per share fair market value of the Company common stock on such date ("Group 1"), 1,000,000 shall have an exercise price equal to 150% of the per share fair market value of the Company common stock on such date ("Group 2"), and 1,000,000 shall have an exercise price equal to 200% of the per share fair market value of the Company common stock on such date ("Group 3") ("Groups 1, 2 and 3 are collectively referred to herein as the B Options"). The A Option shall vest on September 30, 2003. Group 1 of the B Options shall vest on September 30, 2004. Group 2 of the B Options shall vest on September 30, 2005. Group 3 of the B Options shall vest on September 30, 2006. The A Option shall expire on September 30, 2008, and the B Options shall expire on September 30, 2011. Such options shall be subject to, and governed by, the terms and provisions of the Plan except to the extent of modifications of such options which are permitted by the Plan and which are expressly provided for in this Agreement.

There are several details of Eisner's grant that are worth discussing. The first item is the large amount of options granted (8,000,000), which were valued by Disney at $195,583,281 on the date of grant.[6] As will be shown later in the chapter and book, the grant size and value far exceed that of the average option grant. A second

---

[4]Matsunaga (1995, note 6) finds only 5% of his sample firms issued options with an exercise price below the fair market value at the grant date.

[5]As will be discussed later in this book (in particular chapters 6 and 13), when share prices fall after the date of grant, resulting in the exercise price of the option being greater than the share price, companies sometimes grant additional options at the lower price and/or reduce the exercise price on the existing option.

[6]Walt Disney Company proxy statement filed with the Securities and Exchange Commission, January 9, 1997, p. 16.

item that can be noted is that some of the options ("A" options) have an exercise price equal to the current market value, whereas others ("B" options) have exercise prices greater than the current market value. Although the former is most common, the latter, which is referred to as a *premium option,* does occur with some frequency (discussed in more detail in Chapters 6 and 12). The third item is that the options do not vest until September 30, 2003 ("A" options) or September 30, 2004 ("B" options). By vest, it means that the options cannot be exercised until that date has passed. In other words, Eisner cannot exercise his options until either 7 or 8 years have passed from the date of grant. Although most option grants have vesting periods (occasionally corporations grant options that vest or are exercisable immediately), this is an exceptionally long vesting period. In most cases he must also continue to be employed by Disney to be allowed to exercise the options. Consequently, if he leaves prior to vesting, he will forfeit the options and the ensuing profits. Thus, the extended vesting period provides Eisner with incentive to remain with Disney. Finally the options expire on (can no longer be exercised after) either September 30, 2008, or September 30, 2011, giving them a 12- or 15-year life. Although all options have expiration dates, the norm is 10 years. As will be noted in Appendix 2.1, the longer the life, the more valuable the option.

D. Stock Grants

Stock grants occur when corporations give shares to their employees. They differ from stock options in that they have no exercise price. Whereas a stock option only has value if the corporation's share price is above the exercise price, a stock grant has value as long as the share price is above zero. Stock grants can be unrestricted or restricted. An example of a restriction imposed upon a stock grant might be that the employee cannot sell the shares until he or she has worked for the corporation for a period of time. Such a restriction was placed on the grant given to Paul J. Norris when he agreed to become CEO of W. R. Grace:

> 4. You will be granted a restricted stock award covering 170,733 shares of Grace Common Stock on November 1, 1998, with the provision that you will vest in shares and the restrictions will lapse in three equal installments, each covering 56,911 shares, on November 1, 1999, November 1, 2000, and November 1, 2001, respectively; provided, however, all such installments will vest immediately upon termination of your employment by the Company without "Cause" (including termination of your employment by the Company without "Cause" following a "change in control" of the Company, within the meaning of your "Executive Severance Agreement" described below), or upon your death or disability as defined under the Company's Long-Term Disability Income Plan.[7]

[7]Employment agreement between Paul J. Norris and W.R. Grace dated October 26, 1998.

E. Other Stock–Based Forms of Compensation

Although not as popular as stock options and grants, some companies grant *stock appreciation rights (SARs), phantom stock,* and/or *equity units.* Stock appreciation rights are the right to receive the increase in the value of a specified number of shares of common stock over a defined period of time. Economically they are equivalent to stock options, with one exception. With a stock option the executive has to purchase and then sell the shares to receive his or her profit.[8] With an SAR the corporation simply pays the executive, in cash or common stock, the excess of the current market price of the shares over the aggregate exercise price.[9] Thus the executive is able to realize the benefits of a stock option without having to purchase the stock. In most cases, SARs are granted in tandem with stock options where the executive, at the time of exercise, can choose to exercise either the stock option or SAR.

Phantom stock are units that act like common stock, but which do not constitute claims for ownership of the corporation. They entitle the executive to receive the increase in common stock prices *and* any dividends declared on common stock. They are often used in privately held corporations or publicly held corporations, where the owners do not want to dilute existing ownership.

Equity units entitle the holder to purchase common stock at its book value, and then resell the stock to the corporation at their book value at a later date. The owner also gets the dividend payments on the stock. Like phantom stock, equity units are often used in privately held corporations, or publicly held corporations, where the owners do not want to dilute existing ownership.

F. Pensions

Pensions are a form of deferred compensation, whereby after retirement from the corporation, the employee receives a payment or series of payments. These payments may be defined by the pension plan,[10] or based upon the amounts accumulated in the employee's personal retirement account.[11] If the payments are defined by the plan they can be based upon a number of factors including, but not limited

---

[8]In some cases, companies have set up programs with investment bankers that allow (for a commission) the executive to engage in a simultaneous exercise of their options and sale of the shares acquired upon exercise. This allows the executive to avoid having to pay the exercise price on the shares being acquired, and as a result, lowers the costs of the two transactions.

[9]To the executive, a stock appreciation right is preferred to as a stock option, as it allows the executive to avoid transaction costs associated with the exercise of the option and the subsequent sale of the shares acquired upon exercise. The corporation, on the other hand, prefers stock options, which are a source, rather than a use of cash. In addition, the financial reporting treatment for stock options is more favorable than that for stock appreciation rights (see Balsam and Paek 2001 for a discussion of these issues).

[10]These plans are known as defined benefit plans.

[11]These plans are known as defined contribution plans, the most common of which would be a 401(K).

to, number of years with the corporation, earnings while working, and level within corporation. Pensions can be structured in many ways; for example, the payments can be fixed in amount, or they can be adjusted for inflation. Due to Internal Revenue Code limitations, in most cases, executives are covered by more than one plan. That is, they participate in a primary "tax-qualified" plan along with other employees and have at least one "supplemental" plan. The second plan is necessitated by Internal Revenue code limitations on payments from a qualified plan. That is, in order to qualify for favorable tax treatment, the plan must be nondiscriminatory, that is, the benefits cannot be skewed in favor of highly paid employees, *and* the corporation cannot consider compensation in excess of a threshold, which was $170,000 for the year 2000 [section 401(a)(17)], in determining pension benefits, nor make payments in excess of $135,000 [section 415(b)]. The supplemental plan (or plans) provides additional benefits without limitation.[12]

G. Other Compensation

In addition to receiving salary, bonuses, stock-based compensation, and pensions, executives receive a variety of benefits and perquisites, whose value must be reported in the proxy statement.[13] These items include corporate cars; the use of corporate airplanes and apartments; special dining facilities; country club memberships; health, dental, medical, life, and disability insurance; the ability to defer compensation at above-market rates of interest; and the ability to borrow money on favorable terms. The following disclosure from First Union Corporation illustrates that the value of these benefits can run into the hundreds of thousands of dollars.[14]

	Crutchfield	*Thompson*	*McMullen*	*Atwood*	*Adams*	*Georgius*	*Antonini*
Savings plan matching contributions	$ 61,200	$30,000	$29,400	$28,500	$ 27,600	$ 44,000	$28,500
Value of life insurance premiums	239,536	21,820	45,678	61,184	31,509	174,869	3,168

[12]As will be discussed in more detail in Chapter 7, there are costs to these supplemental plans that do not exist for tax-qualified plans. With a tax-qualified plan, the corporation funds the plan and takes an immediate deduction at the time of funding, whereas the employee does not recognize income until the time he or she receives the pension. In contrast, supplemental plans cannot be funded or the employee would have to immediately recognize taxable income. Consequently, since the plan is not funded, the corporation cannot take an immediate deduction.

[13]The corporation need not disclose the value of the benefits if "the aggregate amount of such compensation is the lesser of either $50,000 or 10% of the total of annual salary and bonus reported for the named executive officer" (Securities and Exchange Commission regulation S-K 229.402 (b)(2)(iii)(C)1).

[14]First Union Corporation Proxy statement filed with Securities and Exchange Commission, March 13, 2000, p. 10.

	Crutchfield	Thompson	McMullen	Atwood	Adams	Georgius	Antonini
Value of disability insurance	—	1,130	—	4,269	2,266	1,634	2,886
Above market interest on deferred compensation	10,208	53,070	991	62,488	109,361	202,765	—

Schellhardt (1994) reported that of major employers, 63% provided corporate cars, 62% paid for club memberships, and 53% allowed the use of corporate jets, while Sessa and Egodigwe (1999) noted that many corporations offer their executives interest-free loans to finance their purchases of corporate stock.

III. USAGE OF MAJOR COMPONENTS OF COMPENSATION

Tables 2.1, 2.2, and 2.3 show the frequency with which salary, bonus, stock options, stock grants, and pension plans are included in the CEO compensation package of large corporations.[15] Table 2.1 shows the frequency with which these components are used by year, whereas Table 2.2 shows the frequency across industry, and Table 2.3 shows the frequency by the size of the corporation. With few exceptions, salary is paid to the CEO every year. Between 79 and 83% of CEOs receive annual bonus

[15]Tables 2.1 through 2.3 and most of the other tables in the book are prepared using data from Standard and Poors' Market Insights. The executive compensation component of Market Insights, also known as ExecuComp, includes data for approximately 1500 firms, the S&P 500, S&P MidCap 400, and S&P SmallCap 600.

TABLE 2.1   Fraction of Firms Paying Salary or Bonus or Granting Options, Shares, and Pension Benefits to Their CEOs by Year

Year	Salary	Annual bonus	Long-term bonus	Stock options	Stock grants	Pension
1992	1.00	0.81	0.16	0.50	0.17	1.00
1993	1.00	0.81	0.14	0.62	0.17	1.00
1994	1.00	0.82	0.13	0.64	0.17	1.00
1995	1.00	0.82	0.16	0.63	0.18	1.00
1996	0.99	0.81	0.15	0.67	0.19	1.00
1997	0.99	0.83	0.15	0.68	0.18	1.00
1998	0.99	0.80	0.15	0.71	0.19	1.00
1999	0.99	0.79	0.15	0.75	0.19	1.00
2000	0.99	0.81	0.17	0.79	0.22	1.00

TABLE 2.2   Fraction of Firms Paying Salary or Bonus or Granting Options or Shares to Their CEOs in 2000, by Industry

Industry	Standard industrial classification codes	Salary	Annual bonus	Long-term bonus	Stock options	Stock grants
Mining and construction	1000–1999	1.00	0.92	0.30	0.78	0.27
Manufacturing	2000–3999	0.99	0.83	0.16	0.81	0.19
Transportation, communications, electric, gas, and sanitary services	4000–4999	0.96	0.83	0.34	0.79	0.24
Wholesale and retail trade	5000–5999	0.99	0.79	0.09	0.74	0.24
Finance, insurance, and real estate	6000–6999	0.99	0.82	0.19	0.82	0.34
Services	7000–8999	1.00	0.74	0.06	0.74	0.15

payments in a given year. A smaller proportion of CEOs (between 13–17%) receives payments from a long-term bonus plan (sometimes referred to as a performance plan) in a given year. Stock options are granted to between 50 and 79% of CEOs each year, whereas restricted stock is granted to between 17 and 22% of CEOs in a given year. Finally, all of the CEOs in the database participate in defined benefit pension plans.[16]

[16]Pensions are not included in most of the tables in this book, as the tables are derived from proxy statement data and valuations derived from that data, and the disclosure and valuation of pension benefits in the proxy is not as clear as that of other components.

TABLE 2.3   Fraction of Firms Paying Salary or Bonus or Granting Options or Shares to Their CEOs in 2000, by Firm Size[a]

	Size decile	Salary	Annual bonus	Long-term bonus	Stock options	Stock grants
Smallest	1	0.98	0.62	0.03	0.70	0.15
	2	1.00	0.73	0.10	0.75	0.15
	3	0.99	0.77	0.09	0.69	0.22
	4	0.99	0.87	0.17	0.74	0.17
	5	0.98	0.81	0.19	0.83	0.24
	6	0.98	0.83	0.18	0.80	0.17
	7	1.00	0.86	0.25	0.85	0.21
	8	0.96	0.87	0.24	0.89	0.29
	9	0.99	0.90	0.20	0.83	0.31
Largest	10	0.98	0.89	0.21	0.87	0.31

[a]Firms divided into deciles by market value of equity.

But even these relatively high proportions understate the true percentage of CEOs with bonus plans and stock options. First, with respect to bonuses, the data in the tables reflect bonuses actually paid. A greater percentage of CEOs may have bonus plans, but performance may have not reached the threshold necessary for payout. For example, Donald J. Carty, Chairman and CEO of AMR Corporation, did not receive a bonus in 1999 because "performance failed to satisfy the performance measurements under such Plan."[17] Other examples include Richard B. Cheney, current Vice-President of the United States, and at the time CEO of Halliburton, who did not receive a bonus because "performance did not meet the target level established by the Compensation Committee"[18] R. Brad Martin, Chairman and CEO of Saks, also did not receive a bonus because "the Company did not meet its plans for earnings growth."[19]

With long-term plans, corporations may skip years by definition; for example, a target is set in 1998 for the 3-year period 1999 through 2001. By definition, no long-term bonus payment will be made in either 1999 or 2000 regardless of how well the corporation is doing. Of course corporations can, and do, use overlapping performance periods. That is, the corporation in the example above may also award bonuses for the 3-year periods ending in 1999 and 2000 also.

With respect to stock options and stock grants, the percentages in the table represent the grants in a given year. Sometimes corporations do not make grants every year, but make large grants in one year intended to represent a longer period. For example, as discussed earlier in this chapter, the Walt Disney Company in 1996 awarded its CEO, Michael Eisner, options on 8 million shares with a grant date value of $195,583,281.[20] Prior to that, Disney had not granted Eisner any options since 1989, nor have they granted him any since.[21]

Substantial variation in the composition of the compensation package is observed over time (Table 2.1), with the biggest change involving the percentage of CEOs receiving a stock compensation. As noted above, the percentage of CEOs receiving stock option grants increased from 50% in 1992 to 79% in 2000. Similarly, the percentage of CEOs receiving stock grants increased from 17% in 1992 to 22% in 2000. Both of these increases are consistent with evidence presented later in this book indicating that stock-based compensation has become a more important component of the executive compensation package.

---

[17]Page 12, AMR Corporation proxy statement filed with the Securities and Exchange Commission, April 25, 2000, p. 12.

[18]Halliburton proxy statement filed with the Securities and Exchange Commission April 3, 2000, p. 16.

[19]Saks proxy statement filed with the Securities and Exchange Commission, April 27, 2000.

[20]Walt Disney Company proxy statement filed with the Securities and Exchange Commission January 9, 1997, p. 16.

[21]While Eisner has not received any additional options on Disney stock since 1996, in 2000 he did receive a grant of 2,000,000 options on Disney Internet Group stock valued at $37,740,000 (Walt Disney proxy statement filed with the Securities and Exchange Commission January 12, 2001, pp. 20, 21).

Variation is also observed across industries (Table 2.2). Compensation is likely to be similar within an industry, because corporate characteristics (see Chapter 11) influence compensation package design, and because these corporations are competing to hire and retain the same individuals. In contrast, the amount, as well as the components, of the compensation package will vary across industries, as industries offer different opportunities and challenges and compete for executives with different skill sets. Hambrick and Abrahamson (1995) document differences in managerial discretion across industries. Take, for example, regulated companies. It has been argued that the level of compensation, as well as the composition of the compensation package, varies with the complexity and growth of the corporation. Palia (2000), among others, finds that regulated companies pay less than nonregulated companies, a finding that can in part be attributed to the limited growth opportunities these companies had (until recently), and in part to the regulated environment in which they operate.

In 2000 the percentage of CEOs receiving an annual bonus ranged from a low of 74% in the service industry to a high of 92% in mining and construction.[22] The percentage of CEOs receiving long-term bonuses ranged from a low of 6% in the services industry to a high of 34% in transportation, communications, electric, gas, and sanitary services; whereas the percentage of CEOs receiving stock options ranged from 74% in wholesale and retail trade and services, to 82% in finance, insurance, and real estate; and the percentage receiving stock grants ranged from 15% in services to 34% in finance, insurance, and real estate. As noted above, these differences arise from differences in corporate characteristics across industries that lead to differences in compensation contract design. These differences also arise from firm performance realizations that are similar within an industry. Consider, for example, a scenario where a worldwide oversupply depresses steel prices and causes most steel companies to report losses. As a consequence, companies in the steel industry would be less likely to pay bonuses.

Finally, and perhaps most strikingly, variation is observed by the size of the corporation (Table 2.3). Compensation is likely to be similar within similar-sized corporations because these corporations are competing to hire and retain the same individuals. However, CEO compensation has long been shown, in academic research dating back to Taussig and Barker (1925), to vary or increase with the size of the corporation. In 2000, the percentage of corporations paying annual bonuses increased from 62% for corporations in the smallest decile to 89% for corporations in the highest decile. Similarly, the percentage of corporations paying long-term bonuses, granting stock options, and providing stock grants increased from 3–21%, 70–87%, and 15–31%, respectively, as we move from the smallest to the largest corporations.

---

[22]The industry partitions used in these tables are admittedly not very precise, and thus each classification includes a wide variety of firms. Had a finer partition been used, the variation across industries would have been greater.

IV. RELATIVE IMPORTANCE OF COMPONENTS OF A COMPENSATION PACKAGE

As observed above, corporations normally include multiple forms of fixed and variable compensation in the compensation package. They do so because each component has a different affect on employee motivation and risk, as well as having different costs to the corporation.[23] That is, executives have bonus plans based, to some extent, on controllable variables to offset the risk of stock-based compensation, which is in part driven by uncontrollable market forces. The corporation weighs the cost of using potentially controllable variables against the benefit of reducing executive risk and, hence, the wages demanded. Tables 2.1 through 2.3 showed the fraction of corporations' CEO compensation package, including salary, bonus, stock options, stock grants, and pensions in their CEO's compensation package. Tables 2.4, 2.5, and 2.6 and Figure 2.1 show the relative importance of these components, that is, the proportions of these components in the CEO compensation package of large corporations.

Three things should be noted about Table 2.4 and the remaining tables in this chapter. The first thing to note about Table 2.4 is that, in addition to salary, annual and long-term bonus, stock options and grants, two additional columns are added,

[23]Those benefits and costs will be discussed in detail in Part II of this book.

TABLE 2.4   Proportion of Compensation Package Represented by Components, by Year[a]

Year	Salary	Annual bonus	Other annual	Long-term bonus	Stock options	Stock grants	All other
1992	0.47	0.20	0.02	0.04	0.21	0.04	0.04
	0.43	0.19	0.00	0.00	0.14	0.00	0.02
1993	0.44	0.21	0.01	0.03	0.23	0.04	0.04
	0.41	0.20	0.00	0.00	0.16	0.00	0.02
1994	0.42	0.21	0.01	0.02	0.26	0.04	0.04
	0.38	0.19	0.00	0.00	0.20	0.00	0.01
1995	0.41	0.21	0.02	0.03	0.24	0.04	0.04
	0.37	0.20	0.00	0.00	0.19	0.00	0.01
1996	0.38	0.20	0.02	0.04	0.29	0.04	0.04
	0.33	0.18	0.00	0.00	0.25	0.00	0.01
1997	0.35	0.20	0.03	0.04	0.32	0.04	0.04
	0.28	0.18	0.00	0.00	0.27	0.00	0.01
1998	0.34	0.18	0.03	0.03	0.35	0.04	0.04
	0.27	0.16	0.00	0.00	0.34	0.00	0.01
1999	0.31	0.18	0.02	0.03	0.38	0.04	0.04
	0.25	0.15	0.00	0.00	0.39	0.00	0.01
2000	0.27	0.18	0.02	0.03	0.42	0.05	0.04
	0.20	0.14	0.00	0.00	0.42	0.00	0.01

[a]Means on top, medians below.

TABLE 2.5   Proportion of 2000 CEO Compensation Package Represented by Components, by Industry[a]

Industry	SIC codes[b]	Salary	Annual bonus	Other annual	Long-term bonus	Stock options	Stock grants	All other
Mining and construction	1000–1999	0.23	0.24	0.01	0.08	0.37	0.06	0.03
		0.21	0.21	0.00	0.00	0.46	0.00	0.01
Manufacturing	2000–3999	0.27	0.18	0.03	0.03	0.43	0.04	0.04
		0.22	0.16	0.00	0.00	0.43	0.00	0.01
Transportation, communications, electric, gas, and sanitary services	4000–4999	0.26	0.17	0.02	0.07	0.37	0.07	0.05
		0.21	0.15	0.00	0.00	0.35	0.00	0.01
Wholesale and retail trade	5000–5999	0.32	0.19	0.02	0.01	0.37	0.06	0.04
		0.26	0.16	0.00	0.00	0.36	0.00	0.01
Finance, insurance, and real estate	6000–6999	0.18	0.21	0.02	0.04	0.43	0.07	0.06
		0.13	0.16	0.00	0.00	0.44	0.00	0.01
Services	7000–8999	0.31	0.14	0.01	0.01	0.47	0.04	0.03
		0.20	0.08	0.00	0.00	0.50	0.00	0.01

[a]Means on top, medians below.
[b]SIC, Standard Industrial Classification.

one for other annual compensation and the other for all other compensation. Although small relative to the other components of the compensation package, for some companies (see First Union example above), other compensation can be material. The second item that should be explained is how the variables are valued. Companies report salaries and bonuses earned, whether paid in the current period or not, as well as the value of stock grants, other annual, and all other compensation. These amounts are picked up by ExecuComp and used in this study. The valuation of stock option grants, however, is more subjective. Companies are allowed to report in their proxy statements either their estimate of the grant date value of the options using an option-pricing model, or the potential realizable value of the options assuming the share price grows at a rate of 5 or 10% per year until the option expires. Thus, some companies report grant date values and others report potentially realizable values. ExecuComp, however, using information available about the corporation, estimates the value of all option grants using option-pricing models (Appendix 2.1 explains option pricing models). For consistency across companies, the ExecuComp estimate is used in these tables and throughout the book. The last difference between Table 2.4 and the earlier tables is the addition of a second row for each year (industry, size decile), where the first row represents the mean for that component for that year, and the second row represents the median.[24] Medians are presented beginning in Table 2.4 to demonstrate that the trends ob-

[24]For ease of presentation, the figures will be based upon the means.

TABLE 2.6   Proportion of 2000 CEO Compensation Packages Represented by Components, by Firm Size[a]

	Size decile	Salary	Annual bonus	Other annual	Long-term bonus	Stock options	Stock grants	All other
Smallest	1	0.46	0.15	0.02	0.01	0.27	0.04	0.05
		0.44	0.09	0.00	0.00	0.20	0.00	0.01
	2	0.36	0.16	0.01	0.02	0.38	0.03	0.03
		0.31	0.11	0.00	0.00	0.39	0.00	0.01
	3	0.38	0.19	0.02	0.02	0.32	0.05	0.03
		0.30	0.17	0.00	0.00	0.29	0.00	0.01
	4	0.29	0.24	0.01	0.03	0.34	0.04	0.06
		0.26	0.19	0.00	0.00	0.34	0.00	0.01
	5	0.25	0.18	0.01	0.04	0.40	0.06	0.05
		0.21	0.13	0.00	0.00	0.42	0.00	0.01
	6	0.26	0.21	0.03	0.03	0.42	0.04	0.04
		0.21	0.17	0.00	0.00	0.42	0.00	0.01
	7	0.21	0.15	0.01	0.04	0.49	0.06	0.04
		0.15	0.14	0.00	0.00	0.50	0.00	0.01
	8	0.18	0.17	0.02	0.04	0.50	0.07	0.03
		0.14	0.15	0.00	0.00	0.52	0.00	0.01
	9	0.13	0.18	0.03	0.03	0.53	0.07	0.05
		0.10	0.15	0.00	0.00	0.58	0.00	0.01
Largest	10	0.11	0.18	0.05	0.04	0.55	0.08	0.03
		0.06	0.13	0.00	0.00	0.62	0.00	0.01

[a]Firms divided by deciles by market value of equity. Means on top, medians below.

served are not being caused by outliers; rather, they are representative of the population being examined.

Substantial changes in the composition of the compensation package are observed over time (Table 2.4 and Figure 2.1), with the mean (median) proportion of the compensation package represented by salary dropping from 47% (43%) in 1992 to 27% (20%) in 2000, the mean (median) proportion of the compensation package represented by the short-term bonus dropping from 20% (19%) in 1992 to 18% (14%) in 2000, and the mean (median) proportion of the compensation package represented by stock options increasing from 21% (14%) in 1992 to 42% (42%) in 2000. This change is not driven by decreases in either salary or bonus, but by increases in the value of stock options granted to CEOs (valued at the time of grant), which now make up the largest and fastest growing component of the compensation package over the period covered by the table.[25]

Even more variation is observed looking across industries. For example, in 2000, the mean (median) proportion of CEO compensation represented by salary ranged

[25]Balsam (1995) and Yermack (1995) found that this trend, (stock compensation making up an increasing portion of the compensation package) existed over periods beginning with 1984.

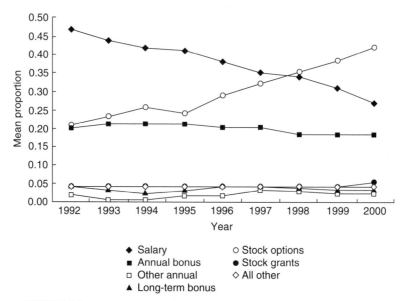

FIGURE 2.1   Mean proportion of compensation package represented by components

from a low of 18% (13%) in finance, insurance, and real estate to a high of 32% (26%) in wholesale and retail trade. Similarly, the proportion of CEO compensation represented by the annual bonus ranged from a low of 14% (8%), in services, to a high of 24% (21%) in mining and construction. Transportation, communications, electric, gas, and sanitary services had the lowest mean and median proportions represented by stock options, 37 and 35%, and services the highest, at 47 and 50%, respectively.

Finally, and perhaps most interestingly, variation is observed by the size of the corporation. In 2000, the mean (median) proportion of the compensation package represented by salary declines from 46% (44%) for the smallest decile of corporations to 11% (6%) in the largest! In contrast, the proportion of the compensation package represented by stock options and stock grants generally increases with the size of the corporation. The proportion of the compensation package represented by stock options increases from a mean (median) of 27% (20%) in the smallest decile of corporations to a mean (median) of 55% (62%) in the largest decile of corporations. The proportion of the compensation package represented by stock grants increases from a mean of 4% in the smallest decile of corporations to a mean of 8% in the largest decile of corporations (in both deciles most companies do not issue stock grants, hence the medians of 0).

As will be shown in Chapter 8, CEO percentage ownership decreases with increases in the size of the corporation. As noted in Chapter 1, executive ownership and the executive compensation package are two of the mechanisms for minimizing the agency costs arising from the separation of the ownership and management of the corporation. Consequently, the trends observed in the composition of the compensation package, that is, the increased used of stock-based compensation as the size of the corporation increases, may be an optimal response to the lower level of incentives provided by equity ownership in larger corporations.

The evidence in Tables 2.1. through 2.6 shows that there is considerable variation in the items included in the CEO compensation package, and the relative importance of those items. These differences occur over time, across industry, and across the size of the corporation.

V. MAGNITUDE OF COMPENSATION PACKAGE

Tables 2.7, 2.8, and 2.9 and Figure 2.2, show the dollar amounts of CEO compensation. Table 2.7 and Figure 2.2 show that the dollar amounts of salary, bonus, stock options and stock grants, as well as total compensation increased dramatically over time. For example, mean (median) total compensation increased from $1,689,000 ($997,000) in 1992 to $8,466,000 ($3,188,000) in 2000, an increase of 401% (220%). The bulk of this increase was driven by the value of stock options. That is, the mean (median) value of stock option grants increased from $592,000 ($110,000) in 1992, to $5,589,000 ($1,214,000) in 2000, an increase of 1004% (844%)! But all the major components increased. Mean (median) salary increased from $454,000 ($394,000) in 1992 to $677,000 ($640,000) in 2000, an increase of 49% (62%), and mean (median) short-term bonuses increased from $316,000 ($176,000) to $1,029,000 ($495,000), an increase of 226% (181%). By contrast, the cumulative inflation rate over that time period was about 20%! Hence total compensation, and the major components of the CEO compensation package, have increased at rates far in excess of inflation over the most recent time period.

Table 2.8 shows the differences across industry. In 2000, the mean (median) CEO compensation package ranged from a low of $5,002,000 ($3,295,000) in mining and construction to a high of $11,169,000 ($4,960,000) in finance, insurance, and real estate. When comparing these two industries it becomes readily apparent that these differences are driven almost entirely by conditional compensation. That is, the mean and median salary across the two industries is nearly identical, $734,000 and $700,000 for mining and construction, versus $755,000 and $735,000 for financial, insurance, and real estate. In contrast, the mean (median) annual bonus received by CEOs in finance, insurance, and real estate of $2,009,000 ($800,000) is approximately double the amount received by CEOs in mining and construction—$1,090,000 ($680,000)—and the mean (median) value of stock option grants received by CEOs in finance, insurance, and real estate of $6,337,000 ($2,407,000) is

TABLE 2.7   Average of CEO Compensation Package in Dollars by Components, by Year[a]

Year	Salary	Annual bonus	Other annual	Long-term bonus	Stock options	Stock grants	All other	Total
1992	454,000	316,000	44,000	77,000	592,000	114,000	42,000	1,689,000
	394,000	176,000	0	0	110,000	0	11,000	997,000
1993	477,000	377,000	37,000	81,000	601,000	136,000	75,000	1,798,000
	416,000	196,000	0	0	156,000	0	14,000	1,076,000
1994	494,000	430,000	49,000	73,000	860,000	127,000	75,000	2,109,000
	433,000	229,000	0	0	222,000	0	15,000	1,198,000
1995	506,000	470,000	74,000	111,000	819,000	142,000	97,000	2,193,000
	450,000	245,000	0	0	215,000	0	17,000	1,245,000
1996	515,000	545,000	77,000	171,000	1,363,000	190,000	93,000	2,947,000
	460,000	255,000	0	0	340,000	0	16,000	1,466,000
1997	523,000	558,000	131,000	161,000	1,745,000	225,000	176,000	3,464,000
	472,000	300,000	0	0	418,000	0	17,000	1,679,000
1998	553,000	564,000	160,000	149,000	1,926,000	281,000	158,000	3,681,000
	500,000	294,000	0	0	554,000	0	18,000	1,865,000
1999	584,000	685,000	117,000	190,000	3,075,000	673,000	212,000	5,474,000
	528,000	344,000	0	0	731,000	0	19,000	2,130,000
2000	677,000	1,029,000	234,000	252,000	5,589,000	609,000	258,000	8,466,000
	640,000	495,000	0	0	1,214,000	0	32,000	3,188,000

[a]Means on top, medians below.

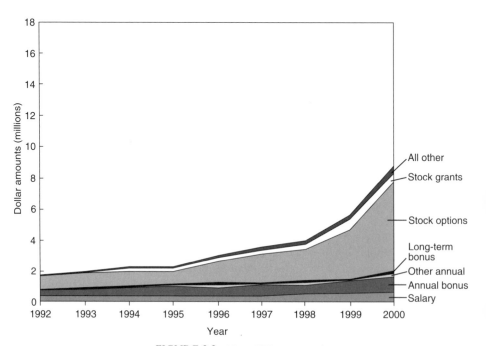

FIGURE 2.2   Mean CEO compensation

TABLE 2.8   Average of 2000 CEO Compensation Package by Components, by Industry[a]

Industry	SIC codes[b]	Salary ($)	Annual bonus ($)	Other annual ($)	Long-term bonus ($)	Stock options ($)	Stock grants ($)	All other ($)	Total ($)
Mining and construction	1000–1999	734,000	1,090,000	30,000	612,000	2,067,000	352,000	120,000	5,002,000
		700,000	680,000	0	0	1,138,000	0	48,000	3,295,000
Manufacturing	2000–3999	664,000	975,000	326,000	202,000	5,981,000	514,000	211,000	8,588,000
		633,000	500,000	0	0	1,189,000	0	34,000	2,958,000
Transportation, communications, electric, gas, and sanitary services	4000–4999	682,000	860,000	96,000	490,000	3,336,000	450,000	422,000	6,284,000
		650,000	405,000	0	0	859,000	0	40,000	2,848,000
Wholesale and retail trade	5000–5999	668,000	688,000	106,000	79,000	3,258,000	385,000	168,000	5,308,000
		631,000	427,000	0	0	790,000	0	24,000	2,613,000
Finance, insurance, and real estate	6000–6999	755,000	2,009,000	346,000	491,000	6,337,000	994,000	483,000	11,169,000
		735,000	800,000	0	0	2,407,000	0	62,000	4,960,000
Services	7000–8999	586,000	566,000	71,000	59,000	7,848,000	499,000	184,000	9,787,000
		507,000	309,000	0	0	1,598,000	0	7,000	3,109,000

[a]Means on top, medians below.
[b]SIC, Standard Industrial Classification.

TABLE 2.9 Average of 2000 CEO Compensation Package in Dollars by Components and by Firm Size[a]

Size decile	Salary	Annual bonus	Other annual	Long-term bonus	Stock options	Stock grants	All other	Total
Smallest 1	426,000	197,000	24,000	16,000	512,000	75,000	72,000	1,321,000
	396,000	129,000	0	0	165,000	0	11,000	942,000
2	468,000	344,000	28,000	41,000	968,000	112,000	55,000	2,002,000
	433,000	150,000	0	0	474,000	0	7,000	1,448,000
3	576,000	493,000	72,000	47,000	1,075,000	193,000	132,000	2,586,000
	558,000	322,000	0	0	533,000	0	23,000	1,866,000
4	562,000	623,000	32,000	76,000	1,670,000	227,000	174,000	3,364,000
	586,000	465,000	0	0	643,000	0	28,000	2,257,000
5	663,000	696,000	39,000	327,000	3,511,000	379,000	176,000	5,782,000
	655,000	519,000	0	0	1,314,000	0	30,000	3,411,000
6	695,000	736,000	95,000	129,000	3,512,000	122,000	171,000	5,384,000
	649,000	567,000	0	0	1,095,000	0	42,000	3,130,000
7	713,000	944,000	230,000	258,000	4,078,000	572,000	481,000	7,173,000
	700,000	510,000	0	0	2,493,000	0	35,000	4,869,000
8	797,000	1,823,000	229,000	255,000	11,427,000	693,000	125,000	15,162,000
	766,000	788,000	0	0	2,299,000	0	45,000	5,460,000
9	826,000	1,347,000	391,000	509,000	10,481,000	789,000	711,000	14,722,000
	875,000	1,168,000	0	0	4,444,000	0	79,000	9,217,000
Largest 10	1,047,000	3,116,000	1,209,000	847,000	18,925,000	2,954,000	420,000	27,405,000
	1,000,000	1,936,000	24,000	0	9,040,000	0	79,000	18,573,000

[a]Firms divided into deciles by market value of equity. Means on top, medians below.

more than double the value of stock option grants received by CEOs in mining and construction—$2,067,000 ($1,138,000).

Table 2.9 shows the differences across the size of the corporation. As would be expected, the average dollar amounts of salary, bonus, stock options, stock grants, and total compensation all increase with the size of the corporation. In 2000 the mean (median) total compensation for a CEO of a corporation in the smallest size decile was $1,321,000 ($942,000), whereas the comparable amounts for a CEO of a corporation in the largest size decile were $27,405,000 ($18,573,000), roughly 20 times as much. This pattern, although consistent across all components of the compensation package, is most pronounced for conditional compensation, that is, bonuses, stock options, and stock grants. It reflects what some consider the added skills needed to run a larger corporation, and to some extent, the added effect on profitability a CEO can have in a larger corporation that is, the dollar gains from his or her actions will be greater the larger the corporation.

VI. RELATIVE PAY OF CEOs TO OTHER TOP EXECUTIVES

The CEO is the leader of the modern corporation. As such, the CEO normally receives higher compensation than his or her subordinates. The amount of this differential can be a source of friction, however. As noted elsewhere in this book, the popular press has noted that CEO pay is out of line compared with that of the average worker. As an illustration, *Time* magazine recently contained the following note: "476:1 Ratio of the average salary of an American CEO to that of an American blue-collar worker."[26]

Tables 2.10, 2.11, and 2.12 provide some descriptive statistics on the variation of the compensation package throughout the executive suite for the 2000 fiscal year.

[26]Hambly (2000).

TABLE 2.10   Median Ratio of 2000 CEO Compensation to Compensation Earned by Next Four Highest Paid Employees

	Rank	Salary	Annual bonus	Other annual	Long-term bonus	Stock options	Stock grants	All other	Total
CEO	1	1.00	1.00	1.00	1.00	1.00	1.00	1.00	1.00
	2	0.63	0.54	0.30	0.46	0.45	0.40	0.64	0.54
	3	0.52	0.38	0.15	0.33	0.31	0.29	0.50	0.41
	4	0.47	0.31	0.08	0.30	0.26	0.25	0.47	0.35
	5	0.43	0.27	0.04	0.25	0.22	0.20	0.41	0.30

TABLE 2.11   Proportion of 2000 Compensation Package Represented by Components and Executive Rank[a]

	Rank	Salary	Annual bonus	Other annual	Long-term bonus	Stock options	Stock grants	All other
CEO	1	0.27	0.18	0.02	0.03	0.42	0.05	0.04
		0.20	0.14	0.00	0.00	0.42	0.00	0.01
	2	0.29	0.20	0.02	0.03	0.39	0.05	0.04
		0.25	0.17	0.00	0.00	0.36	0.00	0.01
	3	0.31	0.18	0.01	0.03	0.38	0.05	0.03
		0.27	0.16	0.00	0.00	0.37	0.00	0.01
	4	0.32	0.17	0.01	0.03	0.38	0.05	0.03
		0.29	0.15	0.00	0.00	0.36	0.00	0.01
	5	0.34	0.16	0.01	0.03	0.37	0.05	0.04
		0.30	0.14	0.00	0.00	0.35	0.00	0.01

[a]Means on top, medians below.

The difference, although not as pronounced as the *Time* magazine quote, is substantial. Looking at Table 2.10, which controls for corporate characteristics, in that pay for the second to fifth highest executive is calculated as a fraction of CEO pay, in terms of total compensation, the second highest paid executive makes a median 54% of what the CEO makes, whereas the fifth highest paid executive makes a median of 30% of the CEO.[27] Viewed from the bottom up, the CEO makes about 89% more than the next highest paid executive, and more than three times the fifth highest paid executive. This differential is consistent with tournament theory—see, for example, Lazear and Rosen (1981), whereby CEO pay is not necessarily based upon the CEO's value or marginal product, but rather held out as an incentive or reward to lower level executives to strive to become CEO. Rosen (1986, p. 714) claims, "Payments at the top have indirect effects of increasing productivity of competitors further down the ladder." Hence the differential is necessary. This differential is greatest for conditional, in particular, long-term compensation, consistent with risk aversion playing a role in the setting of the compensation package, and allowing for the possibility of large payoff if the corporation does well and recognizing, perhaps, that the CEO is the individual with the largest effect on corporationwide payoffs. Table 2.11 provides support for this theory, as salary while making up a mean (median) 27% (20%) of the CEO compensation package, increases monotonically until it makes up 34% (30%) of the compensation package of the fifth highest paid individual. Conversely, the proportion of stock options in the compensation package drops from a mean (median) of 42% (42%) for the CEO to a still substantial 37% (35%) for the fifth highest paid executive. Table 2.12 provides

[27]Because small denominators have the ability to create extremely large ratios, and consequently disproportionately affect the means, only medians are presented in this table.

TABLE 2.12   Average of 2000 CEO Compensation Package in Dollars by Components and by Executive Rank[a]

	Rank	Salary	Annual bonus	Other annual	Long-term bonus	Stock options	Stock grants	All other	Total
CEO	1	677,000	1,029,000	234,000	252,000	5,589,000	609,000	258,000	8,466,000
		640,000	495,000	0	0	1,214,000	0	32,000	3,188,000
	2	439,000	567,000	147,000	130,000	2,554,000	303,000	150,000	4,167,000
		396,000	300,000	0	0	561,000	0	19,000	1,687,000
	3	365,000	393,000	28,000	99,000	1,673,000	208,000	104,000	2,858,000
		325,000	218,000	0	0	435,000	0	14,000	1,274,000
	4	324,000	310,000	18,000	83,000	1,540,000	186,000	65,000	2,527,000
		288,000	175,000	0	0	339,000	0	14,000	1,086,000
	5	294,000	261,000	14,000	70,000	1,315,000	181,000	78,000	2,215,000
		267,000	142,000	0	0	292,000	0	13,000	957,000

[a]Means on top, medians below.

the actual dollar amounts, which for total compensation, range from a mean (median) $2,215,000 ($957,000) for the fifth highest paid executive to $8,466,000 ($3,188,000) for the CEO.

VII. SUMMARY

This chapter provided an overview of the executive compensation package. It began by explaining the major components of the compensation package (e.g., salary, bonus, stock options and grants, pensions, and benefits) and provided examples from publicly held corporations of the use of each component in the executive compensation package. The chapter then provided descriptive statistics of the use of these components in the compensation packages of the corporations comprising the S&P 500, S&P MidCap 400, and S&P SmallCap 600 indices for the years 1992–2000.

In terms of usage, salary is observed in the compensation packages of almost all CEOs across time, industry, and corporate size, whereas other components of the compensation package (e.g., stock option grants) have become more prevalent over the period under examination and vary by industry and with the size of the corporation. Although salary is observed in almost all compensation packages, its importance varies over time, across industry, and depending on corporate size. For example, the mean (median) proportion of the compensation package represented by salary dropping from 47% (43%) in 1992 to 27% (20%) in 2000. Similar variation was observed with respect to the other components of the compensation package.

Examining the amounts involved, CEO compensation appears rather large, with the amounts growing dramatically over the years examined. That is, mean (median) total compensation increased from $1,689,000 ($997,000) in 1992 to $8,466,000 ($3,188,000) in 2000, an increase of 401% (220%). This occurred over a period of fairly stable prices. That is, the consumer price index only increased by about 20% over the same period. Although the bulk of the increase was caused by increases in the value of stock options granted, each component of the compensation package grew over the time period under examination.

APPENDIX 2.1. AN INTRODUCTION TO OPTION PRICING MODELS

A stock option is a right to buy a share of stock at a precontracted price over a predetermined period of time. For example, a stock option might allow its holder the *right* to buy a share of stock for $10 at any time over the next 10 years. The issue faced by academics and nonacademics alike, is how to value that *right*. The right is valuable because, if the share price increases beyond $10 before the right expires, the holder can exercise that right to buy the share at a price less than its worth in the marketplace. As a precursor to explaining option-pricing models, the two components of an option's value,[1] the intrinsic and time values, need to be defined. The intrinsic value of an option is equal to the excess of the current market price of a share of stock over the exercise price of the option at any point in time. Continuing with the above example, if the current market price is $12 per share, and the holder of the option can purchase the share for $10, the intrinsic value of the option is $2. The time value of an option is the value attached to the potential increase in the share price over the life of the option. Although the intrinsic value is easily determinable, the time value is not, and requires the use of an option-pricing model, such as the one developed by Fisher Black and Myron Scholes.

To illustrate the complexity of option pricing models, consider the formula used by Foster et al. (1991) to calculate the value of options under the Black–Scholes model:

$$V = [e^{-\ln(1+k)t}S \, \phi \, (Z) - e^{-\ln(1+r)t}X \, \phi \, (Z - 6\sqrt{t})],$$

where

V = the value of the option,
S = the current stock price,
X = the exercise price,
r = the risk-free rate,
6^2 = the variance of return on the optioned stock,
t = the time until the option matures,
k = the continuous-dividend yield as a constant proportion of the underlying share price,
$\phi \, (.)$ = the cumulative normal density functino,

and

$$Z = [\ln(S/X) + (\ln(1+r) - \ln(1+k) + 6^2/2t]/6\sqrt{t}$$

As can be seen from the formula, the Black-Scholes option pricing model estimates the option's value by considering the current stock price, the exercise price, the time until the option matures, the continuous dividend, the risk-free rate, and

---

[1]The value of the option is equal to the sum of its intrinsic and time values.

the variance of return on the optioned stock. It can be shown that the value of the option increases with increases in the current stock price, the variance of return on the optioned stock, and the time until the option matures; and that it decreases with increases in the exercise price, the risk-free rate, and the continuous dividend yield.

Although few are familiar with the formula itself, readily available computer software can perform the actual calculation. However, effort must be expended to get the inputs for the model, and many of the inputs are subjective. It has been asserted by many (see discussion in Balsam 1994) that these models tend to over-value employee stock options because they assume tradeability, the ability to sell short, and ignore the effect of the continued employment requirement, all of which reduce the value of the option to the employee.

CHAPTER 3

An Introduction to Designing the Executive Compensation Contract

I. INTRODUCTION

This chapter will introduce, in general terms, some of the issues involved in designing an executive compensation contract. The issues are (1) making the offer attractive, (2) providing incentives to increase shareholder value, (3) providing incentives to remain with the corporation, and (4) minimizing the costs to shareholders. Although the discussion that follows will focus on designing a contract to attract a new CEO from outside the corporation, much of the discussion applies to internal promotions, as well as to designing a contract to retain existing executives.

II. MAKING THE OFFER ATTRACTIVE

To illustrate the decisions a corporation must make in designing a compensation package, consider the corporation that wishes to hire a new CEO from outside the corporation. First, the corporation must make the compensation package lucrative enough to entice the targeted executive to take the position. That is, the value of the compensation package offered to the executive should exceed his or her next best opportunity or "opportunity cost." This may be his or her current compensation package or the compensation package being offered by another potential employer. However, simply exceeding the executives' current compensation package may not be enough. Changing jobs is a gamble, and executives, as risk-averse individuals, need to be compensated for taking chances. To induce them to take that chance, a substantial premium may be involved.

As an illustration, consider what Citigroup offered in October 1999 to Robert E. Rubin to become chairman of its executive committee. Rubin had just resigned his position as United States Secretary of the Treasury making approximately $150,000 a year. Citigroup, in addition to giving him options on 1.5 million shares, which Citigroup valued at $18.5 million,[1] promised him an additional 1.5 million options in 2000, and at least $1 million in salary and $14 million in bonus in both 2000 and 2001.[2] While substantially above his salary as Secretary of the Treasury, the amount did not seem unreasonable (to Citigroup at least) given what he had earned prior to his government service or what he could earn if he returned to Wall Street. Prior to entering governmental service, Rubin was Co-Senior Partner and Co-Chairman of Goldman, Sachs & Co. Thus an estimate of his opportunity cost would be the earnings of the current chairman of Goldman Sachs and other Wall Street companies. In 1999 the Chairman and CEO of Goldman Sachs, Henry M. Paulson, Jr., received $300,000 in salary, a bonus of $16,062,153, and restricted stock valued at $8,828,701;[3] the Chairman and CEO of Merrill Lynch, David H. Komansky, received a compensation package of $25,800,000;[4] and the Chairman and CEO of Morgan Stanley Dean Witter, Philip J. Purcell, received $775,000 in salary, a bonus of $12,112,500, restricted stock worth $8,184,303, and stock options valued at $5,556,250.[5]

It should be noted that the value of the compensation package to the executive includes both pecuniary and nonpecuniary factors. An executive may be willing to accept a lesser paying position if the corporation's headquarters is in a preferred location. Alternatively, an executive might be willing to accept less compensation to work for corporation A than for corporation B because corporation A is viewed as more prestigious and/or has more growth potential. For example, in September 1999 George Shaheen left his position as head of Andersen Consulting making a "secure seven-figure annual income"[6] to become Chief Executive Officer and President of Webvan for

> a base salary of $500,000, subject to annual adjustment, and a target bonus of $250,000. In connection with this agreement, Mr. Shaheen was granted 1,250,000 shares of fully vested common stock and was granted an option to purchase an additional 15,000,000 shares of common stock at an exercise price of $8.00 per share.[7]

To illustrate that upside potential,

[1]Citigroup proxy statement filed with the Securities and Exchange Commission, March 17, 2000, p. 26.

[2]Citigroup proxy statement filed with Securities and Exchange Commission, March 17, 2000, p. 26.

[3]Goldman Sachs Group proxy statement filed with the Securities and Exchange Commission, February 14, 2000, p. 8.

[4]Merrill Lynch proxy statement filed with the Securities and Exchange Commission, March 9, 2000, p. 19.

[5]Morgan Stanley Dean Witter proxy statement filed with the Securities and Exchange Commission, February 23, 2000, pp. 10, 12.

[6]Whitford (1999), p. 44.

[7]Employment contract, dated September 21, 1999, between George Shaheen and Webvan Group.

At the high point of the first day of Webvan's November 1999 IPO, Shaheen's 15 million stock options were worth $390 million. Along with the 1.25 million shares he was granted, he was worth some $815 million.[8]

III. PROVIDING THE PROPER INCENTIVES

The corporation wants to design the contract to encourage the CEO to act in a way consistent with its objective, presumably, value maximization. In doing so, the corporation recognizes that the different components of the compensation package have different effects on CEO incentives, risk, political costs, and tax payments, and on its own financial reporting, political costs, and tax payments.

To make things simple and to minimize contracting costs, the corporation could offer to pay the CEO a salary, which would fix compensation regardless of performance. However, in that situation, the CEO has little financial incentive to maximize shareholder value because he or she does not benefit from doing so.[9] And considering that economists view most individuals as work averse (although there are many who would argue that individuals who make it to the executive suite are not work averse, but rather workaholics), the CEO would have incentive to shirk and/or overconsume perquisites. Alternatively, the corporation could offer the CEO a contract whereby his or her compensation is solely based upon corporate performance. Although this would provide the CEO with incentive to maximize shareholder value, it would impose substantial risk on the CEO.[10] As most economists assume individuals are risk averse, the CEO would be unwilling to take the contract unless there was a substantial premium built into it to compensate for the risk involved. For example, the CEO might be willing to accept $1 million if compensation was fixed, but require an expected payout of $3 million if compensation were totally based upon performance. The corporation would then have to decide if the benefits from increased performance that could be expected under the performance-based contract would warrant the extra costs of the contract; that is, do the marginal benefits of the performance-based contract exceed the marginal costs?

In practice, we observe few contracts that are either totally fixed or variable. One famous example is that between Lee Iacocca and the Chrysler Corporation. When Iacocca joined Chrysler in 1978 he took all of his compensation in the form of stock options, which are completely variable in the sense that they only have value

[8]Reingold and Jespersen (2000), p. 112.

[9]Some financial incentive does exist. If the corporation performs well as a result of his or her actions, the CEO could get a raise from his or her current employer, and/or increase his or her reputation or value in the managerial labor market.

[10]As an example of the risk involved, Reingold and Jespersen (2000) reported that starting in 1997 the top five executives of the Borders Group elected to take options in lieu of salaries. They stated that "with his options under water, Vice-Chairman Bruce A. Quinnell had to borrow to pay his living expenses" (p. 100).

if the underlying stock increases in value—so if the stock price did not increase Iacocca would have nothing. Another example is Steve Jobs of Apple Computer. Taking over as interim CEO on September 10, 1997,[11] Jobs received no compensation in 1997, other than 30,000 options granted to all directors,[12] salary of $1 in 1998,[13] and salary of $1 in 1999.[14] However, upon formally accepting the position of CEO in January 2000, Apple granted Jobs options to purchase 10,000,000 shares.[15] While no valuation was disclosed by Apple at the time (under Securities and Exchange Commission requirements they did not have to disclose a value for the options until they file their proxy statement for the 2000 fiscal year), according to Menn (2000),[16]

> The options were priced at $87.188 each. Apple shares closed at $111.31 in Nasdaq trading on Friday. That means the marketing whiz has already earned more than $240 million on paper from the stock's appreciation.

Perhaps the most profitable example of an executive forgoing all other compensation in exchange for stock options is that of Lawrence Ellison, Chief Executive Officer of Oracle, who in 1999, agreed to take no salary and bonus for fiscal 2000 through fiscal 2003, in exchange for options on 10,000,000 shares.[17] *The Wall Street Journal* (2000f) reports that this "arrangement has netted Mr. Ellison a paper windfall of about $1.3 billion." Other examples of executives forgoing salary, along with brief explanations as to why they elected to forgo salary, are included in Table 3.1.

At the other extreme are Warren Buffett and Jeff Bezos. Buffet is the famed investor and CEO of Berkshire Hathaway, whose compensation package primarily consists of salary, a salary that has been fixed at $100,000 per year for about 20 years.[18] And yet Berkshire Hathaway has done extremely well over that period. The secret: Buffett owns approximately 35% of Berkshire Hathaway stock,[19] which pro-

[11]Apple Computer proxy statement filed with Securities and Exchange Commission, March 16, 1998, p. 6.

[12]Apple Computer proxy statement filed with Securities and Exchange Commission, March 16, 1998, p. 8.

[13]Apple Computer proxy statement filed with Securities and Exchange Commission, February 9, 1999, p. 7.

[14]Apple Computer proxy statement filed with Securities and Exchange Commission, March 6, 2000, p. 7.

[15]Apple Computer proxy statement filed with Securities and Exchange Commission, March 6, 2000, p. 19.

[16]More than a year later, on March 12, 2001, Apple disclosed that the 10,000,000 options, which ultimately became 20,000,000 because of a subsequent stock split, were estimated to be worth $548,317,503 if their stock price increased at a rate of 5 percent per year, and $1,389,544,207 if their stock price increased by 10 percent per year (Apple Computer proxy statement filed with Securities and Exchange Commission, March 12, 2001, p. 9).

[17]Oracle proxy statement filed with Securities and Exchange Commission, September 11, 2000, p. 12.

[18]Berkshire Hathaway proxy statement filed with Securities and Exchange Commission, March 19, 2001, p. 4.

[19]Berkshire Hathaway proxy statement filed with Securities and Exchange Commission, March 19, 2001, p. 6.

TABLE 3.1   Additional Examples of Executives Forgoing Salary

Corporation, executive, title	Explanation
Capital One Financial • Richard D. Fairbank, Chairman of the Board and Chief Executive Officer • Nigel W. Morris, President and Chief Operating Officer	In 1997 agreed: "to give up their entire salary plus any benefits under the Stock Purchase Plan, the Savings Plan and the Excess Savings Plan for the next three years in exchange for a non-qualified stock option grant."[a]
El Paso Energy • William A Wise, Chairman of the Board, Chief Executive Officer and President	"Base salary was eliminated in 1996 and replaced with long-term awards of stock options and restricted stock, the majority of which vest only after the expiration of specified time periods and only if certain performance targets are met within those periods."[b]
Viacom • Summer Redstone, Chairman of the Board, Chief Executive Officer and controlling stockholder	". . . has waived payment of any salary or bonus compensation for his services as Chief Executive Officer of the Company."[c]
Pepsico • Roger Enrico, Chairman of the Board and Chief Executive Officer	"At Mr. Enrico's request, the Committee again approved a reduction in Mr. Enrico's annual salary from $900,000 to $1, and recommended to the Board of Directors that it consider using the savings to support front line employees. In January 1999, the Board approved annual charitable contributions of approximately $1,000,000 to fund additional scholarships for children of PepsiCo's front line employees.[d]
Borders Group • Robert DiRomualdo, Chairman • George Mrkonic, Vice Chairman	"Messrs. DiRomualdo and Mrkonic were granted options in lieu of cash for 100% of their fiscal 1999 salary and bonus. The options grants to Messrs. DiRomualdo and Mrkonic covered 194,826 and 94,322 shares, respectively. The salary and bonus to which the named officers were entitled for fiscal 1999 is as follows: Mr. DiRomualdo, $474,553 salary, $474,553 bonus; Mr. Mrkonic, $257,500 salary, $257,500 bonus."[e]

[a]Capital One Financial proxy statement filed with Securities and Exchange Commission, March 17, 1998, p. 18.

[b]El Paso Energy proxy statement filed with Securities and Exchange Commission, March 11, 1999, p. 7.

[c]Viacom proxy statement filed with Securities and Exchange Commission, April 16, 1999, p. 12.

[d]Pepsico proxy statement filed with Securities and Exchange Commission, March 24, 2000, p. 9.

[e]Borders Group proxy statement filed with Securities and Exchange Commission, April 21, 2000, p. 5.

vides sufficient incentive by itself for him to want to increase shareholder value. Bezos, Chairman and CEO of Amazon.com, also receives compensation consisting solely of salary, which was $81,840 in 1998, 1999, and 2000.[20] Like Buffett, Bezos owns about one-third of the outstanding shares of Amazon.com. While the ownership of corporate shares by Buffett and Bezos is not the norm, in considering the effect of compensation on incentives, ownership is a factor that always has to be considered. Academic researchers (for example, Jensen and Murphy 1990a & b; Hall and Liebman 1998; Murphy 1998) have noted that the relationship between pay and performance is driven primarily by ownership, broadly defined as holdings of stock and stock options.

More commonly, compensation packages include both fixed and variable components. Fixed components are included to reduce the risk to the CEO and guarantee a standard of living, whereas variable components are included to provide incentives and to align the interests of management and shareholders. Assuming that the compensation package the corporation designs will include fixed and variable components, the corporation then has to decide how much of each to include, and what forms they should take. Fixed components might include salary and benefits, such as employer paid life insurance, health care, and pensions. Variable components might include bonuses, where the payout may be based on reported accounting numbers, market share, or customer satisfaction, and stock compensation, where the payout is based on stock prices. Each has differing effects on CEO incentives and has differing costs to the corporation.

Referring to the incentives, consider salary and the pension benefit, which are both nominally fixed in amount; however, both provide certain incentives and can influence the decisions the CEO makes, both personally and for the corporation. For example, while salary is nominally fixed in amount, it can be renegotiated *upward or downward,* although the latter is less frequent than the former. And a defined benefit pension plan can be structured so that it does not vest immediately and/or so the benefit increases with the individual's tenure with the corporation. Structuring the pension this way gives the CEO incentive to remain with the corporation. However, if the pension is not fully funded, the CEO has the incentive to reduce the risk of the corporation, which could involve forgoing otherwise profitable projects.[21] Why? Because if the corporation goes bankrupt, not only does the CEO lose his or her job, but also to the extent his or her pension is not fully funded, he or she becomes an unsecured creditor of the corporation. Why not then

---

[20]Amazon.com proxy statement filed with Securities and Exchange Commission, April 13, 2001, p. 7.

[21]As noted in chapter 2, most CEOs are covered by two defined benefit pension plans. The basic plan is at least partially funded, governed by Employee Retirement Income Security Act (ERISA), and guaranteed somewhat by the Pension Benefit Guaranty Corporation (PBGC). However, restrictions imposed by ERISA and the Internal Revenue Code limit the payouts from these plans. Thus most corporations have a supplemental plan for their top executives. Given that the supplemental plan is not tax-qualified, if it were funded, the executive would be taxed immediately. Thus these plans are generally unfunded.

simply make the fixed component all salary? One reason is that our tax code provides incentives for employers to provide things like life insurance, health care, and pensions.[22] Sometimes the tax incentives even exist for the employee to defer salary to future periods.[23] To the extent that the compensation package can be structured to minimize taxes, or more formally, the joint tax burden of the corporation and CEO, both parties can be made better off.

When a corporation is determining the variable components of its compensation plan, that is, determining whether variable compensation should include bonuses, stock compensation, or both, it must also realize that different forms of variable compensation provide different incentives. For example, a bonus plan based upon accounting numbers may lead to higher reported accounting income, but not necessarily lead to higher shareholder value, as management may make cosmetic changes to its financial statements to increase its bonuses (see discussion in Chapter 5, Section II). Similarly, if managers are rewarded for increasing market share, the corporation may get increased market share, but at the cost of reduced profits and reduced shareholder value. In contrast, stock compensation only increases in value when value (narrowly defined as share price) increases, but subjects the manager to market risks, for which he or she will want to be compensated. Theoretically, this market risk can be controlled for with a market-adjusted option whereby the exercise price of the option can be adjusted up or down depending on market movements. However, corporations do not seem to grant market-adjusted options.[24] In practice (see Tables 2.1, 2.2, and 2.3) we see corporations including both bonuses and stock-based compensation in the compensation package as a way of reducing the risks to the executive (Sloan 1993). Alternatively, the bonus might be used as a way to reward the executive regardless of performance. For example, in 1999 Eastman Kodak gave its retiring CEO a $2.5 million bonus "in recognition of the company's financial performance" even though in a bull market the corporation's shares declined 8% in value![25]

If stock compensation is used, the corporation must decide if it should take the form of stock grants or stock options. Stock grants are valuable as long as the share price is above zero, whereas stock options are only valuable if the share price is

---

[22]For example, assuming the requirements set by the Internal Revenue Code are met, payments for employee life insurance and health-care benefits are deductible by the employer but not recognized as income by the employee. Thus, the employee is better off having the employer purchase these items on his or her behalf, than if the employer would have paid those amounts as salary, with the employee purchasing those benefits with his or her after-tax salary.

[23]Miller and Scholes (1982) show this occurs when the corporate tax rate is less than that of the individual.

[24]A plethora of possible explanations exist. One is that under current accounting standards, an expense would have to be recognized for market-adjusted options (whereas none is recognized for most options currently granted), hence accounting treatment has kept corporations from granting these options. The other is that managers want the upside potential associated with unadjusted options and may have other mechanisms, for example, repricing, to control downside risk. These issues are more fully discussed in Chapters 6 and 12.

[25] *Wall Street Journal* (2000b).

greater than the exercise price (the price at which the option allows the holder to purchase shares). In general, stock options will provide the CEO with more incentives to take risks than stock grants (Guay 1999). Yet certain companies, such as Philip Morris, grant restricted stock "in an effort to retain its executives in the face of a steep drop in the company's share price" arguing that options do not "work well for tobacco companies, whose share prices now are influenced more by what happens in courtrooms than by whether management is meeting its goals."[26]

IV. DESIGNING THE CONTRACT TO RETAIN THE EXECUTIVE

To minimize recruiting and training costs and to avoid the downtime associated with an open position, corporations would like to ensure that the executive being recruited stays with the corporation. There are two, nonmutually exclusive tracks it can take. The first approach would be to provide monetary incentives to stay, for example, compensation that vests over a period of time, and hence is forfeited if the executive leaves before the end of the vesting period. This track, which involves long-term components of compensation such as restricted stock, stock options, and pensions, could be referred to as the "golden handcuffs" approach. An example would be the following Special Equity Grant given to Richard A. McGinn, Chairman of the Board and CEO of Lucent Technologies:

> As an incentive for Mr. McGinn to continue providing the company with first-class leadership and to guide the company towards its goal of becoming the pre-eminent supplier of next-generation communications networks, we granted Mr. McGinn an additional stock option in fiscal 1999 covering 1,000,000 shares. This option will vest only if Mr. McGinn stays with the company for five years from the grant date.[27]

This grant is in addition his annual grant of 400,000 options (which vest after three years), and was valued by the corporation at the time of grant at $11,180,000.[28] The intrinsic value of the additional grant at December 31, 1999, was $45,640,600. Being that the grant is not yet exercisable, if McGinn were to leave Lucent he would forgo that entire amount, providing him with the incentive to remain with Lucent.[29]

An example of a corporation compensating an executive for items forfeited at a prior employer is found in the following employment contract of C. Michael Arm-

[26]Fairclough (2000), p. A22.

[27]Lucent Technologies proxy statement filed with the Securities and Exchange Commission, December 21, 1999, p. 28.

[28]Lucent Technologies proxy statement filed with the Securities and Exchange Commission, December 21, 1999, p. 32.

[29]McGinn was replaced as Chairman and CEO of Lucent by Henry Schact in October of 2000, well short of the 5-year vesting. As this book goes to press, it is unclear if Lucent allowed him to retain these options or required they be forfeited.

strong, Chairman of the Board and Chief Executive Officer of AT&T dated October 17, 1997:

> In order to address certain forfeitures experienced when the Executive left his previous employer, the Company shall pay a premium of $2,050,000 to purchase a split-dollar survivorship insurance policy under an Estate Enhancement Program insuring the Executive and his spouse. . . .
>
> Prior to the Company purchasing insurance under this paragraph, Executive will make a reasonable effort (but not including litigation) to obtain all or a portion of his 1997 annual bonus and his long-term incentive bonus for the 1995–1997 performance cycle from his current employer, and he will notify the Company, in writing, of the outcome of such efforts.

The second approach is to limit the executive's alternative employment opportunities with noncompete, nondisclosure, and nonsolicitation provisions. An example of each of these provisions was found in the following employment agreement between Thomas A. Corcoran, President and Chief Executive Officer, and Allegheny Teledyne dated August 17th 1999.

> 6. Restrictions.
>
> (a) Non-competition. During the Term and for a one year period after the termination of the Term for any reason, the Executive shall not, directly or indirectly, engage in or have any interest in any sole proprietorship, partnership, corporation or business or any other person or entity (whether as an executive, officer, director, partner, agent, security holder, creditor, consultant or otherwise) that directly or indirectly (or through any affiliated entity) engages in competition with ATI (for this purpose, any business that engages in the manufacture or distribution of products similar to those products manufactured or distributed by ATI at the time of termination of the Agreement shall be deemed to be in competition with ATI); provided that such provision shall not apply to the Executive's ownership of Common Stock of ATI or the acquisition by the Executive, solely as an investment, of securities of any issuer that is registered under Section 12(b) or 12(g) of the Securities Exchange Act of 1934, as amended (the "Securities Exchange Act"), and that are listed or admitted for trading on any United States national securities exchange or that are quoted on the National Association of Securities Dealers Automated Quotation System, or any similar system or automated dissemination of quotations of securities prices in common use, so long as the Executive does not control, acquire a controlling interest in or become a member of a group which exercises direct or indirect control or, more than five percent of any class of capital stock of such corporation.
>
> (b) Nondisclosure. During the Term and at all times after the termination of the Term for any reason, the Executive shall not at any time divulge, communicate, use to the detriment of ATI or for the benefit of any other person or persons, or misuse in any way, any Confidential Information (as hereinafter defined) pertaining to the business of ATI. Any Confidential Information or data now or hereafter acquired by the Executive with respect to the business of ATI (which shall include, but not be limited to, information concerning ATI's financial condition, prospects, technology, customers, suppliers, sources of leads and methods of doing business) shall be deemed a valuable, special and unique asset of ATI that is received by the Executive in confidence and as a fiduciary, and Executive shall remain a fiduciary to ATI with respect to all of such information. For purposes of this Agreement, "Confidential Information" means information disclosed to the Executive or known by the Executive as a consequence of or through his employment by ATI (including information conceived, originated, discovered or developed by the

Executive) prior to or after the date hereof, and not generally known, about ATI or its respective businesses. Notwithstanding the foregoing, nothing herein shall be deemed to restrict the Executive from disclosing Confidential Information to the extent required by law. None of the foregoing obligations and restrictions apply to any Confidential Information that the Executive demonstrates was or became generally available to the public other than as a result of disclosure by the Executive.

(c) Nonsolicitation of Employees and Clients. During the Term and for a one year period after the termination of the Term for any reason, the Executive shall not, directly or indirectly, for himself or for any other person, firm, corporation, partnership, association or other entity, other than in connection with the performance of Executive's duties under this Agreement, (i) employ or attempt to employ or enter into any contractual arrangement with any employee or former employee of the Employer, unless such employee or former employee has not been employed by the Employer for a period in excess of six months, (ii) call on or solicit any of the actual or targeted prospective clients of the Employer on behalf of any person or entity in connection with any business competitive with the business of the Employer, and/or (iii) make known the names and addresses of such clients or any information relating in any manner to the Employer's trade or business relationships with such customers (unless the Executive can demonstrate that such information was or became generally available to the public other than as a result of a disclosure by the Executive).[29a]

Employees in general, and high-level executives in particular, build up a certain level of corporation- and industry-specific knowledge. Hence, a manufacturing executive at an automaker would be more valuable to a rival automaker than to a computer manufacturer. Thus preventing executives from taking positions (through the noncompete provision) at rival corporations makes them less likely to leave. Further, even if the executive were willing to take a position not in competition with his former employer, he or she would be prohibited, through the nonsolicitation provision, from hiring any of his or her former colleagues. Although the above example pertains to a chief executive officer, similar provisions can be designed for a broad base of executives. For example, as shown below, American Express has restrictions on about 675 employees, requiring they forfeit certain components of their compensation package if they act in a way detrimental to the best interests of the corporation, including but not limited to working for competitors, soliciting customers and/or employees, and disclosure of confidential information.

> DETRIMENTAL CONDUCT. To help protect the Company's competitive position, about 675 employees have signed agreements that require them to forfeit compensation they receive through stock option, restricted share and Portfolio Grant awards if they engage in behavior that is detrimental to the Company. Detrimental behavior covers conduct such as working for certain competitors, soliciting customers or employees after employment ends and disclosure of confidential information.[30]

Of course, if a corporation wants an executive badly enough, they can negotiate with the executive's former employer to release the executive from the above restric-

---

[29a]Employment agreement is Exhibit 10(a) to Allegheny Teledyne Form 10-Q filed with the Securities and Exchange Commission, November 15, 1999.

[30]American Express proxy statement filed with Securities and Exchange Commission, March 10, 2000, p. 27.

tions. Such a case arose when Conseco hired Gary C. Wendt to be its Chairman and CEO. Mr. Wendt, although no longer employed by General Electric, was bound by a noncompete provision. To get General Electric to waive that provision and allow them to hire Wendt, Conseco gave General Electric a warrant to purchase 10.5 million shares of its common stock as described below:

> On June 28, 2000 Conseco, Inc. ("Conseco" or the "Company") elected Mr. Gary C. Wendt its Chairman of the Board and Chief Executive Officer. Mr. Wendt served as the Chairman of the Board and Chief Executive Officer of General Electric Capital Services, Inc. until 1998 and, in connection with his departure, entered into an agreement with General Electric Company ("GE") containing, among other things, obligations of Mr. Wendt not to compete with GE with respect to financial services businesses and non-hire obligations. In connection with his employment by the Company, it was necessary to receive a waiver from GE of the noncompetition obligations. As part of receiving the waiver, a number of benefits Mr. Wendt would have otherwise retained or received from GE were terminated. Conseco also issued a warrant for 10.5 million shares of its common stock to a subsidiary of GE in connection with the waiver. This warrant has an exercise price of $5.75 per share and is exercisable at any time prior to its scheduled expiration on June 28, 2005.[31]

As alluded to in the paragraph above, Mr. Wendt also forfeited certain benefits by taking the position with Conseco. He estimated that if he had fulfilled the remaining 21 months of his noncompete agreement he would have received $65 million![32]

A third approach, if the first two do not work, is to use the legal system to deter potential competitors from hiring your executives. Thurm (2001) discusses some of the legal steps companies have taken to prevent employees from working for competitors, including forcing former employees already working for competitors to leave their new positions. A particularly well-publicized case involved the 1993 hiring by Volkswagen of José Ignacio López de Arriorta. While the case was a bit more complicated than normal because of the allegations of theft of confidential documents, it is an example of how multiple legal systems can be used to deter would-be employers. The hiring of López, who was at the time employed by General Motors, led to Volkswagen being entangled in both the United States and German court systems for 4 years, and ultimately led it to pay General Motors $100 million as a settlement.[33]

V. MINIMIZE COSTS TO THE CORPORATION

In addition to making the package attractive enough to entice the individual under consideration and structuring the package so that the individual has the appropriate incentives, the corporation has to take into consideration a multitude of costs, some

[31]Conseco 8-K filed with the Securities and Exchange Commission, July 10, 2000.
[32]Hallinan (2000a).
[33]Shaifali (1997).

of which are not generally thought of as costs. First, consider the financial costs of different forms of variable compensation. Bonuses normally require the payment of cash, whereas stock compensation only requires the issuance of previously unissued shares, a trade-off that may be important for cash-strapped corporations. Also, the accounting and tax treatments differ among bonuses, stock compensation, and different types of stock compensation. For example, while bonuses are normally recognized as an expense for financial reporting purposes in the period earned, if stock option grants meet certain conditions (see Chapter 6, section VIII) the corporation *never recognizes an expense on its income statement.* Furthermore, under the Internal Revenue Code, bonuses are both taxable to the employee and deductible by the employer in the period paid. However, if stock option grants meet certain conditions (see Chapter 6, section VIII), they are not taxable to the employee until they are exercised *and certain options are not even taxable then!*

Although stock options are treated favorably under the Internal Revenue Code, other forms of compensation are not looked upon as favorably. In particular, subject to certain exceptions, which will be discussed later in this book, Section 162(m) of the code limits tax deductions for compensation paid to the top five executives of the corporation to $1 million per executive per year. Thus, while not limiting the amount of compensation a corporation can pay its executives, Section 162(m) affects the after tax cost to the corporation. In the example cited previously, where Robert E. Rubin was hired by Citigroup, Citigroup may only be able to deduct $1 million of the $15 million it has promised to pay him in 2000 and 2001. However, it appears Citigroup has taken steps to preserve that deductibility. Citigroup, in its proxy statement dated March 17, 2000 (p. 26) noted that Robert Rubin is promised a minimum bonus of $14 million for each of 2000 and 2001 adding "which bonus amounts are being deferred." While not explicitly mentioning Section 162(m), this action is consistent with it, as if the amount is deferred until Rubin is no longer subject to Section 162(m), Citigroup will be able to fully deduct it on their tax return. As with other financial decisions, the corporation must take into account the after-tax cost when designing the compensation package.

Nonfinancial costs have to be considered too. One such cost would be equity. For example, it would be insulting to the outgoing CEO if the new CEO were to make more than he (or she) did. Not only would this be insulting, it would breed resentment and not bode well for a working relationship between the two, with the latter possibly retaining the Chairman position, or at least a position on the Board of Directors. Dechow and Sloan (1991) reported that 57% of their sample CEOs stay on as Chairman after retirement, while Brickley et al. (1999, Table 3) reported that 18% of departed CEOs are still chairman 2 years after retirement. Including those that relinquish the chair position, Dechow and Sloan (1991) found 84% initially remained on the board, whereas Brickley et al. (1999) found almost 50% were still on the board 2 years later.

Similarly, a large gap between the newly hired CEO and the remainder of the executive group would add insult to injury, as not only were they passed over in favor of an outsider, that individual is also being paid much more than they are. While in many cases those passed over for the top slot leave the corporation, it is also true that in many cases the corporation, while not wanting to make them CEO, would like to retain them.[34] These concluding points illustrate that when a contract is being explicitly designed for one person, ramifications beyond that person must be taken into consideration. This issue will be further discussed in the next chapter.

VI. SUMMARY

This chapter was a brief introduction into the design of an executive compensation contract. It was an introduction, as many of the details needed to design a compensation contract will be discussed in subsequent chapters. Thus information in this chapter will be followed up in more detail in Part IV of the book.

Although most of the discussion can be applied to designing contracts to motivate and retain existing executives, the context of the chapter was designing a compensation contract to attract a new executive to an existing corporation. Four broad areas were discussed: (1) making the offer attractive, (2) providing incentives to increase shareholder value, (3) providing incentives to remain with the corporation, and (4) minimizing the costs to shareholders.

In general, for the offer to be attractive to the executive, its magnitude must exceed the executive's opportunity cost, which is either his or her current compensation or the compensation being offered by another competitor for his or her services. Although a large compensation package may attract an executive, it may not provide the proper incentives to increase shareholder value. The corporation must provide these incentives in the compensation package, which it normally does through the use of conditional compensation. However, the corporation must take into account the executive's risk aversion, which can have two adverse effects on the corporation. First, a risk-averse individual will demand a higher level of compensation for greater risk. Second, a risk-averse executive may modify his or her behavior in a manner not consistent with maximizing shareholder value if his or her compensation is at risk. Thus compensation packages normally include fixed components to reduce the executive's risk and conditional components to provide incentives to increase shareholder value.

Assuming the corporation is successful in attracting the executive, they want to make sure that he or she remains with the corporation. The compensation contract can be designed to provide monetary incentives for the executive to remain with

---

[34]Corporations are not always successful in this retention and many acknowledge that when multiple candidates are competing for the same position, the losers in the competition are likely to depart. For example, when Jeffrey R. Immelt was named to be John F. Welch's successor as CEO of General Electric, it took the two other internal candidates, Robert L. Nardelli and W. James McNerney, only 9 days to secure positions as CEOs of Home Depot and Minnesota Mining & Manufacturing, respectively, leaving positions to be filled at GE Power Systems and GE Aircraft Engines (Lublin et al. 2000).

the corporation. One approach is to provide the executive with compensation that vests over a period of time, and hence it is forfeited if the executive leaves before the end of the vesting period. A second approach is to limit the executive's alternative employment opportunities with noncompete, nondisclosure, and nonsolicitation provisions. By limiting the executive's alternative employment opportunities, the corporation can make it more likely the executive will remain with the corporation.

The corporation also wants to minimize the cost to shareholders, with the goal of maximizing shareholder value. It must consider both financial and nonfinancial costs. It must consider that each component of the compensation package can have a differing impact on the cash flow, financial reporting, and tax status of the corporation and executive. It must also consider whether the new executive's contract will have an adverse effect on the morale and motivation of existing executives. That is, attracting a star executive may not be worthwhile if the result will be a poor working relationship between the new executive and the current occupants of the executive suite.

PART II

The Components of the Compensation Package

CHAPTER 4

Salary

I. INTRODUCTION

Salary is the most basic part of the compensation package. It is normally fixed in amount, although it is variable in the sense that it can be renegotiated. That is, an individual can get raises for good performance or take a pay cut for poor performance. It provides riskless compensation to almost all employees, except for employees working solely on commission, and the occasional CEO (see Chapter 3) who elects not to take a salary. At a minimum, salary (along with the other parts of the compensation package) must be set to be competitive with the individual's other opportunities, that is, his or her opportunity cost. This is necessary to recruit new employees and retain those already employed by the corporation. Examples exist of executives leaving one corporation for another, for more lucrative opportunities, and of executive contracts being negotiated upward because of competing offers.

Although salary needs to be competitive, because it is only one component of the compensation package, it need not always be greater than the salaries offered by competitors for the executives' services. Consider the following example. Joseph Galli, Executive Vice President at Black & Decker, takes the position of President at Amazon.com. His salary declines from $475,000 at Black & Decker[1] to $200,000 at Amazon.com.[2] Why did he take the job? Amazon gave him a signing bonus of $7,900,000 payable over a 3-year period, and options to purchase almost 4,000,000 shares over a 20-year period.[3] The intrinsic value (excess of market over exercise price) of those options, all of which were unexercisable, at December 31, 1999, was

---

[1]Black & Decker proxy statement filed with the Securities and Exchange Commission, March 15, 1999, p. 12.

[2]Amazon.com proxy statement filed with the Securities and Exchange Commission, March 29, 2000, p. 12.

[3]Amazon.com proxy statement filed with the Securities and Exchange Commission, March 29, 2000, p. 12.

$71,233,260.[4,5] By comparison, on December 31, 1998, Galli held Black & Decker options with an intrinsic value of $13,331,542.[6]

Another example is Frank Newman, President and Chief Executive Officer of More.com. In accepting his position at More.com, Newman accepted a salary of $500,000,[7] whereas in the previous year he had earned $668,307[8] as Chairman, President, and Chief Executive Officer of the Eckerd Corporation, a subsidiary of J.C. Penney. Why did he take the cut in salary? More.com also guaranteed a first-year bonus of $250,000, a $500,000 relocation grant, a $1,000,000 signing bonus, and options to acquire 1,633,752 shares.[9]

On the other hand, Boeing convinced Alan R. Mulally to remain with the corporation rather than take a position at Raytheon by giving him $5.2 million in restricted stock and 200,000 stock options.[10]

> . . . a senior Boeing official said Mulally, 53, received the options and restricted stock before he was installed as head of the jetliner division to keep him from joining another company. Mulally had been offered a job as chief executive of Raytheon.[11]

As shown in Chapter 2, salary is a major component of the CEO compensation package, a component that is used in almost all compensation packages (see Tables 2.1, 2.2, and 2.3), one that makes up a significant proportion of compensation (see Tables 2.4, 2.5, and 2.6), and is substantial in amount (see Tables 2.7, 2.8, and 2.9). While shrinking as a proportion of the total compensation package (see Table 2.4), salary is increasing in amount (see Table 2.7), and at a rate in excess of inflation (see Table 4.1). Table 4.1 shows the percentage change in salary for CEOs that have been with the same corporation (and in the same position) for at least 2 years, whereas Tables 4.2 and 4.3 show these amounts across industry and the size of the corporation. Table 4.1 and Figure 4.1 show that, for continuing CEOs, salary has increased over time, and at mean (median) rate of between 6 and 28% (5 and 6%) per year, a rate which in each year examined exceeded the rate of increase in the consumer price index (CPI), which increased at rates ranging from 1.6–3.4% per year.

Tables 2.5 and 2.8 show that salary varied in importance and magnitude across industry. Analogously, Table 4.2 shows that the 2000 rate of increase in salary varies

[4]Amazon.com proxy statement filed with the Securities and Exchange Commission, March 29, 2000, p. 9.

[5]To illustrate the risks involved, when Galli left Amazon.com to become CEO of VerticalNet those same options had an intrinsic value of zero.

[6]Black & Decker proxy statement filed with the Securities and Exchange Commission, March 15, 1999, p. 14.

[7]Silverman (2000).

[8]J.C. Penney proxy statement filed with the Securities and Exchange Commission, April 14, 2000, p. 16.

[9]Silverman (2000).

[10]Boeing proxy statement filed with the Securities and Exchange Commission March 19, 1999, p. 16.

[11]Holmes (1999). See also Zuckerman (1999).

TABLE 4.1   Percentage Change in Salary for CEOs with
Same Company for Consecutive Years

Year	Mean change in salary	Median change in salary (%)	Average change in consumer price index (%)
1993	6.00	5.00	2.7
1994	8.00	6.00	2.7
1995	9.00	6.00	2.5
1996	8.00	6.00	3.3
1997	8.00	6.00	1.7
1998	10.00	6.00	1.6
1999	9.00	5.00	2.7
2000	28.00	6.00	3.4

by industry. Although the mean (median) rate of increase in salary for 2000 was 28% (6%), for individual industries that rate was as low as 7% (6%) for wholesale and retail trade, and as high as 184% (8%) for the transportation, communications, electric, gas, and sanitary services. For all industries, the rates of increase in salary exceeded the rate of increase in the CPI, which was 3.4% in 2000.

Tables 2.6 shows that salary as a percentage of total compensation decreases with increases in the size of the corporation, whereas Table 2.9 shows that in absolute terms, salary increases with the size of the corporation. The latter finding is expected because of the increased skills and effort required to run a larger corporation,

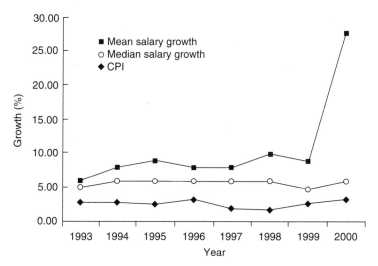

FIGURE 4.1   Growth in salary versus growth in CPI.

TABLE 4.2   Percentage Change in CEO Salary by Industry for 2000

Industry	SIC codes[a]	Mean change in salary (%)	Median change in salary (%)
Mining and construction	1000–1999	10.00	7.00
Manufacturing	2000–3999	10.00	7.00
Transportation, communications, electric, gas, and sanitary services	4000–4999	184.00	8.00
Wholesale and retail trade	5000–5999	7.00	6.00
Finance, insurance, and real estate	6000–6999	12.00	4.00
Services	7000–7999	11.00	5.00

[a]SIC, Standard Industrial Classification.

as well as the larger dollar impact on shareholder value a CEO's actions can have in a larger corporation. The former finding arises because, while salary increases with the size of the corporation, bonuses, stock options, and stock grants awarded increase at a faster rate. Table 4.3 shows some variation in the rate of increase across the size of the corporation, with the rate of increase greater for the larger corporations (mean 10%, median 7%) than for the smallest corporations (mean 5%, median 4%). However, this variation is not monotonic across size deciles. Consistent with the findings reported in Tables 4.1 and 4.2, the rates of increase for corporations of all sizes exceeded the rate of increase in the CPI, which was 3.4% in 2000.

Although this section showed that salary is increasing, and at a rate faster than inflation, because of faster increases in the other components of the compensation package, salary is a declining part of the average compensation package. In particular, as shown in Chapter 2, the pattern is driven by disproportionate increases in the

TABLE 4.3   Percentage Change in CEO Salary by Size for 2000

	Size decile	Mean change in salary (%)	Median change in salary (%)
Smallest	1	5	4
	2	9	6
	3	10	6
	4	8	6
	5	15	6
	6	8	6
	7	12	8
	8	7	5
	9	9	7
Largest	10	10	7

TABLE 4.4   Relation between Changes in Performance and Changes in Next Period Salary

Performance decile	Mean increase in next period salary (%)	Median increase in next period salary (%)	CEOs with increase in salary (%)	CEOs with decrease in salary (%)
Lowest	11.00	5.00	70.00	10.00
2	9.00	5.00	69.00	9.00
3	6.00	5.00	76.00	5.00
4	6.00	5.00	78.00	6.00
5	7.00	6.00	79.00	5.00
6	8.00	6.00	84.00	4.00
7	10.00	7.00	79.00	5.00
8	26.00	6.00	77.00	6.00
9	11.00	7.00	78.00	6.00
Highest	10.00	7.00	78.00	6.00

value of stock option grants. Whether that pattern continues or reverts is uncertain and is partially, if not primarily, dependent on future stock market performance.

II. INCENTIVES

As discussed in Chapter 3, salary has limited incentive effects, as it does not increase with shareholder value. If that were truly the case, in the absence of other forms of compensation, a work-averse individual would merely expend the minimal effort necessary not to get fired. However, there is always the possibility of salary renegotiation. That is, if the corporation does well, the executive can get a raise, which provides some incentive to work hard to increase shareholder value.

Table 4.4 investigates the possibility that CEOs' salaries are adjusted for corporate performance during the years 1993 through 2000. In Table 4.4, corporations are divided into 10 portfolios depending upon their percentage change in income. To the right of the performance decile are mean and median increases in CEO salary for the subsequent year for that portfolio. Viewing the table, it appears there is a weak relationship between salary and performance. That is, the mean increase in next period salary is 10% for the highest and 11% for the lowest performers. However, the median increase is 7% for the highest and 5% for the lowest performers.[12] Further, the percentage of CEOs receiving a raise in their salary increases from 70% for the lowest performers to 78% for the highest performers, whereas the percentage of CEOs seeing their salary go down drops from 10% for the lowest performers to

[12]Correlation analysis confirms this ambiguous result. While the Pearson correlation between percentage change in income and percentage change in salary is insignificant, the Spearman correlation is positive and statistically significant.

6% for the highest. In general, the CEO appears to receive a raise regardless of how well the corporation has performed.

An alternative source of incentives is the "managerial labor market," whereby executives who do well will be sought after by other corporations.[13] In discussing the implicit incentives associated with career concerns, Gibbons and Murphy (1992) noted that, "for young workers it can be optimal for current pay to be completely independent of current performance" (p. 469). Brickley et al. (1999) document that CEOs whose corporations perform well hold more postretirement directorships than CEOs whose corporations perform poorly.

Finally, research (for example, Warner et al. 1988) has shown that turnover is inversely related to corporate performance. That is, CEOs in poorly performing corporations are more likely to be replaced. So it is true that an executive receiving only salary does have some incentives to perform well.

III. AFFECT ON WILLINGNESS TO TAKE RISKS

Although the executive may have the incentive to perform well, he or she may not have the same risk preferences as shareholders. For example, shareholders are assumed to be well diversified, in that losses in one part of their portfolio are expected to be offset by gains in another part of their portfolio. Executives are less diversified in that their human capital, which may be defined as the present value of their future earnings, is largely tied to the prospects of their employer. Poor performance and/or bankruptcy could then have a twofold effect on the executive. First he or she would lose his or her job. Then, he or she would have to enter the job market, a market that would then penalize them for past failures. And this is without considering any shareholdings the executive may have in his or her employer. As is noted elsewhere in this book (see Chapter 8), executives in general, and CEOs in particular, are under pressure, political and otherwise, to own shares in their employer. Some companies (for example, American Express, American General, Black & Decker, Delta Air Lines, Tribune) even have formal requirements that executives own shares worth a multiple of their annual compensation. Thus, if the corporation fails, they would not only lose their job, but also their investments and possibly their pensions, or at least the unfunded supplemental part. For these reasons, executives prefer to take less risk than shareholders. The possibility then exists that executives will elect to pass on projects that increase corporate value because they are risky.

The nonsalary portion of the compensation package can be structured to provide the executive with incentives to take risk. For example, since their payoff increases with share prices, under certain circumstances (to be discussed in Chapter 6) stock options and stock grants will provide incentives for executives to undertake risky but profitable projects. In contrast, an executive compensated solely with salary will

---

[13]See, for example, Fama (1980).

TABLE 4.5   Raises for CEOs Appointed from within the Corporation

	Salary	Annual bonus	Long-term bonus	Stock options	Stock grants	Total
Mean dollar amount	$77,000	$109,000	$12,000	$216,000	$15,000	$458,000
Median dollar amount	$40,000	$27,000	$0	$8,000	$0	$150,000
Mean percentage increase	53.00%	80.00%	51.00%	416.00%	30.00%	105.00%
Median percentage increase	11.00%	14.00%	0.00%	9.00%	−21.00%	19.00%

have the incentive to forgo any projects that increase risk, regardless of how profitable they may be.

IV. HOW MUCH?

The major question with salary, as well as with the other components of the compensation package, is how much to pay. How does the employer determine what to offer a new employee? And how much to pay an existing one? Factors to be considered include, but are not limited to, the size of the corporation (recall from Chapter 2 that there is a positive relationship between size and executive compensation), individual characteristics (for example, education and experience), and the responsibilities of the executive (for example, whether the executive is going to be the CEO or both the CEO and chairman).

In Chapter 3, the situation where a corporation is looking to hire a new CEO was discussed. If the corporation has been operating for several years, they usually have the option to choose between an internal and external candidate. In either case it has been noted that the promotion carries with it a significant raise. This raise should be high enough to attract the outside candidate or to reward the internal candidate, but not so high as to breed resentment within the corporation.[14] The issue then becomes one of equity. At what point will the amount paid to the CEO become a problem with other executives or employees? From Table 2.10 we can see that the second in command, or the second highest paid executive, receives a salary that is, on average, 63% of the salary paid to the CEO. Table 4.5 presents the dollar and percentage raise internal candidates received upon promotion to CEO during the years 1993–2000. The mean (median) increase in salary received in the year of promotion to CEO is $77,000 ($40,000), or 53% (11%) of prior year salary, and an increase in total compensation of $458,000 ($150,000), roughly a 105% (19%) increase over prior year compensation.

[14]Tournament theory suggests that *compensation* should be significantly higher for the CEO. That higher amount provides incentives for lower level executives to strive for the CEO position.

TABLE 4.6   Raises for CEOs Appointed from Outside the Corporation

	Salary	Annual bonus	Long-term bonus	Stock options	Stock grants	Total
Mean dollar amount	$71,000	$200,000	$4,000	$1,793,000	$782,000	$2,928,000
Median dollar amount	$54,000	$65,000	$0	$1,132,000	$0	$1,603,000
Mean percentage increase	35.00%	58.00%	−81.00%	601.00%	908.00%	264.00%
Median percentage increase	13.00%	11.00%	−100.00%	127.00%	131.00%	80.00%

Hiring an external candidate complicates matters even more. To attract a new employee, the corporation must design the compensation package to entice the targeted executive to take the position. Normally, but not always, this requires a raise. This raise may not take the form of salary. There are examples, some of which are cited previously, of individuals taking new positions with a lower salary but more of other forms of compensation. Table 4.6 shows the dollar and percentage raise external candidates get when taking over as CEO. As might be expected due to the risks involved in taking a new position, their raise is significantly greater than that of internal candidates, although the bulk of the raise is stock-based rather than salary. The mean (median) increase in salary upon taking the position of CEO is comparable for external, $71,000 ($54,000), and internal, $77,000 ($40,000), candidates. However, the increase in total compensation is substantially greater: $2,928,000 ($1,603,000) for the external candidate versus $458,000 ($150,000) for the internal candidate, with the bulk of the increase coming in the form of stock options (mean $1,793,000, median $1,132,000) and stock grants (mean $782,000), respectively.[15] The fact that much of the compensation is conditional may make it easier to sell to existing executives; that is, the new CEO will only get that money if our stock price increases, and if that happens we will all be better off. It should also be noted that part of this increase could be the result of the employer compensating its new CEO for compensation forfeited at his or her old employer.

Some of the complications of hiring an external candidate involve the potential animosity between the newly hired CEO and the passed-over internal candidates, who possess valuable firm-specific knowledge not held by the new CEO. Those individuals will be upset not only because they were passed over for the job, but also because the new individual will be making more than they are. But, they need

[15]An alternative explanation for the greater increase in compensation (one consistent with the large part of it being stock based), is that for incentive purposes the CEO needs a certain ownership percentage in the corporation. The internal candidate presumably already owns some shares or options in his or her employer. In contrast, the external hire would be unlikely to own any shares in his or her new employer, and thus what is being measured is that initial grant, the primary purpose of which is to provide incentives rather than compensation.

to be retained and encouraged to remain productive because their firm-specific knowledge cannot easily be replaced.

V. EQUITY ISSUES

This discussion leads to a more generic set of problems involving equity. Vertical equity refers to equity across levels of the organization. That is, equity between upper level management and lower level employees. While most employees are willing to accept the fact that top executives receive higher compensation, too large a spread in compensation levels can lead to conflict, which can result in employee demands for reductions in executive pay or increases in their own compensation. It can also lead to other negative consequences for the corporation. Research has shown (e.g., O'Reilly et al. 1996; Pfeffer and Davis-Blake 1992) that vertical inequity is associated with higher turnover. Cowherd and Levine (1992) show that inequity between top managers and lower level employees may diminish product quality. In an academic context, Pfeffer and Langton (1993) "show that the greater the degree of wage dispersion within academic departments, the lower is individual faculty members' satisfaction and research productivity and the less likely it is that faculty members will collaborate on research" (p. 382).

Horizontal equity refers to equity within a level of the organization. Baker et al. (1988) noted, "Personal executives often espouse the virtues of horizontal equity systems which treat employees at the same level in an organization fairly and equally" (p. 596). Yet no two individuals are identical, and problems will exist if you try to compensate them either identically or differentially. If the corporation pays individuals identically, it has several effects. First, it removes the implicit promise of reward for performance. As noted above, salary, while fixed, can be renegotiated upwards or downward. If salary is fixed within a level, it would be harder to reward an individual for outstanding performance. The corporation could still reward the individual via promotion, but that may not always be possible, as there may not be openings. Thus, at a minimum, fixing salary within a level removes one tool with which to reward performance. Consequently, it would reduce employees' motivation to work hard and excel. It would also make it difficult to recruit talented individuals. As noted by Murphy et al. (1991), "the most talented people will not go into activities where horizontal equity and other ethical considerations prevent them from capturing the quasi rents on their ability" (p. 513).

Alternatively, giving differential salaries or raises can lead to controversy, as those receiving lesser salaries or raises may not agree that they are less valuable to the corporation. An interesting example of this is contained in research conducted by Cross (1977). Cross conducted a survey of college professors, finding that 94% rated their own research above average in quality!

Some companies have elected to disproportionately reward their best performers: "More companies are also giving raises to their most productive managers, even if it means creating disparities among workers with the same title. "We're making sure a larger percentage of our pay goes to the very best performers," said Rick Martino, IBM's vice president for talent."[16]

Gibbons and Murphy (1992, p. 470) suggest that "current pay should be most sensitive to current performance for workers close to retirement and for workers with no promotion opportunities."

Internal equity, the comparison of one's compensation against the compensation of other jobs in the organization, encompasses both vertical and horizontal equity. External equity is the comparison of one's compensation to that of peers outside the corporation. That is, a comparison of compensation with peers in similar jobs, but in different organizations. Employees and executives who see their peers making more than they do are less likely to be satisfied and more likely to seek employment elsewhere, which could lead to "brain drain." It could also lead to a form of "adverse selection," a situation where those who leave (because they were underpaid relative to their skill set) are the most valuable, whereas those who stay (because they are overpaid relative to their skill set) are least valuable. Using matching offers to retain the most valuable employees has its own problems, in that it seems to reward and encourage disloyalty. First, by selectively giving out raises, it creates internal equity problems for the corporation; that is, the person who received the matching offer now earns more than his or her peers. Second, once it becomes known that the employer will match job offers from outside the corporation, employees increase the amount of time they spend looking for such an offer. For these employees there are three potential outcomes, none of which are optimal from the corporate point of view. The first possibility is that the employee receives and accepts an offer from a new employer. The second possibility is that the employee receives an offer from a new employer and uses it to extract concessions from his or her current employer. The final possibility is that the employee does not receive any offers and thus remains with his or her current employer, but becomes demoralized and, hence, unmotivated.

VI. POLITICAL COSTS

Whenever discussing the executive suite of major corporations it would be remiss to ignore the potential political considerations, which have also been referred to as political costs.[17] Participants in the political process are made aware of high executive compensation through public disclosures in proxy statements filed with the Securities and Exchange Commission and reports in the business press.[18] These politicians, regulators, shareholders, and employees have the ability to impose costs

---

[16]Leonhardt (2000b), p. 12.

[17]Watts and Zimmerman (1986) discuss political costs extensively, although Balsam and Ryan (1996) are the first to apply it to executive compensation.

[18]As noted earlier, *Business Week, Forbes,* and the *Wall Street Journal,* as well as regional newspapers such as the *Philadelphia Inquirer,* all publish annual CEO compensation surveys.

on the executive and corporation. For example, after complaints by elected officials of Nassau and Suffolk counties, then Long Island Lighting Company Chairman, William J. Catacosinos declined "a $55,000 raise approved by the utility's board of directors."[19] A more general example of how politicians impose costs on corporations and their executives for paying "excessive compensation" is Section 162(m) of the Internal Revenue Code, which limits the deductibility of executive compensation.

Particularly visible is high compensation at a time when the corporation is losing money, laying off workers, or both. For example, the $76 million pay package Bank of America gave its Chief Executive Officer, Hugh L. McColl Jr., was criticized as occurring "despite a 16 percent earnings shortfall and a stringent bank cost-cutting program, including 19,000 job layoffs."[20] While anecdotal evidence abounds, Hallock (1998) concluded that layoffs do not increase CEO compensation. In fact, DeAngelo and DeAngelo (1991) find the "average CEO salary plus bonus declining 18%" (p. 3) during a period where the steel industry was losing money and asking for union concessions.

Among the components of the compensation package, salary is uniquely vulnerable to political criticism because it is not based on, and therefore cannot be justified by, reference to performance.

VII. FINANCIAL CONSEQUENCES

A. Cash Flows

Each component of the executive compensation package impacts the corporation's cash flows, both directly via the actual payment and indirectly via the corporation's tax returns. Normally the payment of salary is a cash outflow, whereas the benefit from the tax deduction is a cash inflow (alternatively, it can be viewed as a reduction of another cash outflow, income taxes). Sometimes the executive defers part or all of the salary earned. In those cases there is no immediate cash outflow (or inflow). Also, although compensation is normally deductible as an ordinary business expense under Section 162 of the Internal Revenue Code, if the executive is subject to the limitations of Section 162(m), the corporation may not be able to fully deduct salary payments.

B. Tax Deductibility

Specifically, Section 162(m) (reproduced in Appendix 4.1) limits the deductibility of compensation to $1 million per covered individual, where the covered individual is defined as the CEO plus the next four highest paid executives. The $1 million

---

[19]McQuiston (1995), p. B6.
[20]Zuckerman (2000), p. A1.

TABLE 4.7   Number of Firms Where Salary Exceeds $1 million by Executive Rank

Year	CEO	Second highest paid	Third highest paid	Fourth highest paid	Fifth highest paid
1992	39	1	0	0	0
1993	55	3	0	1	0
1994	62	4	1	1	0
1995	69	4	1	1	0
1996	78	6	1	1	0
1997	88	11	2	1	1
1998	108	15	8	1	1
1999	115	20	10	3	2
2000	112	22	7	3	3

limitation is not binding if the amounts involved are specified in a contract executed prior to February 17, 1993 (Section 162(m)(4)(D)). Furthermore, amounts meeting the performance-based criteria set forth in Section 162(m)(4)(B) & (C) are not subject to the limitation. Salary, by definition, is not performance based, thus absent stipulation in a pre-existing (February 17, 1993) contract, amounts in excess of $1 million will not be deductible. A few corporations, for example, IBP, restructured their compensation packages, including cutting salary to meet the requirement of Section 162(m):

> The Chairman and Chief Executive Officer's salary and performance-based bonus for 1994 were established by the Compensation Committee in December of 1993. Mr. Peterson's base salary was decreased to $1,000,000 from $1,240,000. His performance-based bonus was established at 1.3% of the first $100,000,000 of operating income, after adjustments and consistent with the bonus calculations for management generally, and 1% of any operating income that exceeded $100,000,000, this bonus formula was approved by stockholders at the annual meeting. These actions were based on the changes to Section 162(m) of the Internal Revenue Code which requires that any compensation over $1,000,000 be performance-based (or meet other exceptions provided by the Section) to be deductible by the Company. The salary and performance-based bonus were determined pursuant to the changes to Section 162(m) and in order to retain Mr. Peterson as Chairman and Chief Executive Officer. The bonus method was designed to incentivize Mr. Peterson with a performance-based bonus that was competitive with the industry and also allows the Company to take a deduction for federal income tax purposes.[21]

Still, as illustrated by Table 4.7, many corporations pay at least one executive more than $1 million in salary, and this number has been increasing over time. Yet few claim to be able to deduct the full amount due to a pre-existing contract. Corporations paying more than $1 million thus have two choices, the first being to forfeit the deductions, the latter being to defer compensation.

[21]IBP proxy statement filed with Securities and Exchange Commission, March 17, 1995, p.   .

A growing number of companies seem no longer to care about the effects of a 1993 law—the one pay initiative that grew out of the Bill Clinton's 1992 presidential campaign—that limits the maximum amount of base pay they can deduct from taxes for their top five executives to $1 million each. (The law exempts any amount above $1 million that is tied to performance, or that is deferred.)[22]

One such company, Archer Daniels Midland, in their proxy statement filed with the Securities and Exchange Commission on September 15, 1999 (page 11), paid its chief executive, G. Allen Andreas, a base salary of over $2,437,698 last year. In its proxy, the company stated:

The Committee believes, in order to retain the flexibility to compensate its executive officers in a competitive environment in accordance with the principles discussed above, that it would be inadvisable to adopt a strict policy of compliance with Section 162(m) in all cases.

The corporation can preserve the tax deduction if the executive defers compensation to a period in which he or she is no longer subject to the provisions of Section 162(m), that is, a period in which he or she is no longer the CEO or one of the next four highest paid individuals. Wal-Mart CEO David Glass is an example of an executive deferring compensation.

Mr. Glass deferred a portion of his compensation during the fiscal year ended January 31, 2000, so that during the year he actually received less than $1 million in compensation. Because his base salary for the fiscal year ending on January 31, 2001, will exceed $1 million, Mr. Glass has volunteered to defer receipt of that portion of his base salary in excess of $1 million until after his retirement. This allows Wal-Mart to deduct the deferred portion of his base salary when it is paid after his retirement.[23]

Other corporations appear to have responded to section 162(m) by shifting compensation from salary to forms of compensation that meet the performance-based criteria set forth in Section 162(m). Table 2.4 shows that in recent years the proportion of the CEO compensation package composed of salary decreased, whereas the proportion of the compensation package composed of stock option grants (which are generally considered performance based) increased.

C. Financial Reporting

Beyond the cash flow effects, there are the financial reporting or accounting costs involved. Each component of the compensation package has an impact on reported profitability, although the impact for stock option grants is usually limited to footnote disclosures. Salary is recorded as an expense in the period earned, whether deferred or paid currently, and whether deductible for tax purposes or not. In that respect, salary is more expensive for financial accounting purposes than say, stock options, which may not result in any accounting expense at all. Matsunaga (1995) found evidence consistent with corporations increasing stock option grants, and

---

[22]Leonhardt (2000b), p. 12.
[23]Wal Mart proxy statement filed with Securities and Exchange Commission April 17, 2000, p. 9.

implicitly reducing cash compensation, to manage accounting earnings. Similarly, Core and Guay (2000) provided evidence "consistent with cash constrained" corporations using stock options in lieu of cash compensation to conserve cash.

VIII. SUMMARY

The focus of this chapter was on salary, the most basic part of the compensation package. Although normally fixed in amount, it is variable in the sense that it can be renegotiated, as an individual can get raises for good performance, or take a pay cut for poor performance. As shown in Chapter 2, salary is a decreasing portion of an increasingly large compensation package. This chapter showed that even though salary is a decreasing portion of the compensation package, it is still increasing, and at a rate faster than the CPI.

Salary, as a fixed component of the compensation package, has little affect on incentives. For example, it appears that regardless of performance, most CEOs get a raise in salary and few take pay cuts. Similarly, as a fixed component, salary provides executives with no incentive to take risks.

The amount of salary paid to an executive can cause problems both inside and outside the organization. Inside the corporation, concerns about equity and, consequently, disgruntled employees and a potential decrease in productivity arise. Outside the corporation, regulators, politicians, unions, and the press have the ability to take hold of large amounts paid as salary, amounts that cannot be justified based upon performance, and impose political costs on the corporation and executive.

APPENDIX 4.1

Section 162

m) Certain excessive employee remuneration.

(1) In general.

In the case of any publicly held corporation, no deduction shall be allowed under this chapter for applicable employee remuneration with respect to any covered employee to the extent that the amount of such remuneration for the taxable year with respect to such employee exceeds $1,000,000.

(2) Publicly held corporation.

For purposes of this subsection, the term "publicly held corporation" means any corporation issuing any class of common equity securities required to be registered under section 12 of the Securities Exchange Act of 1934.

(3) Covered employee.

For purposes of this subsection, the term "covered employee" means any employee of the taxpayer if—

(A) as of the close of the taxable year, such employee is the chief executive officer of the taxpayer or an individual acting in such a capacity, or

(B) the total compensation of such employee for the taxable year is required to be reported to shareholders under the Securities Exchange Act of 1934 by reason of such employee being among the 4 highest compensated officers for the taxable year (other than the chief executive officer).

(4) Applicable employee remuneration.

For purposes of this subsection —

(A) In general. Except as otherwise provided in this paragraph, the term "applicable employee remuneration" means, with respect to any covered employee for any taxable year, the aggregate amount allowable as a deduction under this chapter for such taxable year (determined without regard to this subsection) for remuneration for services performed by such employee (whether or not during the taxable year).

(B) Exception for remuneration payable on commission basis. The term "applicable employee remuneration" shall not include any remuneration payable on a commission basis solely on account of income generated directly by the individual performance of the individual to whom such remuneration is payable.

(C) Other performance-based compensation. The term "applicable employee remuneration" shall not include any remuneration payable solely on account of the attainment of one or more performance goals, but only if—

> (i) the performance goals are determined by a compensation committee of the board of directors of the taxpayer which is comprised solely of 2 or more outside directors,

> (ii) the material terms under which the remuneration is to be paid, including the performance goals, are disclosed to shareholders and approved by a majority of the vote in a separate shareholder vote before the payment of such remuneration, and

> (iii) before any payment of such remuneration, the compensation committee referred to in clause (i) certifies that the performance goals and any other material terms were in fact satisfied.

(D) Exception for existing binding contracts. The term "applicable employee remuneration" shall not include any remuneration payable under a written binding contract which was in effect on February 17, 1993, and which was not modified thereafter in any material respect before such remuneration is paid.

(E) Remuneration. For purposes of this paragraph , the term "remuneration" includes any remuneration (including benefits) in any medium other than cash, but shall not include—

> (i) any payment referred to in so much of section 3121(a)(5) as precedes subparagraph (E) thereof , and

> (ii) any benefit provided to or on behalf of an employee if at the time such benefit is provided it is reasonable to believe that the employee will be able to exclude such benefit from gross income under this chapter.

For purposes of clause (i), section 3121(a)(5) shall be applied without regard to section 3121(v)(1).

(F) Coordination with disallowed golden parachute payments. The dollar limitation contained in paragraph (1) shall be reduced (but not below zero) by the amount (if any) which would have been included in the applicable employee remuneration of the covered employee for the taxable year but for being disallowed under section 280G.

CHAPTER 5

Bonuses: Short- and Long-Term

I. INTRODUCTION

Bonuses are traditionally considered to be a variable, or at-risk, form of compensation, although the amount of risk the executive is subject to depends upon the parameters of the plan. The payment can be subjective or based upon objective criteria. It can be based upon one or more of the following performance measures: accounting earnings, stock price performance, sales, market share, and/or customer satisfaction. The parameters of the plan include the performance measure or measures, the targets or thresholds for payouts, and the form and timing of payout. One of the more interesting measures, and one used to deal with a specific goal, is that of Coca-Cola basing pay, in part, on the achievement of diversity goals.[1]

Some bonus plans utilize totally quantitative formulas based solely on accounting performance. Appendix 5.1 provides an example of a bonus provision, an extract from the contract signed by David A. Stonecipher, CEO of the Jefferson-Pilot Corporation, on September 15, 1997. The contract provides for the payment of an annual or short-term bonus, denominated as a percentage of base salary, based solely upon one financial factor, growth in operating earnings per share. The contract has a threshold, which is also known as a lower bound, below which no bonus will be paid. That threshold is 5%. That is, if growth in operating earnings per share is less than 5% no bonus will be paid pursuant to the contract. It also has an upper bound, beyond which increases in growth will not increase the bonus amount. That upper bound is 15%. When growth in operating earnings per share equals 5%, Stonecipher will receive a bonus of 30% of base salary. The bonus will increase with growth, reaching a maximum of 110% of base salary when growth in operating earnings per share is 15% (or more).

Although Jefferson-Pilot uses growth in operating earnings as the performance measure, IBP ties its chief executive's bonus solely to operating income. For good

---

[1]McKay (2000).

measure they note that the parameters have been set to meet the requirements of Section 162(m) and guarantee deductibility.

> His performance-based bonus for 1999 was established at 1.627% (pursuant to the five year formula approved by stockholders at the 1995 Annual Meeting) of the first $100,000,000 of operating income, after adjustments and consistent with the bonus calculations for management generally, and 1% of any operating income that exceeded $100,000,000. These actions were based on the 1993 changes to Section 162(m) of the Internal Revenue Code which require that any compensation over $1,000,000 be performance-based (or meet other exceptions provided by the Section) to be deductible by the Company. . . . The bonus method was designed to incentivize Mr. Peterson with a performance-based bonus that was competitive with the industry and also allows the Company to take a deduction for federal income tax purposes.[2]

In contrast, American Express, which has also designed its bonus program to conform to Section 162(m), utilizes multiple financial and nonfinancial factors in determining bonuses. As described below, they use a formula incorporating return on equity and growth in earnings per share to calculate the maximum bonus and then determine the actual award based upon a number of financial and nonfinancial measures. The former meets the requirements of Section 162(m), and the latter is allowed under the negative discretion portion of Section 162(m), that is, the board is allowed downward, but not upward discretion in awarding bonuses.

> For 1999 the Company paid 1999 annual incentive awards to eight executive officers, including the named executives, under an award structure designed to preserve the Company's tax deductions under the Million Dollar Cap. (The Company's Million Dollar Cap policy is described on pages 27–28.) The awards contain a formula based on the Company's 1999 return on equity and growth in earnings per share. The Company may pay the awards in cash or a combination of cash and restricted shares. In assessing performance the Committee applied the formula to determine the maximum amount payable and then used its judgment about annual goal and leadership performance to make actual awards below these maximum values. The Committee gave equal weight to the goal and leadership categories.
>
> The Committee evaluated progress toward goals based on these areas:
>
> • SHAREHOLDER VALUE (50% weight). Includes 1999 shareholder return, earnings growth, revenue growth and return on equity.
>
> • CUSTOMER SATISFACTION (25% weight). Includes customer survey results, expansion and retention of customer base and development of products and services.
>
> • EMPLOYEE SATISFACTION (25% weight). Includes 1999 employee survey results and the Company's and the business units' success in making progress toward long-term, world class targets.
>
> The Committee evaluated leadership by considering a variety of factors, such as innovation, strategic vision, customer focus, management effectiveness, teamwork, integrity, diversity, developing others and managing change, without assigning weights to these factors.[3]

[2]IBP proxy statement filed with the Securities and Exchange Commission, March 21, 2000.
[3]American Express proxy statement filed with Securities and Exchange Commission, March 10, 2000, pp. 24, 25.

The parameters can be set so that the executive bears little or no risk, for example, by basing the bonus on sales rather than profits, or by setting the performance threshold low. Alternatively, executives can be guaranteed "minimum" bonuses. As discussed in Chapter 3, when Citigroup hired Robert E. Rubin as Chairman of their executive committee they guaranteed him a bonus of at least $14 million per year for 2000 and 2001.[4] Another example occurred when Carleton S. Fiorina was hired as President and Chief Executive Officer of Hewlett Packard (HP):

> HP entered into an employment agreement with Ms. Fiorina, President and Chief Executive Officer of HP, as of July 17, 1999. The agreement provides for an initial base salary of $1,000,000 per year. It also provides for a targeted annual incentive award of $1,250,000 per year, with an opportunity to earn up to an additional $2,500,000 per year in annual variable compensation. This variable pay is guaranteed at target for the 2000 fiscal year and was prorated at the target level for the portion of the 1999 fiscal year during which Ms. Fiorina was employed.[5]

Both of these examples involve newly hired executives. For two reasons it may be reasonable to guarantee a bonus for the first year or two of an executives' tenure. First, it reduces the executives' risk, thereby reducing the level of compensation that needs to be paid to attract the executive. Second, given that performance in the early years of an executives' tenure may reflect the actions of his or her predecessor more than his or her own, it would be unfair to penalize the executive for that performance.

Bonuses can be based upon short-term performance, normally one year or annually, as in Ms. Fiorina's contract above, or long-term performance, normally from 3–5 years. Long-term bonus plans are sometimes referred to as performance plans. Among the types of long-term plans are performance unit and performance share plans. With both types of plans, the executive is awarded a number of units or shares at the beginning of the performance period, with the number earned based upon performance during the period. The major difference between the plans is that with performance units the value of those units is usually predetermined, whereas with performance shares the value of those shares is based upon share price at the end of the period. Appendix 5.2 contains the Lucent Technologies 1996 Long-Term Incentive Program, which allows for both performance units and performance shares (see section 5.9). In contrast to the detailed description of plan parameters in Mr. Stonecipher's contract in Appendix 5.1, the Lucent Technologies plan is rather vague about the performance measures, thresholds, and amount of payment. First of all, the plan notes, "Performance Awards in the form of Performance Units or Performance Shares may be issued . . .". That is, they do not have to be used. Recall from Table 2.1, less than 20% of corporations pay long-term bonuses in any given year. Second, the plan does not define the measures or thresholds,

---

[4]Citigroup proxy statement filed with the Securities and Exchange Commission, March 17, 2000, p. 26.

[5]Hewlett Packard proxy statement filed with the Securities and Exchange Commission, January 14, 2000, p. 34.

TABLE 5.1   Comparison of Percentage Change in Salary and Short- and Long-Term Bonuses for CEOs with the Same Company for Consecutive Years[a]

Year	Change in ST bonus (%)	Change in LT bonus (%)	Change in salary (%)	Average change in CPI-U (%)
1993	21	29	6	2.7
	10	0	5	
1994	33	7	8	2.7
	14	−5	6	
1995	60	51	9	2.5
	10	11	6	
1996	20	21	8	3.3
	7	4	6	
1997	45	39	8	1.7
	11	4	6	
1998	20	27	10	1.6
	4	−5	6	
1999	76	101	9	2.7
	7	−12	5	
2000	106	117	28	3.4
	10	−12	6	

[a]Means on top, medians on bottom. ST, short-term; LT, long-term; CPI, Consumer Price Index.

merely noting, "The performance criteria to be achieved during any Performance Period and the length of the Performance Period shall be determined by the Committee upon the grant of each Performance Award or at any time thereafter."

As shown in Chapter 2, bonuses are a major component of the CEO compensation package. Tables 2.1, 2.2, and 2.3 show that short-term or annual bonuses are paid about 80% of the time, whereas long-term incentive payments or bonuses are paid about 15% of the time. Tables 2.4, 2.5, and 2.6 show the proportion of compensation composed of short (approximately 20%) and long-term (less than 5%) bonuses, whereas Tables 2.7, 2.8, and 2.9 show the amounts involved. Although slightly shrinking as a proportion of the total compensation package (see Table 2.4), bonuses are increasing in amount (see Table 2.7) and at a rate in excess of salaries and inflation (see Table 5.1). Table 5.1 shows the percentage change in short-term bonus for CEOs that have been with the same corporation (and in the same position) for at least 2 years, whereas Table 5.2 shows the same percentage changes for the subset of firms that pay long-term bonuses. Tables 5.3 and 5.4 show these amounts across industry and the size of the corporation. Table 5.1 and Figure 5.1 show that, for continuing CEOs, short-term bonuses have increased over time, and at a mean (median) rate of between 20 and 106% (4 and 14%) per year, a rate which, in each year examined, exceeded the rate of increase in salary (mean 6–28%, median 5–6%), and the rate of increase in the consumer price index (CPI) (1.6–3.4%).

TABLE 5.2   Subset of Firms Paying Long-Term Bonuses[a]

Year	Change in ST bonus (%)	Change in LT bonus (%)	Change in salary (%)	Average change in CPI-U (%)
1993	19	58	6	2.7
	10	12	5	
1994	26	51	8	2.7
	14	9	6	
1995	20	77	9	2.5
	13	17	6	
1996	25	53	8	3.3
	18	13	6	
1997	29	70	8	1.7
	15	15	6	
1998	22	67	10	1.6
	9	7	6	
1999	23	168	9	2.7
	10	7	5	
2000	19	191	28	3.4
	13	13	6	

[a]ST, short-term; LT, long-term; CPI-U, consumer price index. Means on top, medians on bottom.

TABLE 5.3   Change in CEO Bonus by Industry[a] for 2000

Industry	SIC codes[b]	Change in ST bonus (%)	Change in LT bonus (%)
Mining and construction	1000–1999	90	43
		30	3
Manufacturing	2000–3999	201	14
		11	−22
Transportation, communications, electric, gas, etc.	4000–4999	38	120
		12	16
Wholesale and retail trade	5000–5999	25	10
		2	−34
Finance, insurance, and real estate	6000–6999	12	715
		9	−14
Services	7000–7999	3	−40
		0	−39

[a]Means on top, medians on bottom.
[b]SIC, Standard Industrial Classification; ST, short-term; LT, long-term.

TABLE 5.4   Bonus and Change in CEO bonus
by Firm Size for 2000[a]

	Size decile	Change in ST bonus (%)	Change in LT bonus (%)
Smallest	1	3	72
		−26	−18
	2	−17	61
		−15	−26
	3	13	3
		9	13
	4	16	−10
		8	6
	5	25	21
		12	−10
	6	33	5
		10	−60
	7	813	25
		13	9
	8	45	746
		21	−6
	9	31	95
		11	−14
Largest	10	56	−10
		13	−12

[a]ST, short-term; LT, long-term.

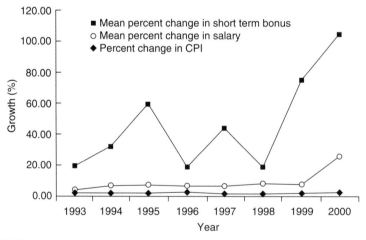

FIGURE 5.1   Growth in short-term bonus versus growth in salary versus growth in CPI.

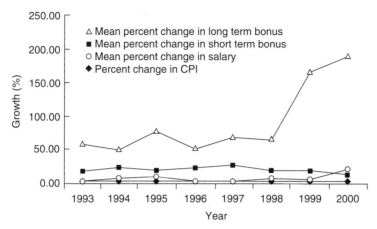

FIGURE 5.2   Growth in long-term bonus, short term bonus, salary and CPI.

Table 5.2 and Figure 5.2 show an even more pronounced pattern for long-term bonuses, with the mean (median) increase ranging from 51% (7%) to 191% (17%).

Tables 2.5 and 2.8 showed that short- and long-term bonuses vary in importance and magnitude across industry. Analogously, Table 5.3 shows that the 2000 rate of increase in short- and long-term bonuses varies by industry. Although the mean (median) rate of increase in short-term bonus for 2000 was 106% (10%), for individual industries that rate was as low as 3% (0%) for services, and as high as 201% (11%) for manufacturing. Similarly, although the mean (median) rate of increase in long-term bonus for 2000 was 191% (13%), for individual industries that rate was as low as a decrease of 40% (39%) in services to an increase of as high as 715% (−14%) in finance, insurance, and real estate.

Although Table 2.6 showed how short-term and long-term bonuses as a percentage of total compensation vary with the size of the corporation, no clear pattern emerges. In contrast, Table 2.9 shows that in absolute terms, both increase with the size of the corporation. Table 5.4 shows some variation in the rate of increase across the size of the corporation, but as with Table 2.6, no clear pattern emerges.

II. INCENTIVES

Bonuses, if appropriately structured, can provide the proper incentives to induce the executive to take actions that maximize shareholder value. Further, as noted by Banker et al. (1999, p. 2),

> performance-based incentives increase an organization's overall productivity by attracting and retaining the more productive employees (selection effect) and/or by inducing employees to increase or to better allocate their effort (effort effect).

If not properly structured, however, the bonus plan itself can lead to dysfunctional behavior. For example, a corporation that has a bonus plan that rewards market share may get increased market share, but at the expense of profitability.[6] Alternatively, depending on the measure or measures used in the bonus plan, executives may be able to manipulate those measures to their advantage. A long line of literature, including Healy (1985) and Balsam (1998), shows managers make accounting choices consistent with increasing their bonus. Bonuses can be based upon stock price performance or returns, which are harder to manipulate. Unfortunately, stock returns are based on factors outside of the control of the corporation's executives, for example, interest rates. Thus, basing the bonus on stock returns imposes risk on the executive, and in equilibrium, the executive must be compensated for this risk. Furthermore, executives are already exposed to this risk via the stock-based portion of their compensation package.

Thus, the choice of performance measure or measures is of utmost importance in setting the proper incentives and encouraging desired behaviors. Lambert and Larcker (1987), Ely (1991), and Sloan (1993), among others, argued that accounting-based benchmarks are useful because they shield executives from fluctuations in stock returns that are beyond the manager's control. Consistent with this theory, they show that the greater the corporations' stock price variability, the larger the cash portion of the CEO compensation package. Bushman, Indjejikian, and Smith (1996) and Ittner, Larcker, and Rajan (1997) argued that subjective or nonfinancial measures are useful for growing, innovative, and nontraditional corporations, for whom the traditional accounting model does not work well.[7]

Once the measure or measures[8] of performance to be used is determined, the parameters to be applied must be decided. For example, in the IBP plan discussed previously, Mr. Peterson gets a bonus of 1.627% of the first $100,000,000 of operating income and 1% of any operating income that exceeded $100,000,000. Other plans may have a threshold or lower bound, below which no bonus is paid. E. I. DuPont De Nemours (DuPont) is an example of a corporation with a lower bound. In discussing their Variable Compensation Plan (VCP), which covers approximately 8600 employees including executive officers, they note that "the VCP limits the

---

[6]Kato (1997) notes that for Japanese companies with financial *keiretsu* affiliation, CEO compensation is positively related to capital investment. Financial *keiretsu* are organized around a main bank, which is the principal lender to member firms and also a major shareholder. Thus structuring executive compensation to encourage capital investment may be optimal, even if it comes at the expense of profitability, because the main bank earns interest on the financing. That is, it maximizes shareholder profit.

[7]The traditional accounting model, developed over hundreds of years, better fits manufacturing firms with lots of fixed assets that can be easily measured and valued. In contrast, firms like Microsoft have little in the way of fixed assets, yet are incredibly valuable, yielding astronomical market-to-book ratios. One of the reasons is that the traditional accounting model undervalues companies like Microsoft, in that it undervalues the intangible assets created by the organization, which includes both the value of the people and products created by those people.

[8]Murphy (1998) Table 2 shows that the majority of firms use multiple measures.

annual maximum funding to 20% of consolidated net income after deducting 6% of net capital employed."[9]

The 6% of net capital employed is the lower bound or threshold. If consolidated net income is below this amount no funds are transferred to the plan. Alternatively, some plans have maximums or upper bounds beyond which no additional rewards may be earned. For example Unocal states "the maximum cash Award to a participant for a year will be 0.25% of the Company's Net Cash Provided by Operating Activities or, if less, $2,000,000."[10] And H.J. Heinz states that "the Incentive Plan also provides that the maximum award payable to an individual for performance in any fiscal year is $4,000,000."[11]

A. Affect of Lower and Upper Bounds

These parameters themselves can affect incentives. Consider the executive who is approaching or over the upper bound of their bonus program, a program based upon accounting income numbers. The incentive exists for them to defer income to a future period. If the executive does this through an income-decreasing choice of accounting methods, the cost to the corporation will be minimal. However, if the executive does so by accelerating future expenditures into the current period and/or deferring sales to the future, there may be real costs to the corporation. As noted by Healy (1985), a similar incentive exists for executives sufficiently below the lower bound. That is, they too have the incentive to defer income to a future period. The incentives for both the executives below their lower bound and above their upper bound are twofold. First, by pushing income to future periods, they increase their bonus in those future periods, while not affecting current period bonus. Second, to the extent that future period bounds or targets are based upon current period performance, lowering current period performance reduces those future targets, also having the affect of increasing future bonuses. This can be illustrated using the contract between David Stonecipher and Jefferson-Pilot contained in Appendix 5.1. Recall Mr. Stonecipher's bonus is based on the growth in operating earnings per share. Thus, implicitly, this period's performance becomes the threshold for determining the bonus paid in the next period. So growth in excess of the upper bound, in this case 15%, not only does not increase his bonus for the current period, but by increasing the threshold for the next period, reduces his expected bonus for that period.

The following example, where an executive is rewarded on growth in reported income, will further illustrate the effect of bounds on incentives. Net income in the

[9]DuPont proxy statement filed with the Securities and Exchange Commission, March 17, 2000, p. 10.
[10]Unocal proxy statement filed with the Securities and Exchange Commission, April 12, 2000, p. 27.
[11]H.J. Heinz proxy statement filed with the Securities and Exchange Commission, August 3, 1999, p. 8.

base year was $100 million, unmanipulated income for the current year is $120 million, and expected income for the next year is $125 million. Assume that this corporation pays its CEO a bonus equal to 1% of the growth in income, up to a maximum of $150,000. If the CEO is unable to manipulate reported income, the bonus in the current year will be $150,000, which is calculated as the lesser of $150,000 or 1% of the excess of $120 million over $100 million, and the bonus in the next year will be $50,000, which is calculated as the lesser of $150,000 or 1% of the excess of $125 million over $120 million. If however, the CEO is able to shift income from the current to the next period, so that income in the current period is $115 million, and income in the next period is $130 million, he or she can receive a bonus of $150,000 in each year. In both cases total income across the two periods is $245 million, yet in the absence of income shifting, the CEO receives a total bonus of $200,000 ($150,000 plus $50,000) over the 2 years, but with income shifting the CEO receives $300,000 ($150,000 in each year).

Empirically, Healy (1985) found corporations below the lower bound and above the upper bound are more likely to make income decreasing accounting choices, whereas Holthausen, Larcker, and Sloan (1995) and Gaver, Gaver, and Austin (1985) only found that corporations above the upper bound are more likely to make income-decreasing accounting choices. A possible explanation for the latter result is that executives who find themselves below the lower bound may be reluctant to reduce income further for fear of losing their jobs. Weisbach (1988), among others, finds that poor accounting performance is associated with subsequent CEO turnover.

Another issue to be considered is the placement of those bounds. Perverse incentives exist if bounds are set too high or too low. If the bounds are too high, then executives can get discouraged and not even try to achieve those goals, adversely affecting corporation performance and value. If they are set too low, especially the upper bound, then there is little incentive to work hard.

How the bounds are set matters, too. As illustrated above, if this year's performance becomes the hurdle for next year's bonus, or the base upon which next year's bonus is computed, then the incentive exists to keep this year's performance down. The frequency with which current year performance is used as a hurdle for next year's evaluation is unclear. However, consistent with current performance being used in future performance evaluation, a long line of accounting and financial literature notes that income smoothing or income manipulation to meet certain goals or targets is prevalent. For example, research by Burgstahler and Dichev (1997) showed evidence consistent with earnings management to avoid reporting losses and decreases in earnings, whereas Burgstahler and Eames (1998), Brown (1999), and Degeorge, Patel, and Zeckhauser (1999) provided evidence consistent with executives manipulating earnings measures to meet analysts' earnings expectations. Further, consistent with the incentives discussed above, these articles find corporations are more likely to report earnings that just meet the threshold under examination.

B. Adherence to Plan

Finally, the incentive effect of the plan will be nullified if the compensation committee does not adhere to the plan. Keep in mind that many plans provide the committee with the ability to override plan provisions and pay different amounts. Alternatively, the committee could adhere to the terms of the plan and not pay, or pay a reduced bonus, but then increase some other component of the compensation package to make the executive whole. One example is J.C. Penney. In 1999, J.C. Penney cut its CEO's bonus by 93%, but more than offset that cut with an increase in salary of 73%, in a year in which its "share price declined by more than half."[12] As noted by J.C. Penney,

> The Company's compensation programs, as revised in February 1999, moved a portion of the Incentive Program payment into base salary. As a result of the Company's weaker performance in fiscal 1999, actual bonus payments for the Named Executive Officers (other than Ms. Castagna) under the Incentive Program and the EVA Performance Plan amounted to only 0% to 2.9% of base salary, depending on the executive's PRL and primary area of responsibility. If the Company had met its planned financial objectives for the year, such payments would have equalled 77% to 107% of base salary, depending on the executive's PRL, with payments in excess of those percentages for results above plan.[13]

The above passage acknowledges the corporation's weaker performance, yet as a result of the above changes, total salary plus bonus increased from $1,062,121 in 1998 to $1,087,240 in 1999. Another example, perhaps an even more explicit example of a corporation offsetting a decreased bonus with some other form of compensation is Tasty Baking. In 1999 Tasty Baking did not pay a cash bonus and used that fact as the justification for a stock grant:

> Under the Company's Management Incentive Plan, cash bonuses are paid upon the attainment of specified financial performance objectives. In 1999, the specified objectives were not achieved and no cash bonuses were awarded under the Plan. In order to provide management with the opportunity to earn compensation in lieu of a cash bonus for 1999 and to provide an incentive to management which is earned as the market value of the Company Common Stock increases, the Committee recommended that the Board conditionally grant 79,304 shares of Company Common Stock to the executive officers and managers eligible to participate in the Plan. Pursuant to the terms of the conditional stock grant, shares will be distributed in one-third installments only if the Company's stock price reaches the target prices of $12, $14, and $16 for five consecutive days prior to December 17, 2002. The Committee and the Board determined that this grant was in the best interests of the Company and its shareholders in order to provide the executive officers and managers with performance incentives which further align their interests with those of shareholders.[14]

[12] *Wall Street Journal* (2000a).

[13] J.C. Penney proxy statement filed with the Securities and Exchange Commission, April 14, 2000, p. 12.

[14] Tasty Baking proxy statement filed with Securities and Exchange Commission, April 3, 2000, pp. 10, 11.

It should be clarified that, on average, corporations do indeed reduce conditional compensation when performance decreases. This has been implied by a long line of academic research (see, for example, Lewellen and Huntsman 1972; Antle and Smith 1985; Lambert and Larcker 1987; Balsam 1998). This is also shown by corporations where executives neither get bonuses nor get an increase elsewhere in their compensation package to make up for it. For example, in 1999 AMR did not pay a bonus because "no payments were made in 2000 under American's 1999 Incentive Compensation Plan because American's performance failed to satisfy the performance measurements under such Plan."[15]

Further analysis of AMR's proxy shows that the omission of the bonus was not offset elsewhere in the CEO's compensation package. To be more precise, the CEO had received a bonus of $1,072,781 and total direct compensation of $14,960,835 as estimated by Standard & Poors for 1998, whereas he received no bonus and total direct compensation of $8,630,350 for 1999.

III. EFFECTIVENESS OF BONUS PLANS

Bonus plans can be and are designed to encourage certain forms of behavior, presumably with a goal of maximizing shareholder wealth. Examining whether they are successful is another story. One approach possible when bonus plans are designed to achieve specific goals is to examine if those goals are met. For example, Larcker (1983) showed that the introduction of long-term incentive plans is associated with subsequent increases in capital expenditures, whereas White (1996) stated that basing bonuses on dividend payout increases dividends paid.[16] Mishra et al. (2000) found that earnings per share growth and return on equity exceed industry medians after adoption of long-term accounting-based performance plans, whereas Leonard (1990) found companies with long-term incentive plans had significantly greater increases in return on equity. However, as noted above, it is possible that an increase in the performance measure is not value increasing, but rather a response to the incentives provided (for example, passing up profitable investments to pay dividends). In general it is hard to measure whether a bonus or other incentive-based compensation arrangement achieves its goal of increasing shareholder value. Empirically, researchers can observe associations, such as the one between compensation and accounting and market performance measures, but have difficulty attributing causality. One approach is the "event study" approach, whereby the market reaction to public disclosure of the plan adoption is used to infer whether or not the plan is value increasing. The event study methodology, which is based upon the assump-

---

[15]AMR proxy statement filed with the Securities and Exchange Commission, April 25, 2000, p. 12.

[16]This is an example of how one component of the compensation can be designed to offset a side or negative effect of another component. As discussed in the next chapter, stock options give managers a disincentive to pay dividends. Thus a provision whereby bonuses are at least partially based upon dividends is useful in that it provides some counterincentive to that provided by the options.

tion that markets are efficient, assumes market participants make unbiased and on average correct predictions about the effect of the plan on shareholder value at the time they first learn about it at public disclosure. Thus if the market reaction is positive, that is, the corporations' share price increases upon announcement, as in Larcker (1983), Brickley et al. (1985), Tehranian and Waegelein (1985), Kumar, Kumar, and Sopariwalla (1992), it is assumed the plan is value increasing.[17] Although while such studies find that on average adoption of long-term incentive plans are associated with an increase in shareholder value, it is hard (once again) to draw those conclusions for any given corporation and plan. One reason is that the positive reaction to plan adoption may not be associated with the expected effects of the plan on firm performance, but rather to the information released by the plan adoption. That is, management is more likely to propose tying its compensation to firm performance when it expects the firm to perform well in the future. Investors realize this tendency and thus react positively when they first learn the plan is being adopted. A second reason is that stock prices are volatile, and the return or price change at any time is affected by many factors, including adoption of the incentive plan. In a large sample study, researchers assume they have randomized away all factors other than those under examination and thus can draw a conclusion, a conclusion that cannot be definitively drawn with a sample size of one.

IV. POLITICAL COSTS

The selection of bonus plan parameters is important for another reason. If the amounts involved are too low, there may be no motivational effect. However, if the amounts are too large, there may be political costs for the corporation and executive. As with salary, large bonuses can be criticized by politicians, regulators, shareholders, and employees. This may explain, in part, the motivation corporations have for putting an upper bound or cap on their bonus payouts. Ford Motor notes that "the limit, approved by you, on the amount of a bonus award for any of the Named Executives for any year under the plan is $10,000,000."[18]

Although Ford limited their bonuses to $10 million per executive, perhaps to avoid the adverse publicity, other corporations have paid larger amounts. Tables 5.5 and 5.6 list the largest short- and long-term bonus payments by year. The largest short-term bonus payment, by far, was the $102,015,000 paid by Green Tree Financial to its Chairman and Chief Executive Officer Lawrence Coss in 1996, whereas the largest long-term bonus was the $31,325,000 paid by General Electric to its Chairman and Chief Executive Officer John Welch in 1999. The short-term bonus

---

[17]Under the efficient market hypothesis the stock price immediately after public announcement is an unbiased representation of the firm's value, and any stock price changes after that point would not be attributable to the plan itself, but to other factors.

[18]Ford Motor proxy statement filed with the Securities and Exchange Commission, April 11, 2000, p. 16.

TABLE 5.5   Largest Short-Term Bonuses

Year	Company	Executive	Position	Short-term bonus ($)
1992	Bear Stearns Companies	Alan Greenberg	Chairman and Chief Executive Officer	11,726,000
1993	Conseco	Stephen Hilbert	Chairman, President, and Chief Executive Officer	14,107,000
1994	Green Tree Financial	Lawrence Coss	Chairman and Chief Executive Officer	28,544,000
1995	Green Tree Financial	Lawrence Coss	Chairman and Chief Executive Officer	65,146,000
1996	Green Tree Financial	Lawrence Coss	Chairman and Chief Executive Officer	102,015,000
1997	Jefferies Group	Richard Handler	Executive Vice President and Manager of the Taxable Fixed Income Division	17,105,000
1998	Marsh & Mclennan	Lawrence Lasser	President, Putnam Investments	17,000,000
1999	Marsh & Mclennan	Lawrence Lasser	President, Putnam Investments	26,000,000
2000	Apple Computer	Steven Jobs	Chief Executive Officer	90,000,000

TABLE 5.6   Largest Long-Term Bonuses

Year	Company	Executive	Position	Long-term bonus ($)
1992	W.R. Grace	Constantine Hampers	Executive Vice President	26,468,000
1993	Louisiana Pacific	Harry Merlo	Chairman, President, and Chief Executive Officer	11,306,000
1994	American International Group	Maurice Greenberg	Chairman and Chief Executive Officer	8,330,000
1995	Federated Department Stores	Alan Questrom	Chairman and Chief Executive Officer	11,049,000
1996	Donaldson Lufkin & Jenrette	Joe Roby	President and Chief Operating Officer	23,984,000
1997	Qwest Communication	Robert Woodruff	Executive Vice President, Chief Financial Officer, and Treasurer	24,137,000
1998	American International Group	Maurice Greenberg	Chairman and Chief Executive Officer	15,460,000
1999	General Electric	John Welch	Chairman and Chief Executive Officer	31,325,000
2000	American International Group	Maurice Greenberg	Chairman and Chief Executive Officer	23,655,000

paid to Steven Jobs, Chief Executive Officer of Apple Computer, in 2000 is interesting in that rather than cash, the bonus took the form of "an aircraft with a total cost to the Company of approximately $90,000,000."[19]

An interesting example of the political costs associated with the payment of large bonuses, and a corporation's response to those costs, involved the securities firm Bear Stearns. After a long history as a privately held partnership, Bear Stearns went public in October 1985. As a partnership their compensation was private information, but as a publicly held corporation their compensation was public knowledge and immediately became an issue. In a *Wall Street Journal* article entitled, "How Embarrassing! Bear Stearns Officials Wallow in a Windfall—Concern Says Its Bonus Plan Has Provided Executives with 'Exorbitant' Sums," it was noted that for the 6 months ending April 30, 1986, which coincided with Bear Stearns first 6 months as a public company, its Chairman and CEO Alan C. Greenberg made $4 million, more than any other executive at a publicly held securities firm made during the entire previous year.[20] The following year the *Wall Street Journal* published a follow-up article entitled "Bear Stearns Aides, Despite Pay Cuts, Can Grin and Bear It—Six Executives at Concern Outearned All Others at Major Public Firms." The article notes that for their fiscal year ending April 30, 1987, the "six top executives of the securities firm earned more last year than any other executive of a major publicly held Wall Street firm."[21] A review of proxy statements for the period shows that Bear Stearns did indeed modify the parameters of their bonus plan, decreasing the percent of adjusted pretax income allocated to the bonus fund. For example, for the fiscal year ending April 30, 1988, the amounts allocated to the fund were determined as follows:[22]

Percentage of Increment of Adjusted Pretax Income

Amount of adjusted pretax income—FY 1988	Allocated to bonus fund (%)
Up to $20,000,000	0
Over $20,000,000 but not exceeding $100,000,000	24.5
Over $100,000,000 but not exceeding $180,000,000	26.0
Over $180,000,000 but not exceeding $260,000,000	28.5
Over $260,000,000 but not exceeding $340,000,000	31.0
Over $340,000,000	33.5

Whereas for the fiscal year ending June 30, 1989, the amounts allocated to the bonus fund were calculated as follows:[22]

[19]Apple Computer proxy statement filed with the Securities and Exchange Commission, March 12, 2001, p. 8.
[20]Swartz (1986).
[21]Swartz (1987).
[22]Bear Stearns proxy statement filed with the Securities and Exchange Commission, August 4, 1988, p. 12.

Percentage of Increment of Adjusted Pretax Income

Amount of adjusted pretax income—FY 1989	Allocated to bonus fund (%)
Up to $15,000,000	0
Over $15,000,000 but not exceeding $85,000,000	7.4
Over $85,000,000 but not exceeding $150,000,000	8.5
Over $150,000,000 but not exceeding $215,000,000	9.2
Over $215,000,000 but not exceeding $275,000,000	11.0
Over $275,000,000	11.9

Given that income before taxes and extraordinary items was $287,383,000 for the year ended June 1989, the change in formula reduced the allocation to the bonus fund by almost two-thirds, from $71,688,730 to $24,758,577!

Another interesting case involved Stephen M. Wolf, Chairman, and Rakesh Gangwal, CEO of US Airways Group. One day after the approval of the US Airways Group, Inc., Long-term Compensation plan by a margin of 63,019,913 to 3,843,023,23[23] the corporation received complaints from unions about the size of their compensation (approximately $34 million and $36 million respectively for 1998).[24] The two men decided not to accept annual cash bonuses,[25] a fact confirmed by the following years' proxy statement: "Both the Chairman and the Chief Executive Officer have declined to accept payments for the performance period ending with fiscal year 1999."[26]

V. FINANCIAL CONSEQUENCES

A. Cash Flows

As noted previously, each component of the executive compensation package impacts the corporation's cash flows, both directly via the actual payment and indirectly via the corporation's tax returns. If paid in cash, a bonus is a cash outflow, whereas the benefit from the tax deduction is a cash inflow (alternatively it can be viewed as a reduction of another cash outflow, income taxes). Sometimes however, the corporation may not pay bonuses immediately or may not use cash to pay those bonuses; that is, it may pay the bonus in stock. For example, Dell Computer allows its executives to convert their cash bonuses into stock options:

[23]US Airways 10-Q filed with the Securities and Exchange Commission, August 6, 1999, p. 23.

[24]US Airways proxy statement filed with the Securities and Exchange Commission, April 1, 1999, pp. 9, 11.

[25]*Wall Street Journal* (1999).

[26]US Airways proxy statement filed with the Securities and Exchange Commission, April 14, 2000, p. 18.

Also, on March 24, 2000, stock options with an exercise price set at 80% of fair market value were granted to 11 executive officers under Dell's Executive Stock Ownership Incentive Program. This program allows executives to elect to forego all or a portion of their pretax annual bonus payouts and receive discounted options. Because of the inherent risk in foregoing a cash payment to receive an option grant, the number of shares granted is calculated by dividing the foregone bonus amount by the amount of the discount (20% of the fair market value of the common stock on the grant date). Although the foregone cash payments would have been unrestricted, the discounted options are subject to a three-year vesting schedule.[27]

B. Tax Deductibility

Sometimes the executive defers part or all of the bonus earned. Also, although compensation is normally deductible as an ordinary business expense under Section 162 of the Internal Revenue Code, if the executive is subject to the limitations of Section 162(m), the corporation may not be able to fully deduct the bonus payment, whether made in cash or stock.

As noted previously, Section 162(m) limits deductibility of compensation to $1 million per covered individual, where covered individual is defined as the CEO plus the next four highest paid executives. The $1 million limitation is not binding if the amounts involved are specified in a contract executed prior to February 17, 1993. Further, amounts meeting the performance-based criteria set forth in Section 162(m) are not subject to the limitation. If bonuses are not paid pursuant to a qualified plan, they are subject to the $1 million deductibility cap (which includes all nonqualifying compensation such as salary). Bonuses, however, may be performance-based and hence may meet those criteria.

As illustrated by Table 5.7, many corporations pay at least one executive more than $1 million in salary and bonus, and this number has been increasing over time. In fact, in 2000, 112 corporations paid each of their top five executives more than $1 million. Yet few claim to be able to deduct the full amount due to a pre-existing contract. When salary is less than $1 million, corporations paying more than $1 million in salary plus bonus have three choices. As with salary, the corporation can elect to forfeit the deductions.

1. Examples of Corporations Forfeiting Deductions

As an example, consider two companies, General Dynamics and Motorola, that elect to forfeit those deductions, first General Dynamics:

The Compensation Committee and one of its compensation consultants have considered the implications of the tax law and of the associated Internal Revenue Service regulations. They have concluded that discretion and sound judgment have been critical elements of

[27]Dell Computer Proxy statement filed with the Securities and Exchange Commission, May 30, 2000, p. 10.

TABLE 5.7   Number of Firms Where Salary Plus
Bonus Exceeds $1 Million by Executive

Year	CEO	Second highest paid	Third highest paid	Fourth highest paid	Fifth highest paid
1992	279	50	14	8	8
1993	421	81	30	17	15
1994	505	110	46	24	20
1995	597	159	72	39	33
1996	677	199	109	69	47
1997	783	270	141	94	71
1998	803	317	172	126	85
1999	816	392	231	162	109
2000	603	353	231	166	112

the Committee's executive compensation philosophy in the past, and the Compensation Committee believes it is in the best interest of the shareholders to maintain discretionary control over the annual cash portion of executive compensation in the future. The creation of the subcommittee is intended to allow the long-term awards to be deductible under Section 162(m), but because of the importance of judgment and discretion, certain portions of salary and bonus will not qualify for deductibility under the law. The Compensation Committee believes that the amount of the deduction foregone for 1999 and in the future will be immaterial.[28]

Two executives, Nicholas D. Chabraja, Chairman of the Board and CEO and James E. Turner, President and Chief Operating Officer, made more than $1 million in nonqualifying compensation in 1999 and thus would be subject to the deduction limitation, with the bulk of the excess pertaining to Mr. Chabraja. Looking at Mr. Chabraja we see that in 1999 he made $837,000 in salary, $1,550,000 in short-term nonqualified bonuses, and $324,163 in other annual compensation, which includes

(i) non-cash items provided to management, including club memberships; executive dining; financial planning services; special travel, accident, and supplementary life insurance; and the use of aircraft and automobiles owned or leased by the Company ("Perquisites"); and (ii) amounts reimbursed for payment of taxes. The amounts shown include: (A) Perquisites for Mr. Chabraja: for 1999 of $255,638, of which $129,600 relates to personal travel and $87,800 relates to club memberships;[29]

Looking at Mr. Turner, we see that in 1999 he made $510,000 in salary, $650,000 in short-term nonqualified bonuses, and $20,891 in other annual compensation. Assuming long-term compensation is fully deductible, as implied by the

---

[28]General Dynamics proxy statement filed with the Securities and Exchange Commission, March 31, 2000, p. 13.

[29]General Dynamics proxy statement filed with the Securities and Exchange Commission, March 31, 2000, p. 16.

above paragraph, approximately \$1,700,000 of Mr. Chabraja's and \$200,000 of Mr. Turner's compensation will be nondeductible. Using the statutory corporate tax rate of 35%, this means that the \$1,900,000 in deductions forgone caused General Dynamics to pay an additional \$665,000 in taxes, an immaterial amount when compared to the \$880 million (less than one tenth of 1%) they earned, or \$136 million (about one-half of 1%) in dividends they paid that year, but material when compared to what the average employee makes.

Now consider Motorola:

> Section 162(m) of the Internal Revenue Code generally limits the corporate tax deduction to one million dollars for compensation paid to named executive officers unless certain requirements are met. The Company has not been entitled to deduct some amount of payments under the Motorola Executive Incentive Plan in the past. The 1999 MEIP awards will not be deductible to the extent they cause the applicable employee remuneration to exceed one million dollars during 1999. MEIP awards fail to qualify as "performance based compensation" exempt from the limitation on deductions that is imposed by Section 162(m) because the Committee exercises discretion in making these awards. The Committee believes that the discretionary component of this plan permits the Committee to make decisions in the best interests of the Company and its stockholders and it intends, therefore, to continue the process by which it determines MEIP awards. The Stock Option Plan of 1996 and the Long Range Incentive Plan of 1994 meet the requirements for exemption under Section 162(m) and compensation paid under these plans in 1999, if any, also will be deductible. The Motorola Incentive Plan of 1998 permits various types of awards, some of which qualify for exemption under Section 162(m) and some of which do not. Stock options, performance shares and stock appreciation rights that are granted under the plan qualify as "performance based compensation" and, as such, are exempt from the limitation on deductions. Outright grants of common stock, restricted stock and/or cash do not qualify for exemption and are subject to the Section 162(m) limitation on deductions.[30]

In contrast to General Dynamics, all five of Motorola's executive officers had nonqualifying (salary plus bonus) compensation in excess of \$1,000,000, with the total nondeductible amount (sum of salary plus bonus in excess of \$1,000,000 per executive) for the five executives estimated at \$4,650,000. Using a statutory tax rate, this would indicate they paid an additional \$1,627,500 in federal taxes. Once again this amount is immaterial when compared to the \$817 million in net income Motorola earned for 1999.

General Dynamics and Motorola are far from being the only corporations forfeiting deductions. Balsam (2001) reported that approximately one-quarter of affected corporations report that they forfeit deductions due to Section 162(m).

2. Examples of Executives Deferring Compensation to Preserve Deductions

Alternatively, the corporation can preserve the tax deduction if the executive defers compensation to a period in which he or she is no longer subject to the provisions

---

[30]Motorola proxy statement filed with the Securities and Exchange Commission, March 22, 2000.

of Section 162(m), that is, a period in which he or she is no longer the CEO or one of the next four highest paid individuals. For example, Citigroup in its proxy statement dated March 17, 2000 (p. 26), noted that Robert Rubin is promised a minimum bonus of $14 million for each of 2000 and 2001, adding "which bonus amounts are being deferred." Although not explicitly mentioning Section 162(m), this action is consistent with it. Other companies reporting that their executives have agreed to defer compensation include Brunswick:

> Brunswick has reviewed its executive compensation plans in response to the Omnibus Budget Reconciliation Act of 1993 (the "Act"), which established a $1.0 million tax deduction limitation in August 1993 for the taxable years beginning on or after January 1, 1994. The limitation applies to compensation in excess of $1.0 million paid to any executive who is employed by Brunswick on December 31 and named in the summary compensation table, with certain exceptions. Mr. Larson and all other Senior Executives will defer receipt of compensation, to the extent it is not deductible by Brunswick, under the terms of an automatic deferral plan established for this purpose.[31]

Balsam (2001) reported that approximately 22% of affected corporations deferred compensation to preserve deductions due to section 162(m).

3. Examples of Corporations Qualifying Their Plans to Preserve Deductions

The final option companies have with their bonus plans is to qualify them as performance based, because if the plan is qualified under Section 162(m), deductibility of those bonus payments is not limited (as long as the payments are made pursuant to the plan). Note that when a corporation qualifies a bonus or other compensation plan it does not assure all compensation paid by the corporation is deductible, only the compensation paid pursuant to the plan. The corporation may still pay salary and other nonqualified compensation in excess of $1 million and hence lose deductions. To qualify a bonus plan under Section 162(m), the plan must be designed so that compensation is paid solely on account of the executive's attainment of one or more performance goals determined by objective formulae; those performance goals must be established by a compensation committee of two or more independent directors; and the material terms of the plan must be disclosed to and approved by shareholders.[32] Because negative, but not positive, discretion is allowed under Section 162(m); the incentive exists for corporations to set loose targets. Subsequently, if the compensation committee desires it can reduce compensation. An

---

[31]Brunswick proxy statement filed with the Securities and Exchange Commission, March 21, 2000, p. 13.

[32]Balsam and Ryan (1996) find that approximately 50% of their sample firms qualify their bonus plans upon enactment of Section 162(m). In contrast, Rose and Wolfram (2000) found that only 40% of the firms in their sample qualified their bonus plans, and 20% their long-term incentive plans. The difference in findings can partially, if not totally, be explained by difference in sample composition. That is, while Balsam and Ryan only included firms paying more than $1 million in cash composition, Rose and Wolfram included firms below that level.

example of a company modifying its bonus plan to meet Section 162(m) requirements is Abbott Laboratories:

> Section 162(m) of the Internal Revenue Code places a limit on the amount of compensation that may be deducted by the corporation in any tax year with respect to each of the corporation's five most highly paid executives. However, certain performance-based compensation that has been approved by shareholders is not subject to this deduction limit. The Plan is designed to provide for this type of performance-based compensation and to permit the corporation to take the corresponding tax deduction.[33]

C. Financial Reporting

Beyond the cash flow effects, there is the financial reporting, or accounting cost involved. Each component of the compensation package has an impact on reported profitability, although the impact for stock option grants is limited to footnote disclosures. Bonuses, like salary, are recorded as an expense in the period earned, whether deferred or paid currently, and whether deductible for tax purposes or not. In that respect salary *and* bonuses are more expensive for financial accounting purposes than say, stock options, which, as will be noted later, may not result in any accounting expense at all. These amounts can be significant. For example, United Parcel Service, in its 2000 annual report (note 6) reported, "Amounts charged to operations for Management Incentive Awards were $735, $588, and $448 million during 2000, 1999, and 1998, respectively."

VI. SUMMARY

This chapter reviewed the issues surrounding executive bonuses. Bonuses are traditionally considered to be a variable or at-risk form of compensation, although the amount of risk the executive is subject to depends upon the parameters of the plan. In some cases the bonus, or a minimum amount of bonus, can be guaranteed, thus there is little risk. The bonus amount can be subjective or based upon objective criteria. It can be based upon financial or nonfinancial measures or a combination of the two.

If structured properly, bonuses can provide the proper incentives to induce the executive to take actions that maximize shareholder value. However, if not structured properly, the bonus plan itself can lead to dysfunctional behavior. For example, if the performance threshold is unachievable, it provides no motivation. Alternatively, if the bonus is based upon a measure over which the executive has some discretion, the executive may manage that measure to increase his or her bonus at

---

[33]Description of 1998 Abbott Laboratories Performance Incentive Plan contained in Abbott Laboratories proxy statement filed with Securities and Exchange Commission, March 9, 1998, p. 16.

the shareholder's expense. Thus, the performance measures, targets, and other parameters must be chosen with extreme care.

Bonuses, like the other components of the compensation package, have political as well as financial reporting costs. Consequently bonuses, and/or bonus plans, should be structured to minimize these costs. For example, the tax deductions associated with bonuses can be maximized if the corporation meets the requirements set out in Section 162(m).

APPENDIX 5.1. BONUS FORMULA FROM CONTRACT BETWEEN DAVID A STONECIPHER AND JEFFERSONPILOT CORPORATION DATED SEPTEMBER 15, 1997

3.3 Annual Bonus Computation. The additional cash compensation payable under Section 3.2 hereof with respect to a Bonus Year shall be in an amount equal to a portion of the Base Salary for such Bonus Year determined as follows:

(a) JP's income from operations (disregarding realized capital gains and losses), as reflected in JP's audited financial statements ("Operating Income"), per share of common stock for the year immediately preceding the Bonus Year (the "Prior Year's Operating EPS") shall be subtracted from JP's Operating Income per share of common stock for the Bonus Year. If the result is negative, no additional compensation shall be payable, and no further computation will be necessary.

(b) The amount determined in clause (a) above shall be divided by the Prior Year's Operating EPS. If the result is less than 0.05 (that is, the growth in Operating Income per share is less than 5%), no additional compensation shall be payable, and no further computation will be necessary.

(c) If the amount determined in clause (b) above is .05 or greater, the amount shall be obtained by straight line interpolation between applicable points shown in the table under (d) below.

(d) The amount determined in clause (c) above shall be multiplied by the Base Salary for the Bonus Year, and the result obtained shall be the additional compensation paid to Stonecipher with respect to such Bonus Year. In making the foregoing computation, appropriate adjustments shall be made for any stock splits and dividends, so that the Company's Operating Income per share of common stock for consecutive years is properly comparable. Without limiting the foregoing, the following table illustrates the application of the foregoing provisions:

Percentage Increase in Operating Income Per Share	*Percentage of Base Salary Paid as Bonus*
less than 5%	0%
5%	30%
10%	55%
15%	110%
more than 15%	110%

Notwithstanding the provisions of this Section 3.3, either Stonecipher or the Compensation Committee of the Board of Directors of the Company may propose adjustments to the annual bonus in light of extraordinary transactions or circumstances that affect materially the Company's income, and any such adjustment agreed to by both Stonecipher and the Compensation Committee of the Company's Board of Directors shall be given effect.

3.4 Adjustment Based on Audited Financial Statements. The parties acknowledge that the Company's audited financial statements might not be available when the annual bonuses under Section 3.2 and 3.3 above are to be calculated and paid. In that event the annual bonus will initially be calculated and paid on the basis of the Company's internal statements for the Bonus Year. If the amount of the bonus ultimately determined to be due for any Bonus Year on the basis of the Company's audited financial statements differs from the bonus that was initially paid for such Bonus Year, Stonecipher shall promptly refund the amount of any excess, or the Company shall promptly pay Stonecipher an additional amount equal to any deficiency.

APPENDIX 5.2. LUCENT TECHNOLOGIES INC. 1996 LONG TERM INCENTIVE PROGRAM

As Amended through July 19, 2000

SECTION 1. PURPOSE. The purposes of the Lucent Technologies Inc. 1996 Long Term Incentive Program (the "Plan") are to encourage selected key employees of Lucent Technologies Inc. (the "Company") and its Affiliates to acquire a proprietary and vested interest in the growth and performance of the Company, to generate an increased incentive to contribute to the Company's future success and prosperity, thus enhancing the value of the Company for the benefit of shareowners, and to enhance the ability of the Company and its Affiliates to attract and retain individuals of exceptional managerial talent upon whom, in large measure, the sustained progress, growth and profitability of the Company depend.

SECTION 2. DEFINITIONS. As used in the Plan, the following terms shall have the meanings set forth below:

(a) "Affiliate" shall mean (i) any Person that directly, or through one or more intermediaries, controls, or is controlled by, or is under common control with, the Company or (ii) any entity in which the Company has a significant equity interest, as determined by the Committee.

(b) "Award" shall mean any Option, Stock Appreciation Right, Restricted Stock Award, Performance Share, Performance Unit, Dividend Equivalent, Other Stock Unit Award, or any other right, interest, or option relating to Shares or other securities of the Company granted pursuant to the provisions of the Plan.

(c) "Award Agreement" shall mean any written agreement, contract, or other instrument or document evidencing any Award granted by the Committee hereunder and signed by both the Company and the Participant.

(d) "Board" shall mean the Board of Directors of the Company.

(e) "Change in Control" shall mean the happening of any of the following events:

(i) An acquisition by any individual, entity or group (within the meaning of Section 13(d)(3) or 14(d)(2) of the Exchange Act) (an "Entity") of beneficial ownership (within the meaning of Rule 13d-3 promulgated under the Exchange Act) of 20% or more of either (A) the then outstanding shares of common stock of the Company (the "Outstanding Company Common Stock") or (B) the combined voting power of the then outstanding voting securities of the Company entitled to vote generally in the election of directors (the "Outstanding Company Voting Securities"); excluding, however, the following: (1) any acquisition directly from the Company, other than an acquisition by virtue of the exercise of a conversion privilege unless the security being so converted was itself acquired directly from the Company, (2) any acquisition by the Company, (3) any acquisition by any employee benefit plan (or related trust) sponsored or maintained by the Company or any corporation controlled by the Company, or (4) any acquisition by any corporation pursuant to a transaction which complies with clauses (A), (B) and (C) of subsection (iii) of this Section 2(e); or

(ii) A change in the composition of the Board during any two year period such that the individuals who, as of the beginning of such two year period, constitute the Board (such Board shall be hereinafter referred to as the "Incumbent Board") cease for any reason to constitute at least a majority of the Board; provided, however, that for purposes of this definition, any individual who becomes a member of the Board subsequent to the beginning of the two year period, whose election, or nomination for election by the Company's shareowners, was approved by a vote of at least a majority of those individuals who are members of the Board and who were also members of the Incumbent Board (or deemed to be such pursuant to this proviso) shall be considered as though such individual were a member of the Incumbent Board; and provided further, however, that any such individual whose initial assumption of office occurs as a result of or in connection with either an actual or threatened election contest (as such terms are used in Rule 14a-11 of Regulation 14A promulgated under the Exchange Act) or other actual or threatened solicitation of proxies or consents by or on behalf of an Entity other than the Board shall not be so considered as a member of the Incumbent Board; or

(iii) The approval by the shareowners of the Company of a merger, reorganization or consolidation or sale or other disposition of all or substantially all of the assets of the Company (each, a "Corporate Transaction") or, if consummation of such Corporate Transaction is subject, at the time of such approval by shareowners, to the consent of any government or governmental agency, the obtaining of such consent (either explicitly or implicitly by consummation); excluding however, such a Corporate Transaction pursuant to which (A) all or substantially all of the individuals and entities who are the beneficial owners of the Outstanding Company Common Stock and Outstanding Company Voting Securities immediately prior to such Corporate Transaction will beneficially own, directly or indirectly, more than 60% of the outstanding shares of common stock, and the combined voting power of the then outstanding voting securities entitled to vote generally in the election of directors of the corporation resulting from such Corporate Transaction (including, without limitation, a corporation or other Person which as a result of such transaction owns the Company or all or substantially all of the Company's assets either directly or through one or more subsidiaries (a "Parent Company")) in substantially the same proportions as their ownership, immediately prior to such Corporate Transaction, of the Outstanding Company Common Stock and Outstanding Company Voting Securities, (B) no Entity (other than the Company, any employee benefit plan (or related trust) of the Company, such corporation resulting from such Corporate Transaction or, if reference was made to equity ownership of any Parent Company for purposes of determining whether clause (A) above is satisfied in connection with the applicable Corporate Transaction, such Parent Company) will beneficially own, directly or indirectly, 20% or more of, respectively, the outstanding shares of common stock of the corporation resulting from such Corporate Transaction or the combined voting power of the outstanding voting securities of such corporation entitled to vote generally in the election of directors unless such ownership resulted solely from ownership of securities of the Company prior to the Corporate Transaction, and (C) individuals who were members of the Incumbent Board will immediately after the consummation of the Corporate Transaction constitute at least a majority of the members of the board of directors of the corporation resulting from such Corporate Transaction (or, if reference was made to equity ownership of any Parent Company for purposes of determining whether clause (A) above is satisfied in connection with the applicable Corporate Transaction, of the Parent Company); or

       (iv) The approval by the shareowners of the Company of a complete liquidation or dissolution of the Company.

    (f) "Change in Control Price" means the higher of (A) the highest reported sales price, regular way, of a Share in any transaction reported on the New York Stock Exchange Composite Tape or other national exchange on which Shares are listed or on NASDAQ during the 60-day period prior to and including the date of a Change in Control or (B) if the Change in Control is the result of a tender or exchange offer or a Corporate Transaction, the highest price per Share paid in such tender or exchange offer or Corporate Transaction; provided however, that in the case of Incentive Stock Options and Stock Appreciation Rights relating to Incentive Stock Options, the Change in Control Price shall be in all cases the Fair Market Value of a Share on the date such Incentive Stock Option or Stock Appreciation Right is exercised or deemed exercised. To the extent that the consideration paid in any such transaction described above consists all or in part of securities or other noncash consideration, the value of such securities or other noncash consideration shall be determined in the sole discretion of the Board.

    (g) "Code" shall mean the Internal Revenue Code of 1986, as amended from time to time, and any successor thereto.

    (h) "Committee" shall mean the Corporate Governance and Compensation Committee of the Board (or any successor committee).

    (i) "Company" shall mean Lucent Technologies Inc., a Delaware corporation.

    (j) "Company Action" shall mean a Company or Subsidiary declared force management program, sale of a unit or portion of a unit, Company or Subsidiary initiated transfer of a Participant to a corporation, partnership, limited liability company or other business entity in which the Company has an equity interest and which does not constitute a Subsidiary or placement of the job function of a Participant with an outsourcing contractor.

    (k) "Covered Employee" shall mean a "covered employee" within the meaning of Section 162(m)(3) of the Code.

(l) "Dividend Equivalent" shall mean any right granted pursuant to Section 14(h) hereof.

(m) "Employee" shall mean any employee of the Company or of any Affiliate. Unless otherwise determined by the Committee in its sole discretion, for purposes of the Plan, an Employee shall be considered to have terminated employment and to have ceased to be an Employee if his or her employer ceases to be an Affiliate, even if he or she continues to be employed by such employer.

(n) "Exchange Act" shall mean the Securities Exchange Act of 1934, as amended from time to time, and any successor thereto.

(o) "Fair Market Value" shall mean, (i) with respect to Shares, the average of the highest and lowest reported sales prices, regular way, of Shares in transactions reported on the New York Stock Exchange on the date of determination of Fair Market Value, or if no sales of Shares are reported on the New York Stock Exchange for that date, the comparable average sales price for the last previous day for which sales were reported on the New York Stock Exchange, and (ii) with respect to any other property, the fair market value of such property determined by such methods or procedures as shall be established from time to time by the Committee.

(p) "Incentive Stock Option" shall mean an Option granted under Section 6 hereof that is intended to meet the requirements of Section 422 of the Code or any successor provision thereto.

(q) "Net Income" shall mean the net income of the Company as determined under generally accepted accounting principles, excluding (a) extraordinary items (net of applicable taxes); (b) cumulative effects of changes in accounting principles; (c) securities gains and losses (net of applicable taxes); and (d) nonrecurring items (net of applicable taxes) including, but not limited to, gains or losses on asset dispositions and sales of divisions, business units or subsidiaries, restructuring charges, gains and losses from qualified benefit plan curtailments and settlements, and income or expenses related to deferred tax assets.

(r) "Nonstatutory Stock Option" shall mean an Option granted under Section 6 hereof that is not intended to be an Incentive Stock Option.

(s) "Officer" shall mean any manager of the Company or any Affiliate holding a position above the executive level (E band) or any future salary grade that is the equivalent thereof.

(t) "Option" shall mean any right granted to a Participant under the Plan allowing such Participant to purchase Shares at such price or prices and during such period or periods as the Committee shall determine.

(u) "Other Stock Unit Award" shall mean any right granted to a Participant by the Committee pursuant to Section 10 hereof.

(v) "Participant" shall mean an Employee who is selected by the Committee to receive an Award under the Plan.

(w) "Performance Award" shall mean any Award of Performance Shares or Performance Units pursuant to Section 9 hereof.

(x) "Performance Period" shall mean that period, established by the Committee at the time any Performance Award is granted or at any time thereafter, during which any performance goals specified by the Committee with respect to such Award are to be measured.

(y) "Performance Share" shall mean any grant pursuant to Section 9 hereof of a unit valued by reference to a designated number of Shares, which value may be paid to the Participant by delivery of such property as the Committee shall determine, including, without limitation, cash, Shares, or any combination thereof, upon achievement of such performance goals during the Performance Period as the Committee shall establish at the time of such grant or thereafter.

(z) "Performance Unit" shall mean any grant pursuant to Section 9 hereof of a unit valued by reference to a designated amount of property other than Shares, which value may be paid to the Participant by delivery of such property as the Committee shall determine, including, without limitation, cash, Shares, or any combination thereof, upon achievement of such performance goals during the Performance Period as the Committee shall establish at the time of such grant or thereafter.

(aa) "Person" shall mean any individual, corporation, partnership, association, joint-stock company, trust, unincorporated organization, limited liability company, other entity or government or political subdivision thereof.

(bb) "Restricted Stock" shall mean any Share issued with the restriction that the holder may not sell, transfer, pledge, or assign such Share and with such other restrictions as the Committee, in its sole discretion, may impose (including, without limitation, any restriction on the right to vote such Share, and the right to receive any cash dividends), which restrictions may lapse separately or in combination at such time or times, in installments or otherwise, as the Committee may deem appropriate.

(cc) "Restricted Stock Award" shall mean an award of Restricted Stock under Section 8 hereof.

(dd) "Shares" shall mean the shares of common stock, $.01 par value, of the Company and such other securities of the Company as the Committee may from time to time determine.

(ee) "Stock Appreciation Right" shall mean any right granted to a Participant pursuant to Section 7 hereof to receive, upon exercise by the Participant, the excess of (i) the Fair Market Value of one Share on the date of exercise or, if the Committee shall so determine in the case of any such right other than one related to any Incentive Stock Option, at any time during a specified period before the date of exercise over (ii) the grant price of the right on the date of grant, or if granted in connection with an outstanding Option on the date of grant of the related Option, as specified by the Committee in its sole discretion, which, other than in the case of Substitute Awards, shall not be less than the Fair Market Value of one Share on such date of grant of the right or the related Option, as the case may be. Any payment by the Company in respect of such right may be made in cash, Shares, other property, or any combination thereof, as the Committee, in its sole discretion, shall determine.

(ff) "Subsidiary" shall mean a "subsidiary corporation" of the Company as defined in Section 424(f) of the Code, an entity in which the Company directly or indirectly owns 50% or more of the voting interests or an entity in which the Company has a significant equity interest, as determined by the Board or the Committee.

(gg) "Substitute Award" is defined in Section 4(a).

(hh) "Term" shall mean the period beginning on February 18, 1998, and ending on February 28, 2003.

SECTION 3. ADMINISTRATION. The Plan shall be administered by the Committee. The Committee shall have full power and authority, subject to such resolutions not inconsistent with the provisions of the Plan as may from time to time be adopted by the Board, to: (i) select the Employees of the Company and its Affiliates to whom Awards may from time to time be granted hereunder; (ii) determine the type or types of Award to be granted to each Participant hereunder; (iii) determine the number of Shares to be covered by each Award granted hereunder; (iv) determine the terms and conditions, not inconsistent with the provisions of the Plan, of any Award granted hereunder; (v) determine whether, to what extent and under what circumstances Awards may be settled in cash, Shares or other property or canceled or suspended; (vi) determine whether, to what extent and under what circumstances cash, Shares and other property and other amounts payable with respect to an Award under this Plan shall be deferred either automatically or at the election of the Participant; (vii) interpret and administer the Plan and any instrument or agreement entered into under the Plan; (viii) establish such rules and regulations and appoint such agents as it shall deem appropriate for the proper administration of the Plan; and (ix) make any other determination and take any other action that the Committee deems necessary or desirable for administration of the Plan. Decisions of the Committee shall be final, conclusive and binding upon all Persons, including the Company, any Participant, any shareowner, and any employee of the Company or of any Affiliate.

SECTION 4. SHARES SUBJECT TO THE PLAN.

(a) Subject to adjustment as provided in Section 4(b), the total number of Shares available for Awards granted under the Plan on and after February 18, 1998 and on or prior to February 28, 2003 shall be one hundred twenty-eight million (128,000,000) Shares; provided, that if any Shares are subject to an Award granted hereunder that is forfeited, settled in cash, expires, or otherwise is terminated without issuance of Shares, the Shares subject to such Award shall again be available for Awards under the Plan, if no Participant shall have received any benefits of ownership in respect thereof; and provided further, that no more than forty million (40,000,000) Shares shall be available for the grant of Incentive Stock Options under the Plan during the Term; and provided further, that no more than forty million (40,000,000) Shares shall be available for the grant of Awards in the form of Stock Appreciation Rights pursuant to Section 7 (excluding for this purpose any Stock Appreciation Right granted in relation to an Incentive Stock Option or a Nonstatutory Stock Option), Restricted Stock pursuant to Section 8, Performance Shares pursuant to Section 9, and Other Stock Unit Awards pursuant to Section 10 that are valued by reference to Shares during the Term; and provided further, that no Participant may be granted Awards with respect to more than twenty million (20,000,000) Shares in the aggregate during the Term. In addition, Awards granted or Shares issued by the Company through the assumption of, or in substitution or exchange for, employee benefit awards or the right or obligation to make future employee benefit awards, in connection with the acquisition of another corporation or business entity ("Substitute Awards") shall not reduce the Shares available for grants under the Plan or to a Participant. Any Shares issued hereunder may consist, in whole or in part, of authorized and unissued Shares or treasury Shares.

(b) In the event of any merger, reorganization, consolidation, recapitalization, stock dividend, stock split, reverse stock split, spin-off or similar transaction or other change in corporate structure affecting the Shares, such adjustments and other substitutions shall be made to the Plan and to Awards as the Committee in its sole discretion deems equitable or appropriate, including without limitation such adjustments in the aggregate number, class and kind of Shares which may be delivered under the Plan, in the aggregate or to any one Participant, in the number, class, kind and option or exercise price of Shares subject to outstanding Options, Stock Appreciation Rights or other Awards granted under the Plan, and in the number, class and kind of Shares subject to Awards granted under the Plan (including, if the Committee deems appropriate, the substitution of similar options to purchase the shares of, or other awards denominated in the shares of, another company) as the Committee may determine to be appropriate in its sole discretion, provided that the number of Shares or other securities subject to any Award shall always be a whole number.

SECTION 5. ELIGIBILITY. Any Employee (excluding any member of the Committee) shall be eligible to be selected as a Participant.

SECTION 6. STOCK OPTIONS. Options may be granted hereunder to Participants either alone or in addition to other Awards granted under the Plan. Options may be granted for no consideration or for such consideration as the Committee may determine. Any Option granted under the Plan shall be evidenced by an Award Agreement in such form as the Committee may from time to time approve. Any such Option shall be subject to the following terms and conditions and to such additional terms and conditions, not inconsistent with the provisions of the Plan, as the Committee shall deem desirable:

(a) OPTION PRICE. The exercise price per Share under an Option shall be determined by the Committee in its sole discretion; provided that except in the case of an Option pursuant to a Substitute Award, such purchase price shall not be less than the Fair Market Value of a Share on the date of the grant of the Option.

(b) OPTION PERIOD. The term of each Option shall be fixed by the Committee in its sole discretion; provided that no Incentive Stock Option shall be exercisable after the expiration of ten years from the date the Option is granted.

(c) EXERCISABILITY. Options shall be exercisable at such time or times as determined by the Committee at or subsequent to grant. Unless otherwise determined by the Committee at or subsequent to grant, no Incentive Stock Option shall be exercisable during the year ending on the day before the first anniversary date of the granting of the Incentive Stock Option.

(d) METHOD OF EXERCISE. Subject to the other provisions of the Plan and any applicable Award Agreement, any Option may be exercised by the Participant in whole or in part at such time or times, and the Participant may make payment of the option price in such form or forms, including, without limitation, payment by delivery of cash, Shares or other consideration (including, where permitted by law and the Committee, Awards) having a Fair Market Value on the exercise date equal to the total option price, or by any combination of cash, Shares and other consideration as the Committee may specify in the applicable Award Agreement.

(e) INCENTIVE STOCK OPTIONS. In accordance with rules and procedures established by the Committee, the aggregate Fair Market Value (determined as of the time of grant) of the Shares with respect to which Incentive Stock Options held by any Participant which are exercisable for the first time by such Participant during any calendar year under the Plan (and under any other benefit plans of the Company or of any parent or subsidiary corporation of the Company) shall not exceed $100,000 or, if different, the maximum limitation in effect at the time of grant under Section 422 of the Code, or any successor provision, and any regulations promulgated thereunder. The terms of any Incentive Stock Option granted hereunder shall comply in all respects with the provisions of Section 422 of the Code, or any successor provision, and any regulations promulgated thereunder.

(f) FORM OF SETTLEMENT. In its sole discretion, the Committee may provide, at the time of grant, that the shares to be issued upon an Option's exercise shall be in the form of Restricted Stock or other similar securities, or may reserve the right so to provide after the time of grant.

(g) COMPANY ACTION. With respect to any Option granted after July 19, 2000, unless otherwise provided in the applicable Award Agreement, if a Participant's employment terminates by reason of a Company Action, then the Company

Action Vesting Portion of any such Option held by that Participant shall not be forfeited and canceled and instead shall become immediately exercisable upon termination until the earlier of ninety days following termination of employment and the original expiration date of the Option. "Company Action Vesting Portion" is determined as of the date of termination of employment and shall be the portion of the Option computed as follows (but not less than zero):

Company Action Vesting Portion = $N \times M/D - E$

where:

N = the number of shares originally subject to the Option,

M = the number of complete months elapsed since the grant date of the Option,

D = the number of complete months between the grant date of the Option and the date on which the Option was originally scheduled to become completely exercisable, and

E = the number of Shares covered by the Option for which the Option has already become exercisable (regardless of whether the Option has been exercised with respect to such Shares).

SECTION 7. STOCK APPRECIATION RIGHTS. Stock Appreciation Rights may be granted hereunder to Participants either alone or in addition to other Awards granted under the Plan and may, but need not, relate to a specific Option granted under Section 6. The provisions of Stock Appreciation Rights need not be the same with respect to each recipient. Any Stock Appreciation Right related to a Nonstatutory Stock Option may be granted at the same time such Option is granted or at any time thereafter before exercise or expiration of such Option. Any Stock Appreciation Right related to an Incentive Stock Option must be granted at the same time such Option is granted. In the case of any Stock Appreciation Right related to any Option, the Stock Appreciation Right or applicable portion thereof shall terminate and no longer be exercisable upon the termination or exercise of the related Option, except that a Stock Appreciation Right granted with respect to less than the full number of Shares covered by a related Option shall not be reduced until the exercise or termination of the related Option exceeds the number of Shares not covered by the Stock Appreciation Right. Any Option related to any Stock Appreciation Right shall no longer be exercisable to the extent the related Stock Appreciation Right has been exercised. The Committee may impose such conditions or restrictions on the exercise of any Stock Appreciation Right as it shall deem appropriate.

SECTION 8. RESTRICTED STOCK. Restricted Stock Awards may be issued hereunder to Participants, for no cash consideration or for such minimum consideration as may be required by applicable law, either alone or in addition to other Awards granted under the Plan. The provisions of Restricted Stock Awards need not be the same with respect to each recipient. Any Restricted Stock Award issued hereunder may be evidenced in such manner as the Committee in its sole discretion shall deem appropriate, including, without limitation, book-entry registration or issuance of a stock certificate or certificates. In the event any stock certificate is issued in respect of a Restricted Stock Award, such certificate shall be registered in the name of the Participant, and shall bear an appropriate legend referring to the terms, conditions, and restrictions applicable to such Award. Except as otherwise determined by the Committee, upon termination of employment for any reason during the restriction period, any portion of a Restricted Stock Award still subject to restriction shall be forfeited by the Participant and reacquired by the Company.

SECTION 9. PERFORMANCE AWARDS. Performance Awards in the form of Performance Units or Performance Shares may be issued hereunder to Participants, For no cash consideration or for such minimum consideration as may be required by applicable law, either alone or in addition to other Awards granted under the Plan. The performance criteria to be achieved during any Performance Period and the length of the Performance Period shall be determined by the Committee upon the grant of each Performance Award or at any time thereafter. Except as provided in Section 11, Performance Awards will be distributed only after the end of the relevant Performance Period. Performance Awards may be paid in cash, Shares, other property or any combination thereof, in the sole discretion of the Committee at the time of payment. The performance levels to be achieved for each Performance Period and the amount of the Award to be distributed shall be conclusively determined by the Committee. Performance Awards may be paid in a lump sum or in installments following the close of the Performance Period.

SECTION 10. OTHER STOCK UNIT AWARDS. Other Awards of Shares and other Awards that are valued in whole or in part by reference to, or are otherwise based on, Shares or other property ("Other Stock Unit Awards") may be granted hereunder to Participants, either alone or in addition to other Awards granted under the Plan. Other Stock Unit Awards may be paid in Shares, other securities of the Company, cash or any other form of property as the Committee shall determine. Shares (including securities convertible into Shares) granted under this Section 10 may be issued for no cash consideration or for such minimum consideration as may be required by applicable law. Shares (including securities convertible into Shares) purchased pursuant to a purchase right awarded under this Section 10 shall be purchased for such consideration as the Committee shall in its sole discretion determine, which shall not be less than the Fair Market Value of such Shares or other securities as of the date such purchase right is awarded. Subject to the provisions of the Plan, the Committee shall have sole and complete authority to determine the Employees of the Company and its Affiliates to whom and the time or times at which such Awards shall be made, the number of Shares to be granted pursuant to such Awards, and all other conditions of the Awards. The provisions of Other Stock Unit Awards need not be the same with respect to each recipient.

SECTION 11. CHANGE IN CONTROL PROVISIONS.

(a) IMPACT OF EVENT. Notwithstanding any other provision of the Plan to the contrary, unless the Committee shall determine otherwise at the time of grant with respect to a particular Award, in the event of a Change in Control:

(i) Any Options and Stock Appreciation Rights outstanding as of the date such Change in Control is determined to have occurred, and which are not then exercisable and vested, shall become fully exercisable and vested.

(ii) The restrictions and deferral limitations applicable to any Restricted Stock Awards shall lapse, and such Restricted Stock Awards shall become free of all restrictions and limitations and become fully vested and transferable.

(iii) All Performance Awards shall be considered to be earned and payable in full, and any deferral or other restriction shall lapse and such Performance Awards shall be immediately settled or distributed.

(iv) The restrictions and deferral limitations and other conditions applicable to any Other Stock Unit Awards or any other Awards shall lapse, and such Other Stock Unit Awards or such other Awards shall become free of all restrictions, limitations or conditions and become fully vested and transferable.

(b) CHANGE IN CONTROL CASH-OUT. Notwithstanding any other provision of the Plan, during the 60-day period from and after a Change in Control (the "Exercise Period"), if the Committee shall determine at, or at any time after, the time of grant, a Participant holding an Option shall have the right, whether or not the Option is fully exercisable and in lieu of the payment of the purchase price for the Shares being purchased under the Option and by giving notice to the Company, to elect (within the Exercise Period) to surrender all or part of the Option to the Company and to receive cash, within 30 days of such notice, in an amount equal to the amount by which the Change in Control Price per Share on the date of such election shall exceed the purchase price per Share under the Option (the "Spread") multiplied by the number of Shares granted under the Option as to which the right granted under this Section 11(b) shall have been exercised.

(c) Notwithstanding any other provision of this Plan, if any right granted pursuant to this Plan would make a Change in Control transaction ineligible for pooling-of-interests accounting under APB No. 16 (or other relevant accounting literature), which transaction (after giving effect to any other actions taken to cause such transaction to be eligible for such pooling-of-interests accounting treatment), but for the nature of such grant, would otherwise be eligible for such accounting treatment, the Committee shall have the ability to substitute for the cash payable pursuant to such right, Shares with an equivalent Fair Market Value.

SECTION 12. CODE SECTION 162(m) PROVISIONS.

(a) Notwithstanding any other provision of this Plan, if the Committee determines at the time Restricted Stock, a Performance Award or an Other Stock Unit

Award is granted to a Participant that such Participant is, or may be as of the end of the tax year for which the Company would claim a tax deduction in connection with such Award, a Covered Employee, then the Committee may provide that this Section 12 is applicable to such Award under such terms as the Committee shall determine.

(b) If an Award is subject to this Section 12, then the lapsing of restrictions thereon and the distribution of cash, Shares or other property pursuant thereto, as applicable, shall be subject to the Company having a level of Net Income for the fiscal year preceding lapse or distribution set by the Committee within the time prescribed by Section 162(m) of the Code or the regulations thereunder in order for the level to be considered "pre-established". The Committee may, in its discretion, reduce the amount of any Performance Award or Other Stock Unit Award subject to this Section 12 at any time prior to payment based on such criteria as it shall determine, including but not limited to individual merit and the attainment of specified levels of one or any combination of the following: net cash provided by operating activities, earnings per Share from continuing operations, operating income, revenues, gross margin, return on operating assets, return on equity, economic value added, stock price appreciation, total shareowner return (measured in terms of stock price appreciation and dividend growth), or cost control, of the Company or the Affiliate or division of the Company for or within which the Participant is primarily employed.

(c) Notwithstanding any contrary provision of the Plan other than Section 11, the Committee may not adjust upwards the amount payable pursuant to any Award subject to this Section 12, nor may it waive the achievement of the Net Income requirement contained in Section 12(b), except in the case of the death or disability of a Participant.

(d) Prior to the payment of any Award subject to this Section 12, the Committee shall certify in writing that the Net Income requirement applicable to such Award was met.

(e) The Committee shall have the power to impose such other restrictions on Awards subject to this Section 12 as it may deem necessary or appropriate to ensure that such Awards satisfy all requirements for "performance-based compensation" within the meaning of Section 162(m)(4)(C) of the Code, the regulations promulgated thereunder, and any successors thereto.

SECTION 13. AMENDMENTS AND TERMINATION. The Board may amend, alter or discontinue the Plan, but no amendment, alteration, or discontinuation shall be made that would impair the rights of an optionee or Participant under an Award theretofore granted, without the optionee's or Participant's consent, or that without the approval of the shareowners would:

(a) except as is provided in Section 4(b) of the Plan, increase the total number of shares reserved for the purpose of the Plan; or

(b) change the employees or class of employees eligible to participate in the Plan.

The Committee may amend the terms of any Award theretofore granted, prospectively or retroactively, but no such amendment shall impair the rights of any Participant without his consent. Except as provided in Section 4(b) and Section 14(e), the Committee shall not have the authority to cancel any outstanding Option and issue a new Option in its place with a lower exercise price.

SECTION 14. GENERAL PROVISIONS.

(a) Unless the Committee determines otherwise at the time the Award is granted, no Award, and no Shares subject to Awards described in Section 10 which have not been issued or as to which any applicable restriction, performance or deferral period has not lapsed, may be sold, assigned, transferred, pledged or otherwise en-cumbered, except by will or by the laws of descent and distribution and all Awards shall be exercisable, during the Participant's lifetime, only by the Participant or, if permissible under applicable law, by the Participant's guardian or legal representative; provided that, if so determined by the Committee, a Participant may, in the manner established by the Committee, designate a beneficiary to exercise the rights of the Participant with respect to any Award upon the death of the Participant.

(b) The term of each Award shall be for such period of months or years from the date of its grant as may be determined by the Committee; provided that in no event shall the term of any Incentive Stock Option or any Stock Appreciation Right related to any Incentive Stock Option exceed a period of ten (10) years from the date of its grant.

(c) No Employee or Participant shall have any claim to be granted any Award under the Plan and there is no obligation for uniformity of treatment of Employees or Participants under the Plan.

(d) The prospective recipient of any Award under the Plan shall not, with respect to such Award, be deemed to have become a Participant, or to have any rights with respect to such Award, until and unless such recipient shall have executed an agreement or other instrument evidencing the Award and delivered a fully executed copy thereof to the Company, and otherwise complied with the then applicable terms and conditions.

(e) Except as provided in Section 12, the Committee shall be authorized to make adjustments in Performance Award criteria or in the terms and conditions of other Awards in recognition of unusual or nonrecurring events affecting the Company or its financial statements, or changes in applicable laws, regulations or accounting principles. The Committee may correct any defect, supply any omission or reconcile any inconsistency in the Plan or any Award in the manner and to the extent it shall deem desirable. In the event the Company shall assume outstanding employee benefit awards or the right or obligation to make future such awards in connection with the acquisition of another corporation or business entity, the Committee may, in its discretion, make such adjustments in the terms of Awards under the Plan as it shall deem appropriate.

(f) The Committee shall have full power and authority to determine whether, to what extent and under what circumstances any Award shall be canceled or suspended. In particular, but without limitation, all outstanding Awards to any Participant shall be canceled if the Participant, without the consent of the Committee, while employed by the Company or after termination of such employment, engages in any activity which is in competition with the Company, as determined by the Committee, one or more Officers of the Company or a committee of Officers of the Company to whom the authority to make such determination is delegated by the Committee.

(g) All certificates for Shares delivered under the Plan pursuant to any Award shall be subject to such stock-transfer orders and other restrictions as the Committee may deem advisable under the rules, regulations, and other requirements of the Securities and Exchange Commission, any stock exchange upon which the Shares are then listed, and any applicable Federal or state securities law, and the Committee may cause a legend or legends to be put on any such certificates to make appropriate reference to such restrictions.

(h) Subject to the provisions of this Plan and any Award Agreement, the recipient of an Award (including, without limitation, any deferred Award) may, if so determined by the Committee, be entitled to receive, currently or on a deferred basis, interest or dividends, or interest or dividend equivalents, with respect to the number of Shares covered by the Award, as determined by the Committee, in its sole discretion, and the Committee may provide that such amounts (if any) shall be deemed to have been reinvested in additional Shares or otherwise reinvested.

(i) Except as otherwise required in any applicable Award Agreement or by the terms of the Plan, recipients of Awards under the Plan shall not be required to make any payment or provide consideration other than the rendering of services.

(j) To the extent permitted by law, the Committee may delegate to one or more directors of the Company (who need not be members of the Committee) the right to grant Awards to Employees who are not officers of the Company for purposes of Section 16 of the Exchange Act or directors of the Company and to amend, administer, interpret, waive conditions with respect to, cancel or suspend Awards to Employees who are not such officers.

(k) The Committee is authorized to establish procedures pursuant to which the payment of any Award may be deferred.

(l) The maximum value of the property, including cash, that may be paid or distributed to any Participant pursuant to grants of Performance Units and/or Other Stock Unit Awards that are valued with reference to property other than Shares made in any one calendar year is $9,000,000.

(m) The Company is authorized to withhold from any Award granted or payment due under the Plan the amount of withholding taxes due in respect of an Award or payment hereunder and to take such other action as may be necessary in the opinion of the Company to satisfy all obligations for the payment of such taxes. The Committee shall be authorized to establish procedures for election by Participants to satisfy such withholding taxes by delivery of, or directing the Company to retain, Shares.

(n) Nothing contained in this Plan shall prevent the Board of Directors from adopting other or additional compensation arrangements, subject to shareowner approval if such approval is otherwise required; and such arrangements may be either generally applicable or applicable only in specific cases.

(o) The validity, construction, and effect of the Plan and any rules and regulations relating to the Plan shall be determined in accordance with the laws of the State of Delaware and applicable Federal law.

(p) If any provision of this Plan is or becomes or is deemed invalid, illegal or unenforceable in any jurisdiction, or would disqualify the Plan or any Award under any law deemed applicable by the Committee, such provision shall be construed or deemed amended to conform to applicable laws or if it cannot be construed or deemed amended without, in the determination of the committee, materially altering the intent of the Plan, it shall be stricken and the remainder of the Plan shall remain in full force and effect.

(q) Awards may be granted to Employees who are foreign nationals or employed outside the United States, or both, on such terms and conditions different from those specified in the Plan as may, in the judgment of the Committee, be necessary or desirable in order to recognize differences in local law or tax policy. The Committee also may impose conditions on the exercise or vesting of Awards in order to minimize the Company's obligation with respect to tax equalization for Employees on assignments outside their home country.

SECTION 15. EFFECTIVE DATE OF PLAN. The Plan first became effective on October 1, 1996.

SECTION 16. TERM OF PLAN. No Award shall be granted pursuant to the Plan after February 28, 2003, but any Award theretofore granted may extend beyond that date.

IN WITNESS WHEREOF, the Company has caused this Plan as amended to be effective July 19, 2000.

LUCENT TECHNOLOGIES INC.

By: _____

    Alan J. Ritchie
    Vice President, Compensation, Benefits & Health Services

Attest: _____

    Richard J. Rawson
    Senior Vice President, General Counsel
    and Secretary

CHAPTER 6

Stock Grants and Options

I. INTRODUCTION

Stock-based compensation, like bonuses, are a variable or at risk form of compensation, although the risk the executive is subject to depends upon the type of compensation. Stock-based compensation normally falls into one of two broad categories: (1) stock options or stock appreciation rights (SARs) or (2) stock grants. Although the ultimate value of either is based upon stock price performance after the date of grant, the payoffs and risks are different. Appendix 6.1 contains an example of a "nonqualified" stock option award, whereas Appendix 6.2 contains an example of a "restricted" stock award; both agreements are between Delta Air Lines and Leo Mullin, its President and Chief Executive Officer.

A. Stock Options or Stock Appreciation Rights

Stock options allow their holder to purchase one or more shares of stock at a fixed "exercise" price over a fixed period of time. That period, however, does not necessarily start on the date the options are granted to the executive. Although some options vest immediately, most of the time the executive does not have the right to exercise some or all of the options until a specified time period has passed or performance goal has been met. At Motorola, for example, options vest 25% per year over a 4-year period: "the options vest and become exercisable over 4 years as follows: 25% on 1/31/01; 25% on 1/31/02; 25% on 1/31/03; and 25% on 1/31/04."[1] In contrast, at DuPont certain senior management options vest with the achievement of performance goals:

> Variable stock option grants have been made to certain members of senior management. These options are subject to forfeiture if, within five years from the date of grant, the

[1]Motorola proxy statement filed with the Securities and Exchange Commission, March 22, 2000, p. 17.

market price of DuPont common stock does not achieve a price of $75 per share for 50 percent of the options and $90 per share for the remaining 50 percent. This condition was met in 1998 for options with a $75 per share hurdle price and, as a result, these options became "fixed" and exercisable.[2]

The options, once vested, can then be exercised until they expire. Most options expire over periods no longer than 10 years from the date of grant, as illustrated by the following extract from Merck's proxy statement:[3]

Option/SAR Grants in Last Fiscal Year

Name	Date of grant	Expiration date
Raymond V. Gilmartin	2/23/99	2/22/09
Edward M. Scolnick	2/23/99	2/22/09
David W. Anstice	2/23/99	2/22/09
Judy C. Lewent	2/23/99	2/22/09
Per G.H. Lofberg	2/23/99	2/22/09

When the stock price increases between the time of grant and the time of vesting (a.k.a., the vesting period), the effect is to tie the employee to the corporation, as the employee would forfeit the increase in value if he or she leaves before the option has vested. Of course, this does not mean the employee never leaves before the option vests. The raise offered by the new employer may be more than sufficient to make up for value of the unvested options. Alternatively, as noted in Chapter 3, if the new employer wants the executive badly enough, it can reimburse the executive for the value of the unvested options. For example, Xerox, in hiring Michael Miron as Senior Vice President,

> . . . agreed to pay Mr. Miron a signing bonus of $250,000 and to recommend to the Executive Compensation and Benefits Committee that Mr. Miron be awarded 235,000 stock options and 14,000 incentive stock rights to compensate him for the forfeiture of unvested stock options and any other compensation from his then current employer.[4]

At any time prior to exercise, the value of an option is composed of its intrinsic and time values (see Appendix 2.1). The intrinsic value of the option is the excess of the current market price of the shares over the exercise price at any point in time. The time value of the option is the value attached to the potential increase in the stock price over the remaining life of the option. Although all options have a positive value at the date of grant (because of the time value), ultimately they will only prove profitable to the executive if the corporation's share price is greater than the exercise price at the exercise date. Otherwise they will expire unexercised. Because the exercise price is normally set at the share price on the date of grant,[5]

---

[2]E. I. Du Pont De Nemours 10-K filed with the Securities and Exchange Commission, March 17, 2000, p. 59.

[3]Merck proxy statement filed with the Securities and Exchange Commission, March 16, 2000, p. 15.

[4]Xerox proxy statement filed with the Securities and Exchange Commission, April 9, 1999, p. 16.

[5]Both Matsunaga (1995, note 6) and Murphy (1998) found about 95% of corporations granting options with an exercise price equal to grant-date fair-market value.

TABLE 6.1   Status of Options Held by CEOs

Year	CEOs with options (%)	CEOs with all options out of the money (%)	CEOs with exercisable options (%)	CEOs with exercisable options all out of the money (%)
1992	66	31	59	16
1993	82	28	73	11
1994	84	37	78	15
1995	81	30	76	15
1996	84	29	78	15
1997	85	26	79	14
1998	88	32	82	16
1999	91	32	86	16
2000	92	24	88	14

the ultimate value of the option depends upon the performance of a corporation's share price subsequent to the date of grant. That is, they can be extremely valuable when the share price rises dramatically, but can also expire worthless if the share price declines.[6] In some cases though, the corporation can guarantee a payoff. When Joseph Galli took the position of president at Amazon.com, Amazon effectively guaranteed him a minimum profit of $20,000,000 over the subsequent 10 years, by promising to make up the difference via a special bonus payment.[7] Table 6.1 shows that the percentage of CEOs that hold options on their employer's common stock has increased over time, reaching a high of 92% at the end of 2000. It also shows that although most CEOs hold options in their employers, a significant percentage of those CEOs, from 24–37% depending on the year, have all of their options out of the money, that is, the exercise price for all of their options exceeds the current market price. Of course, although these options currently have no intrinsic value (cannot be exercised profitably), the possibility exists that at some point prior to their expiration they will be valuable.

Stock appreciation rights are similar to options in their payoff structure; that is, they are only valuable if the stock price increases beyond the exercise price. The difference between stock options and SARs relates to the form of the payoff. With stock options, the executive exercises the options by paying cash and in exchange receives shares of stock. He or she may then turn around and sell those shares at the current market price, the profit being the difference between the price paid (the

[6]As will be discussed later in this chapter, and then again in Chapter 13, when share prices fall after the date of grant, resulting in the exercise price of the option being greater than the share price, companies sometimes grant additional options at the lower price and/or reduce the exercise price on the existing option.

[7]Amazon.com proxy statement filed with the Securities and Exchange Commission, March 29, 2000, p. 12.

exercise price) and the current market price. Alternatively, recognizing that raising cash to pay the exercise price may be a constraint for executives, some corporations grant SARs. When the executive elects to exercise the SAR, the corporation simply pays the executive, in cash and/or shares, the difference between the current market price and the exercise price for the number of SARs held. In most cases SARs are granted in tandem with stock options, so that the executive may exercise one or the other depending upon whether he or she wants to receive shares or cash.[8] Other corporations allow executives to pay the exercise price with previously owned shares of stock and/or loan executives the money with which to buy the shares. For example, Allegheny Technologies has the following program that allows participants to borrow money to purchase shares and secure those loans with the shares being acquired:

> Loans under Stock Acquisition and Retention Programs. Under the terms of the Company's stock acquisition and retention programs, eligible participants may deliver a promissory note, payable to the Company, as payment for the purchase price of shares of Common Stock purchased under the programs. Each note has a term of not more than 10 years and is secured by the shares of Common Stock being purchased with the note. Interest accrues on the notes at a rate, as determined on the applicable purchase date, equal to the lesser of the average borrowing rate of the Company or the prime lending rate of PNC Bank, but not lower than the minimum rate necessary to avoid imputed interest under applicable federal income tax laws. During the 1999 fiscal year, James L. Murdy, Jon D. Walton, Judd R. Cool, and Dale G. Reid delivered promissory notes to the Company to pay the purchase price of Common Stock purchased under the program. The largest amount of indebtedness outstanding under the programs during the 1999 fiscal year and the amount of indebtedness outstanding under the programs as of December 31, 1999 were $1,529,437 and $795,705 for Mr. Murdy; $1,223,845 and $626,087 for Mr. Walton; $248,082 and $116,843 for Mr. Cool; and $366,967 and $193,914 for Mr. Reid.[9]

Some corporations, for example, American Home Products and E.I. Du Pont De Nemours, have gone even further and set up cashless exercise programs for their executives. In a cashless exercise, the executive simply calls the program administrator, which would normally be a brokerage firm like Merrill Lynch, and states that he or she would like to exercise the options and sell the shares. The administrator would then handle the transaction and deposit the profits, less any transaction costs, in the executive's brokerage account or send a check to the executive.

B. Stock Grants

Stock grants differ from stock options in that they have no exercise price. Whereas a stock option only has value if the corporation's share price is above the exercise

---

[8]See Matsunaga (1995) or Balsam and Paek (2001).

[9]Allegheny Technologies proxy statement filed with Securities and Exchange Commission, March 21, 2000, p. 29.

price, a stock grant has value as long as the share price is above zero. Stock grants can be unrestricted or restricted. An example of a restriction imposed upon a stock grant might be that the employee cannot sell the shares until he or she has worked for the corporation for a period of time. For example, when Conseco hired Gary C. Wendt as its Chairman and CEO they gave him "3.2 million restricted shares of common stock which will become unrestricted if Mr. Wendt remains an employee through June 30, 2002."[10]

Other restrictions might be based upon performance. For example, Hercules, Inc., conditions the earning of the shares on stock price performance subsequent to the grant as described here:

> . . . the CEO and each of the other named executive officers received performance shares when they assumed their new roles and responsibilities. These shares will vest only when Hercules stock price closes at or above $50.00 either for five consecutive trading days or for 10 trading days in any 20-day period. Should Hercules stock price not reach either of these targets within three years from the date of grant, the shares will be forfeited.[11]

The risk of forfeiture is real. The following is from Hewlett-Packard's proxy statement:

> In November 1998, the Compensation Committee reviewed the results for the three-year performance period ended October 31, 1998 to determine to what extent the performance objectives associated with performance-based restricted stock granted in fiscal 1996 had been met. The Compensation Committee determined that under the terms of each grant, Mr. Platt, Mr. Wayman, Mr. Barnholt and Dr. Birnbaum were required to forfeit the following shares constituting 75% of the performance-based re-stricted stock granted in 1996: Mr. Platt 52,500 shares, Mr. Wayman 15,000 shares, Mr. Barnholt 12,000 shares and Dr. Birnbaum 6,000 shares. The value of the forfeiture is reflected in the table above as a negative LTIP pay-out in fiscal 1998 based upon the value of HP stock as of the date of the grant in fiscal 1996.[12]

C. Incentive Effects

As with other forms of compensation, stock options and grants can be used to attract and retain employees, an attraction that works well when stock prices are increasing, but not as well when they are decreasing. The reason is that when stock prices are rising executives are reluctant to leave, if by departing they leave some valuable but unexercisable options (options that have not yet vested) or restricted shares behind. Viewed as a way to retain key people, the vesting period then becomes an important factor. As long as the options or shares are unvested, those individuals would suffer a monetary loss when leaving the corporation. Of course,

[10]Conseco 8-K filed with Securities and Exchange Commission July 10, 2000, p. 1.

[11]Hercules proxy statement filed with Securities and Exchange Commission, March 28, 2000, p. 20.

[12]Hewlett Packard proxy statement filed with Securities and Exchange Commission, January 11, 1999, p. 18.

if vesting is too far in the future, executives may leave for a quicker payoff elsewhere. Thus the vesting period is a key factor that must be chosen with care. Furthermore, if those options are "underwater," that is, the exercise price is greater than the current market price, there is no monetary bond to the corporation, and thus employees are more willing to leave the corporation, as discussed in the following example:

> . . . like so many e-tailers, Skymall has seen its stock plunge since the end of last year, leaving Mr. Goldman with options priced at $16 and the stock trading at under $10. So he did what an increasing number of others in his shoes are doing: He quit.[13]

D. Use of Stock Options and Grants in the Compensation Package

As shown in Chapter 2, stock options and grants are a major component of the CEO compensation package, although as shown in Table 2.1, stock options are used much more frequently. Tables 2.1, 2.2, and 2.3 show that both stock options and stock grants are awarded with increasing frequency, as the proportion of firms awarding stock options increased from 50% in 1992 to 79% in 2000, whereas the percentage of firms making stock grants increased from 17% in 1992 to 22% in 2000. Tables 2.4, 2.5, and 2.6 show that the proportion of compensation composed of stock options and stock grants also increases over time, with the percentage of compensation consisting of stock options increasing from a mean (median) of 21% (14%) in 1992 to 42% (42%) in 2000, and that of stock grants increasing from a mean of 4% in 1992 to 5% in 2000.[14] Tables 2.7, 2.8, and 2.9 show the amounts involved, which have increased dramatically through the period. For example, the value of stock options granted increased from a mean (median) of $592,000 ($110,000) in 1992 to $5,589,000 ($1,214,000) in 2000. The mean value of stock grants was much lower, $609,000, in 2000, but also increased dramatically from a mean value of $114,000 in 1992.[15] Stock options and grants have thus been increasing in frequency (Table 2.1) as a proportion of the compensation package (Table 2.4) and in amount (see Table 2.7), and generally, at a rate in excess of the rate of increase in salaries, bonuses, and inflation (see Table 6.2 and Figure 6.1).

Table 6.2 shows the percentage change in the value of stock options and grants awarded to CEOs that have been with the same corporation (and in the same position) for at least 2 years. Tables 6.3 and 6.4 show these amounts across industry

---

[13]Carlton (2000).

[14]The dollar value for the stock option grants are determined by Standard & Poors ExecuComp using the Black–Scholes options pricing model, whereas the dollar value for the stock grants are determined (and reported) by the granting corporations using the market price of the shares on the date of grant.

[15]The median stock grant is zero, because as observed in Table 2.1, only 22% of corporations grant stock to their CEOs in 2000.

TABLE 6.2   Comparison of Percentage Change in Stock Compensation, Salary, Short- and Long-Term Bonuses for CEOs with the Same Company for Consecutive Years[a]

Year	Change in value of stock option grants from prior year (%)	Change in value of stock grants from prior year (%)	Change in salary (%)	Change in ST bonus (%)	Change in LT bonus (%)	Average change in CPI-U (%)
1993	23	56	6	21	29	2.2
	2	−8	5	10	0	
1994	82	34	8	33	7	1.6
	22	−10	6	14	−5	
1995	47	26	9	60	51	2.3
	−17	−28	6	10	11	
1996	62	0	8	20	21	3.0
	12	−8	6	7	4	
1997	88	23	8	45	39	2.8
	2	−11	6	11	4	
1998	355	90	10	20	27	2.6
	11	−16	6	4	−5	
1999	74	24	9	76	101	3.0
	15	−27	5	7	−12	
2000	74	103	28	106	117	3.4
	2	−30	6	10	−12	

[a]Means on top, medians below. ST, short-term; LT, long-term; CPI-U, Consumer Price Index.

and the size of the corporation. Table 6.2 and Figure 6.1 show that for continuing CEOs, the value of stock options granted to CEOs has increased over time, and at a mean (median) rate of between 23 and 355% (−17 and 22%) per year, which compares to increases of 20–106% (4–14%) for short-term bonuses, 6–28% (5–6%) for salary, and 1.6–3.4% for the Consumer Price Index. Similarly, the value of stock grants to CEOs has increased over time, and at a mean rate of between 0 and 103% per year.[16]

Tables 2.5 and 2.8 show that stock options and stock grants vary in importance and magnitude across industry. Analogously, Table 6.3 shows that the 2000 rate of increase in stock options and stock grants varies by industry. Although the mean (median) rate of increase in the value of stock option grants for 2000 was 74% (2%), for individual industries that rate was as low as 9% (−2%) for finance, insurance, and real estate, and as high as 100% (8%) for manufacturing. Similarly, although the mean rate of increase in the value of stock grants for 2000 was 103% for individual

[16]Medians are not meaningful, as the majority of companies do not grant stock in any given year, even those who had granted stock in the previous year.

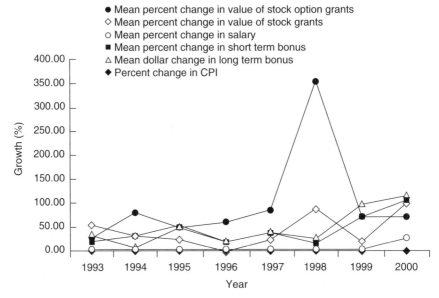

FIGURE 6.1   Growth in components of CEO compensation versus growth in CPI.

TABLE 6.3   Percentage Change in 2000 Stock Compensation for CEOs with Same Company for Consecutive Years by Industry[a]

Industry	SIC codes[b]	Change in value of grants (%)	Change in value of grants (%)
Mining and construction	1000–1999	30	46
		24	36
Manufacturing	2000–3999	100	12
		8	−54
Transportation, communications, electric, gas, etc.	4000–4999	52	366
		−4	−21
Wholesale and retail trade	5000–5999	74	325
		−19	−45
Finance, insurance, and real estate	6000–6999	9	−14
		−2	−19
Services	7000–7999	79	−56
		8	−100

[a]Means on top, medians below.
[b]SIC, Standard Industrial Classification.

TABLE 6.4   Percentage Change in 2000 Stock
Compensation for CEOs with Same Company
for Consecutive Years by Firm Size[a]

	Size decile	Change in value of option grants (%)	Change in value of stock grants (%)
Smallest	1	34	−14
		−18	−36
	2	39	20
		−16	−25
	3	109	−37
		−3	−72
	4	74	−29
		−1	−58
	5	36	4
		7	−51
	6	73	40
		15	−14
	7	68	−19
		−5	−58
	8	99	1144
		18	−70
	9	89	−12
		7	−20
Largest	10	96	9
		6	−8

[a]Means on top, medians below.

industries that rate was as low as a decrease of 56% in services to an increase of as high as 366% in transportation, communication, electric, gas, and sanitary services. Table 2.6 shows that stock options and stock grants as a percentage of total compensation increase with the size of the corporation. Consequently, Table 2.9 shows that, in absolute terms, both increase dramatically with the size of the corporation. That is, the value of stock options granted to the CEO increased from a mean (median) of $512,000 ($165,000) for the smallest corporations to $18,925,000 ($9,040,000) for the largest, and the value of stock grants increased from a mean of $75,000 for the smallest corporations to $2,954,000 for the largest. Table 6.4 shows some variation in the rate of increase across the size of the corporation, but no clear pattern emerges.

II. INCENTIVES

More so than other forms of compensation, stock compensation provides employees with incentives to increase shareholder value. This is because when executives own shares or options on shares, executive wealth increases or decreases with shareholder wealth. Thus, stock compensation (and ownership) aligns the interests of employees with shareholders (see, for example, Jensen and Meckling 1976; Murphy 1985; Abowd 1990; Jensen and Murphy 1990a, b; Murphy 1998). A potential downside to options is that although they provide the incentive to increase stock price, executives may have the incentive to manipulate stock price for short-term gain (for example, they delay disclosing good news until after grant or disclosing bad news until after exercise). Academics have investigated this possibility. Examining the timing of option grants, Yermack (1997) found that "CEOs receive stock option awards shortly before favorable corporate news," (p. 449) while Chauvin and Shenoy (2001) found an abnormal decrease in stock prices during the 10 days prior to option grants. Examining the timing of option exercise, Huddart and Lang (2000) found the level of option exercise inversely related to future stock returns, whereas Carpenter and Remmers (1998) found no evidence of option exercise prior to adverse stock price performance.

Given the riskiness of stock-based compensation, the amount of stock-based compensation included in the compensation package will affect the type of executives attracted to the corporation. In particular, a corporation with a large proportion of stock in its compensation package is more likely to attract executives with low risk aversion. Still, as alluded to in Chapter 3, because of risk aversion, the employer will always have to pay more in stock-based compensation than it would have in fixed cash compensation. Put another way, the employee values stock-based compensation at less than the cost to the corporation. Meulbroek (2000) estimated that "For Internet firms, the estimated value of stock options to undiversified managers is only 53% of their cost to the firm. . . ."

A. Affect on Incentives to Take Risk

Agrawal and Mandelker (1987) found that variance-increasing investments are more likely to be made by managers with larger holdings of common stock and options. Interestingly enough, including stock in the compensation package may or may not provide increased incentive to take risk. Rather, stock options, because their ex-ante value increases with risk, provide managers with incentives to take risk. This can be illustrated with the following simple example. The expected share price of corporation A 1 year from now follows the following probability distribution:

Probability (%)	Share price ($)
50	100
50	50

The corporation has the option to make a risky investment that will alter the above distribution as follows:

Probability (%)	Share price ($)
50	180
50	20

Without the investment, the expected value of a share is $75 (50% of $50 plus 50% of $100); with the investment, the expected value increases to $100 (50% of $20 plus 50% of $180). A risk-averse executive, fearing the repercussions of a bad outcome (that is, getting fired), might be unwilling to take the investment. However, if the executive were awarded options with an exercise price of $75, his or her incentives would change. Without the investment, the expected value of the options would be $12.50 (50% of $25, the value of the option if the share price is $100; the option is worthless if share price is $50). With the investment, the expected value of the options would increase to $52.50 (50% of $105, the value of the option if the share price is $180; the option is worthless if share price is $20). The effect of the options is to provide executives with the incentive to take risks.

Although it is generally assumed that options provide incentives for managers to take risks (DeFusco et al. 1990), this may not be true in all situations (Wiseman and Gomez-Mejia 1998). Although true for options out of (exercise price greater than current market price) and at the money (exercise price equal to current market price), it is not necessarily true for options in the money. If an option is in the money, the executive may become risk averse, in that he or she has something to lose if the stock price decreases. This is also true with stock grants, as the under-diversified manager will not want to take as much risk as diversified shareholders would like. Thus the best way to counter a manager's risk aversion is to make sure the bulk of their equity incentives is from holding at or out of the money options, a situation that can be controlled with reload options (discussed later in this chapter).

B. Effect of Stock Compensation on Ownership

Incentive effects differ across types of stock compensation. First, consider options, the various choices that have to be made, and the effects of those choices on incentives. The corporation can grant, for tax purposes, qualified or nonqualified options. With qualified options, the executive does not pay taxes upon exercise of the option (with a nonqualified option the executive does), but rather pays taxes upon sale of the shares acquired upon exercise. Further, assuming he or she held the shares for 1 year (or more), the gain is taxed at capital gains rather than ordinary income rates. Deferral of taxability with a tax-qualified option provides incentive, similar to the "lock-in effect," to retain shares. In contrast, with a nonqualified option, there is no tax incentive to retain shares, and thus for liquidity and diversification purposes, the executive may sell shares immediately upon exercise. Empirical and anecdotal evidence suggests that employees do sell shares immediately upon exercise, although no research has looked at whether this is affected by the tax status of the option. Huddart (1994) and Giles (1999) reported that over 90% of shares received from exercising options are sold immediately. As noted above, some corporations even facilitate this turnover by setting up "cashless exercise" programs with investment bankers. Yet these corporations often state (for example, Wendy's International, Compaq Computer, Eli Lilly) that encouraging employee ownership is one of the goals of their option programs.

Reload options are used to encourage ownership by employees. In addition, reload options can provide the proper incentives for the executive to take risk; that is, once the options are in the money, the underdiversified executive exercises the option, sells the shares, and gets new at the money options. Consider the following from the Tribune Company:

> To encourage stock ownership by executive officers, replacement stock options ("replacement options") are granted simultaneously with the exercise of the original stock option. Replacement options are intended to encourage an executive officer to exercise a stock option earlier than might otherwise occur, thus resulting in increased share ownership by the executive officer. Replacement options are granted when an executive officer exercises an option by surrendering (or attesting to) currently owned shares to purchase the shares subject to the option as well as to satisfy tax withholding obligations related to the exercise of the option. Replacement options are subject to the same terms and conditions as the original options, including the expiration date, except that the option price of a replacement option is the fair market value on the date of its grant rather than the option price of the original option and replacement options do not become exercisable until one year after award. The grant of replacement options does not result in an increase in the total combined number of shares and options held by an employee and, therefore, does not increase amounts paid by Tribune. As shown in the table beginning on page 16, Mr. Madigan received replacement options during 1999 based on his exercise of previously awarded options.[17]

Although the above passage explicitly states, perhaps for political purposes, that the reload provision exists to encourage share ownership, nothing is mentioned about a requirement that the executive hold onto the shares obtained upon exercise. Without such a requirement, the exercise of the option may not lead to increased share ownership, as noted by Ofek and Yermack (2000). In 1999, Mr. Madigan exercised a total of 1,040,766 options, realizing a profit of $9,852,322,[18] and received a total of 864,382 replacement options.[19] However, as noted below, the number of shares received by Mr. Madigan was substantially lower:

> The number of shares of Tribune common stock acquired upon the exercise of options in 1999 for each of the above officers was offset by the number of existing or newly acquired shares of Tribune common stock the officer used to pay the exercise price and/

[17]Tribune Company proxy statement filed with the Securities and Exchange Commission, March 24, 2000, p. 13.

[18]Tribune Company proxy statement filed with the Securities and Exchange Commission, March 24, 2000, p. 18.

[19]Tribune proxy statement filed with the Securities and Exchange Commission, March 24, 2000, p. 16.

TABLE 6.5   Percentage
of Stock Grants That Are
"Reload" Grants

Year	Percentage
1992	5.99
1993	5.09
1994	5.15
1995	4.83
1996	9.21
1997	11.30
1998	9.63
1999	9.11
2000	9.09

or the applicable withholding tax. The net number of shares of Tribune common stock actually acquired by each of the above officers as a result of option exercises in 1999 was as follows: Mr. Madigan, 132,558 shares . . .[20]

Table 6.5 shows the percentage of new stock grants that are pursuant to reload provisions; that is, new options are issued because old options with reload provisions have been exercised. As shown in table 6.5, this frequency has been increasing over time (although it may have peaked in 1997) and now constitutes fully 9% of new option grants.

C. Choices the Corporation Must Make in Granting Stock Compensation

Other choices the corporation makes are the vesting period, the exercise price, and of course, the number of options. As discussed above, the choice of, or rather, the use of a vesting period provides executives with incentive to remain with the corporation until the options are vested. The choice of exercise price affects the employee's incentives, including risk preferences. If it is set too low, relative to the current market price, the underdiversified employee becomes risk averse, unwilling to take risks. If set too high, again relative to the current market price, the probability of profiting from the option decreases, as does the employee's incentive to work hard to increase the stock price. Also as noted above, if the options are out of the money, they have no retentive effect. For these and other financial reasons detailed next, the vast majority of options are granted with the exercise price equal to the current market price. The number of options can also affect the employee's

[20]Tribune proxy statement filed with the Securities and Exchange Commission, March 24, 2000, p. 18.

incentives. If the grant is large enough, that is, a "mega-grant," even if the stock price increases very little, the executive can become very rich. Thus the executive, while wanting to increase the stock price, does not necessarily want to take the risks necessary to maximize shareholder wealth.

Now consider stock grants. Grants can be restricted or unrestricted. If restricted, the restrictions either expire with the passage of time or the achievement of performance goals. Although both types of restrictions encourage the executive to remain with the corporation, each provides differing incentives. If the restrictions expire with the passage of time, the executive need only concern him- or herself with remaining employed until those restrictions expire. In contrast, if the restrictions only expire with the achievement of performance goals, the executive needs to work towards achievement of those goals. Unrestricted stock grants seemingly do not provide any incentives; however, perhaps they (and restricted stock grants) work towards the goal of increasing employee ownership.

The biggest choice, perhaps, is between stock options and stock grants. Grants can be considered options with a zero-exercise price, with the restriction period being analogous to the vesting period. Both provide incentive for the executive to remain with the corporation, but as noted, they have vastly different effects on the executive's incentive to take risk (Guay 1999), in that while options may make the executive more willing to take risk, stock grants will make the executive less willing to take risks.

They also differentially affect the executives' willingness to pay dividends. Consider the following illustration. An executive holds an option to purchase a share of stock at $75 per share at a time when the shares are trading at $100. The executive is deciding whether to pay a dividend of $10 per share. If the executive decides to pay the dividend, the ex-dividend value of the share will drop to $90 (ignoring taxes and other market imperfections), and the value of the option will drop accordingly. In general, options provide the incentive for the executive not to pay dividends; academic research has shown that corporations where executives hold large numbers of options are likely to pay lower dividends (Lambert et al. 1989; Fenn and Liang 1999). In contrast, if the executive owned shares rather than options, and once again ignoring taxes and other market imperfections, the executive would be indifferent to paying the dividend, as the decrease in value of the share would be offset by an increase in his or her cash holdings.

III. COSTS

A. Dilution

Among the commonalities of stock options and stock grants are that they increase the potential number of outstanding shares and, hence, potentially dilute the proportionate ownership of existing shareholders. This so-called dilution is a major, if not *the* major, cost of stock option and stock grant programs. The term potential is used, as not all options are exercised, nor are all stock grants earned. Some have gone as far to assert, "Option plans are redistributing corporate ownership" (Leonhardt, 2000a, p. 14).

The following passage describes some of the other costs of stock programs, which include dilution; rising debt associated with stock repurchases to minimize that dilution; understatement of expenses; and overstatement of earnings growth:

> As top executives (and other employees) continue to exercise their rising pile of options over the next decade, other stockholders will see their stakes watered down. It seems unavoidable. Already, companies have spent billions of dollars in recent years—and taken on rising levels of debt—buying back shares to minimize the dilution. For the repurchasing to continue at its current pace, a recent Federal Reserve study warned, companies would have to devote virtually all of their future earnings to buybacks.
>
> In essence, the skeptics worry, corporate America is using stock options like a credit card without a spending limit. While every penny in salary is recorded as a cost on company books, hundreds of billions of dollars in stock options aren't counted at all. To the fire of a blazing stock market, companies add the fuel of overly rosy earnings reports, unencumbered by off-the-books promises of future pay.
>
> In a speech last summer, Alan Greenspan, the Fed chairman, said stock options helped "impede judgments about prospective earnings" and, over the last five years, had caused companies to overstate profit growth by one to two percentage points each year.
>
> The level of exaggeration is on the rise, doubling between 1997 and 1998, according to a study by Bear Stearns. At some companies—including Cisco Systems, a new-economy stalwart that briefly last week boasted the highest market capitalization in the world—earnings would be more than 20 percent lower if stock options were accounted for.[21]

Dilution is getting significant attention, at least in the popular press. A recent *Business Week* article included the following passage pertaining to the enormous amount of options granted to Linda Wachner, President, CEO, and Chairman of the Board of Warnaco: "All told, Wachner has received stock options over the last 9 years that could give her ownership of a phenomenal 21% of outstanding shares."[22]

As illustrated by Table 6.6, this potential dilution (that is, the number of options granted) has increased almost linearly over time, both in absolute terms and as a percentage of total shares outstanding. In 1992 the mean (median) number of shares granted by a corporation to all their employees was 1,057,235 (477,577), which was 2% (1%) of all shares outstanding. By 2000 the mean (median) number of shares granted was 20,879,785 (1,827,319), which was 6% (2%) of all shares outstanding. To put these numbers in perspective, at a rate of 2% per year, the number of shares outstanding would double, and hence the proportional holdings of existing shareholders he halved, in 35 years. At a rate of 6% per year, this doubling and halving would occur over 12 years!

Tables 6.7 and 6.8 show that dilution varies across industry and size. Table 6.7 shows, as a percentage of outstanding shares, that total corporation grants range from a mean (median) of 2% (1%) in transportation, communications, electric, gas, and so on, to 11% (2%) in finance, insurance, and real estate. Table 6.8 shows that

---

[21]Leonhardt (2000a), p. 1. Copyright © 2000 by the New York Times Co. Reprinted with permission.
[22]Brady (2000).

TABLE 6.6   Options Granted during Current Year, Both as an Absolute Amount and as a Percentage of Outstanding Shares

Year	Mean number of options granted	Median number of options granted	As a percentage of shares outstanding at year end (mean)	As a percentage of shares outstanding at year end (median)
1992	1,057,235	477,577	2	1
1993	1,503,622	518,361	2	1
1994	1,501,837	556,516	3	1
1995	1,714,172	637,639	3	1
1996	2,789,030	714,286	3	2
1997	6,549,538	837,696	5	2
1998	7,204,517	1,073,653	5	2
1999	10,153,119	1,261,366	5	2
2000	20,879,785	1,827,319	6	2

although the number of options granted increases with the size of the corporation, there is no clear pattern in terms of percentage of shares outstanding. That is, although the mean percentage seems to increase with size, the median decreases. This occurs despite the assertion (for example, see Balsam et al. 2000b) that stock compensation is most important for smaller high-technology companies.[23] Overall,

TABLE 6.7   Options Granted during 2000, by Industry, Both as an Absolute Amount and as a Percentage of Outstanding Shares

Industry	SIC codes[a]	Mean number of options granted	Median number of options granted	As a percentage of shares outstanding at year end (mean)	As a percentage of shares outstanding at year end (median)
Mining and construction	1000–1999	4,392,662	1,374,374	7	1
Manufacturing	2000–3999	17,451,119	1,587,302	5	2
Transportation, communications, electric, gas, etc.	4000–4999	6,601,198	1,554,528	2	1
Wholesale and retail trade	5000–5999	8,638,694	1,826,484	6	3
Finance, insurance, and real estate	6000–6999	53,264,042	2,871,168	11	2
Services	7000–7999	13,304,907	3,227,470	8	5

[a]SIC, Standard Industrial Classification.

[23]The lack of observable pattern may be the result of the fact that what were once small, high-technology companies, for example, Cisco, Intel and Microsoft, are now large, high-technology companies.

TABLE 6.8   Options Granted during 2000, by Size, Both as an Absolute Amount and as a Percentage of Outstanding Shares

	Size decile	Mean number of options granted	Median number of options granted	As a percentage of shares outstanding at year end (mean)	As a percentage of shares outstanding at year end (median)
Smallest	1	885,089	539,568	5	4
	2	948,838	745,000	4	3
	3	1,638,476	888,889	4	3
	4	1,654,505	934,783	4	2
	5	4,929,646	1,636,631	9	3
	6	3,150,118	1,463,415	3	2
	7	6,878,584	2,780,185	6	2
	8	8,264,582	3,012,048	4	2
	9	18,669,620	7,172,428	8	2
Largest	10	146,285,463	24,930,310	12	2

Tables 6.7 and 6.8 demonstrate that stock options have become a major issue and form of compensation for both small and large companies of all industries. This evidence is also consistent with that found in the popular press:

> Last year, the nation's 200 largest public companies handed out options that represented the equivalent of 2.1 percent of their outstanding shares, up from 1.2 percent in 1994, according to Pearl Meyer & Partners, a pay consulting firm in New York. As a result, the average overhang reached 13.7 percent in 1999 . . .[24]

This latter term, *overhang,* is the ratio of stock options granted but not yet exercised to the number of outstanding shares.

B. Cash Outflow

To counter this dilution, many companies have made it a policy to fund their option and grant programs with shares they repurchase in the market. One example is Procter and Gamble:

> The Company maintains a share repurchase program, which authorizes the Company to purchase shares annually on the open market to mitigate the dilutive impact of employee compensation programs. The Company also has a discretionary buy-back program under which it currently intends to repurchase additional outstanding shares of up to $1 billion per year. Current year purchases under the repurchase programs were above normal at $2.53 billion, compared to $1.93 billion in 1998 and $1.65 billion in 1997.[25]

[24]Leonhardt (2000a), p. 14.

[25]Procter and Gamble 10-K filed with Securities and Exchange Commission, September 15, 1999, p. 16.

TABLE 6.9   Amounts Spent to Repurchase Shares

Year	Mean firm ($)	Median firm ($)	Firms repurchasing shares (%)	In aggregate ($)
1992	31,000,000	0	29	28,657,000,000
1993	29,000,000	0	30	38,324,000,000
1994	31,000,000	0	31	46,609,000,000
1995	48,000,000	0	33	76,253,000,000
1996	54,000,000	0	36	91,250,000,000
1997	82,000,000	0	41	141,266,000,000
1998	103,000,000	4,000,000	48	174,843,000,000
1999	120,000,000	6,000,000	51	189,397,000,000
2000	176,000,000	15,000,000	50	177,861,000,000

And some companies, for example, Microsoft, grant so many options even with a multibillion dollar repurchase program ($4.9 billion in 2000) they cannot avoid dilution.

> In addition, cash will be used to repurchase common stock to provide shares for employee stock option and purchase plans. The buyback program has not kept pace with employee stock option grants or exercises. Beginning in fiscal 1990, Microsoft has repurchased 710 million common shares while 1.79 billion shares were issued under the Company's employee stock option and purchase plans.[26]

Table 6.9 documents on a yearly basis how much corporations included in the Standard & Poor's (S&P) 500, S&P MidCap, and S&P SmallCap indices spent repurchasing their own shares. On a per corporation basis, the mean (median) amount increased from $31 ($0) million in 1992 to $176 ($15) million in 2000. Similarly, the percent of corporations repurchasing their own shares rose from 29% in 1992 to 50% in 2000. In aggregate, the corporations under examination spent over $177 billion in 2000 repurchasing their shares. Table 6.10 documents the materiality of those repurchases. Cash spent to repurchase shares ranged from a mean (median) of 14–58% (0–11%) of operating cash flow, and between 24 and 85% (0–19%) of net income. Finally, Table 6.11 shows the percentage increase in shares outstanding on a yearly basis for these corporations. The mean (median) increase, which ranges from 14.12% (0.44%) to 26.2% (1.93%) per year, indicates that all the resources spent on repurchasing shares is not enough to stem the dilution.[27] Table 6.12 shows for a select group of companies the number of and the ratio of options and shares currently outstanding. The ratio varies dramatically. For

[26]Microsoft 10-K filed with Securities and Exchange Commission, September 28, 1999, Exhibit 13.3, p. 5.

[27]This increase may not be entirely attributable to stock options and grants, as corporations may also issue additional shares to the general public to raise equity funds.

TABLE 6.10   Amounts Spent to Repurchase Shares Relative to Operating Cash Flow and Net Income

Year	Amount spent to repurchase shares			
	Divided by operating cash flow (mean) (%)	Divided by operating cash flow (median) (%)	Divided by net income (mean) (%)	Divided by net income (median) (%)
1992	14	0	32	0
1993	26	0	64	0
1994	15	0	42	0
1995	78	0	24	0
1996	19	0	40	0
1997	34	1	50	1
1998	58	5	65	8
1999	58	6	85	11
2000	37	11	65	19

Internet trendsetter Amazon.com, outstanding options represent almost 20% of outstanding shares. In contrast, for brick and mortar retail giant Wal-Mart, outstanding options represent only a little over 1% of outstanding shares.

Stock option plans are normally put to a shareholder vote. This is required by the New York Stock Exchange for all listed corporations and by the Securities and Exchange Commission if the issuer wishes the transaction to be exempt from section 16(b).[28,29] This increasing dilution, among other factors, has led to increased opposition to stock option plans (Lublin and Scism 1999) and to a number of

TABLE 6.11   Changes in Shares Outstanding

Year	Mean change in shares outstanding from prior year (%)	Median change in shares outstanding from prior year (%)
1992	25.48	1.93
1993	22.10	1.41
1994	14.12	0.83
1995	21.19	0.89
1996	24.27	1.26
1997	24.60	1.62
1998	26.20	1.34
1999	24.02	0.66
2000	24.78	0.44

[28]New York Stock Exchange Manual Section 312.03.
[29]17CFR 240.16b-3.

TABLE 6.12   Ratio of Options to Shares Outstanding for Select Companies

	Fiscal year end	Options outstanding at year end	Shares outstanding at year end	Ratio (%)
Amazon.com	Dec. 31, 2000	70,438,000	357,140,000	19.72
America Online	June 30, 2000	356,586,779	2,316,494,480	15.39
Cisco	July 29, 2000	971,000,000	7,138,000,000	13.60
Ford Motor	Dec. 31, 2000	153,700,000	1,837,000,000	8.37
General Electric	Dec. 31, 2000	333,179,000	9,932,006,000	3.35
Intel	Dec. 30, 2000	638,200,000	6,721,000,000	9.50
IBM	Dec. 31, 2000	160,557,003	1,893,940,595	8.48
Lucent Technology	Sept. 30, 2000	458,312,000	3,384,332,104	13.54
Microsoft	June 30, 2000	832,000,000	5,283,000,000	15.75
Wal-Mart	Jan. 31, 2001	49,846,000	4,470,000,000	1.12

corporate proposals regarding stock option plans being voted down by shareholders. For example, the board of directors of Ben & Jerry's, the ice cream maker, proposed to increase the number of shares authorized for its stock option plan from 900,000 to 1,300,000, a proposal that was rejected by shareholders by a vote of 4,800,368 for, 6,551,058 against, with 64,692 abstaining and 1,307,805 broker nonvotes.[30]

IV. INCENTIVE EFFECT VERSUS DILUTIVE EFFECT

In theory, the increase in shareholder value from the incentive effects should out-weigh the dilutive effect of stock-based compensation; that is, existing shareholders should benefit from the increase in shareholder value despite giving up some of their proportional ownership. This may not always be true. A study of Salomon Smith Barney found that most of the heaviest users of options in the S&P 500 actually underperformed the index.[31] Furthermore, the assertion that the incentive effects should outweigh the dilute effect assumes that the individuals who award compensation are acting in the best interests of shareholders and not, for example, in their own self-interest.

Others argue that since options are only valuable if and when the share price increases, there is no downside to shareholders; that is, employees only benefit if shareholders do. Of course, this presumes the options are granted at or above the market price at time of grant, and this does not hold if shares, rather than options, are granted to employees. It also ignores the opportunity costs faced by shareholders.

[30]Ben & Jerry's 10-Q filed with the Securities and Exchange Commission, August 10, 1999, p. 18.
[31]Leonhardt (2000a).

Consider the following example. On January 1, 2000, and each year thereafter, the CEO of XYZ Corporation is granted options, exercisable over 10 years, to purchase 1 million shares at the current market price on the date of grant. The exercise price of the grants fluctuates with the market price, which was $35 on January 1, 2000, $20 on January 1, 2001, $30 on January 1, 2002, and $40 on January 1, 2003. As of January 1, 2003, the CEO has options to purchase 4 million shares with an intrinsic value of $35 million. In contrast, the shareholder who owned the shares on January 1, 2000, earned appreciation of a little over 14% on those shares, less than he or she could have earned with U.S. Treasury Securities.

Although this is a fictional example, truth can sometimes be stranger than fiction. In its proxy statement filed with the Securities and Exchange Commission on March 12, 2001, Apple Computer reported that it had granted its Chief Executive Officer Steven Jobs 20 million options in the previous year, and that if its share price rose at a rate of 5% per year, at the end of the options term, those options would be worth $548,317,503. Of course, if its share price increased by 5% per year, Apple stockholders would have been better off purchasing U.S. Treasury Securities.

V. EFFECTIVENESS OF STOCK–BASED COMPENSATION

As noted in Chapter 5, it is not always easy to measure the effectiveness of various types of compensation. As noted above, more so than other forms of compensation, stock compensation provides employees with incentives to exert the effort and take the risks necessary to increase shareholder value. Unfortunately, since neither can be measured directly, researchers have had to rely on indirect accounting and stock return measures. That is, they measure accounting returns subsequent to plan adoption and stock price reaction at time of public announcement. For example, Mehran (1995) finds that return on assets (an accounting performance measure defined as net income divided by the book value of the corporation's assets) is positively associated with the percentage of compensation that is equity based. In addition, since stock-based compensation can affect risk preferences, they also look at changes in risk over time. Using accounting returns is problematic, though, in measuring the effect of stock option plans. As noted below, no expense is currently recorded for stock option grants. Thus, if they are substituted for other forms of compensation for which expense is recognized, there will be an upward bias in accounting performance measures that is unrelated to improvements in performance. Similarly, as noted in Chapter 5, looking at stock price performance at time of public announcement may be misleading, as the market reaction to plan adoption may not be associated with the expected effects of the plan on firm performance, but rather to the information released by the plan adoption. That is, management is more likely to propose tying its compensation to share price performance when it

TABLE 6.13   Number of Executives Receiving
Stock Option or Stock Grants Valued at More
Than $10 million in a Given Year

Year	Stock option grants valued at more than $10 million	Stock grants valued at more than $10 million
1992	7	1
1993	10	3
1994	27	2
1995	26	1
1996	62	4
1997	117	14
1998	106	17
1999	204	26
2000	264	19

expects the share price to perform well in the future. Investors realize this tendency and thus react positively when they first learn the plan is being adopted.

VI. MACRO–MARKET EFFECTS

It has been said that a rising tide lifts all boats. That is, in a rising market, stock prices go up even if the corporation underperforms the market. And executives benefit. Consider the case of Ralston Purina. In 1986 the corporation granted restricted stock that would vest if within the next 10 years the stock price closed above $100 for 10 consecutive days. Based upon the then current stock price of $63.375, the price had only to rise at a rate of 4.67% per year for the next 10 years for the shares to vest. In fact, $100 was reached within 5 years. However, within its industry, Ralston Purina was somewhat of a laggard. Campbell and Wasley (1999) noted that although executives collected their payoffs, shareholders suffered an industry-adjusted loss of $2.1 billion.

Although this situation has to some extent been repeated throughout the prolonged bull market that began in 1982, it is also true that not all corporations have benefited from the run up in stock prices. It is also true that with the mega-grants that have become prevalent, even a small increase in stock price can lead to large payoff. Arbitrarily defining mega-grant as when the present value of the sum of grants to a senior executive in a year exceeds $10 million, Table 6.13 shows the increase in the number of mega-grants over time. In 1992, seven executives received grants valued by ExecuComp at over $10 million. In contrast, in 2000, 264 executives received stock option grants valued by ExecuComp at over $10 million. Table 6.14 lists the largest grant by year, as valued by ExecuComp. These maximums,

TABLE 6.14   Executives Receiving the Highest Valued Stock Option Grants by Year

Year	Company	Executive	Position	Amount ($)
1992	Primerica	Sanford Weill	Chairman and Chief Executive Officer	36,032,000
1993	RJR Nabisco	Charles Harper	Chairman and Chief Executive Officer	30,285,000
1994	Conseco	Stephen Hilbert	Chairman, President, and Chief Executive Officer	52,096,000
1995	DSC Communications	James Donald	Chairman, President, and Chief Executive Officer	47,472,000
1996	Walt Disney	Michael Eisner	Chairman and Chief Executive Officer	193,532,000
1997	Cendant	Henry Silverman	President and Chief Executive Officer	255,630,000
1998	Citigroup	Sanford Weill	Chairman and Co-Chief Executive Officer	137,044,000
1999	Amazon.com	Joseph Galli	President and Chief Operating Officer	201,356,000
2000	Apple Computer	Steven Jobs	Chief Executive Officer	600,347,000

which ranged in size from $30,285,000 to $52,096,000 between 1992 and 1995, jumped dramatically in 1996 when Michael Eisner, Chairman and Chief Executive Officer of the Walt Disney Company, received a grant valued at $193,532,000. These amounts continue to grow, with Steven Jobs, Chief Executive Officer of Apple Computer, receiving a grant worth over $600 million in 2000. It should, however, be noted, that even these enormous grants do not guarantee a payoff. As shown in Table 6.14, Amazon.com gave Joseph Galli stock options valued at $201,356,000 to join it in 1999. Its stock price dropped dramatically after that point, so in 2000 when Galli resigned to become CEO of VerticalNet, he left Amazon without making a penny off those options.[32]

One issue is, what happens if the market stops rising and drops? This has become a major issue with companies whose stock price has fallen. For example, Microsoft gave out new options to employees after a dramatic fall in stock price that made many of its previously granted options worthless.[33] As noted above, once options are worthless or out of the money, incentives change dramatically. For example, out-of-the-money options no longer tie the employee to the corporation.

What should the corporation do? One response is to grant additional options at the current price, as Microsoft did. Another response is to reprice existing options, essentially lowering the exercise price of the options the executive already holds.

[32]Shortly after arriving at VerticalNet, Galli departed to become President and Chief Executive Office of Newell Rubbermaid.

[33]Buchman (2000).

TABLE 6.15   Firms Repricing Options, by Year

Year	Number of repricers	Firms repricing (%)
1992	13	0.97
1993	30	1.81
1994	39	2.25
1995	40	2.18
1996	59	3.01
1997	80	3.94
1998	86	4.36
1999	37	2.05
2000	6	0.58

The following passage explains the multiple option repricings Apple Computer engaged in during 1996 and 1997:

> In December 1997, the Board of Directors approved an option exchange program which allowed employees to exchange all (but not less than all) of their existing options (vested and unvested) with an exercise price greater than $13.6875, on a one-for-one basis for new options with an exercise price of $13.6875, the fair market value of the Company's common stock on December 19, 1997, and a new four year vesting schedule beginning in December 1997. A total of 4.7 million options with a weighted-average exercise price of $19.90 per share were exchanged for new options as a result of this program.
>
> In July 1997, the Board of Directors approved an option exchange program which allowed employees to exchange all (but not less than all) of their existing options (vested and unvested) to purchase Apple common stock (other than options granted and assumed from NeXT) for options having an exercise price of $13.25 and a new three year vesting period beginning in July of 1997. Approximately 7.9 million options were repriced under this program.
>
> On May 14, 1996, the Board of Directors adopted a resolution allowing employees up to and including the level of Vice President to exchange 1.25 options at their existing option price for 1.0 new options having an exercise price of $26.375 per share, the fair market value of the Company's common stock at May 29, 1996. Options received under this program are subject to one year of additional vesting such that the new vesting date for each vesting portion will be the later of May 29, 1997 or the original vesting date plus one year. Approximately 2.9 million options were exchanged and repriced under this program.[34]

Repricing is extremely controversial, as although it protects executives from declines in share prices, it does nothing for shareholders. Some have gone so far as to assert that repricing destroys the incentive value of options, because employees assume that repricing will occur, or that they will get additional options if the share price falls (Schroeder and Simon 2001). Table 6.15 shows the number of corporations repricing by year. Until 1998, the numbers were steadily increasing, reaching a high of 86 in 1998, before dropping to 6 in 2000. Some have attributed this drop

[34]Apple Computer 10-K filed with Securities and Exchange Commission, December 23, 1998, p. 55.

to recent changes in financial accounting rules, which require that companies recognize expense for options that have been repriced (for example, see Silverman 2000a).

Other choices include more frequent option grants and extending life of options.

> So now some companies are changing the other variable in the options equation—time—by awarding options with longer terms.
>
> At Reebok, for example, the chief executive, Paul B. Fireman, held some 500,000 options that were on the verge of expiring worthless, until Reebok's board extended their term by 10 years, according to the company's recent proxy. Coca-Cola and Procter & Gamble, both suffering from swooning stocks, are issuing options with 15-year exercise terms, instead of 10 years.[35]

Options can be replaced with other forms of compensation, such as cash and stock grants stock. At its 2000 annual meeting, Genesis Health Ventures asked and its shareholders approved the following plan to deal with underwater options.

> . . . a stock option redemption program under which Genesis' employees and directors may elect to surrender Genesis' stock options for unrestricted shares of Common Stock.[36]

Other companies, which have seen their stock price decrease, have added more cash and stock grants.

> Owens Corning, the building materials maker, was typical of old-economy companies that turned more toward cash and restricted stock. Its shares lost more than 40 percent of their value in 1999. But its chief executive, Glen H. Hiner, saw his salary and bonus jump 38 percent, to $4 million. And he received a $2.3 million grant of restricted stock, 10 times what he got in 1998.[37]

Overall, there does seem to be an increase in stock grants, with the grants getting larger in amounts. Table 2.1 showed that the proportion of CEOs getting stock grants increased from 17% in 1992 to 22% in 2000, whereas Table 2.7 showed that the average CEO received stock worth $609,000 in 2000, up from $114,000 in 1992. Interestingly, because of the increase in the compensation package over the same period, stock grants as a percentage of the overall compensation package have remained fairly constant.

> In the highest corporate ranks, companies are increasingly granting restricted stock to executives. These are real shares—not options—that hold value even if the stock is falling, though the executive must hang onto them for a designated period. Thirty-nine percent of large companies gave their chief executives such awards last year, up from 33 percent in 1998, according to a sampling of proxies by Pearl Meyer & Partners, compensation consultants in New York.[38]

[35]Leonhardt (2000b), p. 13.
[36]Genesis Health Ventures proxy statement filed with the Securities and Exchange Commission, January 28, 2000, p. 15.
[37]Leonhardt (2000b), p. 12.
[38]Leonhardt (2000b), p. 12.

VII. ALTERNATIVES

Companies could use alternatives to standard options. Johnson and Tian (2000) discuss six different types of nontraditional options: premium, performance-vested, repriceable, purchased, reload, and indexed options. Whereas a standard option is issued with an exercise price equal to the then market price, premium options are issued with an exercise price exceeding the then market price. Performance-vested options are options whose exercisability depends upon future performance. Repriceable options can have their exercise price lowered if the corporation's stock price falls, whereas with a purchased option the executive pays a portion of the exercise price at the time of grant. Reload options, as discussed above, allow the executive to pay the exercise price with previously owned shares and then receive new options to replace those used to pay the exercise price. Indexed options are options whose exercise price is adjusted for market and/or industrywide movements. When compared to standard options, each of these alternatives has a differing, usually stronger, effect on the incentive to increase share value and risk and reduce dividend yields.

A. Adjusted Options

If options were adjusted for market and/or industrywide movements, then the manager would neither be penalized in a market downturn, nor rewarded in a bull market; rather, they would only be rewarded for above-average stock price growth relative to the benchmark. In other words, they would be paid based upon their performance. Although reasonable in theory, and though research (for example, Gibbons and Murphy 1990) does show that relative performance evaluation is used, market-adjusted options have not caught on in practice. Some (for example, Johnson 1999) explain this unwillingness by pointing to the differential accounting treatments. As explained more fully below, fixed stock options normally do not result in a charge to earnings. In contrast, market-adjusted options would be treated as variable options and, consequently, would result in an expense being recognized on the income statement. For example, RCN in June 2000 adopted its Outperform Stock Option Plan. The following passage from their 2000 annual report (note 12) explains the accounting consequences:

> The Company granted 3,000,000 OSO's to employees during the year ended December 31, 2000 with a fair value under SFAS No. 123 of $42,776. The Company recognized $17,910 of compensation expense during the year 2000 for options granted in 2000. As of December 31, 2000, the Company had not reflected $24,866 of unamortized compensation expense in its financial statements for options granted in 2000.[39,40]

[39]RCN form 10-K filed with Securities and Exchange Commission April 2, 2001, p. 78.

[40]As discussed elsewhere, there is no expense for fixed stock options under APB Opinion No. 25, whereas FASB Statement No. 123 requires an expense be recognized for both fixed and variable options. Coincidentally, during 2000, RCN also adopted the recognition provisions of SFAS No. 123.

Another explanation for the infrequent use of adjusted options is that to date executives have been profiting from the bull market and want to keep doing so. If the market were to decline substantially, they would then simply reprice the options, effectively making the option market adjusted on the downside, but not the upside.

For these reasons, few publicly held companies issue indexed options. One exception is Level 3 Communications. The following description of how they adjust the exercise price is from their proxy statement filed with the Securities and Exchange Commission on June 10, 1998:

> Adjustment of Initial Price
>
> The Initial Price shall be adjusted upward or downward as of the date of exercise of the Award (the "Adjusted Price"), by a percentage equal to the aggregate increase or decrease (expressed as a whole percentage point followed by three decimal places) in the Standard and Poor's 500 Index over the period (the "Period") beginning on the date of grant and ending on the trading day immediately preceding the date of exercise of the Award (the "Aggregate Percentage S&P Performance"). For purposes of determining the Aggregate Percentage S&P Performance with respect to any Period, the Standard and Poor's 500 Index as of the first day of the Period shall be deemed to equal the closing value of such index on the trading day immediately preceding the first day of the Period, and the Standard and Poor's 500 Index on the last day of the Period shall be deemed to equal the average closing value of such index over the ten-consecutive-trading day period immediately preceding the last day of such Period.

B. Premium Options

More companies have used premium options for at least some of their option grants.[41] Premium options differ from market-adjusted options in that their exercise price is set to be greater than market price at date of grant. Thus the executive does not profit from the first dollar increase in stock price. Companies using premium options include Bank of America, Colgate Palmolive, Disney, Masco, Monsanto, and Transamerica. The following passage is from page 14 of Monsanto's proxy statement filed with the Securities and Exchange Commission on March 12, 1998:

> The option strike price is 50% above the value of Monsanto common stock on the date the options were offered, which means that the price of Monsanto common stock will have to increase more than 50% before the premium options have any value.

VIII. FINANCIAL CONSEQUENCES

A. Cash Flow

As noted previously, each component of the executive compensation package impacts the corporation's cash flows. In the case of stock-based compensation, most of

---

[41]Gilles (1999) reported that "about 3 percent of companies use premium-price options, according to a recent William M. Mercer/KPMG survey (p. 42)."

the time there is no direct cash outflow, as the corporation provides stock or options rather than cash as payment.[42] There is an opportunity cost, however. Shares and options that are not given to employees could be sold to outside investors. The opportunity cost is the price these investors would pay for the shares and options.

Stock-based compensation can also increase corporate cash flows. First, stock compensation generates tax savings, as stock grants and certain stock options result in deductions on the corporate return. For example, in their fiscal year ending June 30, 2000, Microsoft reported a tax benefit (that is, savings) associated with employee stock plans exceeding $5.5 billion! Second, cash inflows may result from option exercise (whereby the executive pays the exercise price to the corporation in exchange for the promised shares). Indirectly, stock-based compensation may increase corporate cash flow as it reduces the amount of cash compensation that needs to be paid. Core and Guay (2000) provide evidence "consistent with cash-constrained" corporations using stock options in lieu of cash compensation. However, as discussed above, to counter the dilution associated with stock compensation programs, many corporations repurchase their own stock in the market, a cash outflow. As noted previously, Microsoft spent $4.9 billion repurchasing its own shares during its 2000 fiscal year. It is not the exception. During 1999, Intel spent $4.6 billion and General Motors spent almost $3.9 billion repurchasing its shares.

B. Taxes

Although Microsoft spent significant amounts repurchasing its own shares, it saved even more in taxes: $5.5 billion. Other companies saving significant amounts in taxes during their 2000 fiscal year include International Business Machines—$422 million, Lucent Technology—$1,064 million, and Cisco—$3,077 million. Generally, the corporation gets a deduction for the dollar value of the stock granted, or if options, the profit on exercise.

If the stock grant is unrestricted, the corporation gets an immediate deduction equal to the current value of the shares grants. If the grant is restricted, the executive recognizes income, and the corporation takes as a deduction the fair value when the restrictions expire, although an 83(b) election allows the executive to recognize the income earlier.

With a stock option, or in particular a nonqualified stock option, as long as the exercise price of the option is equal to or greater than the share price at the date of grant, the employee recognizes no income, nor does the corporation recognize a deduction at that time.[43] Rather, at the time of exercise, the employee recognizes

---

[42]An exception would be if the corporation agreed to pay the taxes on the exercise profits, which they occasionally do.

[43]If, however, the exercise price is less than the market price on the date of grant, the employee must recognize ordinary income, and the corporation takes a deduction at that point in time for the excess of the market price over the exercise price.

ordinary income and the employer deducts the difference between the fair value of stock purchased and the exercise price paid.

A special type of option, referred to as a qualified or section 422 (reproduced in Appendix 6.3, which sets the rules options must meet to be considered qualified) option allows the executive to defer taxation at the time of exercise, and it ultimately recognize income as a capital gain if certain conditions are met. However, if these conditions are met, the employer does not receive a tax deduction. The Internal Revenue Code limits the use of qualified stock options to $100,000 of face value (number of options times exercise price) vesting in any particular year.[44] Thus qualified stock options are of little relevance to top executives at large corporations who grant their top executives options with face values that can run into the millions.

Section 162(m), the million-dollar cap, also applies to stock-based compensation. Consequently, the corporation needs to qualify its plans to deduct any compensation over $1 million. Stock options, as long as they are granted at or above the current market price, are easy to qualify as performance based.[45] That is, since they only have value if the share price increases, they are assumed by Section 162(m) to be performance based. In contrast, stock grants are harder to qualify, since they have value as long as the share price is greater than zero. Thus, the shares would have to be earned based on a performance measure for stock grants to be deductible.

C. Financial Reporting

> Warren Buffett has made the point succinctly: if a company has a choice between paying its employees with a currency that counts against its earnings and another currency that does not, there is not a lot of mystery about which one it will pick.[46]

Most companies do not record any expense for financial accounting purposes. In fact, many critics (see for example, Welles 1998) have argued that because companies do not record expense, they overuse options. In contrast to other forms of compensation, such as salary, bonuses, stock grants, and pensions, which are expensed when earned regardless of when they are paid, under Accounting Principles Board Opinion Number 25, stock options do not result in any expense recognition

[44]Section 422 options, while having preferential tax treatment for executives, must satisfy a number of requirements in addition to those mentioned in the text. For example, the exercise price may not be less than the fair-market price at the date of grant, nor may the option be exercisable more than 10 years after the date of grant.

[45]In addition to granting the options with an exercise price at or above the market price on the date of grant, the options must be granted pursuant to a plan approved by shareholders, which specifies the number of options that may be granted overall and to any one individual. While my expectation is that the percentage of corporations qualifying their stock option plans will be close to 100%, Rose and Wolfram (2000) only find 76% of their sample qualify their stock option plans. An explanation for the relatively low percentage of qualifiers is that Rose and Wolfram include corporations not subject to Section 162(m) in their sample, which biases the percentage of qualifiers downward.

[46]Leonhardt (2000a), p. 14.

as long as they are fixed in nature, and the exercise price is greater than the market price at the date of grant. An option is considered fixed if both the exercise price and number of shares obtainable are known at the date of grant. In contrast, if the options have to be earned, that is, the executive's ability to exercise the option is dependent upon performance after the date of grant, then the options are considered variable for accounting purposes. Under Financial Accounting Standards Board (FASB) Interpretation Number 28, companies have to recognize an expense for variable options. It has been asserted that companies prefer fixed to variable options for this reason.[47]

Some accountants, agreeing with the current treatment, argue options are costless, as they do not meet the accounting definition of an expense in that they neither require the expenditure of an asset or the incurrence of a liability.[48] However, the FASB in 1984 concluded that options should be accounted for as an expense.[49] Nine years later, in June 1993, they issued an exposure draft or proposal entitled "Accounting for Stock-based Compensation." This proposal was met with widespread opposition. For example, the FASB received 1786 comment letters on the exposure draft, with the vast majority opposed to any form of recognition for employee stock option grants.[50] Even those amenable to the recognition of an expense questioned the appropriate valuation for the options:

> While compensation consultants have tried to tailor option pricing models to deal with the unique aspects of employee options, no single approach has gained wide acceptance. And since a market confirmation of an employee stock option's value doesn't exist—no trading occurs—it can't really be proved or disproved that the value derived from an option pricing model is accurate or reasonable.[51]

This debate within a debate is particularly important for those arguing about the appropriateness of the level or cost of compensation. Murphy (1996) provided evidence consistent with the hypothesis that companies try to hide the cost of their stock-based compensation. Valuation models, for example, the Black–Scholes or Binomial model, exist that can value the option at the time of grant or at anytime thereafter. Opponents of using these models argue that they were developed for short-lived, tradable options and are not applicable to employee stock options that commonly have 10-year lives and are not tradable. They claim the models, which estimate the option's value by considering the current stock price, the exercise price, the option's life, the expected dividends, the risk-free rate, and the volatility of the stocks price, overvalue employee stock options because they assume tradability, the ability to sell short, and ignore the effect of the continued employment requirement,

---

[47]Gilles (1999).

[48]Statement of Financial Accounting Concepts Number 6, Elements of Financial Statements, Financial Accounting Standards Board, December 1985, paragraph 80.

[49]Invitation to Comment: Accounting for Compensation Plans Involving Certain Rights Granted to Employees, Financial Accounting Standards Board, May 31, 1984.

[50]Statement of Financial Accounting Standards Number 123, Accounting for Stock-based Compensation, December 1995, paragraph 376.

[51]Rouse and Barton (1993), p. 69.

all of which reduce the value of the option to the employee. If valued at time of grant, the true value of the option would be the amount of cash the employee would be willing to forego to receive those options. Lambert et al. (1991) demonstrate that under reasonable assumptions about individual risk aversion and diversification, employees value options at substantially less than that determined by the Black-Scholes option-pricing model.

Alternatively, some have advocated (Balsam 1994) that options be valued based upon profit to employee at time of exercise, which coincidentally is the basis for tax deduction for nonqualified options. There is potentially an enormous difference between the amounts calculated by the valuation models at the date of grant and the actual profits to employees or deductions to the employer at the date of exercise. For example, Microsoft in 2000 disclosed a pro forma reduction in net income of $1.2 billion due to its stock option grants. As noted above, Microsoft disclosed that it saved $5.5 billion in taxes due to stock option exercises that same year. Utilizing the top federal tax bracket of 35%, Microsoft would have had to deduct $15.7 billion on its tax return to save $5.5 billion in taxes. So while they disclosed a cost of $1.2 billion in their financial accounting footnotes, they deducted $15.7 billion on their tax return!

In response to the above described opposition, the FASB withdrew its proposal in December 1994. Then, in October 1995, the FASB issued Statement of Financial Accounting Standards Number 123 Accounting for Stock-based Compensation. Statement 123 requires corporations to provide supplementary disclosure in which the compensation cost associated with employee stock option grants is reflected in pro-forma income statements, and recommends, but does not require, that corporations actually recognize this compensation cost in the income statement.

IX. POLITICAL COSTS

As with other forms of compensation, stock-based compensation is politically sensitive. While critics, including politicians, complain about compensation being unresponsive to corporate performance, and have encouraged corporations to use more performance-based compensation like stock options, they object when those packages lead to big payouts. Sometimes these criticisms take place when the compensation plan is passed or the compensation package is put together, whereas in other cases the criticism only occurs when the enormity of the payouts is realized. For example, the very large and active California Public Employees Retirement System (CalPERs), a major shareholder in many public corporations, objects publicly to compensation packages it deems excessive. One example is the package Bank of America paid its Chief Executive, Hugh L. McColl, Jr., in 1999.

> The California Public Employees Retirement System is taking a public stand against the $76 million pay package Bank of America handed chief executive Hugh McColl last year in what could be a sign of a shareholder revolt.

> The nation's largest public pension fund, one of the biggest holders of BofA stock, will not give its 9.6 million votes to members of the compensation committee of the North Carolina bank's board as a protest against the award to McColl, CalPERS said in a statement posted on its Internet site.[52]

The $76 million included almost $45 million in restricted stock units, over $27 million in option grants (as valued by the corporation), $1,250,000 in salary, and $2,500,000 in bonus. In addition, Kenneth D. Lewis, President and Chief Operating Officer, and James H. Hance, Jr., Vice Chairman and Chief Financial Officer, both received packages of approximately $44 million.[53] Unfortunately CalPERs, even with 9.6 million shares, owns less than 1% of Bank of America, and thus cannot by itself replace the directors in question.

Possibly the most controversial plan involved Computer Associates. Shareholders approved the plan, 1995 Key Employee Stock Ownership Plan, by a vote of 98,427,761 for versus 26,944,563 against, with 1,221,062 abstentions.[54] The criticism, and in this case the lawsuits, began after the corporation awarded its top three executives stock worth over $1 billion in 1998, as noted in their proxy, this

> reflects long-term incentive compensation earned in fiscal year 1999 based on the achievement of stock price targets established in connection with the 1995 Plan. Under that plan, previously described in the 1995 Proxy and approved by the stockholders at the 1995 Annual Meeting, Messrs. Wang, Kumar, and Artzt, were awarded in the aggregate 20.25 million shares. Such share awards, which vested in their entirety on May 21, 1998, were in the amounts of $645,412,050, $322,706,025, and $107,568,675, for Messrs. Wang, Kumar, and Artzt, respectively.[55]

As noted above, the award led to lawsuits and a settlement whereby Messrs. Wang, Kumar, and Artzt returned 4.5 million of the 20.3 million shares previously awarded to the corporation:

> Pursuant to a court approved settlement, Mr. Wang will return to the Company 2,700,000 shares of Common Stock previously issued under the 1995 Plan.
>
> . . .
>
> Pursuant to a court approved settlement, Mr. Kumar and Mr. Artzt will return to the Company 1,350,000 and 450,000 shares, respectively, of Common Stock previously issued under the 1995 Plan.[56]

Although Computer Associates is an extreme case, large profitable exercises are very visible and lead to criticism even if they result from an increasing stock price.

[52]Zuckerman (2000), p. A1.

[53]Bank of America proxy statement filed with Securities and Exchange Commission, March 20, 2000, pp. 10, 11.

[54]Computer Associates 10-Q filed with Securities and Exchange Commission November 2, 1995, Item 4.

[55]Computer Associates proxy statement filed with Securities and Exchange Commission, July 12, 1999, p. 10.

[56]Computer Associates proxy statement filed with Securities and Exchange Commission, July 14, 2000, pp. 7, 8.

Furthermore, as noted above, mega-grants assure large profits even if the stock price appreciates very little. These profits are required to be reported in corporate proxy statements and are then reported in the annual surveys conducted by the business press, that is, *The Wall Street Journal, Business Week, Forbes,* and so on. Consider the following amounts reported in the *Forbes* compensation survey. Charles Wang at just over $650 million was the highest paid CEO in 1999. Michael Eisner of Disney, at over $589 million, most of which consisted of option gains, was the highest paid CEO for 1998. Sanford Weill of the Traveler's Group, at over $227 million, was the highest paid CEO for 1997.

Another issue is the repricing of stock options, the frequency of which was shown in Table 6.15. The repricing of stock options occurs when the corporation reduces the exercise price on a previously granted option, in most cases because the stock price had fallen since the stock option was originally granted. Repricing is controversial because it allows employees to profit even if shareholders lose money. Alternatively, while the shareholders suffer real losses, the employees are made whole. Thus repricing, or even the knowledge that a repricing may occur if the stock price drops, reduces the alignment of interests between employees and shareholders. In many cases companies have repriced their shares more than one time (for example, Cineplex Odeon, Flagstar, Tandem Computer, Live Entertainment).

The reload option, discussed earlier in this chapter, is also controversial. If structured properly, a reload option will provide the employee with the incentives to take the risks desired by shareholders. However, it also allows the employee to cash out periodically. Thus, it may reduce the alignment of interests between employees and shareholders in that the employee can preserve his or her profits and still participate in the upwards potential of the stock, while the shareholder has a harder time doing so.[57]

X. SUMMARY

The focus of this chapter was stock compensation. As noted in earlier chapters, the primary form of stock compensation, both in terms of usage and value, is stock options, although stock grants are used by a growing number of corporations. Stock-based compensation are variable, or at-risk forms of compensation, although the risk the executive is subject to depends upon the type of compensation. For example, whereas a stock option is only valuable when the share price exceeds the exercise price, a stock grant is valuable as long as the share price is positive.

More so than any other form of compensation, stock compensation provides executives with the incentive to increase shareholder value, because as shareholders and as potential shareholders (option holders), they benefit directly from that increase in shareholder value. However, it can, and has been shown, that at some

[57]They could do so utilizing put options, but it is unlikely many shareholders do so.

point, stock compensation may make the executive more risk averse than optimal, as the underdiversified executive becomes fearful of losing what he or she has already gained. Thus, the terms of the grants, for example, vesting period, exercise price, whether the grants have reload provisions, and so on, must be chosen carefully.

Although stock compensation can have financial reporting and political costs, the major cost associated with stock compensation is dilution. Dilution arises because stock compensation programs have the potential to increase the number of outstanding shares, and, hence, dilute the proportionate ownership of existing shareholders. To limit this dilution corporations have spent billions of dollars repurchasing their own shares.

Stock-based compensation has been the fastest growing portion of the compensation package. Whether this growth has been caused by, or been the cause of, the large increases in share prices over the past 20 years, it has certainly been associated with it.

APPENDIX 6.1. NONQUALIFIED STOCK OPTION AWARD AGREEMENT UNDER THE 1989 STOCK INCENTIVE PLAN

EXHIBIT B

August 14, 1997

Leo F. Mullin President & Chief Executive Officer

The 1989 Stock Incentive Plan of Delta Air Lines, Inc., as amended ("Plan"), is intended as an inducement for officers, executives and key employees of Delta Air Lines, Inc. (the "Company") to continue in the employment of the Company, and to provide a greater incentive to such employees to make material contributions to the Company's success by increasing their proprietary interest in the Company through increased direct stock ownership. The Plan, which provides for certain awards to eligible employees, is administered by the Personnel & Compensation Committee of the Board of Directors (the "Committee"). Pursuant to the Plan, the Committee selected you to receive an award of a Nonqualified Stock Option under the Plan, effective as of the close of business on August 14, 1997, and has instructed me, on behalf of the Company, to provide this Agreement to you.

In consideration of the mutual covenants herein contained and for other good and valuable consideration, the Company and you as an employee of the Company (hereinafter called "Employee"), do hereby agree as follows:

1. The Company hereby grants to Employee a Nonqualified Stock Option ("Stock Option") covering 500,000 shares of Stock, as defined in the Plan, a copy of which has been furnished to Employee. This award is in all respects made subject to the terms and conditions of the Plan and, by signing and returning a copy of this Agreement to the Secretary of the Company, Employee acknowledges that he has read this Agreement and the Plan and agrees to all of the terms and conditions thereof for himself, any designated beneficiary and his heirs, executors, administrators or personal representative. Terms used in this Agreement which are defined in the Plan shall have the meanings set forth in the Plan. In the event of any conflict between the Plan and this Agreement, the Plan shall control. Employee also acknowledges receipt of the Prospectus dated January 26, 1995, relating to the Plan.

2. The Option Price of the Stock Option covered by this award shall be $88.3125 per share, which price was the opening price of the Stock on the New York Stock Exchange (the "NYSE") on the date of this award.

3. Subject to the terms and conditions of the Plan and the other provisions of this Agreement, the Stock Option shall become exercisable in installments as follows, provided Employee continues to be employed by the Company on the dates indicated:

Number of shares with respect to which option	*First becomes exercisable date*
200,000	August 14, 1998
100,000	August 14, 1999
100,000	August 14, 2000
100,000	August 14, 2001

In the event of the occurrence prior to August 14, 2001 of (i) a Change in Control or (ii) the termination of Employee's employment (A) by the Company without Cause, or (B) by Employee with Good Reason, the Stock Option shall immediately become fully exercisable. In the event of the termination of Employee's employment for any other reason prior to August 14, 2001, Employee shall forfeit that portion of the Stock Option attributable to Shares with respect to which the Stock Option has not previously become exercisable pursuant to this Paragraph 3. For purposes of this Agreement, the terms "Change in Control," "Cause" and "Good Reason" shall have the respective meanings assigned such terms for purposes of the Employment Agreement between Employee and the Company dated as of August 14, 1997.

4. Subject to the terms and conditions of the Plan and Paragraph 8 below, the Stock Option granted to Employee herein may be exercised during the period beginning as set forth in Paragraph 3 above and ending August 13, 2007, except as provided in Sections 5 and 10 of the Plan. In the event of termination of Employee's employment with the Company (i) by the Company without Cause, (ii) by Employee with Good Reason or (iii) on or after August 14, 2000 for any reason other than death or Disability (to the extent the Stock Option is otherwise exercisable pursuant to Paragraph 3 above), the termination of Employee's employment will be treated, for purposes of determining the terms of exercise of the Stock Option under Section 10(b) of the Plan, as having occurred because of Employee's Retirement. Subject to the terms and conditions of the Plan, Employee (or, if Employee is deceased, a party acting on his behalf pursuant to Section 10 of the Plan) may exercise the Stock Option granted herein in whole or, from time to time, in part by way of a written notice delivered to the Secretary of the Company which includes the following: (i) name, mailing address and social security number of Employee and the date, which shall be the actual date of the notice; (ii) the number of shares of Stock with respect to which the Stock Option is being exercised; (iii) the date of grant and the Option Price with respect to the Stock Option being exercised; and (iv) the signature of Employee or a party acting on behalf of a deceased employee. Payment of the full purchase price of the shares of Stock covered by the exercise shall be made in the manner prescribed by the Committee from time to time. If the Committee, in its sole discretion, shall determine that it is appropriate to do so, such payment may be made in whole or in part by tender of shares of unrestricted Stock, as set forth in Section 5 of the Plan, subject to such requirements or procedures as the Committee may specify.

5. When the Stock Option is exercised, the Company shall make the appropriate calculations under the Plan and deliver to Employee, as soon as practicable, a certif-

icate or certificates representing the net number of shares of Stock due to Employee pursuant to such exercise, calculated in accordance with this paragraph. Unless other tax withholding arrangements are made by Employee and the Company, the Company shall withhold from the shares of Stock issued to Employee a sufficient number of shares of Stock based on its fair market value on the date of exercise to cover any amounts which the Company is required to withhold to comply with withholding requirements of federal, state or local tax laws, rules or regulations. The fair market value for purposes of the second sentence of this paragraph shall be as reasonably determined by the Committee.

6. The Stock Option granted herein is not transferable otherwise than by will, by the laws of descent and distribution, or by a written designation referred to in Section 10(c) of the Plan, and is exercisable during Employee's lifetime only by Employee. In the event that the Stock Option is exercised pursuant to Section 10 of the Plan by any person other than Employee, such notice shall be accompanied by appropriate proof of the right of such person to exercise the Stock Option.

7. The Stock Option granted herein is subject to all terms of the Plan, including but not limited to Section 10(b), which provides for the forfeiture and repayment of certain benefits in certain circumstances in the event of Employee's Retirement prior to his normal retirement date.

8. Employee acknowledges that the federal securities laws and/or the Company's policies regarding trading in its securities may limit or restrict Employee's right to buy or sell shares of Stock, including, without limitation, sales of Stock to exercise the Stock Option or sales of Stock acquired pursuant to the exercise of the Stock Option. Employee agrees to comply with such federal securities law requirements and Company policies, as such laws and policies are amended from time to time.

This Agreement has been prepared in duplicate. Please note your acceptance in the space provided therefor and return the original for the Company's records.

IN WITNESS WHEREOF, the Company, acting through the Committee, has caused this Agreement to be duly executed, and Employee has hereunto set his hand, all as of the day and year first written above.

DELTA AIR LINES, INC.

By _____
Gerald Grinstein, Chairman Personnel & Compensation Committee

EMPLOYEE

_____

Leo F. Mullin

APPENDIX 6.2. RESTRICTED STOCK AWARD AGREEMENT UNDER THE 1989 STOCK INCENTIVE PLAN

EXHIBIT C

August 14, 1997

Leo F. Mullin President & Chief Executive Officer

The 1989 Stock Incentive Plan of Delta Air Lines, Inc., as amended ("Plan"), is intended as an inducement for officers, executives and key employees of Delta Air Lines, Inc. (the "Company") to continue in the employment of the Company, and to provide a greater incentive to such employees to make material contributions to the Company's success by increasing their proprietary interest in the Company through increased direct common stock ownership. The Plan, which provides for certain awards to eligible employees, is administered by the Personnel & Compensation Committee of the Board of Directors (the "Committee"). Pursuant to the Plan, the Committee has selected you to receive an award of Restricted Stock (as defined in the Plan) effective as of the close of business on August 14, 1997, and has instructed me to direct this letter to you.

In consideration of the mutual covenants herein contained and for other good and valuable consideration, the Company and you as an employee of the Company (hereinafter called "Employee"), do hereby agree as follows:

1. Grant of Shares. Pursuant to action of the Committee, the Company has granted to Employee 6,000 shares of Restricted Stock (the "Shares"). This award is in all respects made subject to the terms and conditions of the Plan, a copy of which has been provided to Employee, and by signing and returning a copy of this Agreement to the Secretary of the Company, Employee acknowledges that he has read the Plan and agrees to all of the terms and conditions thereof for himself, any designated beneficiary and his heirs, executors, administrators or personal representative. Terms used in this Agreement which are defined in the Plan shall have the meanings set forth in the Plan. In the event of any conflict between the Plan and this Agreement, the Plan shall control. Employee also acknowledges receipt of the Prospectus dated January 26, 1995, relating to the Plan.

As soon as practicable following Employee's execution of this Agreement and the stock power described below in Section 6, a certificate or certificates representing the Shares and bearing the legend described below in Section 6 shall be issued to Employee. Upon issuance of the certificates representing the Shares, Employee shall have all rights of a stockholder with respect to the Shares, including the right to vote and, subject to Section 10 of this Agreement, to receive all dividends or other distributions paid or made with respect to the Shares; provided, however, that the Shares (and any securities of the Company which may be issued with respect to the Shares by virtue of any dividend reinvestment, stock split, combination, stock dividend or recapitalization, which securities shall be deemed to the "Shares" hereunder) shall be subject to the terms and all of the restrictions set forth in this Agreement.

2. Restriction. Until the restriction imposed by this Section 2 (the "Restriction") has lapsed pursuant to Section 3 or 4 below, Employee shall not be permitted to sell, exchange, assign, transfer, pledge or otherwise dispose of the Shares and the Shares shall be subject to forfeiture as set forth in Section 5 below.

3. Lapse of Restriction by Passage of Time. The Restriction shall lapse and have no further force or effect with respect to 33-1/3% of the Shares (including 33-1/3% of any additional Shares which at the time have been purchased with dividends on the Shares) awarded hereunder on July 1 of each of 1998, 1999 and 2000, provided Employee remains employed by the Company on such dates. If Employee's employment is terminated because of Retirement prior to his Normal Retirement Date as determined under the qualified retirement or pension plan of the Company applicable to Employee, and within two years after any such early Retirement and without the Committee's approval Employee directly or indirectly provides management or executive services (whether as a consultant, advisor, officer or director) to any Person who is in direct and substantial competition with the air transportation business of the Company or its Subsidiaries, Employee shall be required to repay to the Company the cash value of any Shares and any cash which were vested at such early Retirement. The amount of such repayment shall be the closing price of the Company's common stock ("Common Stock") on the New York Stock Exchange ("NYSE") on the day that the Restriction on such Shares lapsed (or, in the event that no sale of the Common Stock takes place on the NYSE on such date, the closing price of the Common Stock on the NYSE on the immediately preceding date on which such a sale occurred) multiplied by the number of such Shares. Because of the broad and extensive scope of the Company's air transportation business, the restrictions contained in this provision are intended to extend to management or executive services which are directly related to the provision of air transportation services into, within, or from the United States, as no smaller geographical restriction will adequately protect the legitimate business interests of the Company.

4. Lapse of Restriction in Certain Cases. The Restriction shall lapse and have no further force or effect with respect to all Shares hereunder upon (a) the occurrence of a Change in Control or (b) termination of Employee's employment (i) by the Company without Cause, (ii) by Employee with Good Reason or (iii) by reason of Employee's death or Disability (as defined in the Plan). For this purpose, the terms "Change in Control," "Cause" and "Good Reason" shall have the respective meanings assigned such terms for purposes of the Employment Agreement between Employee and the Company dated as of August 14, 1997. Employee may provide to the Company written designation naming a person or persons who shall receive the Shares in the event of Employee's death, and such designation must be in a form

approved by counsel for the Company. If there is no such approved designation, Shares shall be distributed upon Employee's death pursuant to Employee's last will and testament or as provided by law.

5. Forfeiture of Shares. In the event of termination of Employee's employment with the Company other than in the circumstances described in clauses (i), (ii) or (iii) of Section 4(b) and prior to lapse of the Restriction under Section 3, Employee shall immediately forfeit all right, title, and interest to the Shares which are still subject to the Restriction, and such Shares shall be canceled or transferred to the Company by Employee, without consideration to Employee or his heirs, executors, administrators or personal representative.

6. Endorsement and Retention of Certificates. All certificates representing the Shares shall be endorsed on the face thereof with the following legend:

"The shares of stock represented by this certificate and the sale, transfer or other disposition of such shares are restricted by and subject to a Restricted Stock Award Agreement dated August 14, 1997 between Leo F. Mullin and the Company, a copy of which is on file with the Secretary of the Company."

All certificates for Shares shall be held by the Company until the restrictions thereon shall have lapsed, and as a condition to this award, Employee shall execute and deliver to the Company a stock power, endorsed in blank and approved by counsel for the Company, relating to the Shares, as set forth in the Plan.

Upon lapse of the Restriction pursuant to Section 3 or 4 of this Agreement without a prior forfeiture of the Shares, a certificate or certificates for an appropriate number of unrestricted Shares shall be delivered to Employee and the certificate with the legend indicated above shall be canceled.

7. Withholding Taxes. Upon lapse of the Restriction on the Shares pursuant to Section 3 or 4 above, unless other tax withholding arrangements are made by Employee and the Company, sufficient Shares shall be transferred to the Company to provide for the payment of any taxes required to be withheld by federal, state, or local law with respect to income resulting from such lapse. The value of the Shares so transferred shall be the closing price of the Common Stock on the NYSE on the date the Restriction lapses (or, in the event that no sale of the Common Stock takes place on the NYSE on such date, the closing price of the Common Stock on the NYSE on the immediately preceding date on which such a sale occurred).

8. Rights Not Enlarged. Nothing herein confers on Employee any right to continue in the employ of the Company or any of its subsidiaries.

9. Succession. This Agreement shall be binding upon and operate for the benefit of the Company and its successors and assigns, and Employee and his heirs, executors, administrators or personal representative.

10. Dividends. Any cash dividends which may become payable on the Shares shall be reinvested by the Company in shares of Common Stock, to the extent Shares are

available under the Plan. If Shares are not so available, dividends shall be paid in cash and held by the Company for the account of Employee until the Restriction lapses. In such event the Company shall pay interest on the amount so held as determined by the Committee, and the accumulated amount of such dividends and interest shall be payable to Employee upon the lapse of the Restriction. Those Shares and any cash held for the account of the Employer shall be governed by the Restriction set forth in the Agreement; the Restriction with respect to such Shares and such cash shall lapse as provided in Sections 3 and 4 of this Agreement; and such Shares and such cash shall be forfeited pursuant to Section 5 to the extent that the Shares on which such dividends were paid shall be so forfeited.

11. Fractional Shares. Upon lapse of the Restriction, certificates for fractional Shares shall not be delivered to Employee, and the value of any fractional Shares which may result from the application of Section 3 or 4 of this Agreement shall be paid in cash to Employee, as determined in the last sentence of Section 7 above.

This Agreement has been prepared in duplicate. Please note your acceptance in the space provided below, and return the original for the Company's records.

IN WITNESS WHEREOF, the Company, acting through the Committee, has caused this Agreement to be duly executed and Employee has hereunto set his or her hand, all as of the day and year first written above.

DELTA AIR LINES, INC.

By:

_____

Gerald Grinstein, Chairman Personnel & Compensation Committee

EMPLOYEE

_____

Leo F. Mullin

APPENDIX 6.3. §422 INCENTIVE STOCK OPTIONS

(a) In general.

Section 421(a) shall apply with respect to the transfer of a share of stock to an individual pursuant to his exercise of an incentive stock option if—

(1) no disposition of such share is made by him within 2 years from the date of the granting of the option nor within 1 year after the transfer of such share to him, and

(2) at all times during the period beginning on the date of the granting of the option and ending on the day 3 months before the date of such exercise, such individual was an employee of either the corporation granting such option, a parent or subsidiary corporation of such corporation, or a corporation or a parent or subsidiary corporation of such corporation issuing or assuming a stock option in a transaction to which section 424(a) applies.

(b) Incentive stock option.

For purposes of this part, the term "incentive stock option" means an option granted to an individual for any reason connected with his employment by a corporation, if granted by the employer corporation or its parent or subsidiary corporation, to purchase stock of any of such corporations, but only if—

(1) the option is granted pursuant to a plan which includes the aggregate number of shares which may be issued under options and the employees (or class of employees) eligible to receive options, and which is approved by the stockholders of the granting corporation within 12 months before or after the date such plan is adopted;

(2) such option is granted within 10 years from the date such plan is adopted, or the date such plan is approved by the stockholders, whichever is earlier;

(3) such option by its terms is not exercisable after the expiration of 10 years from the date such option is granted;

(4) the option price is not less than the fair market value of the stock at the time such option is granted;

(5) such option by its terms is not transferable by such individual otherwise than by will or the laws of descent and distribution, and is exercisable, during his lifetime, only by him; and

(6) such individual, at the time the option is granted, does not own stock possessing more than 10 percent of the total combined voting power of all classes of stock of the employer corporation or of its parent or subsidiary corporation.

Such term shall not include any option if (as of the time the option is granted) the terms of such option provide that it will not be treated as an incentive stock option.

(c) Special rules.

(1) Good faith efforts to value stock.

If a share of stock is transferred pursuant to the exercise by an individual of an option which would fail to qualify as an incentive stock option under subsection (b) because there was a failure in an attempt, made in good faith, to meet the requirement of subsection (b)(4), the requirement of subsection (b)(4) shall be considered to have been met. To the extent provided in regulations by the Secretary, a similar rule shall apply for purposes of subsection (d).

(2) Certain disqualifying dispositions where amount realized is less than value at exercise. If—

(A) an individual who has acquired a share of stock by the exercise of an incentive stock option makes a disposition of such share within either of the periods described in subsection (a)(1), and

(B) such disposition is a sale or exchange with respect to which a loss (if sustained) would be recognized to such individual, then the amount which is includible in the gross income of such individual, and the amount which is deductible from the income of his employer corporation, as compensation attributable to the exercise of such option shall not exceed the excess (if any) of the amount realized on such sale or exchange over the adjusted basis of such share.

(3) Certain transfers by insolvent individuals.

If an insolvent individual holds a share of stock acquired pursuant to his exercise of an incentive stock option, and if such share is transferred to a trustee, receiver, or other similar fiduciary in any proceeding under title 11 or any other similar insolvency proceeding, neither such transfer, nor any other transfer of such share for the benefit of his creditors in such proceeding, shall constitute a disposition of such share for purposes of subsection (a)(1).

(4) Permissible provisions.

An option which meets the requirements of subsection (b) shall be treated as an incentive stock option even if—

(A) the employee may pay for the stock with stock of the corporation granting the option,

(B) the employee has a right to receive property at the time of exercise of the option, or

(C) the option is subject to any condition not inconsistent with the provisions of subsection (b).

Subparagraph (B) shall apply to a transfer of property (other than cash) only if section 83 applies to the property so transferred.

(5) 10-percent shareholder rule.

Subsection (b)(6) shall not apply if at the time such option is granted the option price is at least 110 percent of the fair market value of the stock subject to the option and such option by its terms is not exercisable after the expiration of 5 years from the date such option is granted.

(6) Special rule when disabled.

For purposes of subsection (a)(2), in the case of an employee who is disabled (within the meaning of section 22(e)(3)), the 3-month period of subsection (a)(2) shall be 1 year.

(7) Fair market value.

For purposes of this section, the fair market value of stock shall be determined without regard to any restriction other than a restriction which, by its terms, will never lapse.

(d) $100,000 per year limitation.

(1) In general.

To the extent that the aggregate fair market value of stock with respect to which incentive stock options (determined without regard to this subsection) are exercisable for the 1st time by any individual during any calendar year (under all plans of the individual's employer corporation and its parent and subsidiary corporations) exceeds $100,000, such options shall be treated as options which are not incentive stock options.

(2) Ordering rule.

Paragraph (1) shall be applied by taking options into account in the order in which they were granted.

(3) Determination of fair market value.

For purposes of paragraph (1), the fair market value of any stock shall be determined as of the time the option with respect to such stock is granted.

CHAPTER 7

Deferred Compensation

I. INTRODUCTION

When an employee performs services in one period and receives payment in a subsequent period, the compensation is said to be deferred. The future payment can be in cash, for example, a pension or annuity, stock, or benefits (e.g., the employer continues to pay the employee's health insurance premiums after the employee retires). On some level, stock-based compensation granted in the current period can be considered deferred, as while the options and/or shares are granted in the current period, the executive does not have full rights to them until they vest in some future period. Furthermore with options, if the exercise price is greater than or equal to the market price at the date of grant, executives will not be taxed at least until the options are exercised.[1] Compensation may be deferred to a future period for a number of reasons including, but not limited to, incentives and taxation.

A. Pensions

The most common form of deferred compensation for most employees is their pension, whereby they earn benefits while working and receive payments after they retire. Pension plans fall into two categories, defined benefit and defined contribution.

1. Defined Benefit Plans

As noted in Chapter 2, all of the CEOs in the Standard & Poors' ExecuComp database participate in defined benefit pension plans. Defined benefit plans provide employees with guaranteed payments based upon predetermined benefit formulas,

[1]As noted in Chapter 6, if the options are tax qualified (under Internal Revenue Code section 422) the executive will not realize taxable income until he or she sells the shares acquired upon exercise of the option.

formulas that may take into account retirement age, length of service, and pre-retirement earnings. Formulas include those based on terminal earnings, career earnings, dollar amount, and cash account. Terminal earnings formulas base benefits on average earnings during a specified number of years at the end of a worker's career. In contrast, career earnings formulas base benefits on average career earnings. Dollar amount formulas calculate benefits based on a dollar amount for each year of service, whereas cash account formulas are based on employer contributions plus interest earned on those contributions.

The benefit payment can be fixed in amount at the time of retirement or in certain cases can vary, for example, with increases in the Consumer Price Index. An example of the latter is our social security system, in which payments increase with the rate of inflation. Appendix 7.1, which provides a description of the General Motors retirement plans for its executives, also illustrates the magnitude and materiality of these plans (see Tables I and II).

2. Defined Contribution Plans

In contrast, with a defined contribution plan, the employer's contribution is defined by the plan. The employee may add to those contributions. He or she then directs those contributions into one of the investment vehicles provided by the employer, which may include company stock, professionally managed mutual funds, fixed interest securities, and so on. The employee's benefit is then based upon the investment choices made by the employee, and how well those investments perform.

A corporation may have multiple pension plans; in fact, most large corporations do. They can have both defined benefit and defined contribution plans. They can have different plans for different bargaining units. They can have different plans for the different countries they operate in. The following excerpt from IBM's 1999 10-K discusses, in very generic terms, those U.S. and non-U.S. plans:

> U.S. Plan
>
> U.S. regular, full-time and part-time employees are covered by a noncontributory plan that is funded by company contributions to an irrevocable trust fund, which is held for the sole benefit of participants.
>
> . . .
>
> The number of individuals who were receiving benefits at December 31, 1999 and 1998, was 124,175 and 116,685, respectively.
>
> Non-U.S. Plans
>
> Most subsidiaries and branches outside the U.S. have retirement plans that cover substantially all regular employees, under which the company deposits funds under various fiduciary-type arrangements, purchases annuities under group contracts or provides reserves. Retirement benefits are based on years of service and the employee's compensation, generally during a fixed number of years immediately before retirement. The ranges of assumptions that are used for the non-U.S. plans reflect the different economic environments within various countries.[2]

[2]International Business Machines, 10-K filed with the Securities and Exchange Commission, March 13, 2000, p. 88.

B. Supplemental Executive Retirement Plans

Employees can participate in more than one plan. That is, they may participate in both their employers' defined benefit and defined contribution plans. Executives in particular usually participate in multiple plans. The reasons are partly institutional. Pensions plans are governed by the Employee Retirement Income Security Act (ERISA) and the Internal Revenue Code (IRC), both of which set limits on contributions and payouts. To provide their executives retirement payouts beyond those allowed under ERISA and the IRC, most corporations have set up supplemental executive retirement plans.[3] The following excerpt, from IBM's 2000 proxy statement, discusses its supplemental plan and how it is coordinated with the primary tax-qualified defined benefit plan. In fact, the benefit offset mentioned in the second sentence implies that the supplemental plan exists primarily because of ERISA and IRC limitations on qualified plans.

> Retirement benefits are provided to the executive officers of the Company, including the named executive officers, under an unfunded, non-qualified defined benefit pension plan known as the Supplemental Executive Retention Plan ("SERP"). Benefits under the SERP are offset by benefits under the Company's funded, tax-qualified defined benefit pension plan known as the IBM Personal Pension Plan. The SERP and the IBM Personal Pension Plan are referred to collectively as the "Plans."[4]

The next passage explains in part how the benefit is computed. Given that IBM uses compensation over either the executive's final 5 years or the executive's 5 most highly compensated years, its plan would seem to use a terminal earnings formula.

> For purposes of the Plans, average annual compensation is equal to the average annual salary and bonus over the final five years of employment or the highest consecutive five calendar years of compensation, whichever is greater. The annual salary and bonus for the current year for the named executive officers is indicated in the Annual Compensation column of the Summary Compensation Table. The years of service for each of the named executive officers under the Plans, as of December 31, 1999, are: Mr. Gerstner, 6 years; Mr. Thompson, 33 years; Mr. Palmisano, 26 years; Mr. Ricciardi, 4 years; and Mr. Donofrio, 32 years. No additional benefits are payable under the Plans for years of service in excess of 35 years.[5]

Finally, the following sentence illustrates one of the benefits of a supplemental plan. Unlike the qualified primary plan, for which benefit formulas must be computed in a nondiscriminatory fashion in accordance with ERISA and IRC regulations, a supplemental plan allows the corporation flexibility to deviate from its formulae and negotiate separately with each executive. Thus IBM, rather than setting Louis Gertner's pension based upon the formula, set it by contract: "Mr.

[3]Compensation Resource Group (2000) found that 75% of corporations in their survey of the Fortune 1000 have supplemental plans.

[4]International Business Machines proxy statement filed with Securities and Exchange Commission, March 13, 2000, pp. 17, 18.

[5]International Business Machines proxy statement filed with Securities and Exchange Commission, March 13, 2000, pp. 17, 18.

Gerstner's annual pension from the Company under his employment agreement has been set at approximately $1,140,000 at age 60."[6]

The following from First Union illustrates the relative importance of supplemental versus qualified pension plans.[7] For example, an executive with 35 years of experience and an average annual compensation of $1,250,000 would receive $74,189 from the primary qualified pension plan (PP), and almost ten times that amount, $724,534, from the supplemental plan (SRP).

First Union
Estimated annual retirement benefit, assuming a married
participant, a straight life annuity and the years of service indicated (1)

Average annual compensation	15 years		20 years		25 years		30 years		35 years	
	PP	SRP	PP	SRP	PP	SRP	PP	SRP	PP	SRP
1,250,000	35,095	354,647	46,793	479,123	58,491	603,598	70,189	728,074	74,189	724,534
2,250,000	35,095	678,236	46,793	910,575	58,491	1,142,915	70,189	1,375,254	74,189	1,371,714
3,250,000	35,095	1,001,826	46,793	1,342,028	58,491	1,682,231	70,189	2,022,433	74,189	2,018,893
4,250,000	35,095	1,325,416	46,793	1,773,481	58,491	2,221,547	70,189	2,669,612	74,189	2,666,072
5,250,000	35,095	1,649,005	46,793	2,204,934	58,491	2,760,563	70,189	3,316,792	74,189	3,313,252

(1) For the year ending December 31, 2000, the annual retirement benefit payable under the Pension Plan is limited by federal law to $135,000 and the maximum covered compensation is limited to $170,000. For officers covered under the Supplemental Retirement Plan (currently, a total of 15 in number), any excess annual retirement benefit (based on 30 or less years of service) which could not be paid under the Pension Plan because of such limitations would be payable under the Supplemental Retirement Plan.

To illustrate the complexity involved in these plans and agreements, Appendix 7.2 contains the full text of the "Excess Benefits Agreement," that is the supplemental plan, dated August 14, 1997, between Delta Air Lines and Leo F. Mullin, its President and Chief Executive Officer.

C. Deferred Compensation Plans

In addition to pension plans, many corporations have plans that allow, encourage, or mandate that their executives defer portions of their salary and/or bonuses.[8] For example, in addition to the plans described above, IBM has deferred compensation and supplemental deferred contribution plans as described below. What is particularly interesting, and well illustrated by this example, is the effect the tax code has on the plans. First given the limitation on contributions, which was $10,500 in that

[6]International Business Machines proxy statement filed with Securities and Exchange Commission, March 13, 2000, p. 18.

[7]First Union Corporation Proxy statement filed with the Securities and Exchange Commission, March 13, 2000, p. 13.

[8]Compensation Resources Group (2000) reports that 86% of the firms in their survey of the Fortune 1000 had nonqualified deferred compensation plans.

particular year, IBM has set up the Executive Deferred Compensation Plan. Second, in order to avoid taxation, the Executive Deferred Compensation Plan has to be unfunded, with the participants being general creditors of the corporation.

> The IBM TDSP 401(k) (the "TDSP") (previously known as the IBM Tax Deferred Savings Plan) allows all eligible employees to defer up to 15% of their income on a tax-favored basis into a tax exempt trust pursuant to Internal Revenue Service guidelines. IBM matches these deferrals at the rate of 50% for the first 6% of compensation deferred. The employee accounts are invested by the plan trustee in a selection of investment funds, including an IBM Stock Fund, as directed by the employees. Corporate officers participate in the TDSP on the same basis as all other employees. Internal Revenue Service limits on the TDSP preclude an annual investment of more than $10,500 or an eligible compensation base of more than $170,000 for any one employee.
>
> IBM established the Executive Deferred Compensation Plan (the "EDCP") in 1995. The EDCP formerly was known as the Extended Tax Deferred Savings Plan. The EDCP allows any U.S. executive, including officers, to defer additional monies and receive a Company match on the same basis as the TDSP except that the Company match for the EDCP is credited only in units of IBM common stock, which are not transferable to other investment alternatives during employment. In addition, participants can defer all or a portion of their annual incentive until retirement under the EDCP. In the event that the salary of a Company officer who is subject to the limits of section 162(m) of the Code exceeds $1,000,000, such officer may defer up to 100 percent of his or her salary. The EDCP is not funded and participants are general creditors of the Company. All investments in the EDCP earn income based on the results of the actual TDSP funds' performance, but the income is paid out of Company funds rather than the actual returns on a dedicated investment portfolio.[9]

Another example of a company offering a nonqualified deferred compensation plan to its employees is Dell Computer.

> Dell also maintains a nonqualified deferred compensation plan that is available to executives. Under the terms of this plan, Dell matches 100% of each participant's voluntary contributions up to 3% of the participant's compensation. A participant vests ratably in the matching contributions over the first five years of employment (20% per year). Upon a participant's death or retirement, the funds are distributed in a lump sum or in annual, quarterly or monthly installments over a period of up to ten years.[10]

There are a variety of instruments into which compensation can be deferred. For example, the deferral can be into an account that is credited with interest according to some interest rate, for example, the rate on 6-month Treasury bills; an account that is tied to some stock market index, for example, the S&P 500; or into an account whose payout is dependent on the firm's stock price performance. Sometimes, to encourage executives to take advantage of these plans, corporations provide additional monetary rewards. The Compensation Resources Group (2000) found that 41% of their survey respondents matched at least some of the

---

[9]International Business Machines proxy statement filed with Securities and Exchange Commission, March 13, 2000, p. 19.

[10]Dell Computer proxy statement filed with Securities and Exchange Commission, May 30, 2000, p. 14.

executive deferrals, and 11% used a premium rate. An illustration of employer matching is the Dell example in the previous paragraph, where Dell matches the executive's deferral on a dollar-for-dollar basis up to 3% of the participants' compensation. That is, if the executive earns $100,000 and defers $3,000 or more, Dell will add another $3,000, to be invested on the executive's behalf. An illustration of a premium rate occurs when the rate of return promised equals some market rate, for example, return on long-term Treasury bonds, plus a bonus, for example, 2% per year. These amounts can be significant. For example, American Home Products reported that during 2000, John Stafford, its Chairman and Chief Executive Officer, earned $744,964 from above-market interest rates paid on deferred compensation.[11] Similarly, General Electric reported that during 2000, John Welch, its Chairman and Chief Executive Officer, earned $974,005 from above-market interest rates paid on his deferred compensation.[12] Consequently, both employer matching and the existence of a premium rate increase the monetary reward from, and hence, the desirability of deferring compensation from the viewpoint of the executive.

II. FUNDING LIMITATIONS

Although qualified pension plans are required to be funded by ERISA, nonqualified supplemental pension plans and deferred compensation arrangements are not required to be funded. Furthermore, to avoid current taxation, the executive has to avoid constructive receipt of the amounts involved in both the supplemental retirement plan and nonqualified deferred compensation plan. Thus, formally, the corporation does not fund an "account" at the time of deferral; rather, the corporation promises to pay the amount in the "account" at the end of the deferral period. Many corporations informally fund[13] and secure those benefits via techniques like Rabbi Trusts.[14] A Rabbi Trust sets aside assets to be used to satisfy the employer's obligations to the executive. Similar to an escrow account, it is an irrevocable trust established for the benefit of the participant by an employer. However, although the employer cannot touch those assets, the creditors of the employer can. It is this last provision, the ability of creditors of the employer to attach those assets if necessary, that allows the executive to avoid constructive receipt and current taxation. In the

---

[11]American Home Products proxy statement filed with Securities and Exchange Commission, March 19, 2001, p. 9.

[12]General Electric proxy statement filed with the Securities and Exchange Commission, March 9, 2001, p. 23.

[13]Compensation Resource Group (2000) reports that 66% of firms in its survey of the Fortune 1000 informally fund their nonqualified deferred compensation arrangements and 52% informally fund their supplemental executive retirement plans.

[14]The term *Rabbi Trust* arose because the Internal Revenue Service Private Letter Ruling No. 8,113,107, which approved the technique, pertained to a trust set up by a Temple to benefit its rabbi.

Senior Executive Excess Benefit agreement reprinted in Appendix 7.2 (between Delta Air Lines and Leo F. Mullin, its President and Chief Executive Officer), section nine states that the rights of the executive "shall be no greater than that of a general creditor. . . ."

III. INCENTIVES

Deferral of compensation can affect the executives' incentives, with the affect on incentives depending on the structure of the deferral. For example, different incentives will arise if the deferral goes into an interest-bearing account, or into a stock type account, where the payout is based upon firm performance. Consider first the effect of vesting on the pension benefit.

A. Vesting

The pension benefit, while nominally fixed, or at least independent of performance, does provide certain incentives. Most pension plans are structured so that the benefits do not vest immediately. This provides the executive with the incentive to remain with the firm at least until the pension vests. That is, there is a monetary cost to leaving the firm before then, as the unvested pension would be forfeited. Although ERISA mandates that vesting occur over no longer than 5 years, ERISA does not apply to supplemental plans. Thus, the corporation is free to set its own vesting requirements for its supplemental plans. And given that supplemental plans (see the First Union example above) provide the bulk of retirement income to executives, the supplemental plan is the more important plan in providing incentives to executives.

B. Pension Backloading

Beyond vesting, there are other techniques the corporation can use to encourage executives to remain with the firm (or retire early). For example, the pension plan can be structured so the benefit increases with the individual's tenure with the firm, something referred to as "pension backloading." Kotlikoff and Wise (1989) described it as follows:

> Pension backloading refers to pension plans that provide very little pension accrual up to a specific age and substantial pension accrual after a specific age. This feature of pension plans typically means that pension benefits are much smaller for employees who change jobs than for those who don't. (pp. 1, 2)

Pension backloading may be achieved by basing the pension on final compensation or average compensation over last 3–5 years (see IBM example), that is, using a terminal earnings formula. Alternatively, the pension can be a percentage of final compensation, and that percentage can increase with the number of years employed. In such a case, assuming compensation increases over time, the executive has a double monetary incentive to stay. That is, the pension is an increasing percentage of an increasing amount.

Consider the following example. For employees with more than 20 but less than 40 years of service, the promised annual pension payout is equal to the number of years employed times 1.5% of the executive's final compensation. For employees with 40 or more years of service, the promised annual pension payout is equal to the number of years employed times 2% of the executive's final compensation. An executive with 39 years of service is deciding on whether to return for his or her 40th year. If he or she returns, total compensation other than pension will be $150,000, which is $5,000 more than he or she earned in the previous year. Thus, the promised future pension would be 80% of $150,000 or $120,000, rather than 58.5% of $145,000 or $84,825. The executive's real earnings on returning for year 40 would thus be the $150,000, minus the pension he or she would have received that year, $84,825, plus the present value of the increase in the annual pension payment of $35,175. If by working the additional year, the executive increases the present value of his or her pension annuity, the pension plan provides incentive for the executive to continue working. Given reasonable assumptions as to the length of time the executive will collect the pension, and the discount rates to be applied to that pension, it is likely the present value of an annuity of $35,175 will exceed $84,825; thus, the pension accrual is positive and the pension plan provides incentive for the executive to continue working.[15]

Alternatively, some corporations may decide to structure their plans to avoid giving executives the incentive to stay too long.[16] They could design their plan so that the maximum benefit is reached when the executive reaches a certain age or a certain number of years of service.

Consider the following modification to the above example. Assume the corporation caps the payout at 80% of final salary. The executive is now deciding whether to return for his or her 41st year. If he or she returns total compensation other than pension will be $155,000, which is $5000 more than he or she earned in the previous year. Thus the promised future pension would be 80% of $155,000 or $124,000, rather than $120,000. The executive's real earnings on returning for year

---

[15]It is worth noting that the average individual retiring at age 65 can expect to live an additional 20 years.

[16]The issue arises of why a corporation would even have to consider this situation. That is, they could always fire an executive who refuses to retire. However, it would be politically untenable, both inside and outside the corporation, to fire a previously valued employee in the twilight of his or her career. Given the legal environment in the United States, the corporation might even face an age-discrimination lawsuit.

41 would thus be $155,000, minus the pension he or she would have received in year 41, $120,000, plus the present value of the increase in the annual pension payment of $4000. Given it is unlikely the present value of an annuity of $4000 is unlikely to be anywhere near $120,000[17] the pension accrual in this case is actually negative! That is, the corporation is saving more by not paying a pension this year, than the incremental increase in pension amount they will have to pay out in the future. Hence, the pension plan provides disincentive for the executive to continue working.

C. Affect on Risk Preferences

Pensions or deferred compensation can also affect the executives' risk preferences. As noted above, ostensibly the promised payments are not related to firm or individual performance. However, if the deferred amounts are invested in company stock, then the ultimate payout will depend on corporate performance.[18] Alternatively, if the deferral is not funded, the corporations' ability to make those payments are not guaranteed and become dependent upon future performance. At the extreme, if the firm goes out of business the executive would lose all forms of deferred compensation not fully funded. And note that much of an executive's retirement package comes from supplemental plans, which are not funded. For example, it was noted above that IBM has promised Louis Gerstner an annual pension of approximately $1,140,000. Given that the Section 415b limits the payout from qualified plans to a maximum of $135,000 in 2000, the bulk of that promised amount, $1,005,000, is at risk.[19] Thus, an executive, with large amounts of unfunded deferred compensation, has the incentive to reduce firm risks, which could involve forgoing otherwise profitable projects.[20]

D. Bond on Performance

Deferred compensation, if the corporation can refuse to pay it later, can also work as a bond on performance. For example, if the executive is later found to have embezzled funds or misrepresented results while employed with the company, or violated a noncompete agreement after leaving the company, the company could refuse to pay the amounts deferred. An example of the former situation, that is,

[17]The employee would have to collect the increase of $4,000 in his or her pension for 30 years before the nominal amount equaled $120,000. At a discount rate of 2% per year it would take almost 50 years!

[18]Kadlec (2001) discusses how many 401(K) plans include a disproportionate amount of employer stock.

[19]While it could be funded with a Rabbi Trust, recall that Rabbi Trusts may be attached by creditors of the firm.

[20]Hence the need for other forms of compensation whose value increases with risk.

misrepresentation of results, arose with Waste Management, where the new board resisted making payouts due to accounting misrepresentations occurring under previous management (Bailey 1999). An example of the latter condition, that is, the explicit statement that the benefit spelled out in the agreement may be stopped if the executive takes a position with a competitor, can be found in section eight of the excess benefit agreement between Delta Air Lines and Leo F. Mullin, its President and Chief Executive Officer, found in Appendix 7.2.

E. Resolving Horizon Problems

Depending upon how it is structured, deferred compensation may also help resolve the horizon problem. The horizon problem arises when decisions made by an executive affect performance after his or her retirement. If the executive is paid based upon current performance, he or she has no incentive to care about firm performance after he or she retires, and thus, at a minimum, has no incentive to invest in projects where the payback begins after retirement. Consistent with this theory, Dechow and Sloan (1991) found investment in research and development (R&D) decreases as the CEO nears retirement. While in theory, stock compensation and stock ownership are forward-looking forms of compensation, that is, the value of a share is the present value of expected future cash flows, in the presence of asymmetric information that may not always be the case. To control for this Bizjak et al. (1993) suggested that the executive be paid based on stock-price performance after retirement. This would be achieved if the executive defers compensation into stock units. Stock units qualify as deferred compensation because shares are not issued at the time of grant; rather, an unfunded promise is made by the firm to issue a number of shares in the future. Note that in IBM's Executive Deferred Compensation Plan (above) the Company match was credits in units of IBM stock.

IV. POLITICAL COSTS

Deferred compensation is not as political an issue as other components of compensation plan. First of all, both ERISA and the IRC place limits on qualified pension plans. However, as discussed above, these limits can be bypassed with supplemental plans, and there are no limits on other forms of deferred compensation. Second, payments occur after retirement and therefore are not as visible. For one, they are not reported in proxy statements. Thus, the $1,140,000 IBM has promised to pay Louis Gerstner as an annual pension will not be disclosed when the payments are actually made. An exception in terms of political visibility was when First Union promised to pay its retiring chairman and former CEO, Edward E. Crutchfield, Jr., $1.8 million per year for life, in addition to his regular and supplemental pension that were estimated to pay him $1.3 million per year.[21]

[21]Mollenkamp (2000).

One aspect of pensions that has become an issue is the pensions paid to directors. "Shareholder activists argue that such perks unduly enrich outside directors, encourage them to stay too long and endanger their independence."[22] Thus, they have become an issue, and as will be shown in Chapter 9 (Table 9.2), many firms have eliminated pensions for their directors, substituting cash and stock compensation instead.

V. FINANCIAL CONSEQUENCES

A. Cash Flows and Taxes

Deferred compensation, like the other components of the executive compensation package, impacts the corporation's cash flows, although depending on the type of compensation, cash flow may be affected in either the current or some future period(s). As noted in the introduction to this chapter, taxes, or more precisely, our tax system, provide incentives for employees to defer compensation. At its most basic form, Miller and Scholes (1982) showed that if the employee's tax rate is higher than the corporation's tax rate, it makes tax sense to have the employee defer, and the corporation invest those funds. Deferral also makes tax sense if the executive can postpone the recognition of income to a period in which he or she has a lower tax rate and/or a period in which the corporation has a higher tax rate.[23]

Specific provisions of the tax code encourage deferred compensation. For example, if a pension plan is qualified, the corporation is required to fund the plan while the employee is working and gets to deduct the amount it pays into the pension fund at the time it makes those payments. Those amounts then get to compound on a tax-deferred basis, with the employee only taxed at the future date when he or she receives payments from the pension fund. The ability of the corporation to take an immediate tax deduction, as well as for the amounts invested to grow on a tax-deferred basis, provide incentive for the corporation to provide qualified pensions. In contrast, there are no tax incentives associated with nonqualified pension plans or other nonqualified deferred compensation arrangements. For nonqualified plans, funding will trigger a tax liability on the part of the employee, hence those plans are not usually formally funded.[24] Thus, for those plans both the cash outflow and tax deduction will occur at some time in the future. In the

[22]Selz (1996), p. B10.

[23]Both the executive and the corporation want to minimize the taxes paid on this transaction. For the executive, to whom this is taxable income, that means recognizing income when his or her tax rate is low. For the corporation, to whom this is a tax deduction, that means recognizing the deduction when their tax rate is high.

[24]Funding the plan results in constructive receipt (and hence taxability to the executive) under the Internal Revenue Code. In effect, the executive must be a general creditor of the firm to avoid taxation. As discussed above, funding deferred compensation via a Rabbi Trust provides some security to the executive while avoiding constructive receipt.

situation where the plan is informally funded, the corporation has a cash outflow in the current period, but doesn't receive a deduction until the executive recognizes the income, which would normally be when they receive the cash payments.

Another section of the Internal Revenue Code that encourages deferral of compensation by executives is the million-dollar cap, that is Section 162(m). It encourages deferral of compensation, as amounts that would not be deductible if paid currently, can be fully deductible if payment is deferred until the executive is no longer subject to its limitations, for example, once the executive is retired. To preserve tax deductions some companies require the deferral of any amounts that would not be currently deductible because of Section 162(m). The effect of such a policy is to push the cash outflow to a future period, but more importantly, to preserve a deduction that otherwise would be lost. An example of a company requiring deferral is Temple Inland, which states,

> The Committee has adopted a policy requiring the deferral of any compensation that exceeds the permissible deduction under Section 162(m) of the Internal Revenue Code until such time as the maximum deduction under Section 162(m) may be taken.[25]

B. Financial Reporting Consequences

For financial accounting purposes, amounts deferred are expensed when earned, regardless of when paid. At the same time as the amounts are expensed, the related income tax accounting consequences are recognized. That is, for its financial accounting records, the company records both the expense and income tax deduction when the amounts are earned, rather than when they are paid or actually deducted on the corporate tax return.

If the amounts are recorded at the present value of the future payment, as with pension and other postretirement benefits, or if the corporation pays interest on the amounts deferred, then that increase in the present value of the liability[26] or interest on the deferred amount is also recognized as an expense with the passage of time. These amounts are offset by interest or returns earned on prefunded amounts, if any. For example, as discussed above, qualified pension plans are funded when the employee works. The amount contributed by the company to the pension fund is less than the future promised payment because it is expected that the pension fund will invest that money profitably.

For some companies these returns have been so large that companies have reported pension income in recent years! That is, not only are the returns greater than the increase in present value of the liability, the excess of the returns over the

---

[25]Temple Inland proxy statement filed with the Securities and Exchange Commission, March 24, 2000, p. 12.

[26]As the payment date gets closer, the present value of a liability increases, and at the payment date, it equals the face value of the liability.

increase in the present value of the liability exceeds the benefits earned during that period. For example, General Electric has reported pension income of $1.38 billion in 1999, $1.016 billion in 1998, and $331 million in 1997![27]

VI. SUMMARY

The focus of this chapter was deferred compensation, which occurs when an employee performs services in one period and receives payment in a subsequent period. The most common form of deferred compensation, at least to most employees, is their pension, where the payment is not received until after the employee retires. Pensions can be either defined benefit or defined contribution, with many executives having both types of plans. In addition to their primary tax-qualified plans, which are limited in amount, most upper level executives have supplemental unfunded plans. As illustrated in the chapter, these supplemental plans, which are not subject to Internal Revenue Code or ERISA regulations, provide the preponderance of an upper level executive's retirement benefits. In addition to pension plans, many corporations have plans that allow, encourage, or mandate their executives defer portions of their salary and/or bonuses.

Deferred compensation can be structured to provide incentives. For example, vesting and the formula used to determine retirement benefits can provide incentive for the executive to remain with the corporation. Deferred compensation can also affect risk preferences. In particular, unfunded deferred compensation decreases the executive's willingness to take risk. However, deferred compensation, especially if the payout is tied to the corporation's stock price, can help mitigate the horizon problem.

[27]General Electric 10-K filed with Securities and Exchange Commission, March 17, 2000, p. F-27.

APPENDIX 7.1. EXECUTIVE PENSION BENEFITS FROM GENERAL MOTORS PROXY STATEMENT FILED APRIL 20, 1999

RETIREMENT PROGRAM

The retirement program for General Motors executives in the United States consists of the General Motors Retirement Program for Salaried Employees and two non-qualified plans. Together, these plans are referred to here as the "GM Salaried Program."

The General Motors Retirement Program for Salaried Employees is a tax-qualified plan subject to the requirements of the Employee Retirement Income Security Act (ERISA). The contributory portion (known as Part B) of this tax-qualified plan provides benefits under a formula based on the number of "Years of Part B Credited Service" and upon the average of the highest five years of base salary received during the final ten years of service, subject to certain Internal Revenue Code limitations which may change from time to time. Part B of the tax-qualified plan also provides employees with an annual retirement benefit which is equal to the sum of 100% of the Part B contributions they made after October 1, 1979, and smaller percentages of the contributions they made before that date. If employees elect not to contribute to Part B of the tax-qualified plan, they are entitled to receive only basic retirement benefits equal to a flat dollar amount per year of credited service (essentially equivalent to the General Motors Hourly-Rate Employees Pension Plan). Benefits under the tax-qualified plan vest after five years of credited service and are payable at the normal retirement age of 65, either in the form of a single life annuity or in a reduced amount in joint and survivor form.

Supplemental Executive Retirement Program (SERP). If an executive makes Part B contributions to the tax-qualified plan, the executive may also be eligible to receive a non-qualified Regular SERP benefit. The sum of the tax-qualified plan's benefits plus the Regular SERP benefit will provide an eligible executive with total annual retirement benefits under the GM Salaried Program that are equal to 2% times Years of Part B Credited Service times Average Annual Base Salary, less 2% times years of credited service times the maximum annual Social Security benefit in the year of retirement payable to a person retiring at age 65 ($16,476 for a 65 year old retiring in 1999).

Table I shows the regular form of the estimated total annual retirement benefit payable under the GM Salaried Program (based on Average Annual Base Salary as of December 31, 1998) that would be paid in 12 equal monthly installments per year as a single life annuity to executives retiring in 1999 at age 65. If the executive elects to receive such benefits in the form of a 60% joint and survivor annuity, the single life annuity amounts shown would generally be reduced by 5% to 7.5%, depending upon the age differential between spouses.

TABLE I   Projected Total Annual Retirement Benefits from All Parts of the GM Salaried Program Assuming an Executive Qualifies for Regular SERP Benefits[a]

Average annual base salary[b]	Years of Part B credited service			
	15	25	35	45
$ 750,000	$220,057	$ 366,762	$ 513,467	$ 660,172
$1,070,000	$316,057	$ 526,762	$ 737,467	$ 948,172
$1,390,000	$412,057	$ 686,762	$ 961,467	$1,236,172
$1,710,000	$508,057	$ 846,762	$1,185,467	$1,524,172
$2,030,000	$604,057	$1,006,762	$1,409,467	$1,812,172
$2,350,000	$700,057	$1,166,762	$1,633,467	$2,100,172

[a]The Average Annual Base Salary and the Years of Part B Credited Service (shown in parenthesis) as of December 31, 1998 for each of the Named Executive Officers were as follows; John F. Smith, Jr.—$1,690,000 (38 years); Harry J. Pearce—$942,500 (21 years); G. Richard Wagoner, Jr.—$917,500 (21 years); J. T. Battenberg III—$767,500 (36 years); and Louis R. Hughes—$900,000 (31 years). The Annual Base Salary for the most recent year(s) considered in the calculation reported here are shown in the Summary Compensation Table on page 15 in the column labeled "Salary."

[b]Average Annual Base Salary means the average of the highest five years of base salary paid during the final ten years of service.

Executives may be eligible to receive an Alternative SERP benefit in lieu of the Regular SERP benefit if they satisfy certain criteria, including not working for any competitor or otherwise acting in any manner which is not in the best interests of the Corporation. An eligible executive will receive the greater of the Regular SERP benefit or the Alternative SERP benefit. The sum of the tax-qualified plan's benefits plus the Alternative SERP benefit will provide an eligible executive with total annual retirement benefits under the GM Salaried Program that are equal to 1.5% times Eligible Years of Part B Credited Service (up to a maximum of 35 years) times the executive's Average Annual Total Direct Compensation, less 100% of the maximum annual Social Security benefit in the year of retirement payable to a person age 65.

Table II shows the alternative form of the estimated total annual retirement benefit payable under the GM Salaried Program (based upon Average Annual Total Direct Compensation as of December 31, 1998) that would be paid in 12 equal monthly installments per year as a single life annuity to executives retiring in 1999 at age 65. The amounts shown would be reduced in the same way as under the regular form if the executive elects joint and survivor benefits.

In addition, the Board of Directors has delegated to the Committee discretionary authority to grant additional eligible years of credited service to selected key

TABLE II   Projected Total Annual Retirement Benefits from All Parts of the GM Salaried Program Assuming Executive Qualifies for Alterantive SERP Benefits[a]

Average annual total direct compensation[b]	Eligible years of Part B credited service				
	15	20	25	30	35
$1,450,000	$ 309,774	$ 418,524	$ 527,274	$ 636,024	$ 744,774
$2,220,000	$ 483,024	$ 649,524	$ 816,024	$ 982,524	$1,149,024
$2,990,000	$ 656,274	$ 880,524	$1,104,774	$1,329,024	$1,553,274
$3,760,000	$ 829,524	$1,111,524	$1,393,524	$1,675,524	$1,957,524
$4,530,000	$1,002,774	$1,342,524	$1,682,274	$2,022,024	$2,361,774
$5,300,000	$1,176,024	$1,573,524	$1,971,024	$2,100,172	$2,766,024

[a]The Average Annual Total Direct Compensation and the Eligible Years of Part B Credited Service (shown in parenthesis) which may be considered in the Alternative SERP calculation as of December 31, 1998 for each of the Named Executive Officers was as follows: John F. Smith, Jr.—$3,451,000 (35 years); Harry J. Pearce—$1,792,100 (21 years); G. Richard Wagoner, Jr.—$1,754,100 (21 years); J. T. Battenberg III—$1,453,900 (35 years); and Louis R. Hughes—$1,731,600 (31 years). The Annual Total Direct Compensation for the most recent year(s) considered in the calculation reported here will be found in the Summary Compensation Table on Page 15 in the columns labeled "Salary" and "Bonus."

[b]Average Annual Total Direct Compensation means the sum of Average Annual Base Salary plus the average of the highest five Annual Incentive Awards earned in respect of the final ten calendar years of service prior to an executive's retirement.

executives under such terms and conditions as the Committee shall determine for purposes of computing the regular and alternative forms of SERP for such executives. Both the regular and alternative form of the SERP benefit are provided under a program which is non-qualified for tax purposes and not pre-funded. SERP benefits under the regular and alternative form can be reduced or eliminated for both retirees and active employees by the Committee and/or the Board of Directors.

APPENDIX 7.2. SENIOR OFFICER EXCESS BENEFIT AGREEMENT

EXHIBIT A

THIS EXCESS BENEFIT AGREEMENT ("Agreement") is made and entered into as of the 14th day of August, 1997, by and between DELTA AIR LINES, INC. (hereinafter the "Company") and Leo F. Mullin (hereinafter "Key Employee"):

WITNESSETH:

WHEREAS, the Company has implemented the 1991 Delta Excess Benefit Plan, and the Delta Supplemental Excess Benefit Plan, both as amended (collectively referred to as the "Plans"), and has entered into an Employment Agreement with Key Employee (the "Employment Agreement"); and

WHEREAS, the Company believes it is in the best interest of the Company in seeking to assure itself of Key Employee's best efforts in the future to provide for the payment of full retirement and other benefits to the Key Employee; and

WHEREAS, the Company has agreed in the Employment Agreement to provide Key Employee with specified retirement benefits, as described herein; and

WHEREAS, various sections of the Internal Revenue Code of 1986 (the "Code"), including, but not limited to, Sections 79, 401(a)(4), 401(a)(17), 415, and 505(b) restrict either: (i) compensation that may be taken into account in determining benefits under a qualified pension plan; (ii) benefits that can be paid from qualified pension plans; (iii) compensation that may be taken into account in determining benefits for participants in a Voluntary Employee Beneficiary Association ("VEBA") described in–Section 501(c)(9) of the Code; or (iv) restrict benefits that can be paid from a VEBA (such limitations collectively or individually hereinafter referred to as the "Restrictions"); and

WHEREAS, the Company wishes to make up under this Agreement any reduction in Key Employee's disability or survivor benefits under the Delta Family-Care Disability and Survivorship Plan (the "Disability and Survivorship Plan") which results from the Restrictions, or any other applicable laws, statutes, or regulations which restrict in any way the benefits that can be paid from a VEBA; and

WHEREAS, the Board of Directors of the Company has authorized post-retirement life insurance benefits for senior officers in excess of the coverage provided to other employees of the Company through the Basic Lump Sum Death Benefit under the Disability and Survivorship Plan; and

WHEREAS, certain restrictions imposed by the Tax Equity and Fiscal Responsibility Act of 1982 ("TEFRA") prohibit the Company from providing post-retirement life insurance benefits to officers in excess of that provided to other employees of the Company; and

WHEREAS, the Company wishes to make up any such loss of group life insurance coverage for Key Employee which cannot be provided because of the TEFRA restrictions;

NOW, THEREFORE, the parties hereby agree as follows:

1. Certain Requirements Not Applicable. The parties specifically acknowledge that this Agreement is exempt from certain provisions of the Employee Retirement Income Security Act of 1974 ("ERISA") including, but not limited to, parts 2, 3 and 4 of Subtitle B of Title 1 of ERISA and is also subject to limited reporting and disclosure requirements of part 1 of Subtitle B of Title 1 of ERISA.

2. Incorporation of the Retirement Plan and the Disability and Survivorship Plan. The terms of the Delta Family-Care Retirement Plan (the "Retirement Plan") and the Disability and Survivorship Plan are hereby incorporated into this Agreement by reference, except that changes in those plans which reduce benefits (except such changes as may be required by law) shall be incorporated as to Key Employee only if advance notice of such proposed reduction is given to the Key Employee and the Key Employee agrees to an amendment of this Agreement to incorporate the benefit reduction. The incorporation of the Retirement Plan and the Disability and Survivorship Plan is not intended to modify any provision of this Agreement, and the benefits provided hereunder shall be governed only by the provisions hereof. Unless indicated otherwise, capitalized terms used in this Agreement shall have the meaning given those terms in the Retirement Plan and Disability and Survivorship Plan.

3. Supplemental Retirement Income.

(a) Upon termination of his employment with the Company, in addition to retirement income which Key Employee might be eligible to receive through his participation in the Plans, and subject to the vesting provision in Section 3(c) below, Key Employee will be entitled to receive from the Company supplemental retirement income ("Supplemental Retirement Income") which will provide Key Employee with an aggregate retirement benefit (taking into account the amounts offset as described in Section 3(b) below) in an annual amount (in the form of an unreduced joint and 50% survivor annuity) equal to the aggregate retirement benefits that would have accrued to the benefit of Key Employee under the Retirement Plan and the Plans (which shall provide benefits substantially equivalent to those described in the excerpt from the Company's 1996 Proxy Statement attached as Exhibit 1 hereto (disregarding references to plans maintained primarily for pilots), without regard to any changes after the date of such Proxy Statement), calculated crediting Key Employee with 22 years of service credit plus the number of years of service credit attributable to Key Employee's service with the Company after the date hereof, and calculated without regard to any waiting period which might otherwise apply with respect to the accrual of benefits under the Retirement Plan and the Plans.

(b) The amount of the Supplemental Retirement Income will be offset by (i) the benefits provided Key Employee under any qualified defined benefit retirement plans of the Company, including but not limited to the Retirement Plan; (ii) benefits provided Key Employee under any nonqualified defined benefit retirement plans of the Company, including but not limited to the Plans; and (iii) Social Security benefits and other amounts for which and to the extent offset is provided for under the Retirement Plan. In the event Key Employee commences receiving the Supplemental Retirement Income on or after his attainment of age 60, the Supplemental Retirement Income (prior to actuarial conversion to the form of benefit elected by Key Employee) will be paid without reduction for early commencement. In the event Key Employee commences receiving the Supplemental Retirement Income prior to his attainment of age 60, the Supplemental Retirement Income (prior to actuarial conversion to the form of benefit elected by Key Employee) will be subject to a reduction of 0.25% for each whole or partial month by which 60 years exceeds Key Employee's age as of such commencement of benefits.

(c) Except as otherwise expressly provided in the Employment Agreement, Key Employee's right to Supplemental Retirement Income will be wholly unvested until August 14, 2000, on which date, provided Key Employee remains employed by the Company until such date, such Income will become fully vested. Unless Key Employee's right to Supplemental Retirement Income shall have previously or thereupon become vested, Key Employee's rights thereto will be forfeited upon termination of his employment with the Company prior to August 14, 2000.

(d) If Key Employee dies after the date hereof but before Supplemental Retirement Income becomes payable, his spouse will receive a survivor annuity for her life equal to 50% of the aggregate annual benefit amount which would have been payable to Key Employee under this Section 3 if he had terminated his employment for Good Reason (as defined in the Employment Agreement) on the date immediately before his death (without regard to the additional two or three years of credited service described in Sections 4.01(f) and 5.04(b) of the Employment Agreement), but such survivor annuity will be reduced by the amount of (i) any pre-retirement survivor benefit payable under the Company's qualified and nonqualified defined benefit retirement plans (including but not limited to the Retirement Plan and the Plans) and (ii) survivor benefits under the Company's Disability and Survivorship Plan.

4. Supplemental Disability Income. Subject to Section 8, the Company agrees to pay Key Employee at the time set forth below a supplemental monthly disability income ("Supplemental Disability Income") equal to (a) minus (b), where

(a) equals the monthly disability benefit which the Key Employee would receive under the Disability and Survivorship Plan beginning on the Benefit Commencement Date (as defined below) if the Restrictions were not in effect and taking into account his or her elections under the Delta Air Lines, Inc. DELTAFLEX Plan; and

(b) equals the monthly disability benefit to which the Key Employee actually receives from the Disability and Survivorship Plan beginning on the Benefit Commencement Date, taking into account his or her elections under the Delta Air Lines,

Inc. DELTAFLEX Plan. The amount of Supplemental Disability Income paid under this Agreement will be adjusted as permitted under the Delta Air Lines, Inc. DELTAFLEX Plan, and if the amount in (b) above increases or decreases as a result of a change in the Restrictions.

5. Supplemental Monthly Survivor Income. Subject to Section 8, the Company agrees to pay to Eligible Family Member(s) (as defined in the Disability and Survivorship Plan) of Key Employee at Key Employee's death a supplemental monthly survivor income ("Supplemental Survivor Income") equal to (a) minus (b), where

(a) equals the monthly survivor benefit which the Eligible Family Member(s) of Key Employee would receive under the Disability and Survivorship Plan beginning on the Benefit Commencement Date (as defined below) without considering any Restrictions on any benefit plan; and

(b) equals the monthly survivor benefit which the Eligible Family Member(s) of Key Employee actually receives under the terms of the Disability and Survivorship Plan.

The amount of Supplemental Survivor Income paid under this Agreement will be adjusted as permitted under the Disability and Survivorship Plan and the Code to account for, inter alia, changes in the number of Eligible Family Members.

6. Benefit Commencement Date; Cessation of Benefits. Subject to Section 18 (Change in Control), the Company shall commence payment of the Supplemental Retirement Income as of the Benefit Commencement Date under the Retirement Plan and the Supplemental Disability or Survivor Income as of the Benefit Commencement Date under the Disability and Survivorship Plan. Subject to Section 18, Benefit Commencement Date under this Agreement shall mean the day that the retirement income benefit, disability benefit or survivor benefit, as the case may be, commences under the Retirement Plan or Disability and Survivorship Plan with respect to Key Employee or his Spouse, or Eligible Family Member(s); Supplemental Retirement Income will cease upon the death of the last to die of Key Employee or, if applicable, his Spouse, or if changes in the Restrictions permit the full benefit due under Section 3 hereof to be paid from the Retirement Plan and the Retirement Plan assumes such full payment, or if full payment of retirement benefits due hereunder have already been made. Supplemental Disability Income will cease if the full benefit due under the Disability and Survivorship Plan may be paid from that Plan and the Disability and Survivorship Plan assumes such full payment or when the Key Employee is no longer eligible for disability benefits under that Plan. Supplemental Survivor Income will cease if the full benefit due under the Disability and Survivorship Plan may be paid from that Plan, and the Disability and Survivorship Plan assumes full payment of the benefit amount or when there are no remaining Eligible Family Member(s) under that Plan. Subject to Section 18, all benefits (other than Supplemental Retirement Income benefits) payable hereunder may cease pursuant to Section 8 at any time.

7. Supplemental Lump Sum Death Benefit. Subject to Section 8, the Company agrees to pay to the named beneficiary (as designated by Key Employee for the Basic Life Benefit under the Disability and Survivorship Plan) of Key Employee at Key Employee's death, a supplemental lump sum death benefit in the amount necessary to provide a total lump sum death benefit of $50,000 when combined with the Basic Life Benefit actually provided by the Disability and Survivorship Plan. Such benefit shall be taken into account in determining the Company's compliance with any provision of the Employment Agreement providing for the payment of life insurance benefits, and the Company's obligations under this Section 7 shall be treated as discharged upon the purchase by the Company of a fully paid-up term life insurance policy on Key Employee's life pursuant to Section 5.04 (d)(ii) of the Employment Agreement.

8. Certain Restrictions. Subject to Section 18, or unless waived by the Committee under circumstances the Committee deems appropriate, if Key Employee terminates active employment with the Company prior to his Normal Retirement Date and within two years of such termination directly or indirectly provides management or executive services (whether as a consultant, advisor, officer or director) to any Person (as defined in Section 18) who is in direct and substantial competition with the air transportation business of the Company or any of its subsidiaries, then (a) if Supplemental Monthly Survivor Income or Supplemental Lump Sum Death benefits under this Agreement shall have not yet commenced, no such benefits shall be paid under this Agreement to Key Employee, his Spouse, Eligible Family Member or beneficiary; and (b) if Supplemental Monthly Survivor Income or Supplemental Lump Sum Death benefits under this Agreement have commenced, no further such benefits shall be paid. Because of the broad and extensive scope of the Company's air transportation business, the restrictions contained in this provision are intended to extend to management or executive services which are directly related to the provision of air transportation services into, within or from the United States, as no smaller geographical restriction will adequately protect the legitimate business interest of the Company.

9. Funding of Benefit. Subject to Section 18 (Change in Control) the benefits provided by this Agreement shall be paid, as they become due, from the Company's general assets or by such other means as the Company deems advisable, including a trust or trusts established by the Company, provided however, if such trusts are established, benefits shall be payable from such trusts only as and to the extent provided therein. To the extent Key Employee acquires the right to receive payments from the Company under this Agreement, such right shall be no greater than that of a general creditor of the Company. The Company shall have complete discretion under this Agreement to account for and report, or to refrain from accounting for or reporting, its liabilities under this Agreement. In the event that the Company in its sole discretion establishes a reserve or bookkeeping account for the benefits payable under this Agreement, the Key Employee shall have no proprietary or security interest in any such reserve or account.

10. Nonassignability of Benefits. No benefit payable under this Agreement may be assigned, transferred, encumbered or subjected to legal process for the payment of any claim against Key Employee, his Spouse, Eligible Family Member, or beneficiary.

11. No Right to Continued Employment. Nothing in this Agreement shall be deemed to give Key Employee the right to be retained in the service of the Company or to deny the Company any right it may have to discharge Key Employee at any time, subject to the Company's obligation to provide benefits and amounts as may be required hereunder.

12. Arbitration. The parties acknowledge that any claim or controversy arising out of this Agreement is subject to arbitration in accordance with the Employment Agreement.

13. Governing Law. This Agreement shall be governed by and construed in accordance with the laws of the State of Georgia without regard to its conflict of laws rules.

14. Successors and Assigns. This Agreement shall be binding upon the successors and assigns of the parties hereto.

15. Amendment. This writing and the Employment Agreement, including any terms or documents incorporated herein by reference, supersede any previous excess benefit agreement between Key Employee and the Company. This Agreement may not be modified orally, but only by writing signed by the parties hereto.

16. Notice. All notices, requests, demands and other communications under this Agreement, shall be in writing and shall be delivered personally (including by courier) or mailed by certified mail, return receipt requested. Refusal to acknowledge receipt of such notice shall constitute receipt of such notice upon the date it is returned to the sender. Any notice under this Agreement shall be sent to Key Employee, Spouse, his Eligible Family Member or beneficiary at the last known address of such person as reflected in the Company's records. Notice to the Company or the Committee shall be sent to:

Delta Air Lines, Inc.
Law Department
1030 Delta Boulevard
Atlanta, Georgia 30320

Attention: Robert S. Harkey, Senior Vice President—General Counsel

17. Form of Payment. If Key Employee becomes entitled to Supplemental Retirement Income under this Excess Benefit Agreement, such benefit shall automatically be paid in the identical form that benefits are payable under the Retirement Plan, subject to actuarial adjustment in accordance with the Retirement Plan, commencing with the date payments under the Retirement Plan begin.

18. Change in Control. Notwithstanding anything in this Agreement to the contrary, in the event a Change in Control (as defined below) occurs, the Company shall, if not previously established, establish a grantor trust (the "Trust") to provide

benefits payable under this Agreement. Subject to the following paragraph, the Company shall promptly cause to be irrevocably deposited in such Trust for the benefit of Key Employee and his or her beneficiaries, on the terms set forth below, an amount equal to the balance as of the date of such deposit of Key Employee's accrued benefit under this Agreement, regardless of whether such benefit is vested. From and after the date of such Change in Control, the Company shall cause to be irrevocably deposited in the Trust any additional accruals under this Agreement, regardless of whether such benefit is vested.

The instrument governing the Trust shall, to the extent reasonably necessary to assure that this Agreement will continue to be treated as "unfunded" for purposes of ERISA and the Code, provide that upon insolvency of the Company, the assets of the trust will be subject to the claims of the Company's general creditors. The Trust instrument shall provide that in all other respects the assets of the Trust will be maintained for the exclusive benefit of Key Employee and his or her beneficiaries, and will otherwise be subject to all fiduciary and other requirements of applicable state trust law.

In addition, in the event Employee's employment terminates under circumstances in which Section 5.04 of the Employment Agreement applies, Section 8 of this Agreement shall be deemed waived. Further, the timing and payments of any retirement benefits to be provided hereunder shall be governed by, and subject to, the terms of the Employment Agreement to the extent such Agreement provides for accelerated payments of retirement benefits otherwise payable under this Agreement.

For purposes of this Agreement, "Change in Control" means, and shall be deemed to have occurred upon, the first to occur of any of the following events:

(a) Any Person (other than an Excluded Person) acquires, together with all Affiliates and Associates of such Person, Beneficial Ownership of securities representing 20% or more of the combined voting power of the Voting Stock then outstanding, unless such Person acquires Beneficial Ownership of 20% or more of the combined voting power of the Voting Stock then outstanding solely as a result of an acquisition of Voting Stock by the Company which, by reducing the Voting Stock outstanding, increases the proportionate Voting Stock beneficially owned by such Person (together with all Affiliates and associates of such Person) to 20% or more of the combined voting power of the Voting Stock then outstanding; provided, that if a Person shall become the Beneficial Owner of 20% or more of the combined voting power of the Voting Stock then outstanding by reason of such Voting Stock acquisition by the Company and shall thereafter become the Beneficial Owner of any additional Voting Stock which causes the proportionate voting power of Voting Stock beneficially owned by such Person to increase to 20% or more of the combined voting power of the Voting Stock then outstanding, such Person shall, upon becoming the Beneficial Owner of such additional Voting Stock, be deemed to have become the Beneficial Owner of 20% or more of the combined voting power of the Voting Stock then outstanding other than solely as a result of such Voting Stock acquisition by the Company;

(b) During any period of two consecutive years (not including any period prior to the Effective Date), individuals who at the beginning of such period constitute the Board (and any new Director, whose election by the Board or nomination for election by the Company's stockholders was approved by a vote of at least two-thirds of the Directors then still in office who either were Directors at the beginning of the period or whose election or nomination for election was so approved), cease for any reason to constitute a majority of Directors then constituting the Board;

(c) A reorganization, merger or consolidation of the Company is consummated, in each case, unless, immediately following such reorganization, merger or consolidation, (i) more than 50% of, respectively, the then outstanding shares of common stock of the corporation resulting from such reorganization, merger or consolidation and the combined voting power of the then outstanding voting securities of such corporation entitled to vote generally in the election of directors is then beneficially owned, directly or indirectly, by all or substantially all OF the individuals and entities who were the beneficial owners of the Voting Stock outstanding immediately prior to such reorganization, merger or consolidation, (ii) no Person (but excluding for this purpose any Excluded Person and any Person beneficially owning, immediately prior to such reorganization, merger or consolidation, directly or indirectly, 20% or more of the voting power of the outstanding Voting Stock) beneficially owns, directly or indirectly, 20% or more of, respectively, the then outstanding shares of common stock of the corporation resulting from such reorganization, merger or consolidation or the combined voting power of the then outstanding voting securities of such corporation entitled to vote generally in the election of directors and (iii) at least a majority of the members of the board of directors of the corporation resulting from such reorganization, merger or consolidation were members of the Board at the time of the execution of the initial agreement providing for such reorganization, merger or consolidation; or

(d) The shareholders of the Company approve (i) a complete liquidation or dissolution of the Company or (ii) the sale or other disposition of all or substantially all of the assets of the Company, other than to any corporation with respect to which, immediately following such sale or other disposition, (A) more than 50% of, respectively, the then outstanding shares of common stock of such corporation and the combined voting power of the then outstanding voting securities of such corporation entitled to vote generally in the election of directors is then beneficially owned, directly or indirectly, by all or substantially all of the individuals and entities who were the beneficial owners of the Voting Stock outstanding immediately prior to such sale or other disposition of assets, (B) no Person (but excluding for this purpose any Excluded Person and any Person beneficially owning, immediately prior to such sale or other disposition, directly or indirectly, 20% or more of the voting power of the outstanding Voting Stock) beneficially owns, directly or indirectly, 20% or more of, respectively, the then outstanding shares of common stock of such corporation or the combined voting power of the then outstanding voting securities of such corporation entitled to vote generally in the election of directors and (C) at least a majority of the members of the board of directors of such corporation were members of the Board at the time of the execution of the initial agreement or action of the Board providing for such sale or other disposition of assets of the Company.

Notwithstanding the foregoing, in no event shall a "Change in Control" be deemed to have occurred (i) as a result of the formation of a Holding Company, or (ii) with respect to Key Employee, if Key Employee is part of a "group," within the meaning of Section 13(d)(3) of the Exchange Act as in effect on the Effective Date, which consummates the Change in Control transaction. In addition, for purposes of the definition of "Change in Control" a Person engaged in business as an underwriter of securities shall not be deemed to be the "Beneficial Owner" of, or to "beneficially own," any securities acquired through such Person's participation in good faith in a firm commitment underwriting until the expiration of forty days after the date of such acquisition.

As used in the above definition, "Person" shall mean an individual, corporation, partnership, association, trust or any other entity or organization. "Excluded Person" means (i) the Company; (ii) any of the Company's Subsidiaries; (iii) any Holding Company; (iv) any employee benefit plan of the Company, any of its Subsidiaries or a Holding Company; or (v) any Person organized, appointed or established by the Company, any of its Subsidiaries or a Holding Company for or pursuant to the terms of any plan described in clause (iv). "Affiliate" and "Associate" have the respective meanings accorded to such terms in Rule 12b-2 under the Exchange Act as in effect on the Effective Date. A Person shall be deemed the "Beneficial Owner" of, and shall be deemed to "beneficially own," securities pursuant to Rule 13d-3 under the Exchange Act as in effect on the Effective Date. "Voting Stock" means securities of the Company entitled to vote generally in the election of members of the Board. "Board" means the Board of Directors of the Company. "Exchange Act" means the Securities Exchange Act of 1934. "Holding Company" means an entity that becomes a holding company for the Company or its businesses as a part of any reorganization, merger, consolidation or other transaction, provided that the outstanding shares of common stock of such entity and the combined voting power of the then outstanding voting securities of such entity entitled to vote generally in the election of directors is, immediately after such reorganization, merger, consolidation or other transaction, beneficially owned, directly or indirectly, by all or substantially all of the individuals and entities who were the beneficial owners, respectively, of the Voting Stock outstanding immediately prior to such reorganization, merger, consolidation or other transaction in substantially the same proportions as their ownership, immediately prior to such reorganization, merger, consolidation or other transaction, of such outstanding Voting Stock.

IN WITNESS WHEREOF, the parties hereto have set their hands and seals on the date first set forth above.

DELTA AIR LINES, INC.

By:

_____

Gerald Grinstein Chairman of the Board

KEY EMPLOYEE

_____

Leo F. Mullin

PART III

Related Issues

CHAPTER 8

Ownership of the Corporation

I. INTRODUCTION

It has long been believed that many of the problems associated with the modern corporation arise from the separation of the ownership from the control of the corporation.[1] This separation, and the conflicting incentives of owners (value maximization) and managers (utility maximization) has been termed the *agency problem,* with the resulting costs called *agency costs.* Consequently, many have argued (e.g., Jensen and Meckling 1976) that increasing managerial ownership will reduce those problems by aligning the interests of management and shareholders.

Consider the following example. The CEO of a major corporation is considering the purchase of a corporate jet for $10 million. Although the corporation does not need the jet, the CEO wants it for the status it conveys. If the CEO owns 1% of the corporation, his or her wealth will decrease by $100,000 as a result of the purchase. Consequently, as long as the value placed on the jet by the CEO exceeds $100,000, he or she will have the corporation purchase the jet. However, if the CEO owns 10% of the corporation, his or her wealth would decrease by $1 million as a result of the purchase. Obviously, it is less likely he or she will value the jet at $1 million, and hence the corporation is less likely to purchase the jet. In generic terms, as CEO ownership increases, he or she bears more of the costs of his or her nonvalue-maximizing actions, such as overconsumption of perquisites, and as a result, is more likely to act to maximize firm value.

Many of those making the argument that increasing managerial ownership will reduce agency costs also argue that current levels of ownership are too low (see, e.g., Jensen and Murphy 1990a). Although it has not been empirically established that higher managerial ownership leads to better firm performance (Loderer and Martin 1997; Himmelberg et al. 1999), to increase executive ownership many corporations have instituted stock option and grant programs, and they have set

---

[1] The modern literature on this topic can be traced back to Berle and Means (1932).

minimum levels for executive ownership. For example, Wells Fargo sets ownership goals and provides a stock option program, including reload options, to help executives meet those goals:

> Each executive officer is assigned stock ownership goals to be met by specified dates. Executive officers achieve these goals primarily by exercising stock options and retaining a substantial portion of the stock acquired. Once the basic ownership level is met, the goal continues to increase each time an executive officer exercises a stock option or a restricted stock grant vests. All executive officers named in the Summary Compensation Table have exceeded their ownership goals.[2]

What is particularly interesting is the second sentence of the following paragraph, which alludes to the fact that if the executive does not meet those ownership goals, he or she will be penalized via a reduction in the size of future stock option grants.

> In determining original option grants each year, the 162(m) Committee considers the number of shares of common stock owned by the executive officer compared to the executive officer's ownership goal and the stock option grant practices of the Peer Group at the time of grant. If the executive officer does not meet his or her stock ownership goal, the number of stock options granted by the 162(m) Committee to the executive officer in the future will be less than banking organizations in the Peer Group would grant to their executive officers with comparable positions. The 162(m) Committee also encourages executive officers to achieve their stock ownership goals by including in original option grants a reload feature. If the optionee exercises the original option and pays for the option shares by delivering shares of previously owned common stock or shares purchased in the market, the optionee receives a reload option. Under a reload option, the optionee can purchase the same number of whole shares of stock, at their fair market value on the date the original option is exercised, as were used to pay the option exercise price and related taxes. Reload options are exercisable at any time during the remaining term of the original option. Reload options allow the exercise of the original option early in its term while preserving the executive officer's opportunity for future appreciation in the shares delivered to exercise the original option. The 162(m) Committee believes that the reload feature encourages executive officers to acquire and retain the Company's stock.[3]

Conyon and Murphy (2000) found that in 1997 the average CEO owned 3.1% (median 0.29%) of the shares in his or her corporation. However, once they aggregated ownership, options, and long-term incentives, they arrived at an effective ownership percentage of 4.18% (median 1.48%). Incorporating options and other long-term components of the compensation package provide a better measure of the CEO's incentives to increase shareholder value than looking at ownership alone, as it shows the percentage of the increase in shareholder wealth that would flow to the CEO. Consequently, Tables 8.1 through 8.6 show CEO stock ownership, and stock ownership including stock options, for large United States corporations (firms

---

[2]Wells Fargo proxy statement filed with Securities and Exchange Commission, March 20, 2000, p. 18.

[3]Wells Fargo proxy statement filed with Securities and Exchange Commission, March 20, 2000, p. 18.

TABLE 8.1   Ownership as a Percentage of Shares Outstanding by Year

	Mean			Median		
Year	Shares (%)	Options (%)	Shares + options (%)	Shares (%)	Options (%)	Shares + options (%)
1992	2.85	0.72	3.57	0.20	0.28	0.73
1993	3.30	0.83	4.13	0.36	0.38	1.21
1994	3.29	0.98	4.27	0.44	0.52	1.52
1995	3.20	1.03	4.23	0.41	0.58	1.52
1996	3.22	1.14	4.36	0.41	0.67	1.71
1997	3.42	1.30	4.72	0.39	0.77	1.81
1998	3.24	1.33	4.56	0.40	0.84	1.88
1999	3.45	1.43	4.88	0.44	0.92	1.96
2000	2.53	1.24	3.78	0.30	0.86	1.57

in the S&P 500, MidCap, and SmallCap indexes). Table 8.1 shows ownership as a percentage of outstanding shares. Mean (median) ownership is comparable to that found by Conyon and Murphy, ranging from a low of 2.53% (0.30%) in 2000 to 3.45% (0.44%) in 1999. After including options (both exercisable and unexercisable), this percentage increases to 3.78% (1.57%) in 2000 and 4.88% (1.96%) in 1999. In both cases, it is interesting to note the decline in ownership from 1999–2000, which may be coincidental, or may be associated with the overall market decline observed in 2000. Table 8.2 shows that ownership varies across industries, with wholesale and retail trade having the highest share and option ownership (mean

TABLE 8.2   Ownership as a Percentage of Shares Outstanding by Industry (for 2000)

Industry	Standard industrial classification codes	Mean			Median		
		Shares (%)	Options (%)	Shares + options (%)	Shares (%)	Option (%)	Shares + options (%)
Mining and construction	1000–1999	0.99	1.08	2.08	0.20	0.60	0.80
Manufacturing	2000–3999	2.23	1.32	3.55	0.28	0.94	1.58
Transportation, communications, electric, gas, and sanitary services	4000–4999	1.70	0.67	2.37	0.17	0.40	0.80
Wholesale and retail trade	5000–5999	4.02	1.41	5.43	0.61	1.02	2.13
Finance, insurance, and real estate	6000–6999	2.14	0.96	3.11	0.33	0.57	1.31
Services	7000–7999	3.72	1.59	5.31	0.47	1.28	2.44

TABLE 8.3   Ownership as a Percentage of Shares Outstanding by Size (for 2000)

	Size decile	Mean			Median		
		Shares (%)	Options (%)	Shares + options (%)	Shares (%)	Options (%)	Shares + options (%)
Smallest	1	4.27	2.09	6.36	0.55	1.64	2.74
	2	4.84	1.67	6.51	1.04	1.35	2.64
	3	4.31	1.43	5.74	0.80	1.27	2.36
	4	2.10	1.42	3.52	0.42	0.99	1.80
	5	1.77	1.39	3.16	0.32	1.05	1.74
	6	1.39	1.13	2.52	0.29	0.75	1.26
	7	1.18	1.06	2.25	0.20	0.83	1.18
	8	2.20	1.01	3.22	0.14	0.55	1.11
	9	1.75	0.85	2.59	0.16	0.55	0.82
Largest	10	1.57	0.42	1.98	0.09	0.23	0.40

5.43%, median 2.13%) and mining and construction having the lowest ownership (mean 2.08%, median 0.80%). Table 8.3 shows that mean and median share and option ownership percentage is generally inversely related to size, with ownership dropping from 6.36% (median 2.74%) for the smallest to 1.98% (0.40%) for the largest corporations. The latter finding makes sense given an executive's wealth constraint. That is, it costs more to buy a given percentage of a larger corporation than it does to purchase the same percentage of a smaller corporation. Overall, the ownership percentages are rather low, indicating the potential for agency problems. To be more precise, ownership percentages are low relative to 100%, where the owner–manager bears the full cost and receives the full benefit of his or her actions. As illustrated in the introduction to this chapter, as the ownership percentage increases, the owner becomes less likely to take costly actions (for example, purchasing a corporate jet) that reduce shareholder value because he or she bears a greater percentage of that cost.

Tables 8.4, 8.5, and 8.6 provide the dollar value of CEO ownership as of the end of the year. It is calculated by multiplying the number of shares owned by the year-end price and adding to that amount the intrinsic value of in-the-money options (the intrinsic value of the options is the profit that would be realized if the options were exercised at that point in time). As shown in the table, the amounts are quite large and growing rapidly, with the value of share and option ownership increasing from a mean (median) of $46,878,461 ($5,109,750) in 1992 to $353,437,665 ($18,298,000) in 2000. Thus, CEOs have substantial investments in their firms, even if, as a percentage of total shares outstanding, their ownership is low. Furthermore, it appears that the long bull market greatly increased the value of CEO ownership over the period under examination.

Table 8.5 shows that dollar amounts vary by industry, ranging from a mean (median) of $26,558,835 ($14,379,875) for mining and construction firms to

TABLE 8.4   Dollar Value of Ownership by Year

	Mean			Median		
Year	Shares ($)	Options ($)	Shares + options ($)	Shares ($)	Options ($)	Shares + options ($)
1992	44,314,548	2,563,913	46,878,461	3,165,375	643,000	5,109,750
1993	47,343,917	3,123,426	50,467,343	4,306,875	860,500	6,575,625
1994	44,894,915	2,947,312	47,842,227	4,026,500	641,500	6,535,500
1995	55,442,086	10,552,901	65,994,986	4,631,625	1,181,000	8,369,250
1996	66,605,507	9,012,373	75,617,880	5,103,938	1,833,000	9,622,875
1997	94,767,982	15,334,844	110,102,826	6,382,080	2,643,500	13,180,160
1998	121,648,883	30,769,830	152,418,712	6,087,625	2,144,000	12,349,563
1999	170,549,981	103,030,661	273,580,642	7,303,250	1,955,000	14,716,438
2000	219,470,733	133,966,932	353,437,665	8,613,000	3,750,000	18,298,000

$1,214,930,784 ($35,365,250) for service firms. Table 8.6 shows that the dollar amounts increase with firm size, ranging from a mean (median) of $7,528,392 ($1,404,406) for the smallest firms to $2,448,110,013 ($142,631,375) for the largest firms. This holds despite the inverse relationship between firm size and ownership percentage documented in Table 8.3, indicating that although the dollar value of ownership increases with firm size, it does not increase as much as market value.

II. THE AFFECT OF EXECUTIVE OWNERSHIP ON INCENTIVES

Table 8.7 shows CEO ownership for a sample of well-known U.S. corporations. Firms such as Berkshire Hathaway and Amazon.com, which are at the top of the list, can pay less attention to their compensation packages simply because their ownership structure provides their CEO with the proper incentives. As discussed in Chapter 3, both corporations compensate their chief executives solely with salary.[4] And yet each has done a good job of increasing shareholder wealth. Their large ownership provides the incentive to exert effort and take actions to increase firm value. Thus, ownership can take the place of stock options and grants in providing executives with the proper set of incentives.[5] In fact, a growing body of research shows (Jensen and Murphy 1990a; Hall and Liebman 1998; and Murphy 1998) that CEO ownership (including options) accounts for the bulk of the sensitivity of CEO wealth to firm performance.

[4]This is an oversimplification, as each also receives pension and other benefits. They do not, however, receive any compensation conditioned on performance.

[5]Researchers have looked at whether ownership does take the place of stock options and grants, finding conflicting results. Mehran (1995) found an inverse relation between ownership and stock-based compensation, whereas Lewellen, Loderer, and Martin (1987) and Yermack (1995) did not.

TABLE 8.5   Dollar Value of Ownership by Industry (for 2000)

Industry	Standard industrial classification codes	Mean Shares ($)	Mean Options ($)	Mean Shares + options ($)	Median Shares ($)	Median Options ($)	Median Shares + options ($)
Mining and construction	1000–1999	16,587,921	9,970,914	26,558,835	7,837,500	4,868,000	14,379,875
Manufacturing	2000–3999	96,948,620	99,768,303	196,716,923	6,069,000	3,231,000	16,048,750
Transportation, communications, electric, gas, and sanitary services	4000–4999	130,324,949	70,298,970	200,623,919	4,571,531	3,276,500	14,197,406
Wholesale and retail trade	5000–5999	84,931,815	51,006,612	135,938,427	9,014,250	1,305,000	16,133,750
Finance, insurance, and real estate	6000–6999	496,245,465	112,889,528	609,134,993	21,779,313	12,736,000	52,740,500
Services	7000–7999	719,522,085	495,408,699	1,214,930,784	10,915,875	6,650,000	35,365,250

TABLE 8.6   Dollar Value of Ownership, by Size (for 2000)

		Mean			Median		
	Size decile	Shares ($)	Options ($)	Shares + options ($)	Shares ($)	Options ($)	Shares + options ($)
Smallest	1	6,938,902	589,489	7,528,392	675,844	12,500	1,404,406
	2	22,227,189	2,325,663	24,552,852	4,487,375	928,500	6,313,875
	3	34,617,702	3,027,146	37,644,848	6,055,000	1,335,000	9,204,375
	4	25,902,060	6,581,381	32,483,441	5,475,000	1,956,000	12,519,500
	5	32,689,989	8,629,427	41,319,416	5,904,750	3,583,500	14,228,584
	6	41,052,868	10,439,306	51,492,174	8,057,219	4,618,000	17,768,094
	7	62,529,187	28,976,041	91,505,229	10,042,500	8,129,000	23,246,875
	8	184,573,765	157,323,220	341,896,985	11,336,063	10,452,000	34,678,938
	9	222,449,752	189,849,033	412,298,785	20,002,063	37,312,500	67,896,938
Largest	10	1,531,253,373	916,856,640	2,448,110,013	56,178,938	55,350,500	142,631,375

TABLE 8.7   Examples of CEO Ownership

Corporation	Executive	Position	Ownership (%)
Berkshire Hathaway	Warren Buffett	Chairman and Chief Executive Officer	35.6[a]
Amazon.com	Jeffrey Bezos	Chairman and Chief Executive Officer	33.6[b]
Microsoft	William Gates	Chairman and Chief Software Architect	13.7[c]
Dell Computer	Michael Dell	Chairman and Chief Executive Officer	12.4[d]
Eastman Kodak	George M.C. Fisher	Chairman and Chief Executive Officer	1.0[e]
Xerox	Paul A. Allaire	Chairman	0.5[f]
Cisco	John T. Chambers	President and Chief Executive Officer	0.2[g]
General Electric	John Welch	Chairman and Chief Executive Officer	0.1[h]

[a]Berkshire Hathaway proxy statement filed with Securities and Exchange Commission, March 20, 2000, p. 6.

[b]Amazon.com proxy statement filed with Securities and Exchange Commission, March 29, 2000, p. 5.

[c]Microsoft proxy statement filed with Securities and Exchange Commission, September 28, 2000.

[d]Dell Computer proxy statement filed with Securities and Exchange Commission, May 30, 2000, p. 17.

[e]Eastman Kodak proxy statement filed with Securities and Exchange Commission, March 13, 2000, p. 29.

[f]Xerox proxy statement filed with Securities and Exchange Commission, April 7, 2000, p. 13.

[g]Cisco proxy statement filed with Securities and Exchange Commission, September 28, 2000, p. 7.

[h]General Electric proxy statement filed with Securities and Exchange Commission, March 13, 2000.

It should be noted though that CEO ownership does not have to be high for the shareholders to do well. The last row of Table 8.7 shows that John Welch, CEO of General Electric, who has presided over an enormous increase in shareholder wealth, owns 0.1% of GE's shares, about average for the largest firms (Table 8.3

shows that the median for the largest firms is 0.09%). However, Mr. Welch receives lots of incentives via his compensation package. That is, in contrast to Warren Buffett and Jeff Bezos (respective CEOs of Berkshire Hathaway and Amazon.com who only receive salary, and minimal amounts at that), Welch received, in 1999, $3,325,000 in salary, an annual bonus of $10,000,000, payout from a long-term incentive plan of $31,325,000, and 625,000 stock options.[6]

A. Affect of Executive Ownership on Risk Preferences

The issue, however, is much more complex. Although ownership provides incentive to increase firm value, as any increase in stock price increases the executive's wealth, it also affects risk preferences. An executive with much of his or her wealth tied up in the firm may be more risk averse than optimal, passing up value-increasing investments that also increase firm risk. Thus we observe executives and major shareholders, for example, Michael Dell and Bill Gates, selling shares in their companies from time to time.[7] Consistent with this diversification argument, Murphy (1998, p. 37) found evidence suggesting that "executives with large option holdings rationally reduce their unrestricted stock holdings."

B. Affect of Executive Ownership on Corporate Performance

Academic research is, however, inconclusive as to whether increased executive ownership leads to improved performance. In a recent paper, Himmelberg et al. (1999) noted, "we cannot conclude (econometrically) that changes in managerial ownership affect firm performance" (p. 354). Yet Core and Larcker (2000), who examined a sample of firms that institute ownership requirements, concluded that "for this sample of firms, required increases in the level of managerial equity ownership are associated with improvements in firm performance." And earlier, Mehran (1995) concluded that "Firm performance is positively related to the percentage of equity held by managers" (p. 163).

One possible explanation for these conflicting results is that although insider ownership does affect performance, the relationship is not a linear one. At low levels, increases in ownership improve firm performance, but once ownership increases beyond a certain level, management becomes entrenched (Morck et al. 1988). That is, once their ownership exceeds a certain level, management is unlikely to be fired, and hence, a major incentive to perform well is removed.

[6]General Electric proxy statement filed with Securities and Exchange Commission, March 13, 2000.
[7]For example, on October 10, 2000, Michael Dell filed a form 4 indicating that he had sold or otherwise disposed of, 26,401 shares of Dell Computer Common Stock on September 14, 2000.

C. Executive Ownership Requirements

Despite the inconclusive academic evidence, there has been a trend toward requiring executives to own stock.[8] One example is American General:

> In support of the company's desire to increase employee ownership and foster a "pay for performance" culture, employees eligible for variable compensation are encouraged to acquire and retain shares of Common Stock (within 5 years of becoming eligible for variable compensation) that equal or exceed a multiple of their base salary as follows:

> *Stock ownership guidelines (as a % of base salary)*

Chairman	8x
Vice-chairmen	7x
Other members of the management committee	6x
Salary greater than or equal to $300,000	5x
Salary between $250,000 and $299,999	4x
Salary between $200,000 and $249,999	3x
Salary between $150,000 and $199,999	1.50x
Salary between $100,000 and $149,999	0.75x
Salary between $65,000 and $99,999	0.50x[9]

As shown, American General encourages employees to meet certain ownership guidelines, which are linked to, and decline with, rank and salary. That is, although the chairman of the board is required to own shares valued at eight times (8×) base salary, an individual earning between $65,000 and $99,9999 is only required to own shares worth one-half (0.50×) his or her base salary. Whereas American General encourages ownership, American Express requires it, as illustrated by the following passage:

> SHARE OWNERSHIP. The Company's share ownership policy requires about 150 senior officers to meet share ownership targets. The program includes these key features:
> * Participants have a share ownership target based on a multiple of their base salary, ranging from three times base salary for certain participants to 20 times for Mr. Golub.
> * As an incentive to maximize shareholder value, a participant may count toward his or her target the value of owned shares, 50% of the unrealized gain in stock options and 50% of the market value of restricted shares, with market value based on the market price of the Company's common shares.
> * The Committee expects participants to meet their targets within 5 years and to make pro rata progress each year.[10]

The number of executives required to purchase shares differs across companies. American General, although not disclosing the number of executives covered by

[8]Gilles (1999) reported, "Thirty-five percent of public companies maintain stock ownership guidelines, according to the '1997 Long-Term and Equity Survey' by William M. Mercer/KPMG" (p. 44).

[9]American General proxy statement filed with Securities and Exchange Commission, March 21, 2000, p. 12.

[10]American Express proxy statement filed with Securities and Exchange Commission, March 10, 2000, p. 27.

the guidelines, extends those guidelines to all employees eligible for variable compensation. American Express has guidelines for its top 150 executives, whereas the Tribune Corporation has guidelines for its top 120 executives and has extended those guidelines to their directors, as follows:

> Effective January 1, 1996, the Committee implemented stock ownership guidelines for approximately 85 executives. The guidelines generally range from a high of five times annual salary in the case of Mr. Madigan to two times annual salary. Executives are expected to achieve the suggested ownership level over a 5-year period in increments of 20% per year. Shares held in Tribune benefit plans are counted in satisfying the guidelines but unexercised stock options are not counted. The Committee believes that these guidelines have the positive effect of further aligning the interests of Tribune's executives with those of its shareholders. All of the executive officers named in the summary compensation table have achieved their suggested stock ownership levels. The stock ownership guidelines were revised in February 2000 such that they now range from a high of ten times annual salary in the case of Mr. Madigan to two times annual salary and apply to approximately 120 executives.[11]
>
> Effective March 1, 2000, Tribune established a stock ownership guideline for its outside directors. The suggested stock ownership level is five times the most recent annual stock award paid to outside directors. Based on the 1999 annual stock award of $50,000, the present guideline is $250,000. Outside directors are expected to achieve the suggested ownership level over a 5-year period in increments of 20% per year. Tribune shares held in deferred compensation accounts are counted in satisfying the guideline but unexercised stock options are not. Tribune believes that this guideline has the positive effect of further aligning the interests of Tribune's outside directors with those of its shareholders. All of Tribune's outside directors presently satisfy the suggested stock ownership level.[12]

A somewhat interesting trend is that of corporations, in this case Louisiana-Pacific, requiring executives to own shares, and then lending them the money to make the purchase:

> In November 1999, the subcommittee of the Compensation Committee approved an Executive Loan Program under which up to 1,700,000 shares of the Common Stock were offered by L-P for purchase prior to January 23, 2000, by L-P's executive officers, Business Team Leaders, and other executives designated by its chief executive officer. Participants were permitted to borrow up to 100 percent of the purchase price of the shares to be purchased, which was equal to the closing price of the Common Stock on the New York Stock Exchange (NYSE) on the date of delivery of an election to participate to L-P. The maximum amount an individual was permitted to borrow was three times his or her annual base pay.
>
> The loans bear interest at the annual rate of 6.02%. Interest and principal are due and payable at the earlier of January 23, 2005, or 30 days following the executive's resignation or involuntary termination of employment. The loans are unsecured. If an executive with a loan outstanding remains employed by L-P on January 23, 2005, or dies or becomes disabled while employed prior to that date, one-half of the loan principal and accrued interest will be forgiven if the executive still owns all the shares purchased under the program and the Common Stock has traded on the NYSE at a price of $23 per share (subject to adjustment for stock dividends or other recapitalizations) for at least five consecutive trading days during the preceding 12 months.

[11]Tribune proxy statement filed with Securities and Exchange Commission, March 24, 2000, p. 13.
[12]Tribune proxy statement filed with Securities and Exchange Commission, March 24, 2000, p. 9.

A total of 966,884 shares of Common Stock were purchased by 19 executives during the period from November 29, 1999 to January 21, 2000, for a total purchase price of $11,649,887. The following table provides loan information for L-P's executive officers. The loan amounts shown represent both the original principal amount and the amount outstanding at March 3, 2000.

Name	Loan amount	Share price	No. of shares
J. Ray Barbee	$ 599,991	$13.625	44,036
F. Jeff Duncan	542,191	13.000	41,707
Warren C. Easley	349,994	11.625	30,107
Richard W. Frost	599,990	11.625	51,612
M. Ward Hubbell	416,803	11.625	35,854
J. Keith Matheney	688,491	11.625	59,225
Curtis M. Stevens	719,994	11.625	61,935
Mark A. Suwyn	2,141,999	11.625	184,258
Michael J. Tull	656,999	11.625	56,516
Gary C. Wilkerson	854,996	11.625	73,548
Walter M. Wirfs	569,997	11.625	49,032[13]

Note that under the terms of the plan, participants are allowed to borrow up to 100% of the purchase price of the shares, thus no investment on their part is required. The interest rate is relatively low, the loans are unsecured, and half may be forgiven if certain conditions are met. If the share price declines the company may simply have to forgive the loans. Consider the saga of Conseco. At one time a stellar performer, Conseco arranged for and guaranteed bank loans for its executives to purchase shares of stock. It even loaned the executives money to pay interest on the loans. When the share price declined dramatically, the shares were worth substantially less than the loan balances.[14] Hallinan (2000b) reported that subsequently, two directors of Conseco were removed from the board for failure to pay back these loans.

If the effect of executive ownership on performance is inconclusive, and corporations have to assist their executives in purchasing the shares via loans and the counting of stock option gains, the question arises as to why firms are so concerned with managerial ownership. The answer is simple. Instituting mandatory or voluntary guidelines is good politics; it looks good for both the shareholders and politicians.

III. THE EFFECT OF EXECUTIVE OWNERSHIP ON EXECUTIVE COMPENSATION

Some CEOs who are major shareholders take relatively modest compensation, for example, Warren Buffett, owner of approximately 35% of Berkshire Hathaway, receives an annual salary of $100,000, and Jeff Bezos, owner of approximately 33%

[13]Louisiana-Pacific proxy statement filed with Securities and Exchange Commission, March 20, 2000, p. 25.

[14]Conseco proxy statement filed with Securities and Exchange Commission, May 23, 2000, p. 18.

of Amazon.com, receives an annual salary of $81,840. In contrast, Saul Steinberg owns 31.3% of Reliance Group:[15]

> Since 1991 alone, Mr. Steinberg has received a total of more than $48 million in salary and bonuses from Reliance, according to proxy materials. During that time, Reliance shares have plunged 95%, compared with a gain of 666% at comparable insurers and 334% for the Standard & Poors index . . .[16]

A. Affect of Executive Ownership on the Level of Compensation

CEO ownership provides two sets of incentives with respect to compensation, as illustrated by these divergent examples. This arises from the owner–manager conflict and the ability of the CEO to control the transfer of wealth from shareholders to managers and vice versa. On the one hand, since the pay of subordinates is usually pegged to that of the CEO, a CEO with large shareholdings has the incentive to reduce his or her pay since doing so will decrease that of subordinates and increase shareholder wealth. On the other hand, a CEO with large shareholdings has the ability to control the corporation, and with it, his or her own compensation. If the CEO owns 50% of the corporation, each $1 increase in his or her own compensation decreases the value of his or her shares by only 50 cents.[17] Thus, the CEO has some incentive to increase his or her compensation at the expense of the other shareholders. In this very simple example, the CEO will increase his or her compensation as long as he or she is able to keep the total increase in compensation to lower level employees to $1 or less.[18] Given that few CEOs own anywhere near 50% of their corporations, the latter effect, that is, enriching his or herself at the expense of shareholders, may predominate. Empirical research on this issue is mixed, with Dyl (1988) and Mallette et al. (1995) finding that increases in CEO ownership lead to increases in CEO compensation, and Allen (1981) and Core et al. (1999) finding that increases in CEO ownership lead to lower CEO compensation.

B. Affect of Executive Ownership on the Composition of the Compensation Package

CEO ownership also influences the composition of the compensation package. As noted above, Warren Buffett and Jeff Bezos's compensation packages are solely

---

[15]Reliance Group Holdings proxy statement filed with Securities and Exchange Commission, June 5, 2000, p. 6.

[16]Zuckerman et al. (2000) p. C1.

[17]Ignoring taxes and/or transaction costs, which may make the actual cost higher or lower.

[18]To elaborate, if the CEO who owns 50% of the corporation increases his or her own compensation by $1 and that of subordinates by $1, then the increase in the CEO's compensation will be exactly offset by the decrease in value of the CEO's shareholdings.

composed of cash. There is no need for any form of incentive compensation as their ownership provides all the necessary incentives. At lower levels of ownership, however, incentive compensation is needed. Toyne et al. (2000) find that at low levels of ownership, the proportion of stock-based compensation in the compensation package is positively related to board (including the CEO) ownership. As ownership increases, however, the association between the proportion of stock-based compensation and board ownership decreases, consistent with the marginal incentive affect of additional stock-based compensation being outweighed by the risk to the CEO caused by underdiversification, which reduces the valuation placed on that stock-based compensation by the CEO.

IV. THE EFFECT OF DIRECTOR'S OWNERSHIP ON EXECUTIVE COMPENSATION

As will be discussed more fully in the next chapter, to some extent the agency problem that exists between shareholders and managers also exists between shareholders and directors. In the absence of a substantial equity investment on the part of directors, their interests may lie with those of management, whom they are supposed to supervise, rather than shareholders, to whom they have a fiduciary responsibility. Bhagat et al. (1998) argued the following:

> Without the direct economic incentive of substantial stock ownership, directors, given a natural loyalty to their appointing party and the substantial reputation enhancement and monetary compensation board service came to entail, had little incentive other than their legal fiduciary duties to engage in active managerial oversight. (p. 3)

Both Bhagat et al. (1998) and Core et al. (1999) found the average director owns a relatively small proportion of corporation stock. Bhagat et al. (1998) found mean (median) ownership of 0.57% (0.02%), whereas Core et al. found mean (median) ownership of 0.136% (0.005%). Core et al. (1999) found CEO compensation inversely related to percentage stock ownership per director.

V. THE EFFECT OF LARGE SHAREHOLDERS AND INSTITUTIONAL OWNERSHIP ON EXECUTIVE COMPENSATION

Executives in general, and CEOs in particular, may be able to enrich themselves at the expense of shareholders who, for the most part, lack the resources and/or incentive to resist. The existence of large shareholders and the trend toward institutional ownership [for example, Balsam et al. (2000a) found approximately 50% of shares held by institutions] may mitigate this problem because those shareholders have the incentives and ability to both monitor and resist management, and coalesce to oppose management if necessary. Large shareholders have this incentive because if they can effect a policy change that increases firm value, they will garner a larger portion of that increase than small shareholders. Furthermore, large shareholders, because they cannot sell their shares readily without causing a stock price decline, may have no choice but to be active in monitoring management. They have the ability to impact management in general and executive compensation in particular, through their ability to vote for and elect board members willing to act in their interests.

In fact, the mere existence of a large shareholder or ownership by an activist institutional shareholder, such as CaLPERS (California Public Employees Retirement System), may be enough to persuade executives to moderate their compensation demands. These shareholders may persuade executives to mitigate their compensation demands privately or via a shareholder proposal,[19] which is allowed under Securities and Exchange Commission Rule 14a-8 (§240.14a-8).[20] In addition, if a proposal on executive compensation is made, large shareholders are more likely to pay for and receive advice from voting advisory services, such as Institutional Shareholder Services (http://www.isstf.com/).

A. Affect of Large and Institutional Shareholders on the Level of Compensation

Allen (1981) found CEOs of corporations where no shareholder owned 5% or more of the firm received higher compensation. Both Lambert et al. (1993) and Core et al. (1999) found that the existence of an insider other than the CEO owning 5% of the firm decreased the CEO's compensation, as did the existence of an outside blockholder owning 5% or more of the firm. Hartzell and Starks (2000) found "a significantly negative relation between the level of compensation and the concentration of institutional ownership" (p. 1). David et al. (1998) found that both large noninstitutional shareholders and pressure-resistant institutional shareholders reduce the level of CEO compensation.

---

[19]Thomas and Martin (1999) found that "target companies do not increase average total CEO compensation levels as rapidly in the year after receiving a shareholder proposal (on average two percent increases) as firms not receiving such proposals (on average 22.3% increases)" (p. 1022).

[20]Among other requirements, rule 14a-8 requires that a shareholder continuously hold at least $2,000 in market value, or 1%, of the corporation's securities entitled to be voted on the proposal at the meeting for at least 1 year and continue to hold those securities through the date of the meeting to be eligible to submit a proposal. Consequently, both small and large shareholders have the ability to submit shareholder proposals. However, large shareholders can make more of an impact because of the larger number of shares they vote in support of their proposal and their ability to communicate with other shareholders. Thomas and Martin (1999) find that the higher the level of voting support for a proposal, the smaller the subsequent increases in CEO compensation.

B. Affect of Large and Institutional Shareholders on the Composition of the Compensation Package

Looking at the relationship between pay and performance, Gomez-Mejia et al. (1987) found compensation most tightly linked to performance in firms defined as owner-controlled, which they defined as firms that had a 5% shareholder. Similarly, Hartzell and Starks (2000) found "a significantly positive relation between the pay-for-performance sensitivity of executive compensation and both the level and concentration of institutional ownership" (p. 1).

Looking at the composition of the compensation package, David et al. (1998) found the proportion of long-term incentives to total compensation increasing with the ownership of pressure-resistant institutional shareholders, but decreasing with the existence of a large noninstitutional shareholder. They attribute this finding to the ability of such shareholders to monitor management directly, and thus have less need for incentive mechanisms in the compensation package. Mehran (1995) found a similar result; that is, "firms in which a higher percentage of shares are held by insiders or outside blockholders use less equity-based compensation" (p. 163).

C. Affect of Shareholder Proposals on Executive Pay

Johnson et al. (1997) find that firms targeted by CaLPERS reduce both the level of executive compensation and the sensitivity of that compensation to performance. Although the two findings are seemingly inconsistent, and the latter finding surely is not what CaLPERS intended, the findings are consistent with economic theory; that is, in equilibrium, the only way to reduce compensation is to reduce the risk associated with that compensation. Another interesting result is found by Williams et al. (2000), who examined the effects of shareholder proposals sponsored by public pension funds and labor unions on executive compensation. They found that although there is an increase in option-based compensation, that increase does not appear to enhance the sensitivity of pay to performance. An explanation for their finding is that although options are assumed to be performance based because their value is a function of future share price performance, at the time of grant, the grant date value of the options need not be related to contemporaneous performance. Looking at the effect of antitakeover legislation on executive pay, Bertrand and Mullainathan (2000) found that subsequent to the passage of antitakeover legislation, "firms with a large shareholder increased pay for performance, while firms without a large shareholder increased mean pay" (p. 203). Recall from Chapter 1 that the market for corporate control and the compensation package are two ways to provide executives with incentives to increase shareholder value. Passage of the antitakeover legislation reduced the effectiveness of the market for corporate control in providing those incentives. In response, corporations with large shareholders increased the incentives provided via the compensation package. In contrast, executives in corporations without large shareholders responded by increasing their pay.

VI. SUMMARY

This chapter examined ownership and its effect on the executive compensation package. In percentage terms, CEO ownership is rather small, with mean ownership approximating 3% over time and median ownership well below 1%. Including options to arrive at an effective ownership percentage raises these numbers somewhat, but the percentages are still rather low, always less than 5%. These amounts are rather low, in that they indicate that the CEO bears less than 5% of the cost of his or her actions, and analogously, receives less than 5% of the benefits. However, although low in percentage terms, in dollar amounts, ownership is extremely significant, with the value of shares and options held by the CEO averaging over $350 million (median $18,298,000) in 2000.

As pointed out in Chapter 1, the goals of executives and shareholders can be aligned through executive share ownership. Chapter 8 discusses the steps certain corporations have taken to increase executive share ownership, providing examples along the way. Yet as noted, there is no conclusive evidence that increasing share ownership improves corporate performance. One possible explanation for the lack of association is that in addition to affecting incentives to increase shareholder value, executive ownership affects executive risk preferences as well. An executive who has both his or her human capital and a good portion of his or her financial wealth tied to the firm is not optimally diversified. That makes him or her less willing to take on risky new projects, even when the expected value of those projects is positive.

Executive ownership and the executive compensation package are both ways to provide the incentives to increase shareholder value. Thus, the higher the level of executive ownership, the less the need for conditional compensation in the compensation package to motivate executives to increase shareholder value. Similarly, monitoring by the board of directors and/or large shareholders is a way to provide executives with incentives to increase shareholder value independent of the executive compensation package. Although the evidence on the effect of CEO ownership on the level of CEO compensation is mixed, there is some evidence that the level of CEO compensation decreases as the ownership of an outside director's compensation increases. Similarly, there is some evidence that the level of compensation is lower when there are large shareholders. Looking at the composition of the compensation package, there is also some evidence that the portion of stock in the compensation package decreases with increases in insider, board, and large shareholder ownership.

CHAPTER 9

Corporate Governance

I. INTRODUCTION

A. Statutory Regulations

In the United States, corporate charters are issued by the states. The state of Delaware, home to 324,000 corporations, "including 60 percent of the Fortune 500 and 50 percent of the companies listed on the New York Stock Exchange,"[1] requires that "the business and affairs of every corporation organized under this chapter shall be managed by or under the direction of a board of directors . . ."[2] The major tasks of these directors are the hiring, firing, and compensating of top executives.

When the corporation goes public, that is, has an initial public offering, it also becomes subject to the rules promulgated by the Securities and Exchange Commission (SEC) and the exchange upon which it is listing. For example, the New York Stock Exchange (NYSE) requires each corporation have a qualified audit committee composed "of at least three directors, all of whom have no relationship with the company that may interfere with the exercise of their independence from management and the company."[3] Nasdaq requires companies have a minimum of three independent directors, as well as an audit committee with a minimum of three directors, all of which must be independent.

Additional requirements are imposed by the Internal Revenue Code for those companies wishing to deduct compensation in excess of $1 million per executive. To meet Section 162(m) requirements, the performance goal under which compensation is paid must be established by a compensation committee composed solely of two or more independent or outside directors. Treasury regulation §1.162-27 defines an outside director as a director who (a) is not a current employee of the publicly held corporation; (b) is not a former employee of the publicly held corporation

---

[1]Available: http://www.state.de.us/corp/
[2]Delaware General Corporation Law § 141.
[3]New York Stock Exchange manual 303.01.

who receives compensation for prior services (other than benefits under a tax-qualified retirement plan) during the taxable year; (c) has not been an officer of the publicly held corporation; and (d) does not receive remuneration from the publicly held corporation, either directly or indirectly, in any capacity other than as a director. For this purpose, remuneration includes any payment in exchange for goods or services.

The shareholders of the corporation elect the directors. Legally, the directors of a corporation are responsible to those shareholders; that is, they have a fiduciary duty to put the interests of shareholders first. There are many [for example, Mace (1971) and Crystal (1991)], who believe this does not occur in practice, as the directors themselves are agents, with little or no equity investment in the corporation, and consequently, whose interests are not necessarily aligned with those of shareholders. Pfeffer (1972, p. 220) writes that

> . . . in most cases board members are handpicked by management. In many practical respects, then, management is, therefore, in control of the board.

Bhagat et al. (1998) noted that

> Through control of the proxy process, incumbent management nominated its own candidates for board membership. The board of directors, theoretically composed of the representatives of various shareholding groups, instead was comprised of individuals selected by management. The directors' connection with the enterprise generally resulted from a prior relationship with management, not the stockholding owners, and they often had little or no shareholding stake in the company.

B. Categories of Directors

Few directors are completely independent of the CEO. The board is composed of two broad groups: (a) inside directors, that is, those whose full-time employment is with the corporation, and (b) outside directors. In many cases, an insider, the CEO, is also the chairman of the board,[4] which adversely affects the board's ability to independently monitor and discipline the CEO (see Jensen 1993; Fama and Jensen 1983). For example, Goyal and Park (2000) concluded "that the sensitivity of CEO turnover to firm performance is significantly lower when the CEO and chairman titles are vested in the same individual." Perhaps because of this, Yermack (1996) provided evidence consistent with corporations being more highly valued when the positions are separated.

The other inside directors are executive-level subordinates whose compensation may be linked to that of the CEO. Some believe (Main et al. 1995) the CEO actually controls the wage-setting process of subordinates. At a minimum the CEO has influence over it.

[4]Shivdasani and Yermack (1999) found this duality for 84% of the firms in the Fortune 500.

Outside directors are those for whom the corporation is not their primary employer. They can include former employees of the corporation, relatives of the CEO, individuals with business relationships with the corporation, and individuals who sit on other boards with the corporation's CEO or on whose board the CEO sits, with the latter being known as an interlocking directorate.[5] Sometimes these individuals are referred to as gray directors because, although they are not full-time employees of the corporation, they are not independent of the corporation either (Shivdasani and Yermack 1999). More formally, gray directors, although not directly employed by the company, have business ties or affiliations to the company and/or its executives that may compromise their independence.

Acknowledging this lack of independence, both NASDAQ and the NYSE have tightened their definitions of independent directors for purposes of serving on audit committees. As of December 14, 1999, the following criteria must be met for a NASDAQ company:

A director will not be considered "independent" if, among other things, he or she has:

- been employed by the corporation or its affiliates in the current or past three years;
- accepted any compensation from the corporation or its affiliates in excess of $60,000 during the previous fiscal year (except for board service, retirement plan benefits, or nondiscretionary compensation);
- an immediate family member who is, or has been in the past 3 years, employed by the corporation or its affiliates as an executive officer;
- been a partner, controlling shareholder, or an executive officer of any for-profit business to which the corporation made, or from which it received, payments (other than those which arise solely from investments in the corporation's securities) that exceed 5% of the organization's consolidated gross revenues for that year, or $200,000, whichever is more, in any of the past 3 years; or
- been employed as an executive of another entity where any of the company's executives serve on that entity's compensation committee.[6]

Shivdasani and Yermack (1999) examined new appointments to the boards of the Fortune 500 over the 1994–1996 period. They found that 24% of the appointments were insiders, 11% gray outsiders, and 65% independent outsiders. Of the gray outsiders,

> 69% have disclosed business dealings with the firm either personally or through their principal employers, while 13% have direct interlocking relationships with the CEO (i.e., service on each other's boards) and 24% have interlocking relationships on the board of a third company." (p. 1832)

[5]An extreme case is the interlocking compensation committee where the CEO of ABC sits on compensation committee of XYZ, and CEO of XYZ sits on compensation committee of ABC (Fierman 1990).

[6]Available: http://www.nasdaq.com/about/sec_apvd_amendment_121499.stm. © Copyright 2001, The Nasdaq Stock Market, Inc. All rights reserved. Reprinted with permission.

Shivdasani and Yermack also examined the composition of the board at the beginning of 1994, finding the percentage of insiders and gray outsiders higher (28 and 26%, respectively) and independent outsiders lower (46%) than in their new appointment sample. They provided two potential explanations for the discrepancy between their new appointments and existing board members. The first is that the turnover among independent directors is higher than that of gray and inside directors. The second potential explanation is that more independent directors are being appointed than in the past. Westphal and Zajac (1994, p. 386) cautioned that

> increasing the number and/or proportion of outsiders on the board of directors as recommended by some activists interested in governance reform, could be a more symbolic than substantive action, given that CEO's may simply recruit sympathetic outsiders to the board.

II. DIRECTOR COMPENSATION

A director's compensation can be significant in amount and can include cash retainers (a fixed amount, analogous to salary), board meeting fees, fees for chairing committees, stock options, stock grants, and pensions. The following example is from Ford Motor Company:

> Compensation of Directors
>
> Goal. Ford wants the directors' compensation to be tied to your interests as stockholders. Accordingly, 25% ($10,000) of a director's annual Board membership fee is deferred in the form of common stock units. This deferral, together with the restricted stock given to directors and director stock ownership goals, is part of Ford's commitment to link director and stockholder interests. These compensation programs are described below.
>
> Fees. The following fees are paid to directors, other than the Chairman of the Board, who are not Ford employees:
>
> | | |
> |---|---|
> | Annual Board membership fee | $40,000 |
> | Annual Committee membership fee | $10,000 |
> | Attendance fee for each Board meeting | $1,000 |
>
> The Chairman of the Board is paid a fee for each calendar quarter of $375,000, paid in restricted shares of common stock. These shares cannot be sold for one year and are subject to the conditions of the 1998 Long-Term Incentive Plan.
>
> Deferred Compensation Plan. Under this plan, 25% of a director's annual Board membership fee must be deferred in common stock units. Directors also can choose to have the payment of all or some of the remainder of their fees deferred in the form of cash and/or common stock units. Each common stock unit is equal in value to a share of common stock and is ultimately paid in cash. These common stock units generate Dividend Equivalents in the form of additional common stock units. These units are credited to the directors' accounts on the date common stock cash dividends are paid. Any fees deferred in cash are held in the general funds of the Company. Interest on fees deferred in cash is credited semiannually to the directors' accounts at the then-current U.S. Treasury Bill rate plus 0.75%. In general, deferred amounts are not paid until after the director retires from the Board. The amounts are then paid, at the director's option, either in a lump sum or in annual installments over a period of up to ten years.

Restricted Stock Plan. Nonemployee directors also receive restricted shares of common stock. Each nonemployee director who has served for at least six months receives 2,000 shares of common stock subject to restrictions on sale. In general, the restrictions expire for 20% of the shares each year following the year of the grant. Each nonemployee director receives an additional 2,000 shares on the same terms when the restrictions on all of the prior 2,000 shares end.

Stock Ownership Goals. To further link director and stockholder interests, Ford established stock ownership goals for nonemployee directors in 1995. Each nonemployee director has a goal to own common stock equal in value to five times the sum of the director's annual Board and Committee fees within five years.

Life Insurance. Ford provides nonemployee directors with $200,000 of life insurance and $500,000 of accidental death or dismemberment coverage. The life insurance coverage continues after the director retires from the Board if the director is at least age 55 and has served for at least five years. A director who retires from the Board after age 70, or, with Board approval, after age 55, and who has served for at least five years may elect to have the life insurance reduced to $100,000 and receive $15,000 a year for life. The accidental death or dismemberment coverage may, at the director's expense, be supplemented up to an additional $500,000 and ends when the director retires from the Board.

Matching Gift Program. Nonemployee directors may give up to $25,000 per year to certain tax-exempt organizations under the Ford Fund Matching Gift Program. For each dollar given, the Ford Motor Company Fund contributes two dollars.[7]

Note that Ford pays a base retainer of $40,000, additional amounts for committee memberships ($10,000) and for each meeting ($1000), provides 2000 shares of restricted stock annually, and a life insurance policy that may be converted, under certain circumstances, into an annuity of $15,000 for life. In contrast General Motors (below), pays an annual retainer of $120,000, and additional amounts for chairing committees ($5000) and special services ($1000 per day). While at face value General Motors appears to pay more than Ford, that is, the base retainer of $120,000 is triple the $40,000 paid by Ford, half of that retainer must be deferred into restricted stock. In contrast, Ford provides 2000 shares of restricted stock in addition to the retainer. Valued at the December 31, 1999, closing price of $53.3125 per share, those 2000 shares were worth $106,625, making Ford's base package of $146,625 more valuable than that of General Motors.

DIRECTOR COMPENSATION

Only non-employee directors receive payment for serving on the Board. Since Messrs. Smith, Pearce, and Wagoner are employees of the Corporation, they are not compensated as directors. Non-employee directors are not eligible to participate in the executive incentive program, Savings-Stock Purchase Program, or any of the Retirement Programs for General Motors employees. Other than as described in this section, there are no separate benefit plans for directors. Compensation paid to non-employee directors is as follows:

- Annual retainer $120,000(a)
- Retainer for Committee chair $ 5,000
- Per diem for special services $ 1,000

[7]Ford Motor Company proxy statement filed with Securities and Exchange Commission, April 11, 2000, pp. 13, 14.

TABLE 9.1   Directors' Compensation by Year[a]

Year	Retainer ($)	Meeting fees ($)	Value of stock grants ($)	Value of option grants ($)	Total compensation ($)
1992	17,000	7,000	1,000	8,000	36,000
	17,000	7,000	0	0	31,000
1993	17,000	7,000	2,000	13,000	40,000
	16,000	7,000	0	0	32,000
1994	17,000	7,000	2,000	19,000	47,000
	18,000	7,000	0	0	36,000
1995	18,000	8,000	3,000	20,000	50,000
	18,000	7,000	0	4,000	37,000
1996	17,000	8,000	4,000	30,000	59,000
	16,000	7,000	0	7,000	41,000
1997	17,000	8,000	6,000	34,000	67,000
	16,000	7,000	0	11,000	47,000
1998	18,000	8,000	7,000	38,000	70,000
	18,000	7,000	0	13,000	51,000
1999	18,000	8,000	8,000	46,000	82,000
	18,000	7,000	0	16,000	57,000
2000	21,000	8,000	10,000	81,000	118,000
	20,000	7,000	0	20,000	70,000

[a]Means on top, medians below.

(a) Under the General Motors Compensation Plan for Non-Employee Directors (the "Plan"), non-employee directors are required to defer $60,000 of the above annual retainer in restricted units of GM common stocks or stock options valued at $60,000. In addition, under the Plan directors may also elect to defer all or a portion of the remaining compensation in cash or units of GM common stocks.

Restricted Stock Units under the Plan are credited with dividend equivalents in the form of additional stock units of the same class. Amounts deferred under the Plan are generally not available until after the director retires from the Board at age 70. After the director leaves the Board, payment under the Plan is made in cash based on the number of stock units and the market price of the related GM common stocks at the time of payment.

Mr. John G. Smale is Chair of the Board's Executive Committee, for which he is paid $300,000 annually. In this capacity he serves as an ex-officio member of each of the standing committees of the Board. Pursuant to the director retirement policy, Mr. Smale is not standing for reelection.[8]

Director compensation has increased dramatically over time. Yermack (1996) reported that for a sample of corporations over the 1984 through 1991 period, director compensation averaged just under $30,000 (in 1991 dollars). Brickley et al. (1999) showed that for their sample of corporations over the period 1991–1995, this amount rose to $46,000. Bryan et al. (2000) showed this amount has jumped to an average of $70,450 in 1997. Table 9.1 provides some more recent statistics on

[8]General Motors proxy statement filed with the Securities and Exchange Commission, April 18, 2000, pp. 3, 4.

TABLE 9.2   Percentage of Corporations
with Director Pension Plans

Year	Corporations with director pension plans (%)
1992	26.97
1993	28.45
1994	28.99
1995	27.07
1996	21.11
1997	13.21
1998	9.73
1999	8.54
2000	8.59

director pay. Consistent with the above evidence, the amounts are substantial and have increased throughout the 1990s, from a mean (median) of $36,000 ($31,000) in 1992 to $118,000 ($70,000) in 2000. As with executives, the bulk of the increase is coming in the form of equity-based compensation. For example, although the mean (median) retainer (base remuneration) increased from $17,000 ($17,000) in 1992 to $21,000 ($20,000) in 2000, or less than 25% (25%), the mean (median) value of stock grants increased from $1000 (0) to $10,000 (0), or 1000% (0); and the mean (median) value of stock option grants increased from $8000 (0) to $81,000 ($20,000), more than 1000%! This is consistent with corporations responding to pressures put on them to offer their directors incentive and stock-based compensation (National Association of Corporate Directors 2000; Teachers Insurance and Annuity Association—College Retirement Equities Fund 2000; Lublin 1996; California Public Employees Retirement System 1998). These numbers, and those in Table 9.2, are also consistent with some corporations dropping their director pension plans and replacing them with stock and/or option grants. Table 9.2 shows the number of corporations offering director pension plans dropped from 26.97% in 1992 to 8.59% in 2000.

Table 9.3 shows that in 2000, director compensation varied across industries, ranging from a mean (median) of $74,000 ($57,000) for corporations in the transportation, communications, electric, gas, and sanitary services classification to $141,000 ($85,000) in the services classification. Interestingly, this entire difference is driven by stock-based compensation, as the mean and median retainer for corporations in the transportation, communications, electric, gas, and sanitary services classification exceeds that of the services classification by more than 30%!

As observed with CEO compensation, director compensation also increases with the size of the corporation. Table 9.4 shows that in 2000, mean (median) total director compensation was $42,000 ($41,000) for the smallest decile of corporations, increasing to $245,000 ($128,000) for the largest corporations. In terms of

TABLE 9.3 Directors Compensation by Industry (for 2000)[a]

Industry	SIC codes[b]	Retainer ($)	Meeting fees ($)	Value of stock grants ($)	Value of option grants ($)	Total compensation ($)
Mining and	1000–1999	26,000	9,000	9,000	48,000	95,000
construction		25,000	8,000	0	34,000	90,000
Manufacturing	2000–3999	22,000	8,000	10,000	101,000	140,000
		20,000	6,000	0	23,000	71,000
Transportation,	4000–4999	22,000	9,000	12,000	38,000	74,000
communications,		20,000	9,000	0	10,000	57,000
electric, gas, and						
sanitary services						
Wholesale and	5000–5999	18,000	7,000	7,000	43,000	78,000
retail trade		20,000	6,000	0	15,000	51,000
Finance, insurance,	6000–6999	23,000	9,000	16,000	52,000	105,000
and real estate		22,000	8,000	0	12,000	77,000
Services	7000–7999	16,000	7,000	6,000	125,000	141,000
		16,000	7,000	0	54,000	85,000

[a]Means on top, medians below.
[b]Standard Industrial Classification.

composition, directors in large corporations seem to be getting less of their compensation in the form of retainers and more in the form of stock. As with CEOs, this finding is driven by the magnitude of stock in the compensation package, not by a reduction in the value of the retainer, as directors of large corporations also get larger retainers (mean $34,000, median $35,000) than their smaller corporation counterparts (mean $14,000, median $15,000).

A. Determinants of Director Compensation

If the directors themselves are agents with little equity investment, and if their interests are not necessarily aligned with those of shareholders (a possibility raised previously), then the compensation package may be the only way to align their interests with those of shareholders.[9] Only recently have researchers begun looking at the determinants of director compensation. One of the first studies on the topic is Bryan et al. (2000). As noted in Chapter 2 (discussed further in Chapter 11), prior research had found executive compensation related to the growth opportunities of the firm. Similarly, Bryan et al. (2000) found the level of outside director stock option awards positively related to the corporation's growth opportunities, whereas

[9]An interesting question is who would have the incentives and ability to design such a package, given the divergence in interests between management and shareholders, and the dispersion of shareholders in most companies.

TABLE 9.4   Directors' Compensation by Size (for 2000)[a]

	Size decile	Retainer ($)	Meeting fees ($)	Value of stock grants ($)	Value of option grants ($)	Total compensation ($)
Smallest	1	14,000	8,000	2,000	16,000	42,000
		15,000	6,000	0	12,000	41,000
	2	14,000	7,000	6,000	36,000	65,000
		15,000	6,000	0	20,000	51,000
	3	19,000	8,000	4,000	43,000	74,000
		20,000	6,000	0	18,000	58,000
	4	18,000	7,000	7,000	52,000	77,000
		20,000	6,000	0	17,000	60,000
	5	19,000	7,000	8,000	68,000	101,000
		18,000	7,000	0	25,000	75,000
	6	21,000	8,000	8,000	51,000	89,000
		20,000	8,000	0	23,000	68,000
	7	21,000	9,000	11,000	79,000	123,000
		24,000	8,000	0	18,000	83,000
	8	23,000	8,000	17,000	119,000	170,000
		25,000	8,000	0	36,000	92,000
	9	25,000	8,000	17,000	159,000	193,000
		25,000	8,000	0	28,000	110,000
Largest	10	34,000	9,000	24,000	166,000	245,000
		35,000	7,000	0	33,000	128,000

[a]Means on top, medians below.

the level of director stock grants is negatively associated with the corporation's growth opportunities. As discussed in Chapter 8, institutional shareholdings are also associated with executive compensation. Similarly, Bryan et al. (2000) found the level of outside director stock option awards positively related to the level of institutional shareholdings in the corporation. In general, Bryan et al. (2000) found that firm characteristics that explain executive compensation also explain director compensation a finding consistent with directors being treated as agents of the shareholders who need economic incentives to increase shareholder value.

B. Effect of Director Compensation on Director Independence

In contrast to Bryan et al. (2000), who looked at multiple determinants of director compensation, Moskowitz (1998) focuses on one item and finds that the level of director pay is positively related to CEO overcompensation. The latter leads to a very interesting and controversial hypothesis: a corporate version of "you scratch my back and I'll scratch yours." Board memberships can be quite lucrative, and that may impair the director's objectivity. Further, as with executives, this compensation can serve as a bond to be forfeited if their performance is not satisfactory. However, outside directors do not have any operational duties upon which to be judged. Rather, because outside directors are appointed by and serve with the approval of the CEO,[10,11] their performance may be judged on how well they get along (or go along) with the CEO. For example, Tejada (1997) reported that when Jesse L. Upchurch resigned as director of Tandy, he claimed he was being penalized for criticizing the CEO's performance. Thus for both financial and social reasons, board members may be more loyal to the CEO who has appointed them than to the shareholders they legally represent. Furthermore, the greater the pay, the greater the loyalty.

III. THE EFFECT OF THE BOARD OF DIRECTORS ON CEO COMPENSATION

The lack of an arm's-length relationship between the CEO and the board creates opportunity for self-dealing when determining compensation. However, even with an arm's-length relationship, the CEO has strong incentives to increase his or her compensation, whereas the board, normally not consisting of large shareholders, has little or no incentive to resist. To provide some incentive, rule changes implemented in 1993 by the SEC, required the compensation committee provide a report in the proxy statement, detailing how they set executive compensation. Figure 9.1 contains, as an example of this report, the compensation committee report incorporated into Dow Jones proxy statement filed with the Securities and Exchange Commission on March 17, 2000.

The first section of the report, The Compensation Committee and the Compensation Program, describes the compensation committee; that is, it consists of four nonemployee directors, and the general charge of the committee, that is, to administer the compensation program to enhance stockholder value. The next section, Elements of Compensation Program Considered by the Committee, discusses the focus of the committee, that is senior management, and the elements of compensation considered. The report then goes on to discuss how they establish and administer the program. It is in this section, Establishing and Administering a Competitive Program, that they discuss the use of outside compensation consultants, performance studies, and peer companies. They then go on to explain that the amount of compensation that will be awarded to the CEO in the forthcoming year will be substantially based upon the achievement of predetermined financial objectives, which they describe (e.g., as earnings per share growth) but do not detail (e.g.,

---

[10]See, for example, Mace (1971) and Lorsch and MacIver (1989).

[11]"Directors appointed during the tenure of an incumbent CEO have been termed 'interdependent' directors" (Daily et al. 1998, p. 211).

Compensation Committee Report on Executive Compensation

The Compensation Committee and the Compensation Program

The Committee consists of four non-employee directors. It generally meets five times a year. The Compensation Committee's objective is to establish and administer a "total compensation program" that fairly and competitively rewards Dow Jones executives for current and long-term performance that enhances stockholder value. The purpose of this report is to explain the Company's executive compensation program and the operation of the Compensation Committee.

Elements of Compensation Program Considered by the Committee

The Committee gives special attention to the total compensation of the chief executive officer (Mr. Kann), and certain other members of senior management. We consider four elements of compensation: (1) annual salary; (2) annual incentive award (or bonus); (3) long-term incentive compensation; and (4) retirement and other compensation.

Establishing and Administering a Competitive Program

The Committee retains outside compensation consultants and reviews competitive compensation and performance studies in developing and administering the total compensation program. We give continuing attention to changes in compensation practices, business trends and changes in applicable law and regulations in order to establish and administer a sound competitive compensation program. The competitive universe that we primarily consider includes the six largest newspaper publishers in the Dow Jones U.S. Publishing Index (the "Company's peer group") (see page 18), but we also review data on general industry trends and, from time to time, certain other public companies which compete with one or more of the Company's business segments.

With regard to annual and long-term incentive awards, the Committee, in working with management and its outside compensation consultants, has determined that a substantial portion of executives' awards will be based on the achievement of certain pre-determined financial objectives. For Mr. Kann a substantial portion of his annual incentive award for 2000 will be based on the achievement of these pre-determined financial objectives (earnings per share growth—35%; economic value created—20%; and cash flow margin—15%) and the balance will be based on the achievement of specified strategic goals (30%). For the remaining executive officers, a substantial portion of their annual incentive awards will be based on the achievement of pre-determined financial objectives and the balance will be based on the achievement of strategic goals and, for certain executive officers, individual performance.

Initial awards of contingent stock rights were made under the Company's long-term incentive plan to Mr. Kann and other senior executive officers for the performance period 2000-2003. The final awards to all those receiving these grants will be based in large part on the Company's performance with respect to pre-determined financial objectives (total shareholder return; earnings per share growth; revenue growth; and cash flow margin) relative to the Company's peer group. Determination of final awards will also be based assessment of performance on qualitative criteria.

FIGURE 9.1   Excerpt from Dow Jones proxy statement filed with Securities and Exchange Commission March 17, 2000.

The Committee has retained some measure of discretion under the annual and long-term incentive award programs because it believes that it is difficult to forecast in detail all future developments that will be relevant to an evaluation of executive performance.

Federal tax legislation in effect since 1994 eliminates the deductibility of compensation in excess of $1,000,000 paid to the chief executive officer and certain other executives (i.e., those whose compensation must be detailed in the proxy statement). The law exempts compensation paid under plans that relate compensation to performance. Although our plans are designed to relate compensation to performance, certain elements of them do not meet the tax law's requirements because they allow the Committee to exercise discretion in setting compensation. It may be appropriate in the future to recommend changes in the Company's compensation program to take account of the tax law. However, the Committee is of the opinion that it is better to retain discretion than to give it up in exchange for the tax deduction. For 1999 the deductibility of certain compensation paid to Mr. Kann was affected by this limitation.

Committee Reporting

The Committee makes full reports to the Board of Directors, which approves the structure and general administration of the compensation program. The Board reviews the specific compensation awards for the chief executive officer and each of the other four executives whose compensation is described in the proxy statement.

In 1999 the chief executive officer's salary was $788,000, an increase of $38,000 (or 5%) from his 1998 salary of $750,000. The 1999 salaries for the five officers listed in the table on page 12 were set after evaluating their individual contribution and performance and the value of their jobs in the marketplace based on a review of the competitive compensation guidelines that were developed with advice from our outside compensation consultants.

For 1999 Mr. Kann was granted a bonus of $656,288. That represented a 62.9% increase from his 1998 bonus of $402,885. In determining the bonuses for Mr. Kann and the other officers listed in the table, we compared the Company's results to the financial, strategic and, for certain executive officers, individual performance measures established in early 1999. The bonus awards for 1999 reflect the Company's and business unit's performance measured against the pre-determined financial criteria and the Committee's view that the executives performed reasonably well against the non-financial measures established under the bonus program.

We awarded long-term compensation to the chief executive officer and other members of senior management in February 2000 under the Company's 1992 Long Term Incentive Plan. The Final Awards covered performance for the period 1996-1999 and were made after reviewing the Company's performance on various financial measures (including total stockholder return, return on equity, earnings growth, profit margins, and other financial criteria) relative to the Company's peer group. We also considered progress toward achieving other Company objectives (quality of Dow Jones' publications and services, commitment to innovative products and services, long-term strategic planning, quality of customer service and level of customer satisfaction, development of human resources, and promotion of teamwork

FIGURE 9.1   (continued)

throughout the Company). And, finally, we considered each individual executive's responsibility and performance. In granting final awards, the Committee took into account that the Company's performance trends improved during the 1996–1999 period. In the case of the 1996–1999 performance period, it was expected that fully satisfactory competitive performance would be competitively rewarded if the Final Award approximated 80% of the number of shares in the Initial Award. Exceptional performance would support a Final Award in excess of 80% (up to 100%) of the Initial Award.

Final Awards were made in February 2000 to Mr. Kann and Messrs. Skinner, Ottaway and Crovitz in amounts approximating 55% to 60% of their Initial Awards for the 1996–1999 period. Mr. Kann's Final Award for the 1996–1999 period was 10,500 shares of Common Stock, and constituted approximately 60% of his Initial Award. That represented an increase of 2,200 shares from the Final Award for the 1995–1998 period. The net number of shares of Common Stock received in February 2000 by Mr. Kann, after tax withholding, amounted to 6,613. Mr. Ottaway received his Final Award in cash. Messrs. Skinner and Crovitz received their Final Awards in the form of Common Stock. The fair market value of Mr. Kann's Final Award for the 1996–1999 period was $654,938 (based on a grant date stock price of $62.375), which is approximately 73.9% higher in value than the Final Award for the 1995–1998 period of $376,613 (based on a grant date stock price of $45.375).

In January 2000 we granted members of senior management contingent stock rights and stock options under the 1997 Long Term Incentive Plan for the 2000–2003 performance period. These grants were estimated by our outside compensation consultants to be at the median of general industry practice. The grants tie a significant portion of each senior executive's potential compensation to the Company's long-term objectives and to the market value of the Company's stock. The Committee will determine the actual number of shares of stock payable to an executive under the contingent stock rights at the end of the performance period.

The Committee believes that the number of contingent stock rights and stock options granted to individual executives should be set annually by the committee after consultation with its consultants concerning competitive compensation levels. Accordingly, the Committee does not base the amount of stock options or contingent stock rights to be granted in any given year on the amounts previously granted.

The Committee reaffirms its view that salaries and bonus and other incentive compensation opportunities for the senior executives of the Company generally should not deviate substantially from the median of the competitive guidelines developed with the advice of our consultants and that, particularly with respect to long-term incentive compensation, it is important that the Committee continue to retain a degree of discretion as to the actual amounts paid. The Committee believes that the compensation levels for the chief executive officer and other senior executives reflect these criteria and are appropriate given performance during the periods covered.

Irvine O. Hockaday, Jr., Chairman
Christopher Bancroft
Jane C. MacElree
Frank N. Newman

FIGURE 9.1   *(continued)*

disclose the actual quantitative goal). The last paragraph of the section discusses the affect of Section 162(m) on the deductibility of compensation, noting that the deductibility of certain compensation paid to the CEO was affected, but not disclosing how much compensation was affected or the amount of additional taxes paid as a result. The last section, Committee Reporting, discusses the actual compensation paid during 1999, its relation to 1998 compensation, and the reasons for awarding the compensation, for example, individual contribution and performance, value of jobs in the marketplace, and company performance measured against predetermined financial and nonfinancial criteria.

Note that to justify compensation, the committee refers to vaguely worded financial, strategic, and individual performance goals, without giving details on those goals. Furthermore, in the course of the report the committee refers to the "unnamed" compensation consultants no less than six times! This is not uncommon. Clarke et al. (1998) found the use of external advisors and pay surveys are prevalent among large companies (see also Graef 1991; Thomas and Martin 1999). By surveying the competition, compensation consultants help a corporation determine and justify the compensation paid. Unfortunately, the process is susceptible to biases. For example, if the goal is to justify an increase in compensation, the survey might focus on high paying corporations. Alternatively, if the survey shows that the CEO earns less salary but a larger bonus than his or her peers, the compensation consultants and committee might focus on the relatively low salary to justify a raise, totally ignoring the relatively high bonus. A more general problem with surveys is they can lead to an endless spiraling upwards of compensation. Many corporations state they try to set compensation so that it is above the median, sometimes explicitly stating that it should be in the 50th to 75th percentile relative to their competition. Of course all corporations cannot be above the median. However, in striving to be above the median, corporations can justify continual increases in compensation.

Either before or after the report on executive compensation, in which the compensation committee must explain or justify executive compensation, the company must present a comparison of its shareholder return and those of a peer group. Much research has been conducted on the selection of that peer group for this purpose. For example, Porac et al. (1999) and Byrd et al. (1998) found that corporations select their peer groups to justify the compensation paid. Murphy (1995) noted that "two-thirds of the largest 1000 corporations reported beating the performance of their industry peer groups over the last five fiscal years" (p. 736). An example of this comparison, albeit one in which the corporation does not outperform its peer group (although it does slightly outperform the S&P 500), from the *New York Times* is printed below:

PERFORMANCE PRESENTATION
The following graph shows the annual cumulative total stockholder return for the five years ending December 31, 1999, on an assumed investment of $100 on December 31, 1994, in the Company, the Standard & Poor's S&P 500 Stock Index and an index of

a peer group of communications companies. The peer group returns are weighted by market capitalization at the beginning of each year. The peer group is comprised of the common stocks of the Company and the following other communications companies: Dow Jones & Company, Inc., Gannett Co., Inc., Knight Ridder, Media General, Inc., The Times Mirror Company, Tribune Company and The Washington Post Company. Stockholder return is measured by dividing (a) the sum of (i) the cumulative amount of dividends declared for the measurement period, assuming monthly reinvestment of dividends and (ii) the difference between the issuer's share price at the end and the beginning of the measurement period by (b) the share price at the beginning of the measurement period.

STOCK PERFORMANCE COMPARISON BETWEEN S&P 500, THE NEW YORK TIMES COMPANY'S CLASS A STOCK AND PEER GROUP COMMON STOCK[12]

	12/31/94	12/31/95	12/31/96	12/31/97	12/31/98	12/31/99
NYTimes	100	138	$169	$226	$290	$351
Peer group	100	137	$179	$315	$335	$479
S&P 500	100	128	$157	$244	$255	$336

Given the fact that the corporation must justify the compensation it pays its executives, the question is whether corporate governance, or more precisely, the composition of the board of directors and the compensation committee, affects compensation. Although the assumption is that outside directors, because they are independent, will better represent the interests of shareholders, that need not always be the case. As discussed above, although their primary employer may not be the corporation, they may have relationships with the corporation and/or the CEO that impair their independence. Further, even if they are independent, their low level of shareholdings in the corporation may not provide them with the proper incentives.

Core et al. (1999) conducted a comprehensive study of the effect of corporate governance on CEO compensation. In general, they found that compensation for CEOs was higher at corporations with ineffective governance structures. Mallette et al. (1995), Srindharan (1996), Core et al. (1999), and Conyon and Murphy (2000) all found compensation higher when the same person is both CEO and board chairman. Although this could be the result of the influence the individual holds over the compensation committee, it could also be remuneration for the additional duties the individual holds. Core et al. (1999) also found that compensation increases with board size, that is, number of directors on board. Srindharan (1996) found that compensation increases with increases in the percent of insiders on the board of directors. Although consistent with the finding of Mayers et al. (1997) that mutual insurance companies with more outside directors spend less on salaries and wages, Srindharan's finding is inconsistent with those of Lambert et al. (1993) and Core et al. (1999), who found compensation *decreases* with the

[12]*New York Times* proxy statement filed with Securities and Exchange Commission, April 24, 2000, p. 45.

percentage of insiders on the board.[13] However, Core et al. (1999) found that compensation increases when the CEO has influence over the outside directors, as measured by the percentage of outside directors appointed by the CEO, the percentage of "gray" outside directors, the percentage of outside directors over the age of 69, and the percentage of busy outside directors. Hallock (1997) found the existence of an interlock increases CEO compensation by as much as 52%! In contrast Daily et al. (1998) found no evidence that "captured" directors pay higher levels of CEO compensation. Wade et al. (1990) found the greater the percentage of outside board members appointed after the CEO, the more likely the CEO will have a golden parachute.

Focusing on the compensation committee, Mallette et al. (1995) found (as did O'Reilly et al. 1988), that "the value of compensation received by members of the compensation committee with their primary employer is a significant predictor of CEO cash compensation" (p. 253). In other words, they find that the more highly paid the members of the compensation committee are, the higher will be the compensation they award to the CEO! Among the theoretical explanations for this finding is that compensation committee members use their own pay as a benchmark or reference point in setting CEO pay. Main et al. (1995) found that CEO compensation was higher when the CEO's tenure was greater than that of the chair of the compensation committee. One potential explanation for this finding is that the chair of the compensation committee was only appointed with the approval of the CEO, with whom he or she may have some relationship.

Turning to the relationship between pay and performance, Conyon and Peck (1998) found the relationship between pay and performance to be stronger for corporations whose boards have larger proportions of outside directors. Similarly, Mehran (1995) found that equity-based compensation, which is performance based by definition, is used more extensively in corporations with more outside directors. Yermack (1996) cited evidence that as board size increases, the association between pay and performance decreases, consistent with CEOs receiving "stronger compensation incentives in companies with smaller boards" (p. 205).

As noted in the introduction to this chapter, Section 162(m) of the Internal Revenue Code requires a corporation have a compensation committee consisting of two or more independent directors, if the corporation wishes to deduct compensation in excess of $1 million per executive. This is not an issue with all corporations, as not every corporation pays that much. Furthermore, a number of corporations

---

[13]Hebner and Kato (1997) developed an interesting theory to explain why executive compensation would increase with the number of insiders on the board of directors. In equilibrium, executive compensation consists of explicit compensation plus the implicit profits to be made from trading on inside information. As the number of insiders increases, the ability to profit from inside information decreases, and thus the explicit component of the compensation package must increase. In the absence of direct data on insider profits, they indirectly test their theory using explicit executive compensation, finding that executive compensation does in fact increase with the number of officers.

have elected to forfeit deductions.[14] Thus these corporations can have insiders on their compensation committees. Similar to what they found for the entire board, Conyon and Peck (1998) stated that the link between pay and performance is stronger for corporations with fewer insiders on the compensation committee. Newman and Mozes (1999) found that insider participation on the compensation committee weakens the relation between CEO compensation and corporate performance in poorly performing corporations. In contrast, Lavelle (2000) found that "independent committees are now more likely to dole out raises when the stock tanks than committees stacked with insiders" (p. 106).

IV. THE EFFECT OF THE BOARD OF DIRECTORS ON CEO TURNOVER

As noted, the role of the board is to hire, fire, and monitor the CEO. However, for a multitude of reasons, boards have traditionally been reluctant to fire CEOs. Still there is come evidence that boards do act to remove CEOs following poor performance. Couglan and Schmidt (1985), Warner et al. (1988), and Weisbach (1988) all cited evidence consistent with the theory that outside directors are more willing than inside directors to dismiss CEOs following poor performance. Yermack (1996) showed that the probability of CEO dismissal as the result of poor performance decreases as board size increases, consistent with smaller boards being more effective monitors of management.[15] Goyal and Park (2000), as noted above, found that the sensitivity of CEO turnover to corporate performance is weaker when the CEO is also the chairman of the board.

V. EXAMPLES OF STRONG AND WEAK BOARDS

An article in *Business Week* magazine rated corporate boards.[16] Their survey found General Electric had the best board, whereas Walt Disney had the worst. For Disney, criticism of its board is nothing new.[17] This was the second year in a row that *Business Week* ranked them as having the worst board. Furthermore, institutional investors such as the California Public Employees' Retirement System (CalPERS) have made this an issue, withholding support for directors who draw consulting fees from Disney (Orwall and Lublin 2000).

[14]One such company is Dow Jones, which in the passage reprinted earlier in the chapter reported, "For 1999 the deductibility of certain compensation paid to Mr. Kann was affected by this limitation."

[15]This may be a function of smaller groups being able to arrive at consensus more easily.

[16]*Business Week* (2000).

[17]See, for example, Orwall and Lublin (1997); Orwall (1998); and Lublin (1998).

Let us first consider General Electric, which was praised for having an independent board. Its members, with average shareholdings of $6.6 million in General Electric, have their interests aligned with shareholders. Appendix 9.1 contains an extract from the General Electric proxy statement filed with the Securities and Exchange Commission on March 13, 2000. This extract identifies the members of the board, along with a description of their committee memberships, primary occupation, and shareholdings.

Now let us look at the comparable information for Disney. Appendix 9.2 contains information on the board of directors, which was pulled from the Walt Disney Company proxy statement filed with the Securities and Exchange Commission on January 5, 2000. These pages detail the ownership and election, as well as the qualifications, of those directors.

A comparison of the boards shows that both contain 16 directors who are elected annually at General Electric, and who will be elected annually beginning in 2001 at Disney. Using the information reprinted in Appendix 9.1, we see that the General Electric board contains two current and one retired employee, five gray outsiders, and eight independent directors. Disney in comparison looks even better, with only 2 insiders, 3 gray outsiders, and 11 independent directors. It is in the qualifications of the board where General Electric stands out. Ferris et al. (1999) argued that director quality is positively associated with the number of boards they serve on. Ignoring CEO Jack Welch, the other 15 directors on General Electric's board sit on an average of three corporate boards each (in addition to GEs). On the other hand, the 15 Disney directors other than CEO Michael Eisner sit on an average of one board each. Additionally, the General Electric board includes CEOs of large public companies like Scott G. McNealy of Sun Microsystems and Douglas A. Warner of J.P. Morgan.

How does this affect the compensation paid by Walt Disney? Recall from Chapter 6 that Michael Eisner, Chairman and CEO of Disney, was the highest paid ($589 million) executive in the 1998 Forbes Compensation Survey. Although most of that reflected gains from options granted in previous years, in 1996 he received the highest valued stock option grant $193,532,000. One interpretation is that Disney's board, lacking in stature, is unable to resist Eisner's compensation demands.

Another corporation cited by CalPERS is Tyson Foods:

> In what's shaping up as one of the first big corporate proxy tussles of the year, the California Public Employee's Retirement System (CalPERS) wants to oust Tyson's board of directors and void dual class shares. The 13-member board, stocked with three Tyson family members and five former and current executives, isn't accountable to shareholders, CalPERS says
>
> . . . .
>
> Tyson's board includes former CEO Don Tyson; his son, John; and Barbara Tyson, widow of Don Tyson's brother, Randal. Former executives Leland Tollett, Joe Starr and Gerald Johnston, CEO Wayne Britt and President Don Wray also are directors.
>
> Had Tyson Foods—one of the USA's leading meat marketers—performed better on Wall Street, CalPERS would have nothing to cluck about. But Tyson says in its SEC

filing that its class A stock rose just 27% from 1994–98 vs. 139% for the Standard & Poor's 500 index. Tyson fell 23.5% in 1999 vs. a 19.5% gain for the S&P.

Moreover, Don and John Tyson are no longer involved in day-to-day running of the company but appear to be excessively compensated, says Jamie Heard of Proxy Monitor, a shareholder adviser supporting CalPers.

Don Tyson resigned as CEO in 1991. Yet as senior chairman, he received salary and bonuses of $910,000 in 1999 and nearly $330,000 for travel and entertainment expenses. John Tyson took in $1 million as board chairman and $124,000 for travel and entertainment costs.

The upper tier of Tyson Foods' management, which includes a CEO, president and chief operating officer, also appears bloated, critics say. Britt got $900,000 in 1999 pay and bonuses; Wray, $655,000; and COO Greg Lee, $530,000.[18]

The criticisms of Tyson neatly link the issue of board independence and executive compensation. The board, which contains three family members and five former employees, is clearly not independent. Perhaps as a result, the corporation continues to operate like a family business employing one Tyson as Chairman and another as Senior Chairman, in addition having a nonfamily member as CEO.

VI. AN INTERESTING RESPONSE

It cannot be pointed out often enough that a current board controls the proxy machinery. That is, it nominates directors, which are then rubber stamped by absentee owners with little choice, as there is usually only one nominee per position. Only in the presence of a proxy contest generated by a large shareholder or outsider attempting to gain control of the corporation does the investor have a choice. In response to this environment, Mr. Peter H. Arkison submitted the following proposal, which was incorporated in Walt Disney's 2000 proxy statement, asking that shareholders be given at least two qualified individuals to choose from for each board position.[19]

RESOLVED that the Board of Directors should submit the names of at least two qualified individuals to the shareholders for each position on the board of directors to be voted upon by the shareholders. Each nominee should be submitted in such a manner as to make it impossible for the shareholders to know which is the one preferred by the Board, except that a simple statement may be included indicating that person's time of service on the board. Proxies submitted on behalf of management should be prepared in such a way that each candidate will receive approximately the same number of votes if the shareholders do not make a choice in favor of particular candidates.

STATEMENT IN SUPPORT OF RESOLUTION

It is the legal right and duty of the shareholders to elect the Board of Directors. At the present time, the Board of Directors nominates one candidate for each position to be

---

[18]Straus (2000). Copyright 2000, *USA Today.* Reprinted with permission.

[19]Walt Disney company proxy statement filed with Securities and Exchange Commission January 5, 2000, pp. 22, 23.

filled on the Board. Under the proxy system, the shareholders do not have a meaningful way of saying that they do not like a particular candidate.

It is possible for a shareholder to withhold authority for voting for a particular director; however, since there is not a meaningful alternative choice presented, the chosen candidate wins.

The shareholders have the right to make a choice of whom they want to run their company; this Resolution takes a step towards allowing them to exercise that right. With the vast number of shareholders, only those whose names appear on the proxy ballot submitted with the Notice of the Annual Meeting have a chance at being elected to the board. This Resolution attempts to address this problem by seeking to have the Board submit two equally qualified candidates for each position.

Discretion is left with the Board to determine how information about the candidates is presented; the only requirement is that they be presented in a similar manner.

The proxy ballots are to be designed and distributed in a manner that would result in all candidates receiving approximately the same number of votes. That means that those shareholders who actually take the time and effort to vote for specific candidates will be the ones who choose the new members of the Board. Every vote then becomes very important.

The Resolution seeks to change the way that the company is governed. It seeks return of the control of the corporation to the shareholders. It seeks to terminate the Board of Directors becoming a self perpetuating body by giving shareholders the opportunity to remove the present directors by voting for the alternative choices. The Board then would become more accountable to the shareholders for its actions.

A YES vote is needed for effective shareholder governance.

While a seemingly reasonable proposal, it was opposed by management and turned down by shareholders by a vote of 74,914,596 for and 1,229,835,340 against![20]

VII. SUMMARY

This chapter describes the corporate governance system in the United States. In the United States corporate charters are issued by the states, which are the primary regulators of those corporations. In general, states require that corporations have boards of directors. The shareholders of the corporation elect those directors to oversee the operations of the corporation. When the corporation decides to go public, it then becomes subject to the regulations of the exchange upon which they list and of the SEC. These entities impose additional requirements on the corporation, for example, requiring that the corporation have an audit committee to oversee the financial reporting process and specifying the composition of that committee.

Few directors are completely independent of the CEO. That is, although their fiduciary duty lies with the shareholders who elected them, their true loyalties may lie with the CEO who nominated them in the first place. The board is composed

[20]Walt Disney company 10-Q filed with Securities and Exchange Commission, May 15, 2000, p. 2.

of inside directors, whose full-time employment is with the corporation, and outside directors, who are not currently employed by the corporations. In many cases, an insider, the CEO, is also the chairman of the board, which adversely affects the board's ability to independently monitor and discipline the CEO. Outside directors, although not currently employed by the corporation, may be retired employees or have other business ties or affiliations to the corporation or its executives.

A director's compensation can be significant in amount, averaging $118,000 (median $70,000) in 2000. Like the executive compensation package, it includes multiple components, such as cash retainers, board meeting fees, fees for chairing committees, stock options, stock grants, and pensions. These amounts, although necessary to attract high-quality directors, also may compromise directors' independence. The possibility exists that the board, which is supposed to oversee and set compensation for the CEO, may not be independent of the CEO. And note that, even if they were totally independent, while the CEO has strong incentives to increase his or her compensation, the board has little or no incentive to resist.

Academic evidence generally shows that compensation is higher at firms with ineffective governance structures, for example, when outside directors have ties to the company, or when they hold multiple outside directorships. It also is higher when the same person is both CEO and board chairman, although this finding could be remuneration for the additional duties the individual holds.

APPENDIX 9.1. EXCERPT ON BOARD OF
DIRECTORS FROM GENERAL ELECTRIC PROXY
STATEMENT FILED WITH THE SECURITIES AND
EXCHANGE COMMISSION MARCH 13, 2000

ELECTION OF DIRECTORS

At the 2000 Annual Meeting, 16 directors are to be elected to hold office until the
2001 Annual Meeting and until their successors have been elected and have qualified. The nominees listed on pages 5 to 10 with brief biographies are all now GE
directors. Ann M. Fudge joined the Board in June 1999, and Scott G. McNealy
joined in December 1999. Vice Chairman Eugene F. Murphy, who served as a
director since 1997, retired from GE and the Board at the end of June 1999, and
Vice Chairman John D. Opie, who has served as a director since 1995, will retire
from the Company and the Board at the end of March 2000. The Board knows of
no reason why any nominee may be unable to serve as a director. If any nominee is
unable to serve, the shares represented by all valid proxies will be voted for the
election of such other person as the Board may recommend.

**James I. Cash, Jr., 52, James E. Robison Professor of Business Administra-
tion, Harvard Graduate School of Business, Cambridge, Mass. Director
since 1997.**

A graduate of Texas Christian University with MS and PhD degrees from Purdue
University, Dr. Cash joined the faculty of Harvard Business School in 1976, where
he served as chairman of the MBA program from 1992 to 1995. Dr. Cash is also a
director of Cambridge Technology Partners, The Chubb Corporation, Knight-
Ridder, Inc., State Street Bank and Trust, and WinStar Corporation. He also serves
as a trustee of the Massachusetts General Hospital and Partners Healthcare and as an
overseer for the Boston Museum of Science.

**Silas S. Cathcart, 73, Retired Chairman of the Board and Chief Executive
Officer, Illinois Tool Works, Inc., diversified products, Chicago, Ill. Director 1972–1987 and since 1990.**

Following his graduation from Princeton in 1948, Mr. Cathcart joined Illinois Tool
Works, Inc., a manufacturer of tools, fasteners, packaging and other products. He
was named a vice president in 1954, executive vice president in 1962, and president
and director in 1964; and he served as chairman from 1972 to 1986. From 1987 to
1989, he served as chairman of the board of Kidder, Peabody Group Inc. Mr.
Cathcart is also a director of Cardinal Health, Inc. and serves as a trustee of the
Buffalo Bill Historical Society.

**Dennis D. Dammerman, 54, Vice Chairman of the Board and Executive
Officer, General Electric Company. Director since 1994.**

Mr. Dammerman joined GE after graduating from the University of Dubuque in
1967. He had financial assignments in several GE businesses before being named

vice president and comptroller of General Electric Credit Corporation (now GE Capital Corporation) in 1979. In 1981, he became vice president and general manager of GE Capital's Commercial Financial Services Department and, later that year, of GE Capital's Real Estate Financial Services Division. He was elected senior vice president for finance of GE in 1984, a director of GE in 1994 and, in 1998, was named vice chairman of the board and executive officer of GE and chairman and CEO of GE Capital Services, Inc.

Paolo Fresco, 66, Chairman of the Board, Fiat SpA, automotive and industrial products, Turin, Italy. Director since 1990.

Mr. Fresco received a law degree from the University of Genoa. After practicing law in Rome, he joined GE's Italian subsidiary, Compagnia Generale di Elettricita (COGENEL), in 1962 as corporate counsel, becoming president and general manager of that company in 1972. In 1976, he joined GE's International Group and was elected a vice president in 1977. Mr. Fresco became vice president and general manager—Europe and Africa Operations in 1979. In 1985, he was named vice president and general manager—International Operations. In 1987, he was elected senior vice president—GE International. He became a member of the GE Board in 1990 and was elected vice chairman of the board and executive officer of GE in 1992. Mr. Fresco retired from GE and became chairman of the board of Fiat SpA of Italy in 1998.

Ann M. Fudge, 48, President, Kraft's Maxwell House and Post Division, and Executive Vice President, Kraft Foods, Inc., packaged foods, White Plains, N.Y. Director since 1999.

After graduating from Simmons College in 1973, Ms. Fudge worked in human resources for GE until entering Harvard University, where she obtained an MBA in 1977. She then held marketing positions at General Mills until joining General Foods in 1986, where she was appointed executive vice president in 1991. In 1994, she was named president of Kraft General Foods' Maxwell House Coffee Company, and in 1995, executive vice president of Kraft Foods, Inc. She became president of Kraft's Maxwell House and Post coffee and cereal division in 1997. Ms. Fudge is a director of Honeywell International Inc., Liz Claiborne, Inc. and the Federal Reserve Bank of New York.

Claudio X. Gonzalez, 65, Chairman of the Board and Chief Executive Officer, Kimberly-Clark de Mexico, S.A. de C.V., Mexico City, and Director, Kimberly-Clark Corporation, consumer and paper products. Director since 1993.

Mr. Gonzalez is a graduate of Stanford University. He was employed by Kimberly-Clark in 1956 and by Kimberly-Clark de Mexico, S.A. in 1957. He was elected vice president of operations of Kimberly-Clark de Mexico, S.A. in 1962 and executive vice president and managing director in 1966. He assumed his present position in 1973. Mr. Gonzalez is also a director of Kellogg Company, The Mexico Fund,

Inc., Planet Hollywood International, Inc., Banco Nacional de Mexico, Grupo Carso, Grupo Industrial ALFA, Grupo Modelo, Grupo Televisa and Telefonos de Mexico.

Andrea Jung, 41, President and Chief Executive Officer, and Director, Avon Products, Inc., cosmetics, New York, N.Y. Director since 1998.

Ms. Jung, a graduate of Princeton University, joined Avon Products, Inc., a multi-national cosmetics company, in 1994 as president, product marketing for Avon U.S. She was elected president, global marketing, in 1996, an executive vice president in 1997, president and a director of the company in 1998 and chief executive officer in 1999. Previously, she was executive vice president, Neiman Marcus and a senior vice president for I. Magnin. Ms. Jung is also a member of the Princeton University Board of Trustees and is a director of Catalyst and the Cosmetic, Toiletry and Fragrance Association.

Kenneth G. Langone, 64, Chairman, President and Chief Executive Officer, Invemed Associates, LLC, investment banking and brokerage, New York, N.Y. Director since 1999.

Mr. Langone received a BA from Bucknell University and an MBA from New York University's Stern School of Business. He is the founder of Invemed Associates, LLC, and a co-founder, director and member of the executive committee of Home Depot, Inc. He is also a director of DBT Online, Inc., InterWorld Corporation, TRICON Global Restaurants, Inc. and Unifi, Inc., as well as the New York Stock Exchange. In addition to serving as a director of numerous charitable organizations, Mr. Langone is chairman of the NYU School of Medicine and serves on the Board of Trustees of New York University and the Board of Overseers of its Stern School of Business.

Scott G. McNealy, 45, Chairman of the Board and Chief Executive Officer, Sun Microsystems, Inc., supplier of network computing solutions, Palo Alto, Calif. Director since 1999.

After graduating with an economics degree from Harvard University in 1976, Mr. McNealy worked in manufacturing for Rockwell International before entering Stanford University, where he obtained an MBA degree in 1980. Following Stanford, Mr. McNealy worked at FMC Corporation and Onyx Systems before co-founding Sun Microsystems, Inc., where he became a director and vice president of operations in 1982. Mr. McNealy has been chairman of the Board of Directors and chief executive officer of Sun Microsystems since 1984.

Gertrude G. Michelson, 74, Former Senior Vice President—External Affairs and former Director, R. H. Macy & Co., Inc., retailers, New York, N.Y. Director since 1976.

Mrs. Michelson received a BA degree from Pennsylvania State University in 1945 and an LLB degree from Columbia University in 1947, at which time she joined

Macy's—New York. Mrs. Michelson was elected a vice president in 1963 and senior vice president in 1979, and she was named senior vice president—external affairs in 1980. She served as senior advisor to R. H. Macy & Co., Inc. from 1992 to 1994. She is chairman emeritus of the Board of Trustees of Columbia University and president of the Board of Overseers, TIAA-CREF.

Sam Nunn, 61, Partner, King & Spalding, law firm, Atlanta, Ga. Director since 1997.

After attending Georgia Institute of Technology and serving in the U.S. Coast Guard, Mr. Nunn received an AB degree from Emory University in 1960 and an LLB degree from Emory Law School in 1962. He then practiced law and served in the Georgia House of Representatives before being elected to the United States Senate in 1972, where he served as the chairman and ranking member on both the Senate Armed Services Committee and the Senate Permanent Committee on Investigations before retiring in 1997. Mr. Nunn is also a director of The Coca-Cola Company, Dell Computer Corporation, Internet Security Systems Group, Inc., National Service Industries, Inc., Scientific-Atlanta, Inc., Texaco Inc. and Total System Services, Inc. He also is involved in public policy work as chairman of the board of the Center for Strategic and International Studies (CSIS) and the Sam Nunn School of International Affairs at the Georgia Institute of Technology.

Roger S. Penske, 63, Chairman of the Board, Penske Corporation, Detroit Diesel Corporation, Penske Truck Leasing Corporation, and United Auto Group, Inc., transportation and automotive services, Detroit, Mich. Director since 1994.

A 1959 graduate of Lehigh (Pa.) University, Mr. Penske founded Penske Corporation in 1969. He became chairman of the board of Penske Truck Leasing Corporation in 1982, chairman and chief executive officer of Detroit Diesel Corporation in 1988 and chairman of the board of United Auto Group, Inc. in 1999. Mr. Penske is also vice chairman and a director of International Speedway Corporation and a director of Delphi Automotive Systems Corporation. He serves as a trustee of the Henry Ford Museum and Greenfield Village, is a director of Detroit Renaissance and is a member of the Business Council.

Frank H. T. Rhodes, 73, President Emeritus, Cornell University, Ithaca, N.Y. Director since 1984.

An English-born naturalized U.S. citizen, Dr. Rhodes holds bachelor of science, doctor of philosophy and doctor of science degrees from the University of Birmingham (U.K.). He served as president of Cornell University from 1977 to 1995. Dr. Rhodes was appointed by President Reagan as a member of the National Science Board, of which he is a former chairman, and by President Bush as a member of the President's Education Policy Advisory Committee.

Andrew C. Sigler, 68, Retired Chairman of the Board and Chief Executive Officer, Champion International Corporation, paper and forest products, Stamford, Conn. Director since 1984.

A graduate of Dartmouth College with an MBA degree from its Amos Tuck School of Business Administration, Mr. Sigler joined Champion Papers Inc., a predecessor of Champion International, in 1956. He served as chairman of the board of directors and chief executive officer of Champion International from 1979 until his retirement in 1996. Mr. Sigler is also a director of Honeywell International Inc. and The Chase Manhattan Corporation.

Douglas A. Warner III, 53, Chairman of the Board, Chief Executive Officer and President, J.P. Morgan & Co. Inc. and Morgan Guaranty Trust Company, New York, N.Y. Director since 1992.

Following graduation from Yale University in 1968, Mr. Warner joined Morgan Guaranty Trust Company, a wholly owned subsidiary of J.P. Morgan & Co. Incorporated. He was named an executive vice president of the bank in 1987, executive vice president of the parent in 1989 and managing director of the bank and its parent in 1989. He was elected president and a director of the bank and its parent in 1990 and became chairman and chief executive officer in 1995. Mr. Warner is also a director of Anheuser-Busch Companies, Inc., chairman of the Board of Managers and the Board of Overseers of Memorial Sloan-Kettering Cancer Center, a member of the Business Council and a trustee of the Pierpont Morgan Library.

John F. Welch, Jr., 64, Chairman of the Board and Chief Executive Officer, General Electric Company. Director since 1980.

A 1957 graduate of the University of Massachusetts with MS and PhD degrees from the University of Illinois, Mr. Welch joined GE in 1960. Following managerial assignments in the plastics and the chemical and metallurgical businesses, he was elected a vice president in 1972. In 1973, he was named vice president and group executive of the Components and Materials Group. He became a senior vice president and sector executive of the Consumer Products and Services Sector in 1977 and was elected a vice chairman and named an executive officer in 1979. Mr. Welch was elected chairman and named chief executive officer in 1981. He also serves as a director of Fiat SpA and NBC Internet, Inc.

INFORMATION RELATING TO DIRECTORS, NOMINEES AND EXECUTIVE OFFICERS

The following table includes all GE stock-based holdings, as of February 11, 2000, of the Company's directors and five most highly compensated executive officers. This table indicates the alignment of the named individuals' financial interests with the interests of the Company's share owners because the value of their total GE holdings will increase or decrease in line with the price of GE's stock.

Common Stock and Total Stock-Based Holdings

Name	Stock[1]	Total[2]	Name	Stock[1]	Total[2]
James I. Cash, Jr.	5,607	19,107	Gertrude G. Michelson	36,607[4]	110,017
Silas S. Cathcart	269,203[3]	284,203	Sam Nunn	10,000	27,815
Dennis D. Dammerman	378,021	1,322,416	John D. Opie	589,412[5]	1,622,918
Paolo Fresco	838,238	848,738	Roger S. Penske	29,000	51,521
Ann M. Fudge	553	6,553	Frank H. T. Rhodes	46,003	83,035
Claudio X. Gonzalez	37,886	68,548	Gary L. Rogers	560,260	1,113,590
Benjamin W. Heineman, Jr.	421,783	856,694	Andrew C. Sigler	23,407	38,407
Andrea Jung	3,907	14,407	Douglas A. Warner III	42,607[6]	57,607
Kenneth G. Langone	75,046	81,046	John F. Welch, Jr.	2,666,718[7]	6,788,746
Scott G. McNealy	3,510	9,510			

Common stock holdings of all directors and executive officers as a group were 7,494,9728.[8]

Notes:

[1]This column lists voting securities, including restricted stock held by executive officers over which the officers have voting power but no investment power. Otherwise, each director or officer has sole voting and investment power over the shares reported, except as noted. This column includes 4,500 shares for Dr. Cash, 29,000 shares for Mr. Cathcart, 796,500 shares for Mr. Fresco, 33,000 shares for Messrs. Gonzalez and Warner and Mrs. Michelson, 1,500 shares for Ms. Jung, 9,000 shares for Mr. Nunn, 10,500 shares for Mr. Penske, 45,000 shares for Dr. Rhodes, and 15,000 shares for Mr. Sigler that may be acquired by them pursuant to stock options that are or will become exercisable within 60 days. It also includes 277,499 shares for Mr. Dammerman, 240,000 shares for Mr. Heineman, 315,000 shares for Mr. Opie, 360,000 shares for Mr. Rogers, and 1,680,000 shares for Mr. Welch that may be acquired by them pursuant to stock options that are or will be exercisable within 60 days. No director or executive officer owns more than one-tenth of one percent of the total outstanding shares, nor do all directors and executive officers as a group own more than one percent of the total outstanding shares.
[2]This column shows the individual's total GE stock-based holdings, including the voting securities shown in the "Stock" column (as described in note 1), plus non-voting interests, including, as appropriate, the individual's holdings of stock appreciation rights, restricted stock units, deferred compensation accounted for as units of GE stock, and stock options that will not become exercisable within 60 days.
[3]Includes 10,880 shares over which Mr. Cathcart has shared voting and investment power.
[4]Includes 3,200 shares over which Mrs. Michelson shares voting and investment power.
[5]Includes 25,000 shares over which Mr. Opie's spouse shares voting and investment power but as to which he disclaims any other beneficial interest.
[6]Includes 1,200 shares over which Mr. Warner has shared voting and investment power but as to which he disclaims any other beneficial interest.
[7]Includes 105,000 shares over which Mr. Welch has shared voting and investment power but as to which he disclaims any other beneficial interest.
[8]Includes 950,230 shares over which there are shared voting and/or investment powers.

• Board of Directors and Committees

The Board of Directors held eight meetings during 1999. The average attendance by directors at Board meetings, and Committee meetings they were scheduled to attend, was over 97%.

Among the committees of the Board of Directors are a Nominating Committee, a Management Development and Compensation Committee, and an Audit Committee.

Members of the Nominating Committee are Directors Sigler (Chairman), Cathcart, Michelson, Penske and Warner. This committee's responsibilities include the selection of potential candidates for director and the recommendation of candidates to the Board. It also makes recommendations to the Board concerning the structure and membership of the other Board Committees. The Nominating Committee held three meetings during 1999. This committee will consider share owner recommendations for director sent to the Nominating Committee, c/o Benjamin W. Heineman, Jr., Secretary, General Electric Company, Fairfield, CT 06431.

Members of the Management Development and Compensation Committee are Directors Cathcart (Chairman), Gonzalez, Michelson, Rhodes and Sigler. This committee has two primary responsibilities: (1) to monitor the Company's management resources, structure, succession planning, development and selection process as well as the performance of key executives; and (2) to review and approve executive compensation and changes. It also serves as the committee administering the GE 1990 Long-Term Incentive Plan and the Incentive Compensation Plan. This committee met eight times during 1999.

Members of the Audit Committee are Directors Michelson (Chairman), Cathcart, Penske, Rhodes and Sigler. This committee is primarily concerned with the effectiveness of the audits of GE by its internal audit staff and by the independent auditors. Its duties include: (1) recommending the selection of independent auditors; (2) reviewing the scope of the audit to be conducted by them, as well as the results of their audit; (3) reviewing the organization and scope of GE's internal system of audit and financial controls; (4) appraising GE's financial reporting activities (including its Proxy Statement and Annual Report) and the accounting standards and principles followed; and (5) examining other reviews relating to compliance by employees with important GE policies and applicable laws. There were four meetings of the Audit Committee during 1999.

Non-employee directors are paid an annual retainer of $75,000 plus a fee of $2,000 for each Board meeting and for each Board Committee meeting attended. Half of any portion of the annual retainer that a director has not elected to defer is paid in GE common stock. A director may make an irrevocable election each year to defer all or a portion of annual retainer and fees. At the director's option, his or her account is credited with units accounted for as GE common stock or the dollar amount of the deferral. Accounts are also credited with common stock dividend equivalents or interest equivalents based on the yield for long-term U.S. government bonds. Participants will receive payments from their account in cash or GE stock, in either a lump sum or annual installments, after termination of Board service. Non-employee directors are also paid a travel allowance for attendance at Board meetings.

Any non-employee director who has served as a director for at least five years, is 65 years of age or older, and retires directly from the Board is eligible to elect to receive: (1) an annual retirement benefit for the lives of the director and eligible surviving spouse in the amount of the retainer fee in effect at retirement; or (2) in lieu thereof, a life insurance benefit in the amount of $450,000. GE also provides each non-employee director with group life and accidental death insurance in the aggregate amount of $150,000. The non-employee directors are not eligible to participate in GE's Incentive Compensation Plan, employee stock option plans or in any pension plans of GE or its subsidiaries.

It is the Board's policy that directors should not stand for re-election after their 73rd birthday. In 1998, in light of Mr. Welch's planned retirement, the Board decided to waive temporarily that policy so that all directors serving at that time could continue to participate in the process of selecting a successor to Mr. Welch as the Chairman of the Board.

GE has provided liability insurance for its directors and officers since 1968. Zurich Insurance Company and American International Specialty Lines Company are the principal underwriters of the current coverage, which was extended on June 11, 1997, until June 11, 2002. The annual cost of this coverage is approximately $3.3 million.

As part of the Company's overall support for charitable institutions, and in order to preserve its ability to attract directors with outstanding experience and ability, the Company maintains a plan which permits each director to recommend up to five charitable organizations that would share in a $1 million contribution to be made by the Company upon the director's retirement or death. The directors will not receive any financial benefit from this program since the charitable deductions accrue solely to the Company. The overall program will not result in a material cost to the Company.

To further align the non-employee directors' interests with the long-term interests of the share owners, the share owners approved the 1996 Stock Option Plan for Non-Employee Directors, which automatically provides yearly grants of options from 1997 through 2003 (with each grant becoming exercisable in four equal annual installments) to each non-employee director who is serving on the Board at the time of such grant. Each annual grant permits the holder to purchase from GE up to 6,000 shares of GE's common stock at the fair market value of such shares on the date the option was granted. Under the terms of the Plan, grants were made on January 29, 1999, at an exercise price of $104.875 per share, and on January 31, 2000, at an exercise price of $133.50 per share, and annual grants will be made on the last day of trading of GE stock in each January hereafter through the year 2003. The options expire ten years after the date they were granted or at such earlier date as may be provided by the Plan provisions upon retirement, disability, death or other termination of service. The Plan is administered by a committee of employee directors, none of whom is eligible to receive awards under the Plan.

The directors (other than directors Cash, Fudge, Gonzalez, Jung, Langone, McNealy, Nunn, Opie, Penske and Warner) and certain officers are defendants in a civil suit purportedly brought on behalf of the Company as a share owner derivative action (the McNeil action) in New York State Supreme Court, New York County, in 1991. The suit alleges the Company was negligent and engaged in fraud in connection with the design and construction of containment systems for nuclear power plants and contends that, as a result, GE has incurred significant financial liabilities and is potentially exposed to additional liabilities from claims brought by the Company's customers. The suit alleges breach of fiduciary duty by the directors and seeks unspecified compensatory damages and other relief. The Company and the defendants believe these claims are without merit and are defending the suit.

• **Certain Transactions**

Mr. Penske has an indirect financial interest in Penske Truck Leasing Co., L.P., a limited partnership formed in 1988 between a subsidiary of Penske Corporation and a subsidiary of GE Capital Corporation (GE Capital) in order to operate a truck leasing and rental business. In connection with a 1996 restructuring that increased GE Capital's interest in the partnership from 50% to 79%, the Penske Corporation subsidiary will receive annual payments, declining from $11.3 million to $9.3 million over a ten-year period, with the majority of such payments contingent upon the partnership achieving certain revenue thresholds. GE Capital has also extended acquisition and working capital loans and guarantees to the partnership, which totaled about $3.1 billion at the end of 1999, all on terms substantially equivalent to those extended to similar affiliates and joint ventures. Mr. Penske also has a direct financial interest in and controls Penske Capital Partners, LLC, which in 1997 entered into an investment agreement with GE Capital's Equity Capital Group and other investors. The agreement permits GE Capital to invest up to $100 million of equity in transactions involving selected transportation-related companies in return for its agreement to pay Penske Capital Partners an annual fee of up to $1.5 million for evaluating and, as appropriate, managing such investments. GE Capital also agreed that, after it recovers its investments and receives a preferred return on any such investments, Penske Capital Partners shall then receive a 20% interest in the remaining profits from the GE Capital investments.

GE has, for a number of years, used the services of the law firm of King & Spalding, in which Mr. Nunn is a partner, for a variety of matters. Also, GE and its subsidiaries have obtained investment banking and other financial services from J.P. Morgan & Co. Inc., of which Mr. Warner is Chairman of the Board, Chief Executive Officer and President, and from certain of its subsidiaries. Similarly, GE has obtained brokerage services and GE and its subsidiaries have participated in investments with Invemed Associates, LLC, of which Mr. Langone is Chairman, President and Chief Executive Officer and in which he holds a controlling ownership interest. For several years, GE and its subsidiaries have purchased computer equipment and related services from Sun Microsystems, Inc.

In 1999, GE Capital's Information Technology Solutions business, a Sun distributor and value-added reseller, purchased over $1.9 billion of Sun products and services for resale. GE Capital also has a five-year global vendor financing agreement with Sun under which GE Capital offers to provide loan and lease financing to Sun's customers. Mr. McNealy, who joined the Board in December 1999, is Chairman of the Board and Chief Executive Officer of Sun. GE and its subsidiaries also have purchase, lease, finance, insurance and other transactions and relationships in the normal course of business with companies and organizations with which GE directors are associated, but which are not sufficiently significant to be reportable. Management believes that all of these transactions and relationships during 1999 were on terms that were reasonable and competitive. Additional transactions and relationships of this nature may be expected to take place in the ordinary course of business in the future.

APPENDIX 9.2. EXCERPT ON BOARD OF DIRECTORS FROM WALT DISNEY PROXY STATEMENT FILED WITH THE SECURITIES AND EXCHANGE COMMISSION JANUARY 5, 2000

The following table shows the amount of common stock of the Company beneficially owned (unless otherwise indicated) by the Company's directors, the executive officers of the Company named in the Summary Compensation Table below and the directors and executive officers of the Company as a group. Except as otherwise indicated, all information is as of December 17, 1999.

| Name | Aggregate number of shares beneficially owned[1,2] | | Acquirable within 60 days[3] | | Percent of shares outstanding[4] | |
	Disney group	GO.com	Disney group	GO.com	Disney group	GO.com
Reveta F. Bowers	4,664	—	10,850	—	★	—
John F. Cooke	11,401	—	210,000	—	★	—
Roy E. Disney	17,771,976	—	600,000	—	★	—
Michael D. Eisner	12,387,409[5]	78,000	—	—	★	★
Judith L. Estrin	1,664	—	—	—	★	—
Stanley P. Gold	13,981	—	12,000	—	★	—
Stanley P. Gold	13,981	—	12,000	—	★	—
Sanford M. Litvack	34,252	—	1,050,000	—	★	—
Ignacio E. Lozano, Jr.	17,329	—	12,000	—	★	—
Louis M. Meisinger	72	—	75,000	—	★	—
George J. Mitchell	8,677	—	8,400	—	★	—
Thomas S. Murphy	3,198,672	—	—	—	★	—
Leo J. O'Donovan, S.J	—	—	2,400	—	—	—
Sidney Poitier	5,632	—	12,000	—	★	—
Irwin E. Russell	14,397	—	12,000	—	★	—
Robert A.M. Stern	3,266	—	12,000	—	★	—
Andrea Van de Kamp	1,072	—	—	—	★	—
Raymond L. Watson	37,756	—	12,000	—	★	—
Gary L. Watson	5,339	—	12,000	—	★	—
All current directors and executive officers as a group (20 persons)	33,530,019	80,500	2,698,350	—	1.7%	★

★Represents less than 1% of the Company's outstanding common stock.

[1]The number of shares shown includes shares that are individually or jointly owned, as well as shares over which the individual has either sole or shared investment or voting authority. Certain of the Company's directors and executive officers disclaim beneficial ownership of some of the shares included in the table, as follows:

- Mr. Eisner—88,800 shares held by his wife directly and as custodian for their children, 36,000 shares held in a trust for his children, 4,800 shares held in a trust for other family members, 21,600 shares held in a trust of which Mr. Eisner is a trustee and 9,600 shares held in a trust of which Mr. Eisner is the income beneficiary;

- Mr. Disney—768,960 shares held in trusts for the benefit of his children or grandchildren, of which Mr. Disney is the trustee; and 1,248 shares beneficially owned by Shamrock Holdings, Inc., of which both Mr. Disney and his wife are officers and directors and the shares of which are held by Mr. Disney, his wife, certain of his children, trusts for the benefit of his children and custodial accounts for the benefit of certain of his children and grandchildren;
- Mr. Gold—4,820 shares held by his wife and 1,248 shares beneficially owned by Shamrock Holdings, Inc., of which he is an officer and director;
- Mr. Litvack—450 shares held by a trust of which he is a co-trustee;
- Mr. Lozano—1,320 shares that he holds as custodian for the benefit of his child;
- Thomas Murphy—52,170 shares held in trust for the benefit of a non- family member and 1,320 shares owned by Mr. Murphy's wife; and

All current directors and executive officers as a group disclaim beneficial ownership of a total of 987,536 shares.

[2]For executive officers, the numbers include interests in shares held in the Disney Salaried Savings and Investment Plan, with respect to which participants have voting power but no investment rights: Mr. Eisner—26,458 shares; Mr. Litvack—2,752 shares; Mr. Meisinger—72 shares; Mr. Cooke—11,401 shares; and all current executive officers as a group 47,282 shares. For non-employee directors participating in the Company's 1997 Non-Employee Directors Stock and Deferred Compensation Plan, the numbers include share units credited as of September 30, 1999, to the director's account: Ms. Bowers—3,514; Mr. Gold—2,933; Sen. Mitchell—3,577; Mr. Murphy—5,054; Mr. Poitier—2,857; Mr. Russell—2,397; Mr. Stern—2,341; Ms. Van de Kamp—872; Mr. Watson—2,916; and Mr. Wilson—2,339. Participating directors do not have current voting or investment power with respect to these share units, which are payable solely in shares of common stock upon termination of service.

[3]Reflects the number of shares that could be purchased by exercise of options available at December 28, 1999 or within 60 days thereafter under the Company's stock option plans.

[4]Based on the number of shares outstanding at December 28, 1999.

[5]Does not include 825,000 shares held by The Eisner Foundation, Inc., a charitable not-for-profit corporation in which Mr. Eisner has no pecuniary interest.

Based upon a review of filings with the Securities and Exchange Commission and written representations that no other reports were required, the Company believes that all of the Company's directors and executive officers complied during fiscal 1999 with the reporting requirements of Section 16(a) of the Securities Exchange Act of 1934.

ITEM 1—ELECTION OF DIRECTORS

Directors Standing for Election

The Board of Directors is currently divided into three classes, having three-year terms that expire in successive years. In 1998, the Company amended its certificate of incorporation to provide for the elimination of the classification of the Board by 2001. Under the amended certificate of incorporation, all directors elected by shareholders after the 1998 annual meeting, regardless of class, are elected for a one-year term.

The current term of office of directors in Classes I and III expires at the 2000 annual meeting. The Board of Directors proposes that the nominees described below, all of whom are currently serving as Class I or Class III directors, be re-elected for a new term of one year and until their successors are duly elected and qualified.

Each of the nominees has consented to serve a one-year term. If any of them become unavailable to serve as a director, the Board may designate a substitute nominee. In that case, the persons named as proxies will vote for the substitute nominee designated by the Board.

Class I and Class III Directors. The directors standing for election are:

Class I

Reveta F. Bowers   Director since 1993

Mrs. Bowers, 51, has been an administrator and the Head of School for the Center for Early Education, an independent school for pre-school through sixth grade located in Los Angeles, since 1976. Mrs. Bowers is a member of the Board of Directors of several non-profit educational organizations, including The Institute for Educational Advancement, The Fulfillment Fund, the Coalition for Justice and Independent Educational Services.

Roy E. Disney   Director since June 1984;
                                          also from 1967 to March 1984

Mr. Disney, 69, has been Vice Chairman of the Board of Directors of the Company since 1984, and since November 1985 has also served as head of the Company's animation department. In addition, Mr. Disney is Chairman of the Board of Shamrock Holdings, Inc., which, through its subsidiaries, is engaged in real estate development and the making of investments. Mr. Disney is a nephew of the late Walt Disney.

Ignacio E. Lozano, Jr.   Director since 1981

Mr. Lozano, 73, is Chairman of Lozano Enterprises, which publishes La Opinion, the largest Spanish language newspaper in the Los Angeles metropolitan area. Mr. Lozano was Publisher and Editor of La Opinion from 1953 to 1986, except for the period from 1976 through 1977 when he was the United States Ambassador to El Salvador. Mr. Lozano is a member of the Boards of Directors of Sempra Energy, a holding company, and its subsidiaries Southern California Gas Co. and San Diego Gas and Electric Co., and a number of public service and charitable organizations.

George J. Mitchell   Director since 1995

Senator Mitchell, 66, is special counsel to the law firm of Verner, Liipfert, Bernhard, McPherson & Hand in Washington, D.C. and senior counsel to the firm of Preti, Flaherty, Beliveau & Pachios in Portland, Maine. He served as a United States Senator for fifteen years commencing in 1980, and was Senate Majority Leader from 1989 to 1995. Senator Mitchell is a member of the Board of Directors of UNUM Provident, a disability insurance company; FDX Corporation, an international provider of transportation and delivery services; Xerox Corporation, a manufacturer of photocopier equipment; Unilever, an international food and personal care products company; Staples, Inc., an office supply company; and Starwood Hotels & Resorts. He has also served as Chairman of the Peace Negotiations in Northern Ireland, the Ethics Committee of the U.S. Olympic Committee and the National Health Care Commission.

Gary L. Wilson   Director since 1985

Mr. Wilson, 59, has been Chairman of the Board of Directors of Northwest Airlines Corporation since 1997, having served as Co-Chairman of the Board of Directors from 1991 to 1997 and as a director since 1989. From 1985 through 1989, he was Executive Vice President and Chief Financial Officer of the Company. Prior to joining the Company, Mr. Wilson was Executive Vice President and Chief Financial Officer of Marriott Corporation, a diversified company involved in lodging, food service and related businesses. Mr. Wilson is a director of On Command Corporation, a provider of in-room, on-demand video entertainment and information services to the domestic lodging industry, and CB Richard Ellis Services, Inc., a commercial real estate services company. He also serves on the board of trustees of Duke University and the board of overseers of the Wharton School at the University of Pennsylvania.

Class III

Judith L. Estrin   Director since 1998

Ms. Estrin, 45, is Chief Technology Officer and Senior Vice President of Cisco Systems Inc., a company that develops hardware and software to link computer systems. She was formerly President and Chief Executive Officer of Precept Software, Inc., a developer of networking software of which she was co-founder, from March 1995 until its acquisition by Cisco in April 1998. Ms. Estrin was a computer industry consultant from September 1994 to March 1995, and served Network Computer Devices as President and Chief Executive Officer from October 1993 to September 1994 and as Executive Vice President from July 1988 to October 1993. She also serves as a director of FDX Corporation, an international provider of transportation and delivery services, and Sun Microsystems, Inc., a supplier of network computing products.

Sanford M. Litvack   Director since 1995

Mr. Litvack, 63, currently serves as Vice Chairman of the Board of Directors, having previously served, from August 1994 to September 1999, as Senior Executive Vice President and Chief of Corporate Operations of the Company. He also served as the Company's General Counsel from April 1991 until July 1998. Mr. Litvack was a litigation partner with the law firm of Dewey Ballantine from 1987 until joining the Company in 1991.

Sidney Poitier   Director since 1994

Mr. Poitier, 72, is an actor, director and writer, serving as Chief Executive Officer of Verdon-Cedric Productions, a film production company. Mr. Poitier has won many awards, including the Academy Award® for Best Actor, the American Film Institute's Lifetime Achievement Award and the Kennedy Center Honors. He belongs to numerous civic organizations, including the Children's Defense Fund, the NAACP Legal Defense and Education Fund and the Natural Resources Defense Council. In addition, he is the Ambassador to Japan from the Commonwealth of the Bahamas.

Robert A.M. Stern   Director since 1992

Mr. Stern, 60, is a practicing architect, teacher and writer. He is Senior Partner of Robert A.M. Stern Architects of New York, which he founded, and a Fellow of the American Institute of Architects. Mr. Stern is also Dean of the Yale School of Architecture and previously served as a professor and Director of the Historic Preservation Department at the Graduate School of Architecture, Planning and Preservation at Columbia University. Mr. Stern is the design architect of the Yacht and Beach Club hotels, the Boardwalk Hotel and the Casting Center at the Walt Disney World Resort and the Newport Bay Club and the Cheyenne Hotel at Disneyland Paris. He is also the design architect of the Feature Animation Building at the Company's headquarters in Burbank, California.

Andrea Van de Kamp   Director since 1998

Ms. Van de Kamp, 56, is Chairman of Sotheby's West Coast, a unit of the international auction company, since 1989, and is a member of the Board of Directors of Sotheby's North America. She also serves as a director of City National Bank and Jenny Craig International, and as Chairman of the Board of the Los Angeles Music Center, Inc. In addition, Ms. Van de Kamp is a trustee of Pomona College, in Pomona, California.

Directors Continuing in Office

Class II Directors. The following Class II directors were elected at the Company's 1998 annual meeting for terms ending in 2001:

Michael D. Eisner   Director since 1994

Mr. Eisner, 57, has served as Chairman of the Board and Chief Executive Officer of the Company since 1984. Prior to joining the Company, Mr. Eisner was President and Chief Operating Officer of Paramount Pictures Corp., which was then a wholly owned subsidiary of Gulf+ Western Industries, Inc. Prior to joining Paramount in 1976, Mr. Eisner was Senior Vice President, Prime Time Programming, for ABC Entertainment, a division of the American Broadcasting Company, Inc., with responsibility for the development and supervision of all prime-time series programming, limited series movies made for television and the acquisition of talent.

Stanley P. Gold   Director since 1987;
                                          also from June to September 1984

Mr. Gold, 57, is President and Chief Executive Officer of Shamrock Holdings, Inc. Since 1990, he has also served as President of Trefoil Investors, Inc., the general partner of Trefoil Capital Investors, L.P., an investment partnership, as well as President of Shamrock Capital Advisors, Inc., which acts as manager of the partnership.

Thomas S. Murphy   Director since 1996

Mr. Murphy, 74, was Chairman of the Board and Chief Executive Officer of Capital Cities/ABC, Inc. for 24 years from 1966 to 1990 and from February 1994 until his retirement in February 1996. Mr. Murphy is also a director of Columbia/HCA Healthcare Corp., a provider of health care services, and Doubleclick Inc., a provider of Internet advertising services.

Leo J. O'Donovan, S.J.   Director since 1996

Since 1989, Fr. O'Donovan, 65, has been President of Georgetown University, where he also holds an appointment as Professor of Theology. He serves on a number of higher education boards, including that of the Association of Catholic Colleges and Universities, and is a member of the Steering Committee of Presidents for the America Reads initiative. He is a former member of the National Council on the Arts of the National Endowment for the Arts and past chair of the Consortium on Financing Higher Education.

Irwin E. Russell   Director since 1987

Mr. Russell, 73, is an attorney presently engaged in private practice, who has served as an attorney and executive in the entertainment industry for many years. He serves as an independent member of the Board of Directors of The Lipper Funds, Inc., a mutual fund group, and of the Southern California Tennis Association, a nonprofit association. He also serves as an ad hoc arbitrator for the Federal Mediation and Conciliation Service and the American Arbitration Association.

Raymond L. Watson   Director since 1974

Mr. Watson, 73, has served as Chairman of the Executive Committee of the Company's Board of Directors since 1984 and was Chairman of the Board of the Company from May 1983 to September 1984. Since 1986, Mr. Watson has been Vice Chairman of the Board of The Irvine Company, a land development company. From 1985 to 1986, he was Regents Professor in the Graduate School of Management at the University of California, Irvine. Mr. Watson is also a director of the Public Policy Institute of California, a non-profit public policy research institute.

How are directors compensated?

Base Compensation. Each non-employee director receives a retainer based on an annualized rate of $35,000, together with a fee of $1,000 per Board or Committee meeting attended. Non-employee directors may elect to receive all or part of their retainer and meeting fees either in common stock or in cash or stock unit accounts. Any such elections are effective until termination of the participating director's service as a director. All of the non-employee directors other than Fr. O'Donovan are currently participating in this plan. Directors who are also employees of the Company receive no additional compensation for service as directors.

Options. Each non-employee director receives an automatic grant, on March 1 of each year, of options to purchase 6,000 shares of common stock. For fiscal 1999, Ms. Bowers, Fr. O'Donovan and Messrs. Gold, Lozano, Mitchell, Murphy, Poitier, Russell, Stern, Watson and Wilson received grants under this plan. Each option grant, vesting in equal installments over five years and having a ten-year term, permits the holder to purchase shares at their fair market value on the date of grant, which was $34.91 in the case of options granted in 1999.

How often did the Board meet during fiscal 1999?

The Board of Directors met seven times during fiscal 1999. Each director attended more than 75% of the total number of meetings of the Board and Committees on which he or she served.

What committees has the Board established?

The Board of Directors has standing Executive, Compensation, Audit Review and Nominating Committees, and the Compensation Committee has a standing Executive Performance Subcommittee. During 1999, the Board also established a Capital Stock Committee in connection with the issuance of the GO.com common stock.

Board Committee Membership

Name	Executive committee	Compensation committee	Executive performance subcommittee	Audit review committee	Nominating committee	Capital stock committee
Reveta F. Bowers		★	★	★	★	
Roy E. Disney	★					
Michael D. Eisner	★					
Judith L. Estrin				★		
Stanley P. Gold		★	★★		★★	
Sanford M. Litvack						★
Ignacio E. Lozano, Jr.		★	★	★★		
George J. Mitchell				★	★	★★
Thomas S. Murphy	★	★★				
Leo J. O'Donovan, S.J				★		★
Sidney Poitier		★	★			
Irwin E. Russell	★					
Robert A.M. Stern						
Andrea Van de Kamp					★	
Raymond L. Watson	★★	★		★		
Gary L. Wilson					★	★

★Member.
★★Chair.

Executive Committee. The Executive Committee possesses all of the powers of the Board except the power to issue stock, approve mergers with nonaffiliated corporations or declare dividends (except at a rate or in a periodic amount or within a price range established by the Board), and certain other powers specifically reserved by Delaware law to the Board. In fiscal 1999, the Executive Committee held no meetings, but took action by unanimous written consent four times.

Compensation Committee. The Compensation Committee is charged with reviewing the Company's general compensation strategy (except with respect to matters entrusted to the Executive Performance Subcommittee as described below); establishing salaries and reviewing benefit programs (including pensions) for the Chief Executive Officer and those persons who report directly to him; reviewing, approving, recommending and administering the Company's incentive compensation and stock option plans and certain other compensation plans; and approving certain employment contracts. In fiscal 1999, the Compensation Committee met seven times.

Executive Performance Subcommittee. The Executive Performance Subcommittee of the Compensation Committee has as its principal responsibility to review and advise the Board with respect to performance-based compensation of corporate officers who are, or who are likely to become, subject to Section 162(m) of the Internal Revenue Code. (Section 162(m) limits the deductibility of compensation in excess of $1,000,000 paid to a corporation's chief executive officer and four other most highly compensated executive officers, unless certain conditions are met.) The Subcommittee met seven times during fiscal 1999.

Audit Review Committee. The Audit Review Committee met three times during fiscal 1999. Its functions are to recommend the appointment of independent accountants; review the arrangements for and scope of the audit by independent accountants; review the independence of the independent accountants; consider the adequacy of the system of internal accounting controls and review any proposed corrective actions; review and monitor the Company's policies relating to ethics and conflicts of interests; discuss with management and the independent accountants the Company's draft annual financial statements and key accounting and/or reporting matters, including "Year 2000" matters; and review the activities and recommendations of the Company's management audit department.

Nominating Committee. The Nominating Committee is responsible for soliciting recommendations for candidates for the Board of Directors; developing and reviewing background information for candidates; making recommendations to the Board regarding such candidates; and reviewing and making recommendations to the Board with respect to candidates for directors proposed by shareholders. Any shareholder wishing to propose a nominee should submit a recommendation in writing to the Company's Secretary, indicating the nominee's qualifications and other relevant biographical information and providing confirmation of the nominee's consent to serve as a director. The Nominating Committee did not meet during fiscal 1999.

Capital Stock Committee. The Capital Stock Committee was formed in November 1999 in connection with the issuance of the GO.com common stock. The functions of this Committee include the implementation and interpretation of the Company's "Common Stock Policies," which were adopted by the Board to set out certain policies and procedures relating to the allocation of interests between the "Disney Group" and "GO.com" and other matters that may affect the Company's two classes of common stock. The Committee is charged with overseeing the implementation of these policies, except as they relate to dividends, with respect to which all determinations are made by the Board of Directors as a whole. The Committee is also responsible for adopting additional general policies, as necessary, governing the relationships between the two classes of stock.

Certain Relationships and Related Transactions

During fiscal 1999, Company subsidiaries retained the firm of Robert A.M. Stern Architects, of which Mr. Stern is Senior Partner, for architectural services relating to the Celebration project in Florida and the Edison International Stadium in California. Payments to Mr. Stern's firm for these services aggregated $71,731 during the year. Mr. Stern's firm also provided architectural services during the year to Oriental Land Co., Ltd., the Japanese corporation that owns and operates Tokyo Disneyland and is developing a second theme park, Tokyo DisneySea, and two Disney-branded hotels under license from the Company's subsidiary Disney Enterprises, Inc.

Senator Mitchell provides consulting services to the Company with respect to a variety of matters affecting the Company's international business operations and development efforts. During fiscal 1999, the Company paid Senator Mitchell an aggregate of $50,000 for these services.

PART IV

Considerations in Designing the Executive Compensation Package

CHAPTER 10

Is Executive Compensation Really That High?

I. INTRODUCTION

> *After a decade of seemingly limitless pay increases, the average compensation for chief executives shot up an additional 23 percent, to $11.9 million, last year. Valuing stock options in the most widely used way, a chief executive now makes more in a single day than the typical American worker does in a year.*[1]

Implicit in the above statistic is the argument that American CEOs are overpaid. In reality, whether CEOs are overpaid depends on how the issue is framed. When framed as above, that is as a multiple of blue-collar worker pay, it does appear CEOs are overpaid. The amounts involved are high by most people's standards. However, more interesting is how the amounts compare to corporate profits, dividends, or increases in shareholder wealth, which may be considered surrogates for the value of the CEO to the corporation.

A. CEO Compensation Relative to Corporate Profits

In 2000, James Maguire, Chairman and Chief Executive Officer of Philadelphia Consolidated, realized $64,406,900 in profits from the exercise of stock options,[2] in a year where the company earned $30,770,000,[3] less than half that amount.

---

[1]Leonhardt (2000b, p. 1).

[2]Philadelphia Consolidated Holding Company proxy statement filed with Securities and Exchange Commission, April 9, 2001, p. 7.

[3]Philadelphia Consolidated Holding Company 10-K filed with Securities and Exchange Commission, March 30, 2001, p. 28.

TABLE 10.1   CEO Compensation as a
Percentage of Corporate Profits by Year

Year	Mean (%)	Median (%)
1992	5.89	1.64
1993	6.13	2.34
1994	6.40	2.55
1995	6.43	2.41
1996	7.30	2.73
1997	8.18	2.92
1998	8.19	3.12
1999	8.89	3.04
2000	7.89	2.77

Although these options had been awarded in previous years, and hence would not be considered compensation for the current year, this gain does seem disproportionately large. However, this is only one company.

Tables 10.1, 10.2, and 10.3 show CEO compensation[4] as a percentage of the absolute value of corporate profits for all companies on the ExecuComp database.[5] Table 10.1 shows how CEO pay as a percentage of corporate profits varies over time, whereas Table 10.2 shows how it varies across industry, and Table 10.3 shows how it varies with the size of the corporation.

As can be seen from Table 10.1, mean (median) annual CEO compensation increases from 5.89% (1.64%) of profit in 1992 to 8.89% (3.04%) of profit in 1999, before dropping to 7.89% (2.77%) of profit in 2000. Previously, Table 2.7 showed that in absolute terms, total compensation increased dramatically from 1992 to 2000. The pattern through 1999 is clear; even after controlling for corporate profits, CEO compensation is increasing over time. Determining whether the decrease in 2000 is a reversal in the trend, or simply an anomaly, will take time to tell.

Table 10.2 shows that CEO compensation varies across industries, ranging from a low of 4.00% (median 1.57%) of profit for transportation corporations to a high of 13.38% (median 4.46%) of profit for services corporations. In part this is driven

[4]CEO compensation includes salary, bonus, other annual, value of restricted stock granted, value of stock options granted (valued by ExecuComp), long-term incentive payouts, and all other compensation.

[5]The denominators used to calculate the percentages in Tables 10.1 through 10.9 are corporate profits, common dividends, and increase in shareholder wealth. The possibility of a small or negative value for each of these variables exists, with the potential to disproportionately influence the calculation of the mean. To prevent negative ratios, which would be meaningless, the absolute value of corporate profits and increase in shareholder wealth is used in the denominator (since dividends cannot be negative this was not an issue). To control for the disproportionate influence of outliers, the ratios were capped at 100% before being aggregated across corporations. Still, medians, which are not disproportionately influenced by outliers, may be more representative of the true patterns.

TABLE 10.2   CEO Compensation as a Percentage of Corporate Profits by Industry (for 2000)

Industry	SIC codes[a]	Mean (%)	Median (%)
Mining and construction	1000–1999	4.19	2.38
Manufacturing	2000–3999	8.72	3.18
Transportation, communications, electric, gas, and sanitary services	4000–4999	4.00	1.57
Wholesale and retail trade	5000–5999	7.20	3.14
Finance, insurance, and real estate	6000–6999	4.56	1.45
Services	7000–7999	13.38	4.46

[a]SIC, Standard Industrial Classification.

by the relatively low total compensation in the transportation classification and relatively high total compensation for corporations in the services classification, as shown in Table 2.8.

As found by previous research going back to Taussig and Barker (1925), Table 10.3 shows that CEO compensation as a percentage of profit is inversely related to the size of the corporation, dropping from 11.08% (median 7.26%) of profits for the smallest corporations to 3.06% (median 0.88%) of profits for the largest corporations. This latter finding, when combined with the earlier observation that compensation increases with the size of the corporation (see Table 2.9), indicates that although compensation increases with size of the corporation, the increase is not proportional.

TABLE 10.3   CEO Compensation as a Percentage of Corporate Profits by Size (for 2000)

	Size decile	Mean (%)	Median (%)
Smallest	1	11.08	7.26
	2	10.69	4.96
	3	8.00	3.33
	4	6.86	2.81
	5	9.69	3.18
	6	6.88	2.07
	7	7.39	2.37
	8	7.27	1.52
	9	8.13	1.65
Largest	10	3.06	0.88

TABLE 10.4   CEO Compensation as a
Percentage of Common Dividends by Year

Year	Mean (%)	Median (%)
1992	9.53	2.89
1993	12.64	4.35
1994	14.81	5.29
1995	14.90	5.57
1996	16.24	6.01
1997	17.67	6.93
1998	17.67	6.43
1999	18.74	7.56
2000	17.19	5.69

B. CEO Compensation Relative to Dividends Paid

Tables 10.4, 10.5, and 10.6 show CEO compensation as a percentage of dividends paid to common shareholders. In general, dividends are less than profits because corporations normally retain some profits to internally fund projects. A number of well-known profitable corporations, such as Cisco and Microsoft, don't pay any dividends at all. Thus, the ratios are for all dividend-paying companies included in the ExecuComp database. Consistent with dividends being lower than net income, the percentages in Table 10.4, 10.5, and 10.6 are higher than those in Tables 10.1, 10.2, and 10.3.

Table 10.4 shows mean (median) annual CEO compensation ranges from a low of 9.53% (2.89%) of dividends in 1992 to a high of 18.74% (7.56%) in 1999. Similar to the results presented in table 10.1, CEO compensation as a percentage of dividends increases somewhat dramatically from 1992–1999, with a small decrease registered in 2000.

Table 10.5 shows that across industries, CEO compensation ranges from a low of 7.66% (median 2.08%) of dividends for transportation, communications, electric, gas and sanitary services, to a high of 34.63% (median 12.96%) of dividends for mining and construction. A partial, if not total, explanation for this variation is that corporations in the transportation, communications, electric, gas, and sanitary services classification pay significantly higher dividends than corporations in the mining and construction classification. Note that in Table 2.8, mean total compensation is higher for corporations in the transportation, communications, electric, gas, and sanitary services classification, whereas median total compensation was higher for corporations in the mining and construction classification.

Table 10.6 shows that CEO compensation as a percentage of dividends is inversely related to the size of the corporation, dropping from 30.16% (median 15.47%) of dividends for the smallest corporations to 9.10% (median 2.42%) of

TABLE 10.5   CEO Compensation as a Percentage of Common Dividends by Industry (for 2000)

Industry	Standard industrial classification codes	Mean (%)	Median (%)
Mining and construction	1000–1999	34.63	12.96
Manufacturing	2000–3999	18.53	6.97
Transportation, communications, electric, gas, and sanitary services	4000–4999	7.66	2.08
Wholesale and retail trade	5000–5999	21.59	10.34
Finance, insurance, and real estate	6000–6999	9.89	3.88
Services	7000–7999	31.80	12.84

dividends for the largest corporations. Thus although (as shown in Table 2.9) compensation increases with the size of the corporation, dividends increase at a faster rate.

C. CEO Compensation Relative to Change in Shareholder Wealth

During 2000, Ralph Roberts, Chairman of the Board of Comcast, received $1,102,500 in salary, a bonus of $551,250, other annual compensation of $2,669,177, and all other compensation of $9,611,748,[6] as well as realized $86,671,922, upon

TABLE 10.6   CEO Compensation as a Percentage of Common Dividends by Size (for 2000)

	Size decile	Mean (%)	Median (%)
Smallest	1	30.16	15.47
	2	31.91	15.73
	3	25.95	12.78
	4	20.67	7.62
	5	17.54	7.86
	6	12.42	4.14
	7	7.29	3.18
	8	7.72	2.42
	9	15.81	2.91
Largest	10	9.10	2.42

[6]Comcast Corporation proxy statement filed with the Securities and Exchange Commission, on April 27, 2001, p. 17.

the exercise of stock options,[7] for a total of $100,606,597. This during a year when the Comcast's share price decreased significantly. As noted above with respect to Philadelphia Consolidated and its Chairman and CEO James Maguire, Mr. Roberts received these options in previous years, and hence they should not be considered compensation for the current year. However, even excluding these gains, Mr. Roberts received compensation of over $14 million, as well as 250,000 new options valued by the company at more than $5 million[8] in a year when shareholders lost billions.

Of course markets go up and down, and in years when a corporation's share price goes down, shareholders lose money. During 2000, almost 43% of the companies on ExecuComp had a negative total return to shareholders. However, although shareholders suffered, it is not clear that executives did. For the year 2000, when total return to shareholders was negative, total CEO compensation (including the present value of option grants) averaged $8,196,541 (median $2,673,500). When total return to shareholders was positive, total CEO compensation was slightly higher, averaging $8,756,685 (median $3,800,960). The difference is greater when the present value of option grants are replaced with the realized profit from option exercise. When total return to shareholders was negative, total CEO compensation (including the realized profit from option exercise) averaged $5,939,571 (median $1,489,335), whereas when total return to shareholders was positive, total CEO compensation averaged $8,418,410 (median $2,657,840). This difference, which is driven by the difference in realized profits from option exercise, makes sense in that when share prices decrease, previously granted options are less likely to be exercised, and if exercised, they are less profitable. However, either way, for corporations whose share price decreased, average (mean or median) CEO compensation exceeded $1 million, in a year when shareholders lost money.

Tables 10.7, 10.8, and 10.9 show CEO compensation as a percentage of the absolute value of the change in common shareholder wealth, where the change in common shareholder wealth is defined as the dividends paid to common shareholders plus the increase in the value of their shares. Table 10.7 shows that mean (median) annual CEO compensation ranges from a low of 2.30% (0.51%) of the increase in shareholder wealth in 1992, to a high of 3.29% (1.02%) in 1994. Unlike Tables 10.1 and 10.4, Table 10.7 does not show an increasing pattern over time.

Table 10.8 shows that across industries CEO compensation ranges from a low of 1.37% (median 0.45%) of the increase in shareholder wealth for finance, insurance, and real estate corporations, to a high of 2.91% (median 0.87%) of the increase in shareholder wealth for corporations in wholesale and retail trade. This latter finding is interesting, given that Table 2.8 showed that finance, insurance, and real estate

---

[7]Comcast Corporation proxy statement filed with the Securities and Exchange Commission on April 27, 2001, p. 21.

[8]Comcast Corporation proxy statement filed with the Securities and Exchange Commission on April 27, 2001, p. 19.

TABLE 10.7   CEO Compensation as a
Percentage of Increase in Shareholder
Wealth by Year[a]

Year	Mean (%)	Median (%)
1992	2.30	0.51
1993	2.76	0.73
1994	3.29	1.02
1995	2.41	0.62
1996	3.09	0.78
1997	2.57	0.64
1998	2.53	0.70
1999	2.70	0.63
2000	2.56	0.57

[a]Shareholder wealth is price appreciation plus dividends paid.

corporations paid the highest total compensation and wholesale and retail trade among the lowest.

Table 10.9 shows that CEO compensation as a percentage of the increase in shareholder wealth is inversely related to the size of the corporation, dropping from 5.17% (median 1.47%) of the increase in shareholder wealth for the smallest corporations to 1.34% (median 0.11%) of the increase in shareholder wealth for the largest corporations. Thus, consistent with the findings for corporate profits and dividends, while total compensation increases with the size of the corporation, it does not increase as quickly as the increase in shareholder wealth.

Summarizing Tables 10.1 through 10.9, it appears that CEO compensation is a material component of corporate profits and dividends, but a less significant

TABLE 10.8   CEO Compensation as a Percentage of Increase
in Shareholder Wealth by Industry (for 2000)[a]

Industry	SIC codes[b]	Mean (%)	Median (%)
Mining and construction	1000–1999	1.37	0.61
Manufacturing	2000–3999	2.72	0.59
Transportation, communications, electric, gas, and sanitary services	4000–4999	2.86	0.26
Wholesale and retail trade	5000–5999	2.91	0.87
Finance, insurance, and real estate	6000–6999	1.37	0.45
Services	7000–7999	2.44	0.58

[a]Shareholder wealth is price appreciation plus dividends paid.
[b]SIC, Standard Industrial Classification.

TABLE 10.9   CEO Compensation as a Percentage
of Increase in Shareholder Wealth by Size (for 2000)[a]

	Size decile	Mean (%)	Median (%)
Smallest	1	5.17	1.47
	2	4.86	1.26
	3	2.61	0.95
	4	3.47	0.77
	5	1.47	0.65
	6	1.39	0.40
	7	1.42	0.30
	8	1.77	0.24
	9	0.90	0.18
Largest	10	1.34	0.11

[a]Shareholder wealth is price appreciation plus dividends paid.

proportion of the change in shareholder wealth. Which is the appropriate percentage to use in determining reasonability? Some would argue that since the CEO is an agent of the shareholders that the change in shareholder wealth should be the appropriate benchmark. Using change in shareholder wealth as a benchmark, compensation seems reasonable, with a mean (median) ranging from about 2–3% (0.5–1%) of the change in shareholder wealth (Table 10.7). This is especially true for the largest corporations, where for 2000 the mean is 1.34% and median 0.11% of the change in shareholder wealth (Table 10.9). Others would argue that because stock prices are influenced by factors outside the CEO's control, profits are a more appropriate benchmark. Using corporate profits as a benchmark, CEO compensation appears less reasonable, with a mean ranging from slightly less than 6 to slightly less than 9% of profit over time (Table 10.1). This is especially true for the smallest corporations, where for 2000 the mean is 11.08% and median 7.26% of profit (see Table 10.3). Thus, to some extent, whether compensation is reasonable depends on the base used, that is, increase in shareholder wealth or corporate profits, and a comparison group, that is, small versus large corporations. One item that should be emphasized is that regardless of the base used or the comparison group, these percentages represent the compensation of one individual. The average firm in 2000 employed almost 25,000 individuals!

D. CEO Worth

Although the above numbers provide some descriptive statistics on the relative magnitudes of CEO compensation, they do not address the issue of whether the CEOs are worth those amounts. Hayes and Schaefer (1999) provide some academic evidence on whether executives are worth their pay by examining the effect of executive departures on stock market returns. They reason that if an executive is overpaid relative to his or her marginal product or value to the corporation, the market will react favorably, that is positively, to his or her departure. Conversely, if the executive is underpaid relative to his or her marginal product, the market will react unfavorably to his or her departure. They find that when executives depart for other corporations, the market reacts unfavorably, indicating that those executives were underpaid relative to their contributions to the corporation (which may explain why they were desired by another employer). In contrast, when executives die unexpectedly, the market reacts positively, indicating that those executives were overpaid.[9] Of course, it must be pointed out that the market reaction also takes into account the expected pay and performance of the executive's successor. If an overpaid executive, where overpaid is defined relative to his or her marginal product, is expected to be replaced by another executive who is even more overpaid, then the market will react negatively to the departure. Unfortunately, a direct examination of marginal product is not possible. Thus whether or not executive pay is excessive depends upon your perspective. The following quote, which is from a shareholder proposal by Robert McClellan III requesting that the Board of Directors institute a "comprehensive Executive Compensation Review," takes the view that the compensation of George Fisher, Chief Executive Officer of Kodak, was excessive and unrelated to financial performance.

> In 1998, Kodak's CEO, George Fisher, earned approximately $3,127 an hour, including stocks, shares and salary, according to Kodak's 1998 Annual Meeting and Proxy Statement to shareholders. Yet, a severe drop in earnings has resulted in Kodak's decision to cut payroll by many thousands of workers, a restructuring plan that Kodak states it will continue. Is it fair that comparatively low-wage workers lose their income while top executives salaries do not reflect financial performance?[10]

E. Well-Compensated Disappointments

Feeding this perspective is the perception that executives make enormous amounts whether they perform well or not. In several well-publicized instances, top executives who were forced to leave their companies received multimillion dollar severance packages. For example, Jill Barad, the former Chairman and Chief Executive Officer of Mattel, who resigned her position as of February 3, 2000, received a severance package of approximately $47 million,[11] excluding the value of 6,440,759

---

[9]An alternative explanation is the sudden departure makes the firm more likely to be acquired at a premium to the current stock price.

[10]Eastman Kodak proxy statement filed with the Securities and Exchange Commission on March 13, 2000, p. 19.

[11]Koudsi (2000).

unexercised stock options. The details are contained in the following excerpt from Mattels' proxy statement:

> Separation Agreement with Jill Barad. In connection with Ms. Barad's departure from Mattel, the Compensation/Options Committee negotiated and the Board of Directors approved a separation agreement with Ms. Barad, the principal terms of which implement the separation provisions of her 1997 employment agreement. Pursuant to her employment agreement, Ms. Barad was entitled to receive cash payments of: (1) five times the sum of her annual base salary as of February 2000 and a maximum annual bonus under the MIP; (2) one-twelfth of her maximum annual bonus under the MIP; and (3) the full term maximum payout under the LTIP, which together resulted in an aggregate cash payment, confirmed in the separation agreement, of approximately $26.4 million. Ms. Barad's separation qualified her for benefits of $708,989 per year during her lifetime under Mattel's SERP adopted in 1994, as amended, which amount was confirmed in the separation agreement. Ms. Barad's employment agreement provided that the entire balance due from Ms. Barad with respect to the November 1, 1994 loan from Mattel of $3.0 million at 4.12% per annum for the purchase of a home would be forgiven on her termination. In the separation agreement Mattel agreed to pay Ms. Barad approximately $3.31 million to make her whole for the Federal and California income taxes and Medicare tax payable by her with respect to the income she will recognize as a result of the forgiveness of the home loan. Under the separation agreement, Mattel also forgave the May 29, 1997 loan of $4.2 million at 6.1% per annum which it had given Ms. Barad in connection with the Board of Directors' request that she not sell any of the 292,968 shares of restricted stock which had been granted to her in December 1993 and which had become vested in January 1997 in order to pay the income taxes resulting from such vesting. As provided in her employment agreement: (1) Mattel will continue to provide Ms. Barad with life insurance with a basic fixed death benefit of $5.0 million under Mattel's Key Executive Life Insurance Program for the rest of her lifetime; (2) Ms. Barad may acquire her company car for a nominal sum; and (3) until Ms. Barad accepts other full-time employment, Mattel will provide Ms. Barad at Mattel's expense (a) medical and related health insurance, (b) outplacement services, (c) continuation of certain memberships and transferal of such memberships to Ms. Barad, and (d) financial counseling services. The separation agreement provides that: (1) Mattel will sell Ms. Barad certain artwork at the prices recently paid for such artwork by Mattel; (2) Mattel will continue to provide security services to Ms. Barad for a limited period of time, and (3) Mattel will allow Ms. Barad to retain the personal office equipment provided by Mattel to Ms. Barad. Additionally, the separation agreement provides that options to acquire Mattel stock held by Ms. Barad, to the extent not already vested, became vested in full as of February 3, 2000, and will remain outstanding and exercisable until the expiration of the original terms of the grants. As of February 3, 2000, Ms. Barad held options to purchase 6,440,759 shares of Mattel common stock. 4,082,946 of Ms. Barad's options have exercise prices of $42.31 or $44.87. The remaining options have prices ranging from $15.76 to $26.62. In the separation agreement, Ms. Barad provided Mattel with certain releases and agreed to certain confidentiality and non-competition provisions. She also agreed to provide consulting services to Mattel for up to 40 hours per month until December 31, 2000.[12]

As described in this excerpt, much of Barad's package, for example, cash payments of five times the sum of her annual base salary and maximum annual bonus under the management incentive plan, were required under her previously negoti-

[12]Mattel proxy statement filed with Securities and Exchange Commission, April 28, 2000, pp. 24, 25.

ated employment agreement. Thus, at the time of separation, the board had little discretion. Still, the amounts seem exorbitant when you consider that Barad received this severance payment after Mattel's stock price dropped from $27.75 at the end of December 1996 (Barad was appointed CEO in January of 1997) to $12.125 on the day of her resignation.

Shortly after Barad resigned at Mattel, Douglas Ivester resigned (February 17, 2000) as Chairman of the Board and Chief Executive Officer of Coca-Cola. Mr. Ivester's retirement package, estimated by *Fortune* magazine[13] at $166 million, is detailed below:

> In connection with Mr. Ivester's retirement as a Director, Chairman of the Board and Chief Executive Officer and his agreement to remain for a transition period after December 5, 1999, the Board of Directors negotiated and the Compensation Committee approved a separation arrangement with Mr. Ivester. As amended during the transition process, the arrangement provides that Mr. Ivester is to receive the following benefits: (a) the following benefits that other employees who are retiring in the current realignment are also receiving: immediate vesting of the options granted in October 1999, which vesting includes waiver of the grant provision that such options must be held one year before termination of employment; modification of the exercise period of such options so that the exercise period will be the exercise period provided in the option grant (rather than a short period applicable in the case of termination of employment); release of restrictions on all shares previously awarded under the 1983 Restricted Stock Award Plan; release of restrictions on one-half of the shares awarded under the 1989 Restricted Stock Award Plan; addition of three years to age and years of service under the Retirement Plan and the Supplemental Plan; continued retiree medical coverage for himself and his spouse during their lifetimes; eligibility for the Company's matching gifts program; payments of deferred amounts, plus interest, from the Long-Term Incentive Plan for the periods 1995–1997 and 1996–1998; and (b) the following additional benefits: payments of $1,500,000 in February 2000, 2001 and 2002 in lieu of any amounts that may have been payable under the annual and long-term incentive plans through and including 2002; in addition to amounts to be paid under Company retirement plans, beginning March 2000 through and including the month when Mr. Ivester reaches age 55 in March 2002, monthly payments of approximately $66,300; in addition to amounts to be paid under Company retirement plans, beginning April 2002 and continuing for the lifetime of Mr. Ivester and his wife, monthly payments of approximately $56,300 per month; release of the restrictions on the remaining one-half of the shares awarded to Mr. Ivester under the 1989 Restricted Stock Award Plan; title to his Company automobile, mobile telephones, laptop computer and the like; and until May 1, 2001, suitable office space and secretarial services, maintenance of home security systems and club dues for existing clubs. Further Mr. Ivester and the Committee agreed that he will provide consulting services to the Company from 2002 through and including 2007 for an annual payment of $675,000.[14]

Ivester received this package after Coca-Cola's stock price dropped from $59.375 on January 22, 1997 (Ivester was appointed CEO January 23, 1997) to a $52.3125 on the day of his resignation.

---

[13]Koudsi (2000).

[14]Coca-Cola proxy statement filed with Securities and Exchange Commission, March 3, 2000, pp. 30, 31.

What is rather interesting is that in the year prior to departure, both Barad and Ivester received increases in their base pay of $150,000[15] and $250,000,[16] respectively, presumably as a reward for a job well done. One thing to be noted, in their defense, is that both Barad and Ivester had long and successful careers with Mattel and Coca-Cola, respectively. This is in contrast to the short but costly 15-month tenure of Michael Ovitz at Walt Disney, a debacle that cost Disney $38,869,000 in severance[17] and led to the filing of several shareholder lawsuits, which are described in the following excerpt from Disney's proxy statement:

> CERTAIN LEGAL PROCEEDINGS
>
> On January 3, 1997, two purported stockholders, Richard and David Kaplan, filed a putative derivative action in the Superior Court of the State of California, Los Angeles County (the "California Court"), alleging that certain current and former directors of the Company breached their fiduciary duties of loyalty and care and wasted corporate assets in connection with entering into and terminating the Company's employment agreement with its former president, Michael S. Ovitz. On January 7, 1997, two other purported stockholders, William and Geraldine Brehm, filed a substantially identical complaint in the Court of Chancery for the State of Delaware, New Castle County (the "Delaware Court"), and another purported stockholder, Michael Grening, filed a similar complaint in the Delaware Court. On January 14, 1997, Mr. Grening, together with other purported stockholders Michelle De Benedictis, Peter Lawrence and Judith B. Wohl, filed a similar complaint in the California Court. On February 7, 1997, other purported stockholders, Thomas Malloy, Richard Kaser, Carol Kaser, Melvyn Zupnick, Michael Caesar, Robert S. Goldberg and Michael Shores, filed a similar claim in the California Court.
>
> On May 28, 1997, all these claimants together filed an amended complaint in the Delaware Court, which names as defendants all of the Company's current directors, together with Mr. Ovitz and Stephen F. Bollenbach, the Company's former Chief Financial Officer and a former director. The complaint seeks, among other things, a declaratory judgment that Mr. Ovitz's employment agreement was void or, alternatively, that Mr. Ovitz's termination should be deemed a termination "for cause" and any severance payments to him forfeited, and compensatory or rescissory damages and injunctive and other equitable relief from the named defendants. It also seeks class action status to pursue a claim for damages and invalidation of the 1997 election of directors, based upon allegations of insufficient disclosures concerning, among other things, Mr. Ovitz's termination and Mr. Eisner's compensation.[18]

II. THE RELATIONSHIP BETWEEN EXECUTIVE COMPENSATION AND FIRM PERFORMANCE

The following quotation, which implies that compensation is not related to performance, at least poor performance, is from Taussig and Barker (1925):

[15]Mattel proxy statement filed with the Securities and Exchange Commission, April 28, 2000, p. 14.

[16]Coca-Cola proxy statement filed with the Securities and Exchange Commission, March 3, 2000, p. 26.

[17]Walt Disney proxy statement filed with the Securities and Exchange Commission, January 9, 1997, p. 14.

[18]Walt Disney proxy statement filed with the Securities and Exchange Commission, January 2, 1998, p. 10.

Executive salaries are subject to few and infrequent changes. What movement appears in the individual cases is almost entirely upward. In part this upward movement is accounted for by the circumstance that prices and money incomes in general advanced during the period in question. But no doubt it is chiefly accounted for by the fact that while salaries are raised in the course of time, even tho not promptly, for an efficient and money-making staff, in the reverse case they are not likely to be reduced. Poor management leads to a change in personnel, not a decrease in salary. (p. 20)

Since that time a long line of literature has argued that compensation should be related to performance.[19] The reasons for the linkage are both normative and positive. In a normative sense, compensation is considered fair if it has been "earned" through superior performance. In a positive sense, agency theorists argue that linking compensation to firm performance measures provides incentive to increase firm value.

More recent research has shown that CEO compensation is related to firm performance measures. For example, Masson (1971) showed that CEO compensation is significantly associated with stock market performance. Lewellen and Huntsman (1972) found that compensation is significantly related to both profits and market value. In Murphy (1985), compensation was related to stock returns and sales growth, whereas Coughlin and Schmidt (1985) stated that compensation was related to cumulative abnormal returns.[20] Looking at relative performance, Antle and Smith (1986) showed that compensation is related to both systematic (industry related) and unsystematic components of stock market returns and accounting return on assets; Gibbons and Murphy (1990) showed that compensation is related to stock market returns after both industry and market returns are filtered out. Some researchers (e.g., Tosi et al. 2000) have found that although performance has some explanatory power for compensation, firm size explains more of the variation in compensation. The difference in findings between the more recent research and the early findings of Taussig and Barker (1925) may have to do with changes in the compensation package over time. Taussig and Barker examined compensation in the early twentieth century before the widespread use of conditional compensation, such as bonuses and stock options. Even today decreases in salary are infrequent. An analysis of year-to-year changes in salary for the corporations available on the ExecuComp database found about 93% of the changes to be increases, and only 5% to be decreases!

Although researchers generally agree that there is a statistical relationship between compensation and performance, some argue that the size of the relationship is too small. For example, Jensen and Murphy (1990b) found that CEO wealth increases by $3.25 for every $1000 change in shareholder wealth. Hall and Liebman (1998), however, reexamined this relationship, finding "the level of CEO compensation and the sensitivity of compensation to performance have risen

---

[19]While this is true, most of the theories introduced in Chapter 1, for example, tournament theory, do not posit a linkage between compensation and performance.

[20]Abnormal returns are returns in excess of those explained by market movements.

dramatically . . . largely because of increases in stock option grants" (p. 653). They note the following:

> Our main empirical finding is that CEO wealth often changes by millions of dollars for typical changes in firm value. For example, the median total compensation for CEOs is about $1 million if their firm's stock has a thirtieth percentile annual return (-7.0 percent) and is $5 million if the firm's stock has a seventieth percentile annual return (20.5 percent). Thus, there is a difference of about $4 million dollars in compensation for achieving a moderately above average performance relative to a moderately below average performance. The difference in compensation between a tenth percentile firm performance and a ninetieth percentile performance is more than $9 million. (p. 654–655)

It should be noted that both Jensen and Murphy (1990b) and Hall and Liebman (1998) looked not at responsiveness of compensation to corporate performance, but of the association of CEO wealth (which includes compensation as well as stock and option holdings) with corporate performance. Hall and Liebman (1998) concluded the following:

> stock and stock option revaluations increase median CEO wealth by about $1.25 million in response to a 10% increase in firm value. This is 53 times larger than our estimated $23,400 increase in salary and bonus emanating from the same change in firm value. . . . (p. 685)

Although much of this literature looked at the contemporaneous association between pay and performance, Boschen and Smith (1995), focusing on salary and bonus, showed that CEO compensation responds to firm performance with a lag, that is, over a period of 4–5 years, with the "cumulative response of pay to performance . . . roughly 10 times that of the contemporaneous response" (p. 577). Additionally, Hayes and Schaefer (2000) noted that if compensation contracts incorporate measures unobservable to outsiders, measures that are correlated with future performance, then current compensation will be correlated with future performance. Consistent with their theory, they showed that current compensation is associated with future performance. Consequently, both articles demonstrated that by examining the contemporaneous relationship between pay and performance, the prior research has underestimated the strength of the relationship.

In concluding this section, one additional caveat should be made. Most of the above studies, in particular Jensen and Murphy (1990b), focus on stock price as a measure of performance. Yet it is well known that stock price movements are caused by many factors, some of which are outside of the control of management and thus not reflective of management performance. Maximizing shareholder value in the principal–agent model requires a trade-off between incentive alignment and risk sharing, whereby the principal must compensate the agent for risk imposed upon the agent. Tying managerial pay to a variable out of the control of management imposes additional risk upon the agent, and thus may be an inefficient (and costly) way to align incentives. Consequently, the observed linkage between pay and performance, although low, may be optimal. Consistent with this logic, Aggarwal and

Samwick (1999) demonstrated "the pay–performance sensitivity for executives at firms with the least volatile stock prices is an order of magnitude greater than the pay–performance sensitivity for executives at firms with the most volatile stock prices" (p. 65).

III. THE POLITICS OF EXECUTIVE COMPENSATION

In the U.S., executive compensation is a political issue, and has been for some time. Scores of bills and resolutions have been introduced in Congress (see Appendices 10.1 and 10.2 for some examples) to directly limit compensation, and although none have passed, as discussed in earlier chapters, Congress did pass Section 162(m) of the Internal Revenue Code in 1993, which limited deductibility of executive compensation in general, and Section 280(g) of the Internal Revenue Code in 1984, which limited deductibility of and imposed excise taxes on "golden parachutes" (see Appendix 10.3).[21] Another bill that did pass, the Comprehensive Thrift and Bank Fraud Prosecution and Taxpayer Recovery Act of 1990 (public law no. 101-647), added section 18(k)(1) to the Federal Deposit Insurance Act, which permitted the Federal Deposit Insurance Corporation to prohibit golden parachutes, which it did on February 15, 1996.[22]

Although most of the bills did not pass, many of them achieved their intended goals indirectly. For example, the goal of the Corporate Pay Responsibility Act (Bill number S. 1198, introduced June 4, 1991) was "to provide that the compensation paid to certain corporate officers shall be treated as a proper subject for action by security holders, to require certain disclosures regarding such compensation, and for other purposes."

Although the bill did not pass, shortly thereafter on October 21, 1992, the Securities and Exchange Commission promulgated rules achieving the same goal.[23] Companies must now include increased disclosure of executive compensation in their proxy statements (for current rules see Appendix 1.1), and include a report from the compensation committee (or equivalent) explaining how executive compensation was determined (see Chapter 9, section 9.3, for a discussion and example of this report). Further, shareholders may now raise issues pertaining to executive compensation at the annual meeting. Similarly, the goal of the Corporate Executives' Stock Option Accountability Act (Bill numbers S. 259 and H. R. 2878) was "to require that the stock option compensation paid to corporate executives be recorded as a compensation expense in corporate financial statements."

---

[21]Golden parachutes, which will be discussed in more detail later in this chapter, are payments to executives if they lose their jobs as part of a change in control of the corporation.
[22]61 Federal Register 5927.
[23]SEC Act Release no. 33-6962, 57 Federal Register 48,126.

Once again, although the bill did not pass (actually neither of the bills made it to the floor of their respective chambers), at approximately the same time the Financial Accounting Standards Board made a similar proposal,[24] and beginning in 1997 required disclosure of the costs of stock option grants in the footnotes to the financial statements.[25]

IV. THE EFFECT OF THE POLITICAL PROCESS ON EXECUTIVE COMPENSATION

Although executive compensation is an extremely political issue, and actions have been taken by politicians and regulators, the effect of those actions is unclear. Take for example the increased or improved disclosure of executive compensation in proxy statements beginning in 1993. As shown in Table 2.7, executive compensation has increased dramatically during the 1990s, thus it does not appear the increased disclosures had the effect of reducing compensation (of course we do not know what compensation would have been in the absence of those disclosures). Similarly, there is no evidence that the footnote disclosure of the cost of employee stock option grants has decreased the number of options granted (see Table 6.6).

Moving on to actual legislation, there are some who believe the tax code changes involving executive compensation have had perverse effects. For example, Harris and Livingstone (1999) argued that Section 162(m) has had the effect of raising compensation of CEOs earning less than $1 million, by setting that number as a benchmark. Rose and Wolfram (2000) concluded that the "limit on the deductibility of executive pay has led firms near the $1 million cap to restrain their salary increases, and perhaps to increase the performance components of their pay packages" (p. 201). Other researchers, for example, Balsam (2000), Johnson et al. (1997), and Perry and Zenner (2000), examined CEOs earning more than $1 million and found contradictory results as to whether Section 162(m) made compensation more responsive to firm performance.

Research also suggests that the limit on the deductibility of golden parachutes has not had the intended effect. Originally intended to counter the incentives of executives to fight takeovers,[26] Straus (1999) noted that

> the golden parachute, which has traveled far beyond its initial target of providing a financial safety net to top executives ousted by hostile takeovers. New breed of parachutes reward

[24]Financial Accounting Standards Board. 1993. Proposed Statement of Financial Accounting Standards: Accounting for Stock-based Compensation. Norwalk, CT: FASB.

[25]Statement of Financial Accounting Standards No. 123: Accounting for Stock-Based Compensation is required for all fiscal years beginning after December 15, 1995.

[26]Accumulated research (for example, Walsh 1988; Walsh 1989) finds that executives of acquired firms are likely to lose their jobs as a result of the takeover. Thus, in the absence of any countervailing incentives, executives are likely to resist the takeover. Golden parachutes, in theory, by providing executives with financial payments if they lose their job as a result of the acquisition, supply those countervailing incentives.

retiring execs, hasten the departures of poor performers or simply provide payoffs for those who want out. And they often go beyond boilerplate standards of three years' serverance and automatic vested stock options. (p. 1B)

He continued, stating that ". . . generous parachutes are more pervasive that ever. More than 80% of Fortune 500 companies now have CEOs strapped into parachutes, up from 41% in 1988 . . ." (p. 1B).

V. INTERNATIONAL COMPARISONS

Rules governing executive compensation vary across the globe. For example, although stock options are and have been a major part of the executive compensation package in the United States, it was illegal for companies in Germany and Finland to use stock options to compensate executives until 1998 (Ratnesar 2000). Similarly, although (nonqualified) stock options result in a tax deduction for the granting corporation in the United States, in Britain no tax deduction is allowed (Conyon and Murphy 2000).

A study by the consulting firm Towers Perrin estimated pay as of April 1, 1999, in industrial companies with approximately $500 million in sales. They estimated that CEOs for U.S. companies of that size earn $1,350,567, whereas Japanese CEOs earn $486,669, German CEOs $533,676, French CEOs $571,613, and UK CEOs $667,593, with much of this difference being driven by stock and other variable forms of compensation. Their finding is consistent with the general notion that executive compensation in the United States exceeds that of the rest of the world, although recent years have seen other countries adopting more of the "American" approach. An explanation for other countries adopting more of the American approach is the globalization of business and the mobility of executives. That is, just like other scarce resources, executives are attracted to the highest bidders, as noted by Kroll (1998):

> The once yawning gap between US chief executives and their counterparts abroad is fast closing. The stock options mania has spread globally. In an era when big business seeks talent wherever it can find it, companies no longer restrict their search to their own nationals. With this internationalizing of the executive talent market, companies everywhere must pay international scales.
>
> . . .
>
> Call it globalization of talent. In an era when big business seeks talent wherever it can find it, companies no longer restrict their search to their own nationals. Ford Motor is today headed by an Australian, Compaq Computer by a German. Hartford Insurance's chief executive, Ramani Ayer, was born in India (pp. 220, 221). Reprinted with permission of *Forbes Magazine*. © 2001 Forbes Inc.

Yet others, for example, Ewing et al. (1999), question if the rest of the world will catch up.

> Still, it will be years—if ever—before Europeans make as much as Americans. That's because a combination of government restrictions, prohibitive taxes, and political opposition

continues to hamper the use of options. In France, for example, a government attempt at quiet liberalization of the rules for stock options last year ran afoul of angry communists and other members of Premier Lionel Jospin's coalition. The Netherlands imposed capital-gains taxes on stock options last year after Prime Minister Wim Kok, a former labor leader, blasted "exhibitionist" stock bonuses paid to executives such as Kees Storm, CEO of insurer Aegon. (p. 40)

A. International Politics of Executive Compensation

As in the United States, executive compensation in other countries has become very politicized, sometimes causing action on the part of regulators. For example, after an uproar over executive compensation in Britain, Kenneth Clarke, Chancellor of the Exchequer, "decreed that henceforth share options would not be subject to capital gains tax but income tax" (Blackhurst 1995). A comparable example occurred when Spain, in response to the political uproar associated with the $17 million in stock option gains of Juan Villalonga of Telefnica, and his unwillingness to renounce that profit, doubled the tax on share-option gains (Ratnesar 2000). In France the so-called Jaffé affair, which occurred when the CEO of Elf-Aquitaine, Philippe Jaffé received a stock option package worth $35 million when his company was acquired by TotalFina, derailed government plans to lower the tax rate on stock option earnings from 40 to 26% and led to an unsuccessful campaign to increase the rate to 50% (Ratnesar 2000).

Although the Securities and Exchange Commission requires United States companies to disclose compensation paid to their top five executives, other countries are not as open in their disclosures (Orr and Holloway 1999). Thus, evidence on the level and performance sensitivities of executives in other countries is not as easy to obtain. Consequently, the following discussion is based upon a much more limited data set than that available for U.S. companies.

B. Britain

Conyon and Murphy (2000) noted that in 1997, Disney's Michael Eisner single-handedly outearned "the aggregate paycheques of the top 500 CEOs in the UK" (p. F640). While Eisner is clearly an outlier, they found "CEOs in the United States earn 45% higher cash compensation and 190% higher total compensation," (p. F640) although they also note that the association between cash compensation and performance for United States CEOs is "more than double the elasticity for UK CEOs" and that United States CEOs have much larger ownership (p. F660). They attribute many of the differences in pay packages to the greater use of stock options in the United States.[27] In terms of the composition of the compensation package, they found that

---

[27]It is worth noting that Conyon and Schwalbach (1999) find that, in their study of European countries, the use of long-term incentives is the most prevalent in the UK.

"CEOs in the UK receive 59% of their total pay in the form of base salaries, 18% in bonuses, 10% in share options (valued at grant-date), and 9% in LTIP shares (valued at grant-date, with a 20% discount for performance contingencies). In contrast, base salaries comprise a much smaller percentage of total pay for United States executives (only 29%), while share option grants comprise a much larger percentage (42%). (p. F646)

In terms of levels, the median base salary is 30% higher in the United States, median bonus in the United States is triple that in the U.K., and the "median option grant in the US . . . is nearly *twenty times* the median grant for UK CEOs. . ." (p. F648).

Still, compensation of United States executives does not always exceed that of their British counterparts. For example, in Britain, Glaxo Wellcome's chairman, Sir Richard Sykes, earned $2.9 million in 1997, which was more than the $2.6 million in salary and bonus earned by his counterpart at U.S.-based Merck (Kroll 1998). Other examples of well-paid executives in the United Kingdom include Marjorie Scardino, chief executive of the Pearson Group, who earned $1.6 million, Michael O'Neill, chief executive of Barclays, guaranteed $24 million over 3 years, and Jan Leschly, chief executive officer of SmithKline Beecham PLC, who "received a $140 million package" (Ewing et al. 1999, p. 40). Pay is, nonetheless, generally more restrained, with the general rule being "the value of stock options may not amount to more that four times an executive's base pay" (Ewing et al. 1999, p. 40), and the tax code has been revised to make such options less appealing (Ratnesar 2000).

C. Canada

When comparing corporations in Canada with those in the United States, Zhou (1999) found that there is "a marked difference between the two countries in both the level and structure of CEO compensation" (p. 5). In examining the period 1993–1995, he found Canadian CEOs earn lower pay, with the median CEO in his sample earning $560,000 in U.S. dollars versus $2.45 million for U.S. corporations in the S&P 500, $1.27 million for corporations in the S&P 400 Mid-Cap Industrials, and $752,000 for corporations in the S&P 600 Small-Cap Industrials. He also found that when comparing Canadian to U.S. corporations, salary made up a higher proportion and bonuses and options a lower proportion of the compensation package for Canadian corporations. Overall he concluded that the relationship of pay to performance is weaker in Canada than it is in the United States.

D. Germany

In Germany, "the typical chief executive of a blue-chip company like Siemens earns $550,000 in salary and bonus" (Kroll 1998, p. 220). Although, as noted above, until

1998 it was illegal for German corporations to use stock options, that is rapidly changing. Ewing et al. (1999) noted,

> all the companies on the DAX 30 have either linked the pay of top managers to share performance or are planning to do so soon. . . . The main reason is globalization. When Daimler Benz took over Chrysler Corp. last year, CEO Jurgen E. Schrempp had to confront the fact that Chrysler CEO Robert Eaton, who earned over $11 million in 1997, including exercised options, appears to have made more than the rest of Daimler's management board members put together. Worse, Daimler had to pay out $395 million, primarily in stock, to Chrysler's top 30 executives to cash out their options. Since cutting the pay of Chrysler managers wasn't possible, Daimler was forced to boost pay for its own execs. (p. 40)[28]

Some cynics may wonder if this was indeed the motivation for the merger!

E. Japan

Bremner (1999) found that "for years the pay package of Japanese chief executives, whose base salaries range from $330,000 to $800,000 at the top companies, have lagged badly behind those in the U.S." (p. 39). Furthermore, until recently, Japanese companies did not make much use of stock options. However, a new law allowing companies to hold more of their own shares has resulted in an upsurge of companies offering stock options. Although much more restricted than in the United States for example, the law requires that corporations at the date of grant own enough shares to cover the options granted, formerly Japanese companies were only allowed to hold a maximum of 3% of their own shares, and for no more than 6 months at a time. In contrast, the new rule allows them to hold as much as 10% of their own shares for up to 10 years, effectively allowing them to grant options (*The Economist* 1997). Now 160 listed companies offer stock options. Compared with U.S. corporations, the amounts are modest. For example, Sony, somewhat of a leader in using stock options in Japan as of August 1998, had issued stock options worth a total of $21 million (Bremner 1999). In contrast, in 1996 Walt Disney gave its Chairman and Chief Executive Officer, Michael D. Eisner, 8,000,000 options valued at $195,583,281.[29]

F. Why Do These Differences Exist?

Some of the reasons for these differences are cultural, some regulatory, and some related to taxation. It is taboo in many countries to earn the amounts American

---

[28]These changes are not limited to the DAX 30. Woodruff (2001) reports that 50% of the firms in the DAX 100 and 85% of the firms on the Neuer Market now have option plans.

[29]Calculated based upon values reported in Walt Disney's proxy statement filed with the Securities and Exchange Commission, January 9, 1997, p. 16.

executives make. This culture is reinforced by, or perhaps results in, a system that restrains and taxes such compensation. For example, as noted above, until rather recently few Japanese and German corporations were able to issue options. As alluded to above, in Japan, a corporation had to purchase and hold in its own treasury sufficient shares to fund its stock option program. However, both the amount they could hold and the period they could hold it for was extremely limited. Even now they are limited to owning 10% of their stock, a large amount, but much less than many U.S. companies (Carpenter and Yermack [1999] noted that the typical large U.S. corporation reserves more than 10% of its equity for stock plans). Other countries have their own laws and regulations that make options less valuable. For example, in Germany, shares have to beat an index before the holder can profit from his or her options, whereas in Singapore, options are limited to 5 years in length (Yeo et al. 1999). Also making the options less valuable are differences in taxation. There are differences in the timing of taxation. For example, although in the United States option profits are generally taxed at the time of exercise, in Holland options are taxed upon vesting, and in Belgium and Switzerland, "individuals usually must pay tax on the potential gain from options at the time they are granted" (Woodruff 2001, p. A18). Similarly there are differences in tax rates. While the maximum tax rate on long-term capital gains in the United States is 20%, in France the capital gains tax rate is 50% (Woodruff 2001).

G. Can These Differences Continue to Exist?

As corporations and markets become increasingly global, these differences will to some extent dissipate. As with Ford, Compaq, and Hartford Insurance, American corporations will increasingly search worldwide for executives. This will have two effects. That is, increasing the potential supply of executives should decrease the wages paid to executives in the United States. Similarly, to compete, foreign corporations will have to raise their compensation levels to retain their executives. Additionally, as foreign corporations enter the United States market, they will have to increase their levels of compensation and change the composition of their compensation packages to attract American executives to staff their United States subsidiaries. It is likely they will then have to increase compensation in their home country to avoid having the executives in their United States subsidiary making more than their corporate superiors. This may not always be the case, however. Conwell (2001) reported that Fred Goodwing, Chief Executive Officer of the Royal Bank of Scotland, made $3 million in 2000. This amount, which made him the highest paid banking chief executive in Britain and led to criticism from Royal Bank's institutional shareholders, was less than one-fifth the $15 million paid to Lawrence Fish, Chief Executive of the Royal Bank's Boston-based subsidiary, Citizens Financial Group!

VI. COMPARISONS TO OTHER OCCUPATIONS

If you compare executives to others at the top of their professions, their compensation does not seem as outrageous as when you compare them to the average worker.

A. Wall Street

Examples abound on Wall Street of traders, analysts, and fund managers that make more than many CEOs. For example, Browing (2000) reported that Frank Quattrone, a specialist in mergers and stock offerings for technology companies at Credit Suisse First Boston, "agreed to an arrangement that extended his contract for three years and allowed him to make as much as $30 million a year . . ." (p. A1). Many Wall Street firms are organized as partnerships rather than corporations. In partnerships, profits per partner are the equivalent of average partner compensation. Ip (2001b) reported that "profits averaged $16 million per partner in just nine months at one specialist firm last year, Spear Leeds & Kellogg" (p. A1).

B. Lawyers

Average profits per partner at the top-earning 100 law firms was $755,000 in 1999, with Wachtell, Lipton, Rosen & Katz leading the list at $3,390,000 per partner (*Wall Street Journal* 2000e). Examples also exist of class-action lawyers winning paydays exceeding that of all but a few of the most highly paid CEOs. For example, it has been estimated (Cohen 2000) that Dickie Scruggs will receive "about a third of the $1.2 billion being paid to his firm" as a result of the tobacco settlement. Other highly paid attorneys include Gerald Hosier $40 million, Fred Baron $21 million, Joseph Jamail $20.7 million, Willie Gary $12.1 million, and Philip Corboy $11.6 million (Freedman 2001).

C. Sports and Entertainment

> In 1930 Babe Ruth was asked to justify his new annual salary, $80,000 for which he was paid to hit baseballs a long way, in light of the fact that the President of the United States was making a mere 75 grand. "I had a better year than he did," Ruth replied.[30]

One of the interesting things about this quote is that in 1930 it was newsworthy that Babe Ruth, by any definition, one of the greatest athletes of his time, was being questioned for earning $5000, or less than 7% more, than the President of the United States. Today the average major league baseball salary is estimated to be

[30]Sullivan (2000/2001, p. 144).

$2 million (Sullivan 2000/2001), which works out to more than 400% more than the President of the United States, who earns $390,000.[31] However, this is no longer news, because in the world of sports and entertainment, individuals barely out of, or still in, their teens can make millions.

For example, 18-year-old tennis star Anna Kournikova's estimated 1999 income was $11 million (Klein 2000), whereas 20-year-old Venus Williams earned $14 million (*Parade Magazine* 2001). Before the 2001 baseball season, Alex Rodriguez signed a 10-year contract with the Texas Rangers for $252 million, or an average of $25.2 million per year (Sullivan 2000/2001). On a yearly basis, that is less than the $29.5 million that will be received by basketball's Shaquille O'Neal, under his recently signed 3-year contract extension worth $88.5 million dollars (*Philadelphia Inquirer* 2000). And that is still less than the $33.14 million received by Michael Jordan during the 1997–1998 basketball season (Du Pree 2000). Golfer "Tiger Woods signed a five-year endorsement contract with Nike . . . believed to be worth $85 million, making it the richest endorsement deal in sports history" (Brown 2000, p. C1). That's an estimated $17 million a year before tournament winnings or other endorsements! Overall it was estimated that Tiger earned $47 million in 1999.[32]

The world of entertainment, Flint (2000) reported that the cast of *Friends* accepted a deal whereby each would be paid $750,000 per episode or $18 million for the 24-episode season. Not mentioned are the additional millions the cast members make from their movies and other activities. Stars such as Julia Roberts can make $20 million or more for a single movie (Rickey 2001). Lippman (2001) estimated that actor Tom Hanks made more than $40 million from his performance in the movie *Cast Away*. Other entertainers earning noteworthy amounts include Bruce Willis at $54.4 million, Shania Twain $48 million, Cher $40 million, Adam Sandler $28 million, Rosie O'Donnell $25 million, Britney Spears $15 million, and Barbara Walters $10 million (*Parade Magazine* 2001). Authors Dean Koontz and John Grisham were estimated to have earned $34 million and $36 million, respectively (*Parade Magazine* 2001).

The March 20, 2000, issue of *Forbes* magazine reports the following earnings for the following athletes and entertainers for 1999

Athlete or entertainer	Earnings ($ million)
George Lucas	400
Oprah Winfrey	150
Georgio Armani	135
David Kelly	115
Tom Hanks	71.5
Tiger Woods	47
Michael Jordan	40

[31]H.R.5658, Treasury and General Government Appropriations Act of 2001, raised the compensation of the president from the $200,000 earned by William Jefferson Clinton.

[32]See March 20, 2000, issue of *Forbes*.

D. One Big Difference

A major difference between executive pay and the earnings of any of the people in the list on the preceding page is that unlike the executive, the above individuals have little control over the parties that pay them. That is, they do not set their own pay or exercise influence over those that do set their pay. For example, when Warner Brothers agreed to pay the cast of Friends $750,000 per episode, it was an arm's-length transaction between two independent parties. On the other hand, when the board of directors of a major corporation awards compensation to its chairman of the board and chief executive officer, the parties are not independent. They are not independent for many reasons. First of all, as noted in Chapter 9, directors may be employees of the corporation and hence answer to the CEO. Or while the director may be an outside or "independent" director, he or she may still not be independent of the CEO. For example, the director may be an executive of another corporation upon whose board this CEO serves. This is known as an interlocking directorate. In some extreme cases the CEOs will sit on each other's compensation committees (Fierman 1990). Alternatively, the outside director may have some other business relationship with the corporation, such as being a partner in the corporation's outside law firm. In these situations, the outside director is not totally independent of the corporation on whose board he or she serves, and hence has been termed a "gray" outside director (see Chapter 9). Even a truly independent outside director has little incentive to oppose a CEO's compensation demands. Rather, the director has incentive to acquiesce to those demands to please the CEO and retain his or her lucrative position on the board of directors (Chapter 9 contains descriptive statistics on the compensation of directors). In summary, although the amounts paid to top performers in other occupations may be comparable to the amounts paid CEOs, the process of determining those amounts is quite different.

VII. SUMMARY

This chapter examined the reasonableness of executive compensation relative to corporate profits, dividends, and increases in shareholder wealth, as well as comparing executive compensation in the United States to that outside of the United States, and executive compensation to compensation in other professions. Although the CEO is but one individual, and the average firm in 2000 employed almost 25,000 individuals, their compensation alone is a material component of corporate profits, dividends, and the change in shareholder wealth. Further, whether the shareholders profit or not, CEOs seem to. During 2000, almost 43% of the corporations on ExecuComp had a negative total return to shareholders. Yet regardless of how compensation was defined, the CEOs of these corporations averaged more than $5 million (median greater than $1 million) in compensation in 2000. Even executives that fail, that is, are replaced, are well compensated. The chapter discussed the multimillion-dollar severance packages of three of these CEOs. In general, the evidence on the link between executive compensation and corporate performance is not as strong as many would like it to be.

The combination of large amounts and seemingly lack of relation to performance has made compensation a political issue both inside and outside the United States, although the effect of these actions on executive compensation is unclear. While compensation in the United States is higher than compensation in other countries, even those lesser amounts are high enough to bring about criticism and in some cases tax and regulatory changes. Still, although executive compensation is also affected by cultural norms, and regulations governing executive compensation vary across the globe, over time, in a global marketplace, price, or in this case, compensation, must converge. The chapter concludes with a discussion of compensation paid to top performers in other occupations. Although the amounts are also large, a major difference between executive pay and the earnings of investment bankers, lawyers, athletes, and entertainers, is that unlike executives, these individuals have little control over the parties that pay them. That is, they do not set their own pay or exercise influence over those that do set their pay. Thus, while the amounts paid to top performers in other occupations may be comparable to the amounts paid CEOs, the process of determining those amounts is quite different.

APPENDIX 10.1. SELECTION OF BILLS INTRODUCED, BUT NOT PASSED, WITH THE POTENTIAL TO AFFECT AMOUNTS, DEDUCTIBILITY OR DISCLOSURE OF COMPENSATION

Bill number	Date introduced	Goals
H. R. 740	February 11, 1999	To amend the Internal Revenue Code of 1986 to deny employers a deduction for payments of excessive compensation.
H. R. 3562	March 26, 1998	To amend the Internal Revenue Code of 1986 to allow a credit against income tax to C corporations that have substantial employee ownership and to encourage stock ownership by employees by excluding from gross income stock paid as compensation for services, and for other purposes.
H. R. 2788	October 31, 1997	To amend the Internal Revenue Code of 1986 to promote the grant of incentive stock options to nonhighly compensated employees.
S. 576	April 15, 1997	To amend the Internal Revenue Code of 1986 to provide that corporate tax benefits from stock option compensation expenses are allowed only to the extent such expenses are included in corporate accounts
H. R. 687	February 11, 1997	To amend the Internal Revenue Code of 1986 to deny employers a deduction for payments of excessive compensation.
H. R. 620	January 20, 1995	To increase minimum wage and to deny employers a deduction for payments of excessive compensation.
H. R. 3278	October 13, 1993	To increase the minimum wage and to deny employers a deduction for payments of excessive compensation
H. R. 1725	April 20, 1993	To limit excessive compensation and bonuses paid by the Resolution Trust Corporation and for other purposes.
S. 565	March 11, 1993	To amend the Internal Revenue Code of 1986 to improve disclosure requirements for tax-exempt organizations.
S. 259	January 28, 1993	To require that stock option compensation paid to corporate executives be recorded as a compensation expense in corporate financial statements.
H. R. 2878	August 5, 1993	
H. R. 3331	September 12, 1991	To amend the Internal Revenue Code of 1986 to simplify the definitions of highly compensated employee and compensation for pension plan purposes, and for other purposes.
H. R. 3056	July 25, 1991	To amend the Internal Revenue Code of 1986 to deny employers a deduction for payments of excessive compensation
S. 1198/	June 4, 1991	To provide that the compensation paid to certain corporate officers shall be treated as a proper subject for action by security holders, to require certain disclosures regarding such compensation, and for other purposes.
H.R. 2522	June 4, 1991	

APPENDIX 10.2. RESOLUTIONS INTRODUCED TO LIMIT EXECUTIVE COMPENSATION

Resolution number	Date introduced	Resolution
H. Con. Res. 118	July 1, 1993	Expressing the sense of the Congress that any limitation under Federal tax law on the deductibility of compensation exceeding $1 million paid to executives individually should be expanded to apply to compensation paid to entertainers and athletes.

APPENDIX 10.3. LAWS THAT RESTRICT EXECUTIVE COMPENSATION

Public law number	Date enacted into law	Restrictions placed upon executive compensation
98–369	July 18, 1984	Limits tax deductibility of payments made contingent on a change in the ownership or control of the corporation (i.e., golden parachutes). No deduction is allowed for "excess" parachute payments, which are defined as payments equal to (Internal Revenue Code Section 280G), and a 20% excise tax is imposed upon such payment (Internal Revenue Code Section 4999).
101–647	November 29, 1990	Authorizes the Federal Deposit Insurance Corporation to prohibit or limit golden parachute or indemnification payments.
103–66	August 10, 1993	Disallowance of deduction for certain employee remuneration in excess of $1,000,000 (Internal Revenue Code Section 162(m))

CHAPTER 11

The Effect of Corporate and Executive Characteristics on Designing an Optimal Compensation Contract

I. INTRODUCTION

A good compensation package is customized to take into account the characteristics of the corporation and executive. Trade-offs need to be made based upon those characteristics. In particular, the optimal contract involves a trade-off between incentive alignment and risk sharing. That is, although the corporation wants to provide the executive with incentives to increase firm value (incentive alignment), they do not want to put too much risk on the executive, as (1) it may affect executive decision making in a suboptimal way,[1] and (2) in equilibrium, the corporation must increase remuneration to compensate the executive for bearing that risk. Yet to provide incentive alignment, a portion of the compensation package should be linked to firm performance. Consequently, to minimize executive risk, the corporation may want to use multiple measures of firm performance. The measures used and the weights allocated to those measures should take into account the informativeness of those measures, as well as the noisiness of those measures in evaluating executive performance. Research shows (e.g., Lambert and Larcker 1987; Sloan 1993; Aggarwal and Samwick 1999) that the weights placed on performance measures in contracts are consistent with this trade-off between noise and informativeness.

Consider the following example. An oil exploration company is designing a CEO compensation package. To simplify things, we assume that future firm profitability

---

[1]Mishra et al. (2000) found that when too much risk is placed on the CEO, firm performance suffers.

is a function of only two factors, the company's success in finding oil and the price of oil. Although the CEO has some impact on the former, for example, by deciding where to drill, he or she has little impact on the latter. However, the traditional performance measures (accounting earnings and stock prices) though affected by the former are also greatly impacted by the latter. While providing some information about CEO performance, accounting earnings and stock prices are thus noisy measures. Further, they reflect oil discoveries at different points in time. Assuming market efficiency, stock prices increase at the time the oil is discovered. In contrast, accounting earnings only reflect the discovery when the oil is produced, which could be over a period of years.

Despite the weaknesses of these measures, oil companies continue to use them to measure performance and reward executives. For example, Exxon-Mobil uses accounting measures such as net income, earnings per share, return on capital employed, and return on equity in determining short-term bonus awards.[2] Although not explicitly using stock price as a performance measure, it makes grants of both restricted stock and options to its executives, effectively tying compensation to stock price performance. Among the large integrated oil companies, Exxon-Mobil is not alone in its use of accounting and stock price performance measures. Texaco uses earnings, earnings growth, cash growth, and return on capital employed,[3] whereas Chevron uses "earnings, return on capital employed (ROCE), cash flow and operating expense."[4] Only Chevron, in their discussion of the CEO's annual bonus, even mentions the proved reserves replacement ratio, which is a more direct and, hence, better measure of the company's exploration success, and one unaffected by oil prices, accounting regulations, or broad stock market trends.

Why do companies persist in using accounting earnings and stock prices, which are known to be noisy measures? One reason is that any indirect measure of performance is imperfect, and that direct observation of performance is impractical and perhaps impossible. We assume here that only two factors influence performance: success in finding oil and the price of oil. Yet only one of the corporations above even alluded to oil reserves in their discussion of compensation. A potential explanation is that oil exploration is risky, and directly tying compensation to success in finding oil imposes too much risk on the CEO. For example, because of the boom or bust nature of oil exploration, major oil finds do not occur every year. Thus, tying compensation to those finds would result in an extreme variation in compensation from one year to the next. Thus, the fact that few corporations use a measure indicates that they feel the noise in the measure, or that the risk imposed upon the executive by the using the measure outweighs the benefit from using the measure to provide incentives to the executive.

[2]Exxon Mobil proxy statement filed with the Securities and Exchange Commission, April 14, 2000, p. 16.

[3]Texaco proxy statement filed with the Securities and Exchange Commission, March 14, 2000, p. 17.

[4]Chevron proxy statement filed with the Securities and Exchange Commission, March 22, 2000, p. 13.

As noted above, to minimize risk and maximize incentive effects, corporations may use a combination of measures, both subjective and objective, to evaluate performance. For example, Texaco's compensation committee report on executive compensation contained the following discussion of its incentive bonus program.

> Participants in the incentive bonus program can earn more or less than the target bonus, depending on the achievement of the following financial objective measures:
> - Earnings Growth vs. Peers
> - Cash Growth vs. Peers
> - Return on Capital Employed vs. Peers
> - Earnings vs. Plan
>
> and the following non-financial measures:
> - Respect for the Individual
> - Safety
> - Diversity
>
> The bonus formula also contains additional subjective elements including:
> - Overall contribution to corporate and/or business unit performance
> - Managerial ability
> - Initiative
> - Fostering the Company's "Vision and Values"
> - Compliance with the Corporate Conduct Guidelines
> - Fostering Diversity[5]

In addition, Texaco's long-term incentive program consists of stock option and restricted stock grants. Thus, although its short-term program uses accounting and nonaccounting performance measures, its long-term program uses stock-based compensation to provide the proper incentives. To reduce the riskiness of any one measure, Texaco, like most companies, uses multiple market, accounting, and non-financial measures. They also use objective measures, such as earnings and safety, and subjective measures, such as fostering diversity. Baker et al. (1994) showed that the use of both objective and subjective performance measures can reduce risk, as the "firm can subjectively evaluate the incentive distortions caused by the imperfect objective performance measure" (p. 1128).

The remainder of this chapter addresses the impact of corporate goals and corporate and executive characteristics on the optimal contract. In particular, the focus is on determining how much and how to pay. How much is important, because setting pay too high imposes unnecessary costs upon the corporation, whereas setting it too low increases the probability of executives being lured away by competitors.[6] How to pay is equally important, because the compensation package is used to provide the proper incentives to executives; the form of compensation also affects accounting earnings, cash flow, and the after-tax cost to shareholders.

---

[5]Texaco proxy statement filed with the Securities and Exchange Commission, March 14, 2000, pp. 17, 18.

[6]With the ensuing cost of either matching the offer or recruiting and training a replacement.

II. GOALS

A precursor to designing the executive compensation package is to determine the goals of the package, that is, what forms of behavior would the board of directors like to encourage. While a maintained assumption is that all boards want to encourage the maximization of shareholder value, they may have different approaches, depending on the characteristics of the corporation and the market(s) in which it operates. For example, if the corporation operates in a mature industry, the board may seek increased efficiencies, growth in market share in existing markets, or expansion into new markets. They may also want to encourage (or minimize) risk taking on the part of management. Once these goals are set, the board then tries to achieve them at a minimum cost to shareholders, which involves minimizing cash outflows and/or maximizing tax deductions. An important item to be recognized in designing the package is that the different components of the package must be coordinated, both with each other and with the goals of the corporation.

III. THE EFFECT OF CORPORATE CHARACTERISTICS ON THE OPTIMAL CONTRACT

Having established that most corporations use multiple forms of compensation and multiple performance measures, what corporate characteristics influence the level of pay, the components of the compensation package, and the performance measures to be used, as well as the extent to which they are to be used?

A. Size

The size of the firm influences the compensation package in several ways, some of them subtle. First, in general, the larger the corporation, the greater the set of skills necessary to manage it effectively. Second, the larger the corporation, the greater the effect of the manager in dollar terms. That is, a managerial decision that increases shareholder value by 10% translates into a greater dollar increase in value for a billion dollar corporation than for a million dollar corporation. Both of these factors should increase the level of compensation. In fact, Table 2.9 shows that in 2000, mean (median) total CEO compensation increases from $1,321,000 ($942,000) for corporations in the smallest decile to $27,405,000 ($18,573,000) for the largest corporations. On a more subtle level, as the size of the corporation increases, percentage managerial ownership drops due to wealth constraints. Referring to Table 8.6, the mean (median) value of shares and options held in 2000 by CEOs in the smallest corporations was $6,846,579 ($2,496,313), whereas the mean (median) value of shares and options held by CEOs in the largest firms was

$10,155,500,000 ($286,338,813)! In contrast, Table 8.3 shows that the mean (median) percentage ownership of shares and options of CEOs in the smallest corporations was 6.33% (2.74%), while the mean (median) percentage ownership of shares and options of CEOs in the largest firms was 7.63% (0.81%). Thus the composition of the compensation package must be adjusted to provide incentives to increase equity value.[7] This, of course, can be accomplished by adding or increasing the amount or proportion of stock-based compensation in the compensation package. In fact, Table 2.6 shows that for the smallest corporations, the mean (median) proportion of the value of the 2000 CEO compensation package composed of stock options was 27% (20%), whereas for the largest corporations it was 55% (62%).

B. Political Costs

Related to the size of the corporation are its political costs. Everything about a large publicly traded corporations is visible, including its executive compensation, which is publicly available via proxy statements filed with the Securities and Exchange Commission, and widely disseminated via surveys published in such business publications as *Forbes, Business Week,* and the *Wall Street Journal.* When compensation is high, political costs may be imposed upon the corporation and executive. Political costs include the taxes the corporation and the executive pay and regulations that either require or prohibit the corporation from taking certain actions. An example of a cost imposed upon corporations and their executives because of executive compensation is Section 162(m) of the tax code, which limits deductions for executive compensation, consequently increasing the corporation's tax bill. To minimize political costs, boards in designing or adding components to existing packages must "justify" that compensation to stakeholders (Zajac and Westphal 1995). They do so in one of two ways. One approach is to justify the package in terms of the need to attract and retain qualified executives. The second approach is to justify the components by making reference to how the components will align the interests of management and shareholders. Microsoft, in proposing its 2001 Stock Plan to shareholders, incorporated both. That is, Microsoft states that the plan will "allow the Company to continue to attract and retain the best available employees and provide an incentive for employees to use their best efforts on the Company's behalf."[8]

Westphal and Zajac (1994) actually suggested that some corporations may add incentive-based compensation plans for symbolism rather than substance. That is, they adopt long-term incentive plans to "symbolically" control agency costs.

---

[7]Both dollar and percentage ownership are important in terms of incentives. The differing incentives and effects of each are discussed below.

[8]Microsoft proxy statemement filed with the Securities and Exchange Commission September 28, 2000.

Political costs have the potential to reduce executive compensation. Depending upon the market for executive services, executives may be made to bear all, some, or none of the political costs in the form of lower compensation and/or higher risk. For example, if the market for an executive's services is perfectly inelastic (that is, demand is constant regardless of the price), the executive bears none of the cost, and the corporation bears the entire cost. This would arise when there is a competitive market for his or her services, for example, from entities not subject to similar political constraints, such as privately held corporations, consulting firms, investment banks, or law firms, none of which must disclose compensation to the public. In this environment, to get an executive to accept lower compensation, the corporation would have to reduce the risk of the compensation package. Thus, one side effect of the political pressure to reduce executive compensation is to make the compensation package less responsive to performance, that is, reduce incentives to increase shareholder value. Alternatively, the executive might be willing to accept less explicit compensation if combined with more perquisites, for example, a bigger office. However, if the executive values a dollar spent on perquisites less than a dollar in compensation, the increase in the amount the corporation spends on perquisites will exceed the decrease in compensation, reducing shareholder value.

In contrast, if the market for an executive's services is perfectly elastic, the executive will bear all the costs. In reality, the market for an executive's services is neither perfectly elastic nor perfectly inelastic. Thus both the executive and corporation will bear some of the costs and hence, have the incentive to work together to reduce those costs.

C. Risk

The riskier the corporation, the greater the amount of risk imposed upon an underdiversified executive via performance-based compensation and stock ownership. Consequently, risk-averse executives will demand greater levels of compensation to compensate themselves for bearing that risk. Risk can take many forms. For example, there is the risk of bankruptcy, whereby the most likely outcome is that the executive loses his or her job, and most, if not all, of his or her investment in the corporation. More generally, there is the riskiness of the corporation's share price, which impacts executives via their stock ownership and stock-based compensation. This risk can be broken into systematic and unsystematic components, where the former is market related and the latter a function of the corporation's unique characteristics.

The systematic risk of the corporation, also known in finance circles as Beta, is the movement of the corporation's share price in response to overall market movements. For example, the share price of a corporation with a Beta of 1, which is by definition average, will increase by 20% in response to an overall increase in the market of 20%. In contrast, the share price of a corporation with a Beta of 2 will increase by 40% for that same market increase of 20%. As noted elsewhere, stock price movements are a noisy measure of a corporation's or an executive's performance. The higher the systematic risk, the noisier a measure it is. Consequently, when Beta is high, compensation should not be based upon share price performance nor on the stock-based component of the compensation package (Lewellen et al. 1987).

In contrast, the effect of unsystematic risk on the compensation package is a bit more ambiguous. While unsystematic risk reduces the desirability of stock ownership and stock-based compensation to the executive, unsystematic movements in a corporation's share price reflect the performance of the corporation, and hence, are less noisy than systematic movements that mirror those of the overall market. Consistent with this, Lewellen et al. (1987) found that although the proportion of stock in the compensation package decreases with Beta, they found it increases with the variance of stock returns.

From the above discussion it is clear that structuring stock-based compensation to filter out the systematic risk would be optimal. As discussed in Chapter 6, such market-adjusted options have not been observed in practice, perhaps because of their unfavorable accounting treatment, or because corporations can always informally adjust for downside risk via repricings.

Share price fluctuation is not the only risk a corporation should be concerned with when designing the executive compensation contract. They need to be aware of the riskiness of all measures used in performance evaluation and bonus allocation. For example, if conditional compensation is based upon accounting income, and certain drivers of accounting income are beyond an executive's control, then accounting income becomes a noisy measure of performance.

D. Growth and Liquidity

Empirical research shows that the level of compensation and the use of conditional compensation vary with the investment opportunity set of the corporation. Finkelstein and Boyd (1998) noted that in corporations where managers have a large amount of discretion, their potential impact on the organization is greater, as will be their marginal product and compensation. Smith and Watts (1992) and Gaver and Gaver (1993, 1995) showed that corporations with more growth options have higher executive compensation. Smith and Watts (1992) also showed that corporations with more growth options have a greater use of bonus and stock option plans, whereas Gaver and Gaver (1995) found that corporations with more growth options pay a larger portion of their total compensation in the form of long-term incentives. Baber et al. (1996) found stronger associations between pay and performance and more use of market, rather than accounting-based performance indicators, for high-growth corporations.

Unfortunately, stock-based compensation is most risky for these same growth corporations. As an illustration, Pulliam and Thurm (2000) noted that in 2000 the "25 worst-performing Internet stocks . . . are down a staggering 95.7%" (p. A1). Because of this risk, one might expect growth corporations to use less market-based compensation. Although some might argue that this market risk implies the need for more accounting-based compensation, for many growth companies the traditional accounting model does not work well.

Consider the following example. A newly established company invests significant amounts in product development and marketing, with the goal of establishing a brand name for its products and itself. If the investments are successful, the corporation will acquire a large market share and be able to charge a premium price in the future. Generally accepted accounting principles, while allowing the current capitalization (and future expensing) of expenditures on fixed assets, requires the immediate expensing of most research and development and marketing expenses. Thus although a $100,000 expenditure on a new warehouse will only reduce current income by the current depreciation expense, which could be $2500 if the company depreciated the warehouse over 40 years, a $100,000 expenditure on marketing would reduce current income by $100,000. Basing compensation, or a large portion of compensation, on accounting-based measures would provide disincentive to invest in product development and marketing. This problem is greatest for growth firms, or alternatively, firms with the most investment opportunities.

If there are problems and risks associated with using market and accounting-based compensation, it would imply that growth corporations should include more fixed cash compensation in their compensation packages. But from both the empirical research cited above and anecdotal evidence, this does not appear to be the case. One potential explanation revolves around another corporate characteristic, liquidity.

Fast growing corporations, with many investment opportunities, are often cash constrained. Thus, many have argued that because of liquidity constraints they can only pay minimal cash compensation, and instead they must give large stock and option grants to attract employees.[9] This added risk may in part, or in whole, explain the above findings of Smith and Watts (1992) and Gaver and Gaver (1993, 1995) that growth corporations pay higher levels of compensation. Mitigating this risk may also be an explanation for the stock option repricings and additional grants of options, often observed after the share price drops. For example, Horn (2000) reported that Sprint will allow "employees to cancel stock options granted to them in 2000 in exchange for an equal number of new options in the future" (p. E1) and that "Microsoft doubled its annual stock-option grants to 3,400 full-time employees in a bid to keep workers after its stock price tumbled on a variety of bad news" (p. E6).

---

[9]As noted earlier, Core and Guay (2000) found that firms who are cash constrained are more likely to use stock options to compensate their employees.

E. Labor Intensity

Growth corporations are not the only corporations for whom the accounting model does not work well. The accounting treatment of expenditures affects a wide range of corporations, and consequently, the affect of using accounting measures in compensation packages. Consider labor-intensive firms, whose investments in training (also known in academic jargon as *human capital*) are expensed immediately rather than capitalized and expensed over time. Using accounting measures in setting compensation provides a disincentive to invest in human capital.

F. Ownership and Board Composition

As noted in earlier in the book, concentrated ownership and monitoring by the board of directors can act to provide incentives to maximize shareholder value, independent of the compensation package.[10] Thus, the existence of large, nonmanagement, shareholders and/or an active board of directors may mitigate the need for the compensation package to provide those incentives. Large shareholders, because they internalize more of the gains from monitoring, are more likely to expend resources on monitoring management. Consistent with the reduced need for the compensation package to provide executives with incentives, Beatty and Zajac (1994) found that the existence of a large shareholder is associated with a lower percentage of the compensation package being performance based. Kraft and Niederprum (1999) stated that when a large shareholder dominates a corporation, the corporation pays less, and has a lower pay–performance sensitivity. Kato (1997) pointed out that the ownership and control structure of financial *keiretsu,* which are groups of firms organized around their major lender and having extensive cross-shareholdings, is an effective constraint on executives and executive pay. To that extent he provides evidence that pay is lower for executives in these firms than those in Japanese firms not affiliated with any financial *keiretsu.*

Concentrated shareholdings may in fact substitute for other forms of monitoring. Hebner and Kato (1997) noted that the average corporate board in Japan includes less than one (0.7 to be exact) outside director, perhaps because of the extensive cross-shareholdings of financial *keiretsu.* Kaplan (1999) suggested that in Japan, where capital markets are relatively illiquid and hence market-oriented control mechanisms are less useful, corporate and bank ownership plays the major monitoring and disciplinary role.

The ability and incentive of the board to monitor executives affects the need to use the compensation package to align the interests of executives and shareholders. An example of where monitoring may be weak, and thus the compensation package

---

[10]This section will discuss ownership by individuals not employed by the firm, whereas the next will discuss the effect of executive ownership on incentives.

especially important in providing the proper incentives, occurs when the CEO also holds the position of chairman of the board. Research summarized in Chapter 9 has found that whether it is because of the additional responsibilities they shoulder or the influence they have over the remainder of the board, CEOs who are also chairmen of the board earn higher compensation than their counterparts who are not also board chairs. Other research cited in Chapter 9 shows that the sensitivity of CEO turnover to corporate performance was lower when the same person holds both jobs. Considering the evidence, and incentives, when the CEO is also the board chair, his or her compensation package should consist mainly of performance-based compensation. Beatty and Zajac (1994) found empirical evidence consistent with this hypothesis.

The composition of the remainder of the board of directors influences the ability of that board to monitor executives, and hence, the importance of the compensation package in providing incentives. An independent board, where independent directors are defined as directors whose primary employment is not with the corporation and who do not conduct business with the corporation, has the ability to monitor executives. However, the directors may lack the incentives to do so. Perhaps the relevant factor in terms of incentives is the amount of shares they own. If one or more directors own a significant amount of stock, they have the incentive to monitor executives to look after their investment. Alternatively, if board ownership is low, and most, if not all, of the directors have been appointed by the current CEO, then they lack the incentive to monitor the CEO and the importance of the compensation package in providing incentives is paramount. Beatty and Zajac (1994) found the percentage of incentive compensation increases with the percentage of inside or nonindependent directors.

G. Regulated Industries

As noted in Chapter 1, the need for incentive alignment via the executive compensation package arises from the fact that monitoring by definition is imperfect. That is, the board cannot review every decision made, and even if it could, it may lack the expertise and/or firm specific knowledge necessary to evaluate those decisions. Variation exists nonetheless in the ability of boards and shareholders to monitor executive behavior across corporations. This variation may arise from variation in the ability or incentives of the board and/or from the variation in the investment opportunity set of the corporation. The better able boards and shareholders are to monitor management, the less need there is for incentive alignment via executive compensation packages. Consider, for example, regulated or government-owned firms. Managers of these firms may find their decision-making ability limited by an inability to lay off workers, increase prices, or shift production overseas. In some cases if they do too well, regulators may even force them to reduce future rates and/or return excess profits to rate payers.

Consider the following example of a rate-regulated utility, which also faces a ceiling on the amount of profit it can report, a profit that is a function of its rate base (normally capital investment). Basing compensation on reported profit may not be optimal, as there are political and regulatory constraints upon how much profit the utility can make. However, since the amount of allowed profit increases with the rate base, the plan needs to provide incentive for capital investment. Yet the plan should only encourage relatively low-risk investments, as the payoff function to the firm is asymmetric; that is, regulators limit the upside payoff to investments but may not necessarily limit the downside losses.[11] Thus for two reasons, stock options, also with an asymmetric payoff function, but tied to the upside potential of the corporation, are a suboptimal compensation strategy. The first reason is that the payoff structure of at- or out-of-the-money stock options encourages risk taking. The second reason is the limited upside potential for the share price of a regulated utility. Rather, the optimal package, from the view of shareholders, needs to encourage managers to minimize the variances of cash flows and earnings. Such a package is likely to include more fixed components, that is, salary, than that of the average unregulated corporation. Consistent with this, evidence has shown that regulated corporations use less incentive compensation. Abdel-Khalik (1988), in examining executive compensation in regulated utilities, noted that few firms in his sample use stock options. He also found that compensation is positively associated with overcapacity, consistent with the incentive noted above to increase the rate base. Similarly, an analysis of 1999 compensation for public utilities (Standard Industrial Classification [SIC] code 4900–4999) shows that the portion of the compensation made up of salary (mean 31%, median 29%) is at the high end, and that of stock options (mean 34%, median 30%) is at the low end when compared to the industry groupings shown in Table 2.5.[12] Interestingly, the percentages of long-term bonus (6%) and that of stock grants (8%) were also higher than that observed in Table 2.5. It should be noted that these percentages have changed dramatically to reflect the deregulation that has taken place during the 1990s. Just 7 years earlier, in 1992, the corresponding percentages were 49% (51%) for salary, and 21% (12%) for stock options.

This finding is consistent with the academic research showing changes in the compensation package when regulations are lifted. For example, Cragg and Dyck (2000), who examined British firms that were privatized from 1982–1984, found that prior to privatization, when managers were relatively constrained in their decision making, there was no pay for performance. In contrast, after privatization,

---

[11]Examples abound in the 1980s of regulated power utilities, for example, the Long Island Lighting Company and the Public Service Company of New Hampshire, investing billions in nuclear power generating facilities that were never opened. Because these facilities were never opened they were never included in the rate base (or only partially included in the rate base), which pushed the companies into bankruptcy and caused major losses to shareholders.

[12]SIC codes 4900–4999 are included in the broader industry grouping 4000–4999 in Table 2.5 (and other tables).

when many of the political constraints on their decision making were lifted, both the level of compensation and intensity of their pay for performance measure increased. Bryan et al. (1999) found similar results for electric utilities and Ezzell and Miles (1995) for banks in the United States.

H. Financial Distress

Corporations in financial distress, that is, in bankruptcy or close to it, have many problems. From a compensation and employment viewpoint, there are two major issues. The first is that they impose more than the normal amount of risk on employees, in terms of both job loss (e.g., if the corporation shuts down the employees lose their jobs) and the loss of any amounts directly (stock, options) or indirectly (pensions) invested in the corporation. The second is that they may have little cash with which to pay those employees. Furthermore, in order for the corporation to maximize its survival chances, it needs to retain key employees. Although the above applies to all employees in the corporation, executive departures are particularly painful because they may cause a ripple effect. That is, a well-publicized executive departure can send negative signals[13] about the corporation's chances of survival and lead to lower level employees departing.

How should the corporation in financial distress structure the compensation package? The first and second issues provide conflicting directions. That is, because of the risk involved, the employee would place an extremely high discount rate on the value of any equity-based compensation. In other words, the employee would require much more in the way of uncertain stock-based compensation than he or she would in the form of certain cash compensation. Unfortunately, because of its financial circumstances, the corporation normally would need to conserve cash.

The situation is somewhat similar with start-up corporations; that is, the risk of failure is great, and the amount of cash is normally low. Thus, the compensation package at these corporations will normally have a large equity component. However, there are several differences between a start-up and a corporation in financial distress. The first is the optimism surrounding a start-up, which contrasts with the pessimism surrounding a corporation in financial distress. That is, employees are optimistic about the chances of success for a start-up and, hence, a large payoff when the corporation makes it big, for example, when the corporation goes public. Employees are less likely to envision a big payoff for a corporation already in financial distress. Another difference is that a start-up, by virtue of its ability to start with a clean slate, is able to attract employees who are less risk averse (more willing to endure risk) than an existing corporation whose employees may have been attracted to it because of its stability.

---

[13]The higher the level of the executive, the more information that executive is perceived to have (by other employees, investors, lenders, and suppliers) about the firm and its chances for survival.

Because of its risk, the corporation in financial distress must include a risk premium in its compensation package, that is, additional remuneration to compensate for the risk. Depending upon its cash situation, it may have to pay much of it in the form of equity, promising a large portion of the firm to employees if the corporation succeeds.

IV. THE EFFECT OF EXECUTIVE CHARACTERISTICS ON THE OPTIMAL COMPENSATION CONTRACT

This section builds upon that earlier discussion by more fully incorporating executive characteristics into the design of the compensation package. Factors to be considered include the executive's opportunity cost, risk aversion, horizon, and share ownership.

Although executive characteristics are important, it should be noted that incorporating individual characteristics into the package is more difficult than incorporating the characteristics of the corporation. Although the corporation can tailor its package(s) to its circumstances, or the characteristics of its executives as a group, tailoring the package to specific individuals becomes expensive from a design and political point of view. From a design point of view, the board or the consultants it hires has to analyze each executive's characteristics and then design a plan for that particular individual. From a political viewpoint, designing individual plans can be costly if it breeds the perception of favoritism, or inequity, across the executive ranks.

Still, incorporating executive characteristics, including tailoring the contract to the specific characteristics of an individual, can be beneficial. A prudent approach would be to tailor the plan to the general characteristics of the group, making modifications where appropriate and justifiable.

A. Opportunity Cost

In the context of attracting a new CEO, Chapter 3 briefly discussed the need for the value of the compensation package offered to exceed the executive's next best opportunity, which is his or her opportunity cost. When an individual's opportunity cost is "established" the contract can, but does not have to, be customized to the individual executive. Consider the following example. The vice-president of marketing, highly regarded inside and outside the corporation, is offered a comparable position at a competitor, but at a 20% raise. His (or her) opportunity cost has been established, and given the corporation wants to retain the executive, they match the offer. Previously, all vice-presidents (marketing, finance, manufacturing) were making comparable compensation. The corporation has justification for tailoring it package, that is, paying this vice-president more than the others, because he (or she) has attracted an outside offer and the corporation needs to do so to retain him (or her). Unfortunately, as discussed in an earlier chapter of this book, paying one executive more than his or her colleagues on the same level breeds resentment and the perception of inequity. In the extreme, the executive is viewed as being rewarded for being disloyal, that is, seeking out alternative employment. The other vice-presidents may then look for competing offers, diverting their attention from their corporate responsibilities. If they are successful in attracting new offers, the corporation then must decide whether to match them or lose the executive. If they do not attract new offers, they may become discouraged, which may affect their job performance adversely. Thus, when increasing the compensation of one executive, the corporation may find it wise to increase the pay of all executives at that level, to maintain internal equity. One factor that should influence the decision to increase the compensation of executives on the same level is the number of executives on that level. That is, it is more costly to the corporation if there are 100 executives at the same level then it is if there are three executives at the same level.[14] Another factor that should influence the decision is whether the corporation determines its current pay is too low.

But how does a corporation make the determination that pay is too low? In some cases, where the corporation is trying to attract a new executive who is currently employed elsewhere, or is trying to retain an executive who is being offered a position outside the company, that individual's opportunity cost is usually easy to determine.[15] Usually, but not always.

Consider that when attempting to hire an executive from outside the corporation, one measure of the executive's opportunity cost is his or her current compensation. The example, given in Chapter 3, of Robert Rubin and Citigroup illustrates that this is not always the case. Rubin was previously employed as the United States Secretary of the Treasury, earning $151,800 per year. Yet, for 2000 alone, Citigroup promised him a $1 million salary, $14 million bonus, and 1.5 million stock options. In this case, Rubin's opportunity cost was best measured by what he could have earned elsewhere, rather than what he was earning as Secretary of the Treasury.[16]

---

[14]This same factor, the number of contemporaries of the executive in question, should influence whether or not the corporation matches the offer. As the number of contemporaries increases so does the cost of matching the offer, either in terms of disgruntled contemporaries who are paid less, or in terms of the cost of increasing the pay of those contemporaries.

[15]Where the executive is employed at another company, his or her opportunity cost is his or her existing compensation. When a current executive is offered a position outside the company, his or her opportunity cost is the new offer.

[16]Individuals often take high-level jobs in the government that pay substantially less than they could make in the private sector. Another example is Richard Cheney, who resigned as Chairman and CEO of Halliburton to run for Vice President of the United States. In his final full year at Halliburton, Cheney received a salary of $1,283,000, other compensation of $640,914, and options for 300,0000 shares, with a potential realizable value of between $7,452,401 and $18,885,848 (Halliburton proxy statement filed with the Securities and Exchange Commission, April 3, 2000, pp. 20, 21). Now as Vice President he earns a salary of $171,500 per year.

However, this case is the exception; usually current compensation is the opportunity cost.

In most other circumstances, that is, executives without competing offers, determining the opportunity cost is not that simple. But it is important. Paying the executive too much reduces shareholder value. Paying too little makes it more likely the executive leaves or gets a more costly offer the corporation elects to match. Corporations can, and do, use a variety of means to determine an executive's opportunity costs. On a regular basis (Clarke et al. 1998), corporations, or more likely, the consultants they hire (Ezzamel and Watson 1998), conduct surveys of what comparable firms (based on size and industry) pay their executives, using that information to set compensation accordingly. In addition, the media conduct and publicly report on executive compensation (for example, *Forbes, Business Week, The Wall Street Journal, The Philadelphia Inquirer*). Surveys in trade journals often report compensation for lower level executives.

B. Risk Aversion

The effect of risk aversion on the compensation package is complex and originates with the effect of risk aversion on executive incentives. Risk aversion, in the absence of any incentives (monetary or otherwise) to take risk, will cause executives to pass up projects that increase their risk, even those that increase shareholder value. The solution is to provide compensation where value increases with the risk of the corporation, such as stock options. However, Beatty and Zajac (1994) noted that "linking a manager's compensation too closely to firm performance might lead to risk-avoiding behavior on the part of the manager" (p. 315). They suggest "the ability of firms to use executive compensation contracts to address managerial incentive problems is hampered by risk-bearing concerns that stem from the risk aversion of top managers" (p. 313).

The primary effect of executive risk aversion is on the composition of the compensation package, that is, the compensation package will contain less conditional or risky compensation than it would if the executive was risk neutral. This occurs because a risk-averse individual will demand a higher expected payout if the compensation package is risky than he or she would if the package was risk free. This expected payout will increase with both the risk of the payout and the executive's risk aversion. In equilibrium, corporations will use risky compensation only up to the level where the marginal benefits, that is, alignment of incentive effects, of the additional risky compensation equals their marginal cost, which is the higher level of expected compensation. Similarly, in equilibrium, executives will self-select into positions appropriate for the level of risk they are willing to bear.

The corporation must be extremely careful in designing a package to control for this risk aversion. Conventional wisdom is that stock options, because their value increases with the risk of the firm, provides incentives to take risk. However, consider the case where an executive holds in-the-money stock options, that is, options where the exercise price is less than the current market price. The executive then has something to lose if the share price goes down, which may make him or her reluctant to take risks. For this reason, at- or out-of-the money options provide the appropriate incentive for the executive to take the risks necessary to increase firm value. One mechanism to ensure that an executive's option portfolio does not provide disincentive to take risk is to grant reload options. As discussed earlier, reload options enable the holder to exercise in-the-money options and receive new at-the-money options, that is, new options exercisable at the current market price.

C. Horizon and Age

An executive's horizon is the amount of time he or she expects to spend in a particular job, for example, the time remaining prior to retirement. It has been noted in the literature (for example Dechow and Sloan 1991; Murphy and Zimmerman 1993; Pourciau 1993) that executives approaching retirement have differing incentives; in particular they have less incentive to invest in a project whose payback comes after their retirement. For example, Dechow and Sloan (1991) find evidence that CEOs spend less on research and development in their final years in office. Although in an efficient market, the present value of those payoffs should, theoretically, be reflected in the stock price at the time of investment, the market may not be efficient, or the decision maker may not believe it is. In addition to passing up potentially profitable projects whose payoffs take place after retirement, executives have the incentive to manipulate accounting income to pull future income into current periods. This would increase their bonuses and if they can fool the market, potentially inflate the corporation's stock price. Of course, pulling income from the future into the current period reduces future income and potentially the future stock price. One way to mitigate these incentives is to tie the executives' payoffs to income and/or stock price after retirement. For example, the executive may be given options and/or restricted stock that do not vest until after retirement, at which time any manipulation will presumably be revealed. Consistent with this theory, Lewellen et al. (1987) found that the percentage of current compensation in the compensation package decreases with executive age.

An additional consideration that increases the importance of the compensation package is the decreased incentives provided by the managerial labor market as the executive gets older. In general, although the managerial labor market provides some discipline and incentives in the form of attracting outside offers, the older the executive, the less relevant those incentives are (Beatty and Zajac 1994; Lewellen et al. 1987). This can be because an older executive is less likely to attract an offer or even if he (or she) does receive an offer, he (or she) would have fewer years to earn the new higher level of compensation associated with that offer, thus making it less valuable than it would have been to a younger executive.

D. Ownership

Executive ownership theoretically provides the incentive to increase shareholder value. In the extreme it provides all the incentives necessary. Thus, firms like Berkshire Hathaway and Amazon.com, because their CEOs own such large stakes in the firm, do not need to use their compensation package to align the interest of those CEOs with shareholders. As noted earlier, both Warren Buffett of Berkshire Hathaway and Jeff Bezos of Amazon.com, receive relatively small salaries and no conditional compensation at all. However, there is still the need to provide incentives to lower level executives who will not have such a large stake in the firm. For example, in 1999, Amazon.com provided option grants to each of its next four highest-ranking executives, Richard L. Dalzell, Joseph Galli, Jr, Warren C. Jenson, and Jeffrey A. Wilke.[17] Still, when the CEO has such a large stake in the firm, he (or she) has the incentive, and presumably the ability, to monitor lower level executives. Thus, there is both less need for incentive compensation in the compensation package of these lower level executives, and less need for other shareholders to monitor executives.

Both dollar and percentage executive ownership play a role in determining executive incentives and the need to augment those incentives through the compensation package. When executive ownership is large in dollar terms, it is likely that the executive has a large portion of his or her wealth tied to the firm. In that case, the executive, although having the incentive to maximize shareholder value, will also be more risk averse than a diversified shareholder would like. As noted by Beatty and Zajac (1994), "the magnitude of the existing equity positions held by top managers may influence their willingness to accept further risk bearing." To provide the executive with the appropriate incentives, two divergent approaches might be tried. The first is the standard approach of giving the executive more options, as out-of- or at-the-money options encourage risk taking. This may only have a marginal effect on an executive with an already large investment in the firm. An alternative, which is consistent with the empirical evidence in Lewellen et al. (1987), Beatty and Zajac (1994), and Toyne et al. (2000), would be to reduce the equity portion and increase the cash-based portion of the executive's compensation to reduce his or her risk.

When executive ownership is large in percentage terms, it is likely that the executive's incentives are aligned with those of shareholders, as he or she shares in wealth gains and losses to that extent. Once again, there is less need for incentive compensation. There is one caveat, however. Research has shown (for example, Denis et al. 1997) that as executive ownership increases, executives are less likely to be replaced. Thus the incentive to work hard to avoid being fired is lessened.

---

[17]Amazon.com proxy statement filed with the Securities and Exchange Commission, March 29, 2000, p. 8.

In contrast, when executive ownership is low, ownership provides little incentive to increase firm value. Thus the compensation package must provide those incentives via stock options and stock grants.

V. THE EFFECT OF JOINT CHARACTERISTICS ON THE OPTIMAL CONTRACT

A. Tax Status

The effect of taxes on the compensation package is discussed separately from the firm and executive characteristics above, because the tax status of the corporation and the executive jointly influence the compensation package. Taxes matter, because if the compensation package can be structured to minimize the taxes paid by the corporation and the executive, which is referred to as the joint tax burden, those tax savings can be shared by the two parties, making both better off. However, the corporation and executive must be careful and not ignore the incentives provided by the compensation package. That is, although tax savings are important, they should not be pursued without taking incentive effects into consideration.

B. Tax-Qualified Options

We begin with a discussion of tax-qualified options. Tax-qualified options provide certain benefits to employees; that is, if the employee need not pay taxes on the exercise profit until the shares are sold, and if the shares are held for more than a year, the gain is taxed at capital gains rates. However, the employer does not receive a deduction if the option is tax-qualified. The use of tax-qualified options thus increases the corporate tax burden. However, if the corporation is in a low tax bracket, or more appropriately, anticipates being in a low tax bracket at the time of exercise,[18] tax-qualified options minimize the joint tax burden. In many cases, especially when the corporation is in the top tax bracket, the increase in corporate taxes may exceed the savings to the executive from the option. Yet tax-qualified options have certain incentive effects that may still make them worthwhile. The ability to defer taxation as long as the executive owns the shares creates what is known as the lock-in effect, a disincentive to sell those shares, and consequently

---

[18]Recall that with nonqualified employee stock options the corporation takes a tax deduction at the time of exercise. Thus, in deciding which type of option minimizes the joint tax burden, the corporation must estimate the time of exercise and tax rate at that time. Given the difficulties involved in such estimations, the corporation could always grant qualified options and later, if nonqualified options appear to be more advantageous, induce employees to disqualify those options, which would allow those options to be treated as nonqualified for tax purposes. Matsunaga et al. (1992) document such activity after the Tax Reform Act of 1986, which reduced the relative tax advantages of qualified stock options.

may also increase the possibility the executive remains with the firm. As Balsam et al. (1997) showed, in some cases the benefits from incentive alignment and executive retention outweigh the tax costs and cause firms to grant what appears to be tax-disadvantageous compensation.

C. Deferred Compensation

In minimizing the joint tax burden, both the current and future tax rates of the executive and the corporation must be taken into consideration. An interesting situation surrounded the adoption of the Tax Reform Act of 1986. The act, which was phased in from 1986 to 1988, dramatically reduced the top marginal tax rate for both corporations and individuals. An individual in the top bracket saw his or her rate drop from 50% in 1986 to 28% in 1988, whereas a corporation in the top bracket saw its rate drop from 46–34%. Because of the lower tax rates on income for an individual in the top bracket, deferring income from 1986–1988 saves $22,000 in taxes for every $100,000 deferred. However, from the corporation's perspective, because of the lower tax rates, deductions are less valuable. That is, although a $100,000 deduction in 1986 saves $46,000 in taxes, one in 1988 only saves $34,000 in taxes, a difference of $12,000. The joint tax savings for every $100,000 deferred from 1986–1988 is $10,000, the difference between the $22,000 the executive saves and the additional $12,000 the corporation has to pay.

A more common situation arises when an executive defers income until retirement, under the assumption that he or she will be in a lower bracket at that time. In this situation, the assumption is that the corporation's tax status does not change, thus the deduction is equally valuable, but the executive's tax rate drops resulting in less tax paid.

D. Fringe Benefits

The use of nontaxable fringe benefits, for example, health and life insurance, almost by definition reduces the joint tax burden. The reason is that although the payments are deductible to the corporation, they are not taxable to the employee. Holding total compensation constant, taxes paid by the corporation are unchanged, whereas those paid by the executive are lower because some of his or her compensation is in the form of a nontaxable fringe benefit. However, as noted by Scholes and Wolfson (1992), while tax beneficial, the contracting costs of these plans may outweigh the tax benefits. First are the compliance costs. These are the costs of drawing up plans and ensuring that they meet Internal Revenue Code requirements. A major cost is the requirement that to qualify for favorable tax treatment, that is, exclusion from income by the executive, the benefits have to be offered on a nondiscriminatory basis to essentially all employees. The corporation is willing to incur these costs because, in equilibrium, the executive will accept less explicit compensation. To be more precise, the corporation is *only* willing to incur these costs if they are less than the reduction in explicit compensation the executive(s) are willing to accept. However, although the benefits have to be offered across the board, the valuation of the benefits, and hence the reduction in compensation the employee is willing to accept, differ by employee. For example, while health insurance might be valued highly by an executive with a nonworking spouse and two dependent children, a single employee would place a lower valuation on those benefits and the valuation for someone with a working spouse covered by the spouse's plan would be even lower.

E. Corporate Tax Status

Consider now the corporation's tax status. Because of the structure of our federal tax system, the marginal tax rate for most profitable corporations is 35%. But some corporations pay no federal taxes; for example, newly established corporations that have yet to achieve profitability or established companies that are in financial distress. Those corporations cannot currently use the tax deductions associated with executive compensation.[19] Their preference would be for forms of compensation that generate future, rather than current, deductions. These forms could include stock options and restricted stock, or more simply, the deferral of salary and bonus. That is, nonqualified stock options generate tax deductions in the future when they are exercised, restricted stock generates tax deductions when the restrictions expire, and deferred compensation generates deductions when payment is actually made.

VI. SUMMARY

The focus of this chapter was on how corporate goals and corporate and executive characteristics influence the level and composition of executive pay. Corporate characteristics that influence executive pay include size, political costs, risk, growth, liquidity, tax status, ownership, board composition, regulation, and degree of labor intensity. Executive characteristics include opportunity cost, risk aversion, horizon, and ownership.

In general, larger corporations should and do pay a higher level of compensation. In addition, because the wealth constraint limits the percentage ownership in the corporation, larger corporations should and do make a higher proportion of the compensation package equity based. Fast-growing corporations, perhaps because of

---

[19]While the tax code allows losses (the excess of deductions over taxable income) to be carried forward for 20 years, the present value of a future deduction is less than one, and if the company never becomes profitable, those deductions will never be used.

the risk involved, pay a higher level of compensation, with a larger component of that compensation being equity based. To mitigate some of the risk involved, these corporations often resort to additional option grants or option repricing after share price decreases. When ownership is concentrated or the board of directors takes an active role in monitoring, there is less need to provide incentives via the executive compensation package. Labor-intensive corporations and corporations with large investments in marketing or research and development should minimize their use of accounting numbers in performance evaluation and reward, or alternatively, adjust those numbers before using them. Regulated corporations, given the constraints on their operations, have less need for conditional compensation. Furthermore, performance measures have to be carefully tailored to what the regulatory environment allows. Corporations in financial distress, because of cash constraints, must include a large equity component in their compensation package, despite the risks involved.

Additionally, the executive compensation contract should consider the characteristics of executives individually and as a group. Although it is costly to tailor contracts to individual executives, in some circumstances it may be worthwhile. In those circumstances the corporation should take into account the executive's opportunity cost in setting the level of compensation. The corporation should also consider the executive's risk aversion, horizon, and ownership in determining the composition of the compensation package.

It is important to recognize in designing the package that the different components of the package should be coordinated, so that the incentives they provide do not conflict with one another or with the goals of the corporation. For example, a corporation trying to encourage long-term growth, which requires major investments in research and development, should utilize long-term performance measures. It should not utilize short-term measures of accounting performance, due to the accounting requirement that research and development be expensed immediately, the effect of which would be to discourage such investment if the executive were compensated based upon accounting income. Alternatively, if accounting measures are to be used, adjustments should be made for research and development. For example, rather than using reported accounting income, the corporation could use income before research and development.

Decisions have to be made as to participation in plans. For example, is the bonus plan limited to the CEO, the top five executives, or all executives earning above a certain amount? A related decision is how much, in either dollars or shares, the corporation wants to spend on the plan. The decisions are related in that, all else equal, the greater the number of participants, the greater the cost to the corporation. And how are amounts allocated from the plans? Do all participants get equal allocations, or are the allocations based upon rank, salary, performance, and so on. In many corporations bonus targets are set based upon the participant's salary. For example, American Standard, in its contract with Frederick M. Poses, its Chairman and CEO states the following:

The base salary for your position will be $1,000,000 per year, and will be subject to annual review for increase at the discretion of the Board of Directors. In addition, you will be eligible for an Annual Incentive with a target award of 100% of your base salary.[20]

Related to the allocation is what, if any, performance criteria should be used in determining the size of the plan and allocating amounts to participants. For example, a corporation can set aside a specific proportion of profits for its bonus plan. It may then allocate the bonus to participants based upon rank, individual performance evaluations, etc.

[20]Letter dated October 13, 1999, from American Standard Company to Frederick M. Poses, its newly hired Chairman and CEO.

CHAPTER 12

Designing a
Compensation Contract

*The key to a company achieving its strategic goals often lies in its ability to
attract and retain experienced senior executives—and this, in turn often
depends on the quality of its compensation and benefits programs.*[1]

I. INTRODUCTION

This chapter will extend and be a more detailed discussion of the factors that enter
into the design of the executive compensation contract. As discussed in Chapter 3,
the executive compensation contract has four major objectives. It must be (1) attractive enough to employ the executive initially, (2) provide the proper incentives,
(3) tie the executive to corporation, and (4) minimize the costs to the corporation.
In designing the compensation contract, these four objectives must then be integrated with the corporation's goals and the corporate and executive characteristics
discussed in Chapter 11.

II. SALARY

As noted in Chapter 2 (see Table 2.1), the overwhelming majority of compensation
contracts include a salary component. The issue is then, how much, or what portion,
of the compensation package should be salary? Many factors, both executive and
corporation specific, are incorporated into the decision. An underlying constraint
in determining salary is that an individual's salary is not determined in isolation.
That is, other executives' salaries and reactions must be taken into consideration.

A. Impact of Executive Characteristics

1. Opportunity Cost

Let's start by considering the impact of executive characteristics on salary. Whether
the individual is a current employee or one the corporation wishes to recruit, the

---

[1]Compensation Resources Group (2000).

individual's opportunity cost must be taken into consideration. Generally, an individual will not accept a lower salary than is offered elsewhere, although if the other components of the package are more attractive, the individual may accept the lower salary. However, the onus is on the corporation to make those other components more attractive, as many times those other components are tied to salary. As an example, consider the following passage linking bonus to base salary, which appeared in a letter from Eastman Kodak to Daniel A. Carp, its new President and Chief Executive Officer, dated November 22, 1999:

> 2. Management Variable Compensation Plan
> Your target annual award under Kodak's Management Variable Compensation Plan ("MVCP") will be 105% of your base salary, making your new total targeted annual compensation $2,050,000.

2. Risk Aversion

An executive's risk aversion must be considered in determining salary. A risk-averse individual always prefers a certain to an uncertain amount. Thus, holding the value of the compensation package constant, he or she would prefer that the salary, which is the certain component, to be as large as possible. In equilibrium, he or she would even be willing to accept a lower amount in exchange for reducing the uncertainty or risk of the package. This desire on the part of the executive must be weighed against the goals of the corporation. If risky investments are needed to achieve the corporations' goals, then the compensation package must include some risky compensation. On the other hand, if the executive already has a substantial investment in the corporation, then the necessary incentives may already be present. In that situation, including a risky component in the compensation package may be counterproductive, because it would increase the executive's risk beyond the optimal level.

3. Executive Ownership

As alluded to in the immediately preceding paragraph, executive ownership affects the need for incentives to be provided via the compensation package. In particular, the greater an executive's ownership the less the need for conditional compensation. Thus the amount and proportion of salary in the compensation package should increase with executive ownership.

4. Horizon

The executive's horizon also must be considered in determining salary. If the executive is approaching the traditional retirement age, he or she may be reluctant to make long-term investments that pay off after his or her retirement. To provide incentive for the executive to make such investments, the corporation should consider reducing the amount of current salary and replacing it with deferred compensation conditional upon the performance of the corporation after the executive retires.

B. Impact of Corporate Characteristics

1. Size

In general, it has been observed that the dollar amount of salary increases with the size of the corporation (Table 2.9), although salary as a percentage of the total compensation package decreases with the size of the corporation (Table 2.6). As noted in Chapter 11, this latter finding may be due to the fact that the percentage of the corporation owned by executives decreases with increases in the size of the corporation, and thus, the compensation package has to increasingly provide those equity-related incentives. The finding that salary (and total compensation) increase with size is attributable to the greater set of skills required to run a more complex organization, and the greater demand and willingness to pay for people who can run those organizations.

2. Growth

Similarly, the growth of the corporation must be taken into consideration. As noted in Chapter 11, growth corporations, while in general paying a higher level of compensation, make more of that compensation conditional on performance. Providing incentives in the compensation package is more important for growing corporations because as the amount of discretion an executive has increases, it becomes harder for shareholders and directors to effectively monitor the executive. Thus salary becomes a smaller part of the compensation package.

3. Financial Considerations

The financial circumstances of the corporation also affect the composition of the compensation package. Salary, if currently paid, reduces the corporation's cash availability, financial accounting income, and taxable income. If the corporation is cash constrained, it may substitute noncash items, such as stock grants and options, for cash salary (see Core and Guay 2000). Similarly, if the corporation wishes to increase financial accounting income, it can substitute stock options, which usually do not reduce reported income, for salary (see Matsunaga 1995). While corporations rarely seek to increase taxable income, if the corporation has little taxable income, it may seek to replace salary, which yields current tax deductions, with components that yield tax deductions in the future when the corporation can utilize them. Finally, if the executive is subject to Internal Revenue code Section 162(m) limitations, the corporation may want to either defer salary until the executive is not subject to those limitations, and/or substitute other forms of compensation that meet the performance-based criteria specified in Section 162(m) (see Rose and Wolfram 2000).

4. Ownership and Board Composition

Monitoring from large shareholders and/or an active board of directors may lessen the role of the compensation package in motivating executives. In the absence of active monitoring, a large portion of the compensation package should be performance based to provide executives with incentives to increase shareholder value. However, when performance-based compensation is used, executive risk aversion requires an increase in the expected value of the compensation package. Active monitoring allows corporations to reduce the amount of performance-based compensation in the compensation package, and hence, the expected value of the package. Thus, salary should be both higher and a larger component of a smaller compensation package when there are large shareholders or an active board of directors.

III. BONUS

Approximately 80% of corporations pay their CEOs bonuses in a given year (see Table 2.1). While some of the remaining companies may not have bonus plans, others may have them and not pay bonuses because performance standards were not met. For example, the following passage, from page 16 of the Halliburton proxy statement (filed with the Securities and Exchange Commission on April 3, 2000) explains that no bonus was paid because the performance target was not met.

> In 1999, consolidated CVA performance did not meet the target level established by the Compensation Committee and, accordingly, Mr. Cheney and the other executives named in the Summary Compensation Table earned no incentive award under the provisions of the Annual Performance Pay Plan.

Because of situations like this, the 81% of corporations that paid their CEOs bonuses in 2000 (Table 2.1) understates the number of corporations that have bonus plans.

The standard procedure is to set a target bonus as a percentage of salary, with the percentage of salary usually increasing as the executive moves up through the executive ranks. Thus, consistent with economic theory, as the executive moves up the ranks, more of his or her pay is at risk. For a CEO, the target bonus might be 100% of salary, if the target is met. If the target is exceeded by a certain amount, the executive might get more, for example, 120% of salary, whereas if the target is missed the executive might get less, perhaps 80% of bonus. Generally speaking, these plans are nonlinear; that is, to achieve a higher bonus the executive or corporation must achieve a series of thresholds. Additionally, plans may have upper bounds beyond which increased performance does not increase the bonus, and/or lower bounds below which no bonus is paid. The following passage describing the contract between

Robert Morrison and Pepsico illustrates both the linkage between salary and bonus, that is, bonus is expressed as a percentage of salary, and the use of an upper bound.

> Mr. Morrison will be entitled to an annual base salary of no less than $1,107,750 and will have an annual bonus target equal to at least 100% of base salary, with a maximum payout of 200% of base salary.[2]

This lack of linearity causes problems, as it provides executives with incentives to manipulate performance measures to maximize the present value of bonus payments, even if the current period's bonus cannot be affected. For example, assume the bonus is based on accounting earnings and the corporation is either above the upper bound or below the lower bound. The executive has the incentive to reduce current period income, so that he or she may shift that income to future periods, increasing the bonus paid in those future periods.[3] An extreme example of this has been referred to as the "big bath" (Kinney and Trezevant 1996). A big bath occurs when a corporation having a loss year takes a series of accounting charges to increase the magnitude of the loss. The benefit of the big bath is that because those charges do not have to be taken in the future (and in some cases may be reversed), income and bonuses in future periods will be higher.

The compensation committee, assuming it decides to pay bonuses or have a bonus plan, must make the following determinations. First, should the bonus be implicit or explicit. If the bonus is implicit, no formal plan exists and the committee determines the bonus after the end of the period in question based upon whatever criteria, objective and/or subjective, they decide to use. If the bonus is explicit, a formal plan must be drawn, normally prior to the start of the period in question. Although an implicit plan has advantages in terms of flexibility, explicit plans have advantages in terms of clarity; that is, the executive knows his or her goals; and the payoff if he or she achieves those goals.[4] The plan, if explicit, must address the targeted bonus payout; the performance period, that is, will performance be judged quarterly, annually, or over a longer period; the performance measure or measures to be used; the target or thresholds for those performance measures; and the means of payment. As will be illustrated below, characteristics of the executive and corporation should be taken into consideration in making these determinations.

A. Targeted Bonus Amount

For those corporations that have a bonus plan, the corporation must decide how much, and what proportion of the compensation package, the targeted bonus

---

[2]Pepsico Form S-4 filed with the Securities and Exchange Commission, on January 9, 2001, p. I-77.
[3]Healy (1985) discussed these incentives in more detail.
[4]Further, in order to qualify for exemption from the million-dollar deductibility limit under Internal Revenue Code Section 162(m), bonuses must be paid based upon an explicit performance-based plan approved by shareholders. If the bonuses are not deductible, the after tax-cost to the corporation is increased.

amount should be. As noted above, most explicit bonus plans state that the bonus will be a percentage of salary if a certain level of performance is achieved. Casual observation notes that for CEOs the target bonus is normally 100% of salary.

The target bonus should depend on a number of factors. Consider first, two generic factors. If salary is relatively low, to raise total compensation to the level required to attract and retain executives, bonuses must be higher. The following example, which ignores executive risk aversion and assumes that the targeted bonus is the expected bonus, illustrates the need to consider salary when setting the targeted bonus amount. Corporation A pays its CEO $1 million in salary and will pay a bonus of 100% of salary if the performance targets are met, leading to expected salary plus bonus of $2 million. Corporation B pays its CEO $0.5 million in salary. To be competitive with Corporation A, Corporation B needs its expected bonus to be $1.5 million. Thus it should pay a bonus of 300% of salary if the performance targets are met. A second factor to be considered is the performance goals themselves. The targeted bonus amount should take into account the ease with which the goals can be achieved. If the goals are easy to achieve, there is little risk involved and the bonus becomes akin to salary. Alternatively, if the goals are difficult to achieve, then the actual payment is uncertain, and a risk premium should be built into the targeted bonus amount.

1. Affect of Executive Characteristics on Targeted Bonus Amount

Executive characteristics influence the targeted bonus amount. The executive's risk aversion may influence the breakdown of compensation between certain salary and uncertain bonus, with the amount of bonus decreasing with risk aversion. Similarly, an executive's opportunity cost may influence the targeted bonus amount, as the greater the executive's opportunity cost, the greater total compensation. If an executive has significant share and/or option ownership, the current compensation package should reflect that and mitigate some of the market-based risk, via more bonus and less stock based compensation. In contrast, if an executive is nearing retirement, the corporation may want to increase the percentage of compensation that is forward looking, that is, stock based, consequently decreasing the targeted bonus amount.

2. Affect of Corporate Characteristics on Targeted Bonus Amount

As with salary, the magnitude of bonus will increase with the size of the corporation. Similarly the amount of bonus will be affected by liquidity and tax considerations. That is, a corporation with liquidity constraints may be more likely to pay a smaller cash bonus and to devote a larger portion of the compensation package to stock-based compensation.[5] Analogously, a corporation wishing to report higher financial accounting income will pay less bonus, which is recorded as an expense, and grant more stock options, for which the corporation normally does not recognize any expense. Similarly, if the corporation has little taxable income, even if it is not cash constrained, it may seek to replace the bonus, which yields current tax deductions, with components like stock options that yield tax deductions in the future when the corporation can utilize them.[6] If the executive is subject to Internal Revenue code Section 162(m) limitations, the corporation should either structure its bonus plan to qualify for the performance-based exceptions under Section 162(m), defer the bonus until the executive is not subject to those limitations, and/or substitute into other forms of compensation, such as stock options, that meet the performance-based criteria specified in Section 162(m). Finally, the noise and informativeness of performance measures, in particular share prices, affect the decision to use bonuses versus stock-based compensation. That is, if share prices are very noisy and/or do not provide much information on the performance of an executive, then the conditional compensation component of the compensation package should primarily be composed of bonuses (and share price should not be the performance measure).

B. Performance Period

In general, the longer the performance period or time frame the bonus is calculated over, the greater the retentive effect (Kole 1997). That is, the greater the window, the greater the monetary amount forfeited if the executive leaves. Consider the following illustration of the effect of a 1-year versus 3-year plan. An executive has a bonus plan that pays him (or her) 1% of net income. Income in the first year is $250 million, in the second year the corporation incurs a loss of $75 million, and in the third year the corporation has a profit of $150 million. If the plan is based on yearly income, the executive receives $2.5 million in the first year, 0 in the second, and $1.5 million in the third. If the plan is for 3 years, the executive receives a bonus of $3.25 million at the end of 3 years. Under the 3-year plan the executive gets a smaller bonus, but also somewhat surprisingly, at times has a greater incentive to remain with the corporation. If the plan is annual, it provides no monetary incentive for the executive to remain with the corporation during year two. In contrast, if the plan is based upon 3 years of performance, and hence no payout is made at the end of year one, if the executive leaves during year two, he or she forfeits the accumulated bonus at that point in time, which despite the loss, is still $1.75 million at the end of year two. Of course sometimes the incentives work in reverse. For example,

---

[5]Alternatively, the corporation facing liquidity constraints can require the bonus be deferred to a future period.

[6]Alternatively, rather than replace the bonus, the corporation could require or provide incentives for the executive to defer the bonus until a future period in which it expects to have taxable income.

if the corporation loses money in the first year of the 3-year term the executive has incentive to leave, as in order to earn a bonus, not only does the corporation have to earn money in years two and three, that amount must exceed the losses in year one. The executive, if he or she has the choice, may simply prefer to go elsewhere and start with a clean slate.

A longer period also minimizes the opportunity for shifting income across periods. Consider the example above, where net income is $250 million in the first year, a loss of $75 million in the second year, and $150 million in the third year. If the executive receives bonuses based on yearly income, he or she has the incentive to shift expenses (revenues) from year three (two) to year two (three), thereby increasing the loss in year two (Big Bath), but more importantly increasing income and bonus in year three. In contrast, there are fewer monetary incentives to shift income if the bonus is based on income for the 3-year period. That is, although there are no incentives to shift income across the 3 years, there are still incentives to shift income from earlier and later periods.

1. Affect of Executive Characteristics on Choice of Performance Period

What factors should influence the performance period to be used? Risk aversion would probably cause the executive to prefer a shorter period for the simple reason that the amount of the bonus, or even the existence of the bonus, is uncertain until completion of the performance period. In addition, the executive would prefer more frequent payments to smooth his or her income. That is, if the performance period is 3 years, the executive will not receive a payment in 2 of the 3 years, creating fluctuations in income. Then, of course, there is the issue of present value, that is, a dollar received today is worth more than a dollar received in the future. Assuming that the nominal value of the bonus is the same regardless of the performance period,[7] the present value of the bonus is greater if paid yearly, rather than if paid at the end of 3 years. If the executive has other opportunities, he or she may elect the one that selects the one with the shortest payout period. While it is difficult, first, to measure those other opportunities, and second, to tailor the contract to one executive, the corporation can proxy for those opportunities by examining the terms used by their competitors. These competing corporations, because of executive's industry-specific expertise, are the most likely alternative employers for a corporation's current executives.

An approach used by many corporations that mitigates the problems discussed above (i.e., uncertainty about and fluctuations in executive income) is the use of overlapping periods. A corporation may measure performance over 3 years, but have three performance periods accumulating at the same time. For example, one

---

[7]This may not always be true. Recall in the example above, because of the loss in year two, the total bonus paid over three years was $4 million if a one-year performance period was used, and $3.25 million if a 3-year period was used.

period may consist of years one through three, a second period consist of years two through four, and a third period consist of years three through five. Thus, assuming performance is satisfactory, the executive could expect to receive a bonus every year. In terms of executive income, this may create a smoother income stream than basing the bonus on income for a single year, as the longer time period can filter out fluctuations in the performance measure.

2. *Affect of Corporate Characteristics on Choice of Performance Period*

The corporation's investment opportunities influence the choice of performance period. The greater the corporation's investment opportunities, the more important it is to the corporation to retain existing executives. So the length of the performance period should be positively associated with growth. In addition, the choice of performance period should be positively associated with the corporation's operating cycle. Consider two companies, one that constructs housing and one that sells clothing. The time from initiation of a housing development till its completion could be a period of years. In contrast, the operating cycle for a clothing retailer is less than a year. If direct observation of an executive's actions is impossible or impractical, to properly evaluate the performance of an executive requires the completion of an operating or production cycle.

C. Performance Measure(s)

The choice of performance measure or measures must be made with extreme care, as the compensation committee does not want to provide the wrong set of incentives or impose unnecessary risk on the executive. For example, rewarding managers based upon market share or sales growth alone may yield unprofitable sales that decrease shareholder value. Nor does a corporation want to use accounting earnings as a measure if it provides incentives to avoid certain investments, or if the accounting model does not accurately represent the corporation's true performance. In general, the goal is to maximize the informativeness and minimize the noise and riskiness in the performance measures chosen. Assuming that the measures chosen are not perfectly correlated with each other, and are positively correlated with true, yet unobservable performance, using multiple measures can be more informative than using a single measure. Basing compensation on these measures can also reduce executive risk, and consequently, the level of compensation the corporation is required to pay.

1. *Affect of Executive Characteristics on the Choice of Performance Measures*

Executive characteristics play a role in determining the measures used. If an executive has significant share and option holdings, the corporation should not use share price as a performance measure, as doing so would increase the executive's risk.[8] Conversely, for an executive nearing retirement, share price would be a good measure, as, if markets are efficient, share price reflects the long-run consequences of an executive's actions.

2. Affect of Corporate Characteristics on Choice of Performance Measures

A growing corporation might want to use revenues, rather than net income or cash flows, because the investments required to sustain growth decrease those measures of performance. Similarly, as noted in Chapter 11, a corporation whose profits are capped by regulators would not want to use net income as a performance measure. Generally, corporations want to use measures that are informative and under the executives control. That is, not only should the measure be informative about corporate performance, but it should also reflect the efforts of the executive. For example, airline profits are highly influenced by factors, such as fuel prices, outside of the CEO's control. Should a CEO be punished if an increase in fuel prices leads to a decrease in net income? As noted above, using multiple measures can be beneficial, both in measuring performance, and in reducing executive risk. These measures can include both financial and nonfinancial metrics. Consider again the airline. Customer service provides another measure of performance, one more controllable, or at least responsive to the CEO's actions, than fuel prices are. In general, a corporation dealing with the ultimate consumer, like an airline, might want to include one or more measures of customer service, whereas a manufacturer might want to include one or more measures of product quality.

D. Performance Targets

Targets or thresholds can be absolute, or they can be relative to either prior performance or the performance of competitors. An example of an absolute target is when no bonus is paid unless return on equity equals or exceeds 12%. An example of a relative target is when no bonus is paid unless the growth in earnings per share equals or exceeds 6%. Absolute and relative targets can be combined. For example: No bonus will be paid unless return on equity equals or exceeds 12% *and* equals or exceeds the median return on equity for the benchmark group of corporations.

1. Affect of Corporate Characteristics on Choice of Performance Target

Corporate characteristics will influence whether the target is absolute or relative. If the corporation is growing, then the target can be expressed in terms of growth, that is, the level of performance relative to prior years. In contrast, if the corporation

---

[8]It would also serve no purpose, as the share and options holdings already provide the incentive to maximize share price.

is mature, absolute performance would be a better measure. That is, if the corporation is not expected to grow, and thus, the change in the level of performance is expected to be zero, then using the change in net income to measure performance provides no incentives. Analogously, if the corporation has many close competitors, it should measure performance relative to those competitors to control for industry-specific risks that may be outside of the executive's control. In contrast, the lack of similar corporations, where similarity is defined as size, industry, product line, and so on, suggests the use of absolute measures.

The magnitude of the target, that is, whether the goal is 10% growth in earnings per share, or a 15% return on shareholders equity, should be dependent on the historical growth rate of the corporation and industry in which it operates. That is, certain corporations and industries have higher rates of return than others. For example, pharmaceutical companies traditionally have high return on equity relative to industrial corporations. Taking these differences into account is important, as a threshold that is too low and is thus easily achieved provides no motivation. Neither does a threshold that is too high, and thus, unachievable.

E. Method of Payment

Both corporate and executive characteristics will influence the method of payment. If the corporation is cash constrained then it would be more likely to (a) defer the bonus, (b) pay the bonus in stock, or (c) both. Deferring the bonus also provides a bond if the executive is found to have misstated current period results and/or later decides to breach his or her contract by, for example, going to work for a competitor. Independent of whether the corporation faces cash constraints, deferring bonuses can help with retention and the horizon problem. Deferring the bonus, which some companies require in whole or in part, helps with retention; if the executive does not remain with the corporation for the period required, he or she loses the amount deferred. Deferring the bonus, in particular making the bonus dependent on the future share price, may help mitigate the incentive problems associated with a looming retirement, as the ultimate value of the bonus is dependent on the stock price after the executive retires. Halliburton, as illustrated by the following passage, requires executives defer half of their annual bonus into stock units, which are then payable in cash over the subsequent 2 years.

> In order to maximize the link between the compensation earned under the Annual Performance Pay Plan and shareholder value creation and to focus executives' attention on a time frame longer than one year, only one-half of the bonus earned in the current year is paid in cash. The remaining one-half of the bonus is converted into Halliburton Common Stock equivalents and paid in cash in annual installments in each of the next two years, each installment based on the then value of one-half the stock equivalents.[9]

[9]Halliburton proxy statement, filed with the Securities and Exchange Commission, April 3, 2000, p. 16.

IV. STOCK COMPENSATION

The corporation must decide whether to grant any stock-based compensation, and if they decide to, whether that compensation should be in the form of options, grants, or both. They also must decide on how much, and consequently, what proportion of the compensation package should be stock based. As shown in Table 2.1, most companies (79% in 2000) award stock options to their CEOs, and roughly 20% also issue share grants.

A. Amount of Stock Compensation

There are two separate issues here. The first is how much and what portion of the compensation package should be stock based. The second, which perhaps should precede the first, is how to value that stock compensation. Consider the following example. A corporation decides that the compensation package should be composed of one-third salary, one-third bonus, and one-third stock options. They set salary at $1,000,000, targeted bonus at $1,000,000, and wish to grant $1,000,000 worth of options, with an exercise price equal to the current share price of $25. Theoretically, the most appropriate way to value the option is with an option-pricing model. Assuming the value of the option is $10 per share, the corporation would then grant 100,000 options. However, although theoretically a correct measure of the cost to the corporation (in that these options could have been sold to investors for this value), research such as Lambert et al. (1991) show that undiversified executives, who cannot sell the options, place a much lower value on the options than that generated by an option pricing model.[10] Another approach would be to value the options at their nominal value, that is, their exercise price. In that situation, given the exercise price of $25, the corporation would grant 40,000 options. Yet a third approach would be to value the option based upon the expected gain upon exercise, that is, as some corporations choose to do in their proxy statements. Assuming a 10-year exercise period and appreciation of 5% per year, the expected profit from each option would be just under $16 per option, thus the corporation would need to issue about 64,000 options. But is 5% the correct rate of appreciation? At a rate of 10% the expected profit per option jumps to almost $40, thus the corporation would only need to grant about 25,000 options. The last couple of sentences illustrate that not only is the valuation of the option subject to the method chosen, that is, grant date option model valuation versus nominal value versus expected gain upon exercise, it is also highly influenced by the inputs into those models. Valuation is also an issue with restricted stock grants. Although un-

---

[10]Consequently, the cost of the option to the corporation is greater than the value placed upon the option by the executive.

restricted stock grants should be valued at the current market price on the date of grant, restricted stock grants, because of the restrictions imposed, are less valuable to executives.

1. *Affect of Executive Characteristics on Amount of Stock Compensation*

Assuming the corporation can satisfactorily resolve the valuation issue, the corporation can then return to the issue of how much and what portion of the compensation package is composed of stock-based compensation. If an executive owns few shares, it would be optimal to make a large portion of the compensation package stock based. However, as noted above, it is difficult politically to tailor a specific package to each executive. Thus, the relevant benchmark would be shares owned by executives as a group. If their ownership was low (high), the corporation should make a larger (smaller) portion of the compensation package stock based.

The risk aversion of the executive group will also influence the portion of the compensation package that is made up of stock-based compensation. The difference in the value placed upon stock-based compensation by the executive, and the cost to the corporation, arise, in part, from executive risk aversion. That is, because of risk aversion, the corporation will have to replace $1 of fixed compensation with stock compensation costing more than $1. The corporation will do this as long as the marginal benefits from the improved incentives exceed the marginal cost. However, the greater the risk aversion, the greater the amount of stock the executive will demand to substitute for $1 of fixed compensation. Alternatively, as executive risk aversion increases, the lower the amount of fixed compensation the executive will accept in lieu of a given amount of stock compensation. Either way, using stock-based compensation becomes more costly to the corporation as executive risk aversion increases. Consequently, the portion of stock-based compensation should decline with executive risk aversion.

The horizon of the executive(s) will influence the composition of the compensation package. As noted above, an executive has little incentive to make investments that pay off after his or her retirement. This problem becomes greater as the executive approaches retirement age. Stock-based compensation may mitigate this problem because stock prices, in an efficient market, reflect the expected benefits and the costs of investments at the time the investment is made. Thus, as an executive approaches retirement age, the amount and portion of stock-based compensation in the compensation package should increase.

Also relevant is opportunity cost. As noted above, in many cases, the most likely employer of a corporation's executives are the corporation's industry competitors. Thus, to retain executives, not only should the corporation's level of compensation be comparable with those of its competitors, but the composition of the package should also be comparable. So the portion of compensation package composed of stock-based compensation should be influenced by industry norms.

2. *Affect of Corporate Characteristics on Amount of Stock Compensation*

Growing corporations should grant a large amount of stock-based compensation, due to the value implications of managerial decisions (Kole 1997). However, consider a corporation in a nongrowth industry that basically pays out all of its earnings as dividends. There is little or no expectation for stock price appreciation. Thus standard stock options provide no incentives. The corporation needs to grant restricted stock or a special dividend protected option. Although this type of option would provide the proper incentives and counteract the incentive to reduce dividends (Lambert et al. 1989), they are not observed in practice due to the accounting, tax, and implementation issues. For example, for accounting purposes they would be defined as variable options under Financial Accounting Standards Board Interpretation No. 28, and thus, an expense would have to be recognized, whereas no expense is recognized for most traditional options under Accounting Principles Board Opinion No. 25. For tax purposes, the executive would recognize income each time the option's exercise price were reduced, if that price were below the current market value. And implementation would have to be done carefully. Recall the confusion and ensuing lawsuits when Computer Associates (see Chapter 6, Section IX) adjusted the number of shares given to its top executives for stock splits, an adjustment that was not stipulated in the original plan submitted to shareholders (Johnston 1999).

As noted above with respect to bonuses, the use of a performance measure depends in part on the noise relative to the informativeness of that measure with respect to executive performance. The performance measure implicit in all stock-based compensation is share price. As discussed in Chapter 11, the greater the association between share prices and overall market movements, referred to as Beta, the more noisy share prices are as a measure of executive performance. Thus as Beta increases, the percentage of stock compensation in the compensation package should decrease.

A corporation's financial circumstances can also affect its preferences for stock-based compensation. As neither options nor restricted stock require a cash outflow, the use of stock-based compensation can conserve cash. In fact, stock compensation can be a source of cash, in that executives must pay to exercise their options,[11] and that both shares and options lead to tax savings (recall that Microsoft was able to reduce its tax bill by $5.5 billion dollars in 2000 due to tax deductions associated with their stock plans). Stock options, if the exercise price is set at or above the market price on the grant date, result in no expense for financial reporting purposes.[12] Thus, if the corporation desires to increase current cash flow and/or financial reporting income, it could substitute stock-based compensation for salary and bonus. Similarly, a corporation with little need for current tax deductions should

---

[11]Some corporations allow the executive to pay the exercise price with shares already held, in which case payment of the exercise price would not be a cash inflow to the corporation.

[12]Although no expense is recognized on the income statement, under the Financial Accounting Standards Board, Statement of Financial Accounting Standards No. 123: Accounting for Stock-Based Compensation, the cost of those options must be disclosed in the footnotes to the financial statements.

increase the amount of stock, either options or restricted stock grants, in the compensation package, as it allows the corporation to push those deductions into the future, when they may better be able to utilize those deductions. In the extreme case where the corporation does not anticipate being able to utilize those deductions in the future, it should consider granting tax-qualified stock options, which give the executive tax benefits in lieu of tax deductions for the corporation.

The amount of monitoring of executives should influence the amount of stock in the compensation package. As noted earlier in this book, monitoring in the form of active board members and/or owners can provide incentives for executives to increase shareholder value. In the absence of this monitoring, the compensation package must provide the incentives for executives to increase shareholder value. Thus, corporations with limited monitoring from owners and directors should issue a large amount of stock-based compensation.

B. Share versus Option Grants[13]

Once the corporation decides on the amount of stock-based compensation to include in the executive compensation package, it needs to decide on whether the stock component should be shares, options, or some combination of the two. Although both are valuable to employees, each possesses attributes that make them more or less valuable than the other. First, a share is implicitly an option with a zero exercise price. Thus, it is more valuable than an option. Holding the value of stock-based compensation constant, the employee would receive a larger number of options than shares. Further, as noted in Chapter 6, a share has value as long as the share price exceeds zero, whereas an option is only valuable when the share price exceeds the option's exercise price. Consequently, while a share grant imposes less risk on the executive, it also has less of an impact on the executives' willingness to take risk.

1. Impact of Executive Characteristics on Choice between Option and Share Grants

There is less risk with the shares because as long as the market price is positive, the employee is guaranteed the shares will have value. In contrast, options can, and do,

---

[13]Other forms of stock compensation exist but are omitted for brevity, and to focus on the most important and commonly used forms. For example, a third possibility is stock or share appreciation rights. Stock appreciation rights, which are sometimes offered in tandem with stock options, can be structured to provide the same incentives and payoffs as options. The major difference is that with a stock appreciation right the corporation pays, in either cash or stock, to the executive the difference between market and exercise price at the time of exercise, whereas with an option the executive has to pay cash and then may either retain the shares or sell them in the market. Thus, while payment of the exercise price with a stock option is a source of cash to the corporation, a stock appreciation right may result in a cash outflow. A second difference is that a financial reporting expense must be recognized for stock appreciation rights, but not for stock options.

expire out-of-the-money, effectively making them worthless to the executive. Thus as executive risk aversion increases, so does the executive's preference for shares over options.

To some extent the decision to grant options or restricted shares will be influenced by the executive's opportunity cost, as proxied for by industry norms. That is, if one potential employer grants shares and the other grants options, the executive will choose the form of compensation he or she perceives to be more valuable. As noted in Table 2.2, while virtually all corporations in all industries grant options to their CEOs, there is substantial variation in the use of share grants across industries.

2. Impact of Corporate Characteristics on Choice between Option and Share Grants

Options and shares, because of their different payoff structures, have different effects on executive incentives and decision making. Shares can actually decrease an executive's incentive to take risk, as the executive can suffer monetary losses as a result of the investment. In contrast, options, as long as they are not in-the-money, provide incentives to take risk, as the executive profits from increases in the corporation's share price, but does not suffer any monetary loss from a decrease in share price. Thus corporations with a lot of investment opportunities should primarily grant options, to provide incentive to take risk.

As alluded to above, for a corporation with a relatively fixed share price, that is, little upward potential or growth, options have no incentive effect. In those situations the corporation should grant shares. Yet as shown in Table 2.1, most corporations grant options to their CEOs in every year. Perhaps these corporations grant shares in addition to, rather than in place of, options.[14]

The corporation's financial circumstances can also influence the choice between share and option grants. First, share and option grants have differing cash and financial reporting consequences. Although options may result in a cash inflow when the executive exercises his or her options, if the corporation pays dividends, share grants may lead to cash outflows. Thus, a corporation with little cash will prefer options to grants. Similarly, although an expense must be recognized for value of shares granted to employees, options generally do not result in an expense for financial reporting purposes. Thus, corporations wishing to increase their accounting income should grant options rather than shares. Tax considerations are subtler, as both options and shares, assuming they are restricted, result in deductions in the future. Because future taxable income is uncertain, there is a chance the corporation will not be able to utilize those deductions. If that is a possibility, options may be more efficient in terms of minimizing the joint taxes paid by the corporation and executive. Consider first share grants. Assuming the section 83(b)

---

[14]Alternatively, perhaps corporations are unwilling to admit or accept a stagnant share price and thus grant options regardless.

election is not taken, income will be recognized by the executive and a deduction taken by the corporation at the time the restrictions expire, for the fair value of those shares at that time. Although the executive will always pay tax on that income, the possibility exists that the corporation will not be able to utilize the deduction. Consider now stock options. Assuming they are granted with an exercise price equal to the then market price, options are only valuable if the market price rises. This will generally occur only if the corporation is profitable, which will generally coincide with the corporation having taxable income. Thus, in scenarios where the corporation would be unable to benefit from additional tax deductions, the option would be out-of-the-money and hence the executive would not have any taxable income.[15] A second approach would be to grant tax-qualified options. Thus, although the corporation would not receive any deductions from those options, the executive would receive preferential tax treatment. If in the future the corporation needs tax deductions, it could provide monetary incentives to the executive to disqualify them for tax purposes. If the executive agrees and disqualifies those options, they are then treated as nonqualified and then he or she recognizes ordinary income upon exercise, and the corporation gets a deduction for that same amount.

C. Restrictions and Vesting

Shares and options may be granted with restrictions, some of which may expire with the passage of time (also known as the vesting period), and some of which require the executive and/or corporation to meet certain performance hurdles. Consider first share grants. These grants are commonly referred to as restricted stock because the executive does not have full rights to the shares until the restrictions expire. For example, although the executive may have voting and dividend rights immediately, he or she will not be able to sell the shares until the restrictions expire. These restrictions may expire with the passage of time, achievement of performance objectives, or some combination of the two. Consider next options. Options can have two levels of restrictions, the first imposed on the executive's ability to exercise the option, and the second on the executive's ability to sell the shares obtained upon exercise.

These restrictions affect the incentive and retentive effects. That is, assuming the shares and/or options are valuable, the longer the restriction period, the longer the executive is tied to the corporation. Of course, as mentioned in Chapter 6, if vesting is too far in the future, the executive may leave for a quicker payoff elsewhere. Further, as the restrictions on the executive's ability to sell the shares and diversify his or her risk increase, a risk-averse executive will decrease the value he or she

---

[15]Recall, however, that in equilibrium, the executive will receive a larger amount of options than share grants to make up for both this risk, and the fact that he or she needs to pay an exercise price with options.

places on the stock-based compensation. Additionally, forcing an executive to hold shares and options that are in-the-money can make the undiversified executive less likely to take on new risky projects. Thus, as the restriction period increases, the corporation would have to provide additional incentives to make the executive willing to take on new risks.

1. Affect of Executive Characteristics on Restrictions

Restrictions on the ability to sell the shares, whether restricted shares and/or shares acquired upon exercise of options, will be important if the corporation feels it necessary to increase executive share ownership for incentive or political purposes. Thus when executive ownership is low, the corporation should grant more stock-based compensation and impose restrictions on the ability of executives to sell those shares.

These restrictions will also be important as the executive nears retirement, to guard against policies that lead to short-term gains in the corporation's stock price at the expense of long-term profitability. Thus, restrictions on the ability of the executive to dispose of the shares should extend beyond normal retirement age. The time frame for which the restrictions remain in effect depends on a number of factors, including the gestation period for an investment.

As noted above, imposing restrictions on the ability to exercise options and/or sell shares increases the risk of the executive. Consequently, the executive will place a lower value on those options or shares than if there were fewer restrictions. Similarly, the increased risk may cause the executive to be less willing to take on risky projects. These issues become more important as executive risk aversion increases.

Finally, the executive's opportunity costs must be taken into consideration when determining these restrictions. All else equal, the executive will select the alternative with the fewest constraints. Thus, if a competitor offers the same compensation package with fewer constraints, the executive will elect to work for the competitor. Given that the most likely employer of an executive are the corporation's industry competitors, industry norms should be taken into consideration in setting restrictions.

2. Affect of Corporate Characteristics on Restrictions

The investment opportunities of the corporation should also affect the restriction decisions. The greater the growth opportunities and, in particular, the longer the gestation period of the corporation's projects, the more important it is to retain executives and, consequently, the longer the restriction period should be.

The corporation's financial circumstances affect the restrictions. Consider restricted stock. In the absence of a section 83(b) election, the executive will recognize income and the corporation will receive a deduction when the restrictions expire. Similarly, with nonqualified options, the executive will recognize income, and the corporation will receive a deduction when the shares are exercised. A corporation that does not foresee a need for these deductions in the near future will try to push these deductions as far as possible into the future by extending the restriction and vesting period. In contrast, a corporation in need of cash may want to make the vesting period for its options as short as possible and require payment of the exercise price in cash to improve its liquidity.

Financial accounting treatment also influences the type of restriction. For example, if the options vest with the passage of time, then they are fixed-type options accounted for under Accounting Principles Board Opinion No. 25, whereas if they vest with the achievement of performance goals, they are variable-type options accounted for under Financial Accounting Standards Board Interpretation No. 28. The former measures the costs of the options as the intrinsic value at the grant date, which is usually zero, whereas the latter measures the cost of the options as the intrinsic value at the date the performance goals are achieved, which would normally be positive. Thus making options performance based would result in an expense being recognized on the financial accounting income statement. Many have argued that a corporation's reluctance to record this expense causes them not to use performance conditions with options.[16] Thus, a corporation wishing to maximize its accounting income would not impose performance requirements on the executive's ability to exercise his or her options.[17] The accounting treatment also influences the restriction period for share grants. The cost of restricted shares is recognized as an expense over the restriction period. Hence, the longer the restriction period, the less expense is recognized in each period. So if the corporation desires to increase its accounting income, it will increase the length of the restrictions.

D. Grant Frequency

Shares and options should be granted as frequently as practical. More frequent grants work like the investment technique referred to as "dollar cost averaging." That is, the executive receives options with a variety of exercise prices. This portfolio of options makes it likely that at least some are in-the-money at any point in time. Consequently it reduces the risk due to market fluctuations and minimizes the need to engage in costly repricings!

The frequency of grants will also be related to the restrictions referred to in the previous section. Given that shares and options provide incentives to increase shareholder value, the corporation wants to make sure executives always have some stock-based incentives. Thus a corporation that grants shares and/or options every other year, but only imposes a 1-year restriction or vesting period, would have a

[16]Of course, an alternative interpretation is that executives want their ability to exercise and profit from their options to be subject to as few conditions as possible. Thus, the accounting treatment is an excuse, but not the cause of their reluctance.

[17]Perversely, restrictions that make the options less valuable to the executive increase the accounting expense to the corporation.

problem if executives exercised their options and sold their shares as soon as they were eligible to. The problem would arise as the executives would have no incentives to increase shareholder value in the second year of the cycle.

Related to grant frequency is the use of reload options. Recall from Chapter 6, that as the stock price increases beyond the exercise price, executives become more risk averse in that they now have something to lose if the share price drops. To control for this possibility, corporations should use reload options, which allow executives to exercise their existing options and get replacement options with an exercise price equal to the current share price.

E. Exercise Price

The vast majority of options are granted whereby the exercise price is fixed and equal to the current market price on the date of grant.[18] They need not be. As discussed earlier, it is possible to adjust the exercise price to some market or industry index, to filter out market or industrywide movements that have nothing to do with performance of the corporation or its executives. Alternatively, options can be granted at a fixed price, but at a price that is at a premium to the then existing market price. This premium could be set so that the executive does not benefit unless shareholders do well. As noted in Chapter 6, both are infrequently observed in practice. And yet, both have strong theoretical justifications and would play well in the political arena.[19] Consider the following proposal by the AFL-CIO contained in the Chubb corporation proxy statement filed with the Securities and Exchange Commission on March 24, 1999:

> That the shareholders of The Chubb Corporation (the "Company") urge the board of directors to adopt an executive compensation policy that all future stock option grants to senior executives shall be performance-based. For the purposes of this resolution, a stock-option is performance-based if its exercise price is either 1) linked to an industry index, such as Standard and Poor's Property-Casualty Insurance Index; or 2) significantly above the current market price of the stock at the grant date.

Although the proposal was not approved, it did receive almost 39 million votes, approximately one-third of the total cast,[20] indicating the proposal had appeal beyond the AFL-CIO, which owned only 26,900 shares.[21]

---

[18]For example, Matsunaga (1995, note 6) finds only 5% of his sample corporations issued options with an exercise price below the fair-market value at the grant date. Similarly, Hall and Murphy (2000) found that "94 percent of options grants to S&P 500 CEO's in 1998 were at-the-money grants" (p. 209).

[19]While there are strong theoretical justifications for granting premium and/or indexed options, Hall and Murphy (2000) argue that setting the exercise price at the grant date exercise price is optimal. They assert that risk averse executives discount the value of the option based upon the probability of payout, "and setting exercise prices at (or near) the grant-date market price maximizes incentives by ensuring a relatively high probability of ultimate payout" (p. 209).

[20]Chubb form 10-Q filed with Securities and Exchange Commission on August 13, 1999, p. 20.

[21]Chubb proxy statement filed with Securities and Exchange Commission on March 24, 1999, p. 22.

Adjusted options, that is, options whose exercise price is adjusted for movements in a selected index after the grant date, reduce an executive's risk by removing items that are out of the executive's control. To some extent, executives have been able to control their downside risk via repricings, while at the same time benefiting from upward marketwide movements, which may be why adjusted options have not been observed more frequently. Furthermore, adjusted options have implementation issues. For example, if the exercise price is to be adjusted, what index should be used: that is, should adjustments to the exercise price be based on market or industry returns; should those returns be calculated based upon the relative market values of the companies in the index or an equal weighting of all the corporations in the index; should the returns be adjusted for risk, etc. Additionally, an expense would have to be recognized for financial accounting purposes, as the options would be considered variable.

Premium options, or options granted with an exercise price greater than the share price on the date of grant, have fewer implementation problems, for example, no accounting cost need be recognized. The corporation could simply select a hurdle below which the executive should not benefit, and then price the option accordingly. Although executives would obviously prefer options at a lower price, the corporation could make the executive whole by increasing the number of options granted. Furthermore, premium options would provide more incentive to take risks. However, if it appears the options will expire out-of-the-money, which is more likely with a premium option, they have no retention effects.

Consider the following example, which illustrates the intuitive benefit of premium options. At the time the options are granted, the current market price is $100 a share and the rate of return on 10-year United States Treasury bonds is 7.2%. If the options are granted with an exercise price of $100, executives will profit from any appreciation in share price. Shareholders will not, however, in that there is an opportunity cost for their money. That is, they could invest in another corporation or in Treasury bonds, to name just two possibilities. If they invest in 10-year Treasury bonds, at the end of 10 years they would have $200. So at any price below $200 they would have been better off investing in risk-free Treasury bonds, whereas executives benefit whenever the price exceeds $100.[22] There is a range, when the share price is between $100 and $200, where executives benefit, whereas investors suffer opportunity losses.[23] Thus, setting the exercise price at a premium, $200, aligns the payouts of executives and shareholders.

Options can also be issued at a discount to the current market price. Effectively, a cross between a stock grant, which has a zero exercise price, and a market or premium priced option, discount options have both incentive problems, in that

[22]The example assumes the corporation does not pay any dividends.

[23]In advocating its above proposal, the AFL-CIO noted that Chubb stock price had lagged behind the S&P 500 and other relevant indexes over the previous five years, and that "Chairman and CEO Dean O'Hare stands to gain nearly $3.8 million from last year's grant of 99,250 stock options by achieving a mere 5% annual shareholder return over the term of the grant."

they discourage executive risk taking and are costly from both an accounting and tax viewpoint. Perhaps for these reasons they are not frequently observed.

V. DEFERRED COMPENSATION

Corporations have both tax and incentive motivations to offer pensions and other forms of deferred compensation.[24] As discussed in Chapter 7, tax benefits can arise from the executive's deferral of taxation from the current to a future period. For example, if the executive expects his or her tax rate to drop in the future, he or she will prefer to receive that income in that future period. While the tax benefits accrue to the executive whose tax bill is being deferred, implicitly the corporation will benefit by paying a lower level of compensation than it would have otherwise. In contrast, when the tax benefits accrue to the corporation, for example, where the deferral is motivated by Internal Revenue Code Section 162(m), the corporation may have to provide a monetary incentive for the executive to engage in the deferral, perhaps matching a portion of the deferral or paying a premium rate on the amounts deferred. In either case, the corporation has to be careful that the cost of obtaining those tax benefits, that is, the cost to the corporation of complying with Internal Revenue Code (for example, making the plan nondiscriminatory) and Employee Retirement Income Security Act (ERISA) requirements, do not exceed the value of those benefits.

In addition to being used to minimize the joint tax burden, deferred compensation can be structured, for example, via vesting requirements, to provide monetary incentives to executives to remain with the corporation. Focusing on pensions for the moment, recall from Chapter 7 that for highly paid executives, the majority of their pension comes from supplemental plans not subject to ERISA regulations. Thus the corporation is free to design the plan to improve incentives and retain employees.

A. Amount Deferred

When the executive defers compensation, the ultimate payout is determined by the amount deferred and the returns on that amount. In some cases, the corporation mandates the deferral, for example, to comply with Section 162(m). Most of the time however, it is the executive who determines the amount deferred, although the corporation can encourage deferral via matching and premium interest rates. From the viewpoint of the executive, deferral is beneficial for tax purposes, if he or

---

[24]The primary focus of this section is on nonqualified deferred compensation, for example, supplemental executive retirement plans, which make up the vast majority of deferred compensation for top executives of major corporations.

she expects a lower tax rate in the future. From the viewpoint of the corporation, deferral may be beneficial for tax purposes, for example, preserving deductions under Section 162(m), or to help provide the proper incentives. For example, as discussed earlier, to counteract the horizon problem, the corporation should provide compensation that is paid after retirement, with the ultimate payout tied to corporate performance after the executive retires.

B. Length of Deferral

For tax purposes, the maximum benefit may be achieved if the executive defers compensation until retirement when he or she will possibly be in a lower tax bracket and will no longer be subject to Section 162(m) requirements. However, taxes are not the only consideration. To the executive, the deferral is also a way of providing retirement income. Thus he or she may prefer that the payout be in the form of a lifetime annuity that begins after retirement. For incentive purposes, the corporation may want the deferral to continue for a period after retirement, so that its value might more fully reflect the actions of the executive took prior to retirement.

C. Deferral Vehicle

The returns can be based upon a fixed interest rate agreed to in advance; an interest rate that varies with some published rate, for example, the rate on U.S. Treasury Bills; the rate of return on a stock index, for example, the Standard & Poor's 500; or the rate of return on the corporation's own shares. As executives are risk averse, all else equal, they would generally prefer the more certain payout of the fixed interest rate or the rate of return on Treasury Bills to the more uncertain payouts associated with the rates of return on the stock index or a corporation's shares. However, all else is not equal, as the expected return on the market, that is, the stock index, is generally higher than the expected return on Treasury Bills. Furthermore, the corporation can offer premiums to encourage executives to defer their compensation into corporate shares. If executive ownership is low, making the payout dependent upon the corporation's share price provides incentives for the executive to increase shareholder value. Thus, the corporation may want to provide incentives to defer compensation into corporate stock, for example, by offering that stock at a discount. Of course, if executive ownership is high, then tying the payout to the corporation's share price imposes unnecessary risk on the executive, possibly causing them to take suboptimal actions to reduce their risk. Similarly, if the executive is nearing retirement, and hence, his or her horizon is affecting his or her incentives to invest in projects that pay off subsequent to retirement, the corporation wants to encourage deferral into corporate stock.

If the executive is risk averse, he or she is also concerned that the corporation have the wherewithal to make the promised payments in the future. While as noted earlier, funding the deferral results in adverse tax consequences, the corporation can use a Rabbi Trust to provide some security for the deferred compensation, although even a Rabbi Trust does not guarantee payment.[25]

D. Restrictions

As noted above, the bulk of deferred compensation is not governed by ERISA. Consequently the corporation is free to impose any restrictions it chooses, subject to the caveat that those restrictions will reduce the value of the deferred compensation to the executive. Consider the following example, which illustrates how restrictions can be used to encourage retention. The corporation has a lot of investment opportunities and, consequently, wants to structure the deferral to encourage the executive to remain with the corporation until retirement. Thus, it makes payment conditional upon the executive remaining with the corporation until age 65. The executive, while valuing those benefits, places a lower value on those benefits than he or she would have in the absence of restrictions. In particular, the executive will discount for the possibility that he or she does not remain with the corporation until retirement, and hence does not receive the benefit.

VI. BENEFITS

Corporations normally provide benefits including, but not limited to, health and life insurance to their executives. One reason is that these benefits have become so common that they are expected, not only by executives, but by lower level employees as well. Given that individuals can buy these "benefits" directly, why have they so often become associated with employment? One reason is the Internal Revenue Code encourages them. Consider the following example. An executive in the 40% tax bracket wishes to purchase a health insurance policy that costs $6000. To obtain the funds to pay for the policy the individual has to earn $10,000. Of the $10,000, $4000 will go to taxes, while the remaining $6000 will then go towards the purchase of the insurance policy. Alternatively, the employer can purchase the insurance policy directly and pay $4000 to the employee. The tax code encourages the latter. The reason is, from the employer point of view, whether they directly pay the executive $10,000, or they pay the executive $4000 and buy them an insurance policy costing $6000, the corporation has a tax-deductible expense of $10,000. In

[25]Recall that the only reason the executive is able to avoid taxation when the corporation funds the Rabbi Trust, is because the funds are available to the general creditors of the corporation in case of bankruptcy.

contrast, in the first situation the executive has taxable income of $10,000, whereas in the second, if the corporation meets certain requirements (to be discussed below), the executive only has taxable income of $4000. After the payment of $1600 in taxes, the executive has $2400 left under the second alternative, whereas under the first alternative nothing remained. So the executive is $2400 better off. In theory, the tax savings that arise from minimizing their joint tax burden will be shared between the executive and the corporation, thus while the corporation will buy the policy, it may not pay the executive the full remaining $4000.

It would be remiss not to, at least in general terms, discuss the requirements necessary for health insurance plans, and similar types of benefits, to qualify for this preferential tax treatment. A primary requirement is that the plan is nondiscriminatory, that is the plan does not discriminate in favor of highly paid executives. Effectively, for the executive benefit to qualify for favorable tax treatment, benefits must be offered to all. If not, then the premiums paid by the corporation will be taxable to the executive. Thus, if they do not have a qualified plan, corporations should weigh the benefits (tax savings to employees, some of which the corporation may be able to capture) against the costs to the corporation of implementing a qualified plan. If the corporation is not able to capture any of the benefits then obviously the costs outweigh the benefits.

As noted in Chapter 11, a problem arises in that the benefits must be offered across the board on a nondiscriminatory basis, whereas employees value those benefits differentially. In equilibrium, the largest amount by which the corporation can reduce explicit compensation by is the valuation placed upon the benefits by the employee. In some cases the valuation placed upon the benefits by the employee is less than the cost to corporation, hence there are no benefits to capture. Scholes and Wolfson (1992) and Jones (2001) noted that the use of "cafeteria plans" may mitigate this problem by giving the employee the choice between a menu of taxable and nontaxable benefits, and taxable salary. Thus, at a minimum, the corporation can reduce its explicit salary by the amount it provides employees via the cafeteria plan.

VII. SUMMARY

The focus of this chapter was on designing a compensation contract. The various components of the compensation package, that is, salary, bonus, stock compensation, deferred compensation, and benefits, were reviewed with an eye towards how the executive and corporate characteristics identified in Chapter 11 influenced the inclusion of the component in the compensation package, as well as the amount of the component.

The overwhelming majority of compensation contracts include a salary component, thus the issue is not whether to pay salary, but rather how much to pay. Salary, the primary fixed component of the compensation package, is important, not just because it is a major component of the compensation package, but because other components are sometimes linked to it, for example, when the target bonus is a percentage of salary. In general, salary should increase with increases in an executive's opportunity cost, risk aversion, and ownership. As a proportion of the compensation package, salary should increase with the executive's risk aversion and ownership and decrease as the executive approaches retirement age. Salary should also increase with the size of the corporation and the degree of monitoring, and be lower for firms that are cash constrained.

Although most corporations pay bonuses to their executives, in most cases the amount is neither fixed in advance nor guaranteed. Thus, bonuses are conditional compensation. The payments are made conditional upon implicit or explicit performance measures in order to provide the executive with the proper incentive to exert effort to increase shareholder value. Unfortunately in some cases, the existence of an explicit performance measure provides executives with dysfunctional incentives, for example, to manipulate results to increase the performance measure. Thus, the performance measure should be chosen with care, and consideration should be given to using multiple financial, as well as nonfinancial, measures. Also to be chosen with care are the targeted bonus amount, performance period, performance target, and method of payment. Executive characteristics, as do corporate characteristics, influence these choices. For example, the targeted bonus amount, or the bonus as a portion of the compensation package, will decrease with risk aversion and increase with the executive's opportunity cost. Similarly, a corporation with liquidity constraints is more likely to pay a smaller cash bonus and devote a larger portion of the compensation package to stock-based compensation.

As noted many times in this book, stock compensation is the fastest growing portion of the compensation package. In designing their executive compensation packages, a corporation must decide not only whether it will award stock compensation, but also if it does should that compensation take the form of stock options or grants. They must also decide on the amount of compensation, which will involve valuation issues, and the terms of the compensation. For example, if the stock compensation takes the form of stock options, the corporation needs to decide if the options should be tax qualified or nonqualified, what the exercise price should be, and the length, if any, of the vesting period. The corporation will also have to decide on the frequency with which it makes grants. Given that stock-based compensation provides a direct incentive for the executive to increase shareholder value, the choices made are essential in providing the proper incentives. As with salary and bonus, executive and corporate characteristics influence these choices. In general, if executive ownership is low, it would be optimal to make a large portion of the compensation package stock based. However, other factors need to be considered, such as executive risk aversion, the systematic risk of the corporation's shares, and the corporation's financial circumstances. For example, as executive risk aversion increases, so does the executive's preference for shares over options.

Deferred compensation, while not as sexy or politically visible as the other components of the compensation package, can be both material in amount, note the million-dollar-plus retirement packages discussed in Chapter 7, and valuable in providing executives with the proper incentives. For example, the choice of vesting period, as well as the benefit formula, can be chosen to provide executives with monetary incentive to remain with the corporation. Other choices that need to be made are the amount to be deferred, the length of the deferral, the deferral vehicle, and whether the corporation will match part or all of the deferral or provide a premium rate on the deferral. If used effectively, deferred compensation is also a way to maximize corporate tax deductions and minimize taxes paid by the executive.

PART V

Conclusion

CHAPTER 13

Recent Trends and Their Implications for the Future of Executive Compensation

I. RECENT TRENDS

Executive compensation, while always high, increased dramatically in the last decade of the 20th century. As illustrated in Table 2.7, mean (median) compensation more than quintupled (tripled) over just an 8-year period from 1992–2000.[1] This despite the outcry in the early part of the decade over excessive compensation, an outcry which led to increased Securities and Exchange Commission disclosure requirements, Internal Revenue Code restrictions on the deductibility of executive compensation, and Financial Accounting Standards Board modifications in the accounting treatment for employee stock options. Table 2.7 also shows that although each component of the compensation package increased over the 8-year period, the increase in compensation was primarily driven by stock options. That is, while mean total CEO compensation increased from $1,689,000 in 1992 to $8,466,000 in 2000 for an increase of $6,777,000, the value of stock option grants increased from $592,000 in 1992 to $5,589,000 in 2000 for an increase of $4,997,000. Thus, just under 75% of the increase in the value of the CEO compensation package came from the increase in the value of stock options granted.

This increased level of compensation from stock options was driven by both the increase in the value of the options granted[2] and an increase in the number of options granted. Holding the number of options granted constant from year to year,[3] a rising stock market, as occurred during the 1990s, leads to successive grants

---

[1]This increase is not specific to the corporations examined in this book. For example, Rappaport (1999) found similar results.

[2]Share price at the time of grant is an input into common option valuation models.

[3]Reingold and Grover (1999) report that 40% of large corporations grant options for a fixed number of shares.

being more and more valuable. Simply put, in dollar terms, a given percentage increase in a corporation's stock price leads to greater (dollar) option profits as stock prices increase. In addition, Table 6.6 shows that the number of options granted, both in absolute number and as a percentage of shares outstanding, also increased during the 1990s. Furthermore, Table 6.13 shows that the number of megagrants, defined as grants valued at $10 million or more, simply exploded during the 1990s, increasing from 7 in 1992 to 264 in 2000. Table 6.14 shows, by year, the executive with the highest valued grant in that year, which increased from the grant valued at $36,032,000 in 1992, to the grant valued at $600,347,000 in 2000. And the rising bull market made the exercise date value of these options even greater, as evidenced by the $650 million Charles Wang, Chairman and Chief Executive Officer of Computer Associates, made in 1999, the $589 million made by Michael Eisner, Chairman and Chief Executive Officer of Walt Disney in 1998, and the $227 million made by Sanford Weill, Chairman and Chief Executive Officer in 1997. These observations are consistent with evidence found by Hall and Liebman (1998), among others, who noted that "the dramatic rise in CEO compensation has been driven to a large extent by increases in annual stock option grants" (p. 679)

II. THE FUTURE

To predict the future, one needs to interpret the past. At many points over the last 30 years (see Baker 1977, 1978; Kraus 1980; Unger 1984; Patton 1985; and Crystal 1991) critics have asserted that executive compensation was excessive and out of control. Yet it continues to grow. More so, it continues to grow at rates far in excess of the rates of inflation and the growth of the economy. Why has this happened? Can this trend continue in the future?

A. Use of Compensation Surveys

It has been suggested (for example, see Williams 1985) that a corporation's use of pay surveys and their use of that information to pay above-average compensation (many corporations aim to pay between the 50th and 75th percentile) "impart an upward bias on compensation" (Ezzamel and Watson 1998, p. 222).[4] Given that no one expects consulting firms to stop conducting these surveys or for corporations and their executives to stop using them as justification for compensation packages, theoretically there is no end in sight, short of restructuring the corporation and its

---

[4]Thomas and Martin (1999) suggested that the increasing disclosure and dissemination of information about executive compensation could have the perverse effect of increasing compensation, as knowledge about what others are receiving could fuel pay demands by executives.

control processes. That is, short of ending the separation between the ownership and control of the corporation, executive compensation will continue to climb.[5]

B. Perfomance

Another potential explanation for the vast increase in compensation is the incredible performance of the firms. Hence, the increase in compensation represents pay for performance. For example, at the end of 1992, the Dow Jones Industrial Average was 3301, the Standard & Poors 500 Index was 433, and the NASDAQ Index 677. By the end of 2000 the Dow Jones Industrial Average had increased to 10,786, the Standard & Poors 500 Index to 1320, and the NASDAQ to 2470. Thus although mean CEO compensation increased by 401% over an 8-year period, the Dow increased by 227%, the Standard & Poors 500 by 205%, and the NASDAQ by 265% over that same period.[6,7]

C. Increased Demand for Executives

An alternative economic explanation for the growth in executive compensation requires executives to be viewed as products in limited supply (see for example, Kay 1998). That is, few people are qualified to be CEO of a public corporation. As demand for the product increases, the price will rise. Consistent with this hypothesis explaining some or all of the rate of change in executive compensation, the number of U.S. corporations traded on the New York and American Stock Exchanges, and NASDAQ, has increased from 6,712 on January 1, 1990, to 9172 on December 31, 1998. Although this trend may or may not continue, a trend that is sure to continue for some time is the increasing globalization of capital markets, which will increase the demand for professional managers to run companies outside the United States. For example, in 1990 there were 6000 companies included in Global Vantage, a database maintained by Standard & Poors of large publicly traded corporations around the world. By 2000 Global Vantage included over 13,000 corporations!

[5]Interestingly, the increase in stock compensation and the associated dilution could achieve this goal by transferring the ownership of the corporation from the shareholders to the executives, if the executives were then required to hold on to those shares.

[6]This growth has also increased the demands on the CEO (Murray 2001).

[7]Had this analysis been done at the end of 1999, prior to the market declines in 2000, the comparison would have looked more favorable for the CEO. That is, for the 7 years ending with 1999, mean CEO compensation increased by 227%, whereas the Dow increased by 248%, the Standard & Poors 500 by 240%, and the NASDAQ index by 501%.

D. Increased Use of Stock Compensation

Another factor in the increase in compensation over the past 30 years is the increase in the amount and proportion of stock-based compensation.[8] The huge increase in stock-based compensation has been driven by a number of factors. For example, academics, politicians, and shareholders, among others, have argued for the increased alignment of shareholder and management interests. That is, granting stock-based compensation will make executives act like shareholders, thereby remedying the problems associated with low executive ownership. In addition, stock compensation satisfies the call for "pay for performance," as the ultimate value of stock-based compensation is theoretically based on firm performance. Beyond this, the bull market has caused executives to think of stock compensation as riskless; the lack of accounting recognition has caused corporations to think of stock options as costless; and their tax deductibility has caused corporations to view stock compensation as a source of cash.

E. Increased Risk

Risk, both of compensation and of turnover, has increased over time. Compensation risk has increased as the package has shifted towards conditional and stock-based compensation. In particular, it has been argued by many that because of risk aversion, underdiversification, nontransferability, and the consequent early exercise, the value placed upon employee stock options by executives is substantially less than the cost to the firm (for example, see Hall and Murphy 2000). Consequently, the value placed on the compensation package by the executive is less than that which is reported in the proxy statement and popular press. In addition, the risk of being replaced has increased, as shareholders have become more involved and boards more proactive (Lear 2000).[9] In equilibrium, CEOs have to be compensated for these increased risks via increased monetary rewards.

F. Can These Trends Continue?

Can these trends continue? As noted above, consultants will continue to produce, and corporations continue to use (or misuse) compensation surveys, driving pay higher. In addition, the increased globalization of business and demand for professional managers should continue to increase, at least for the near future. Both of

---

[8]However, it should be noted that even though stock comprises the bulk of the increase in compensation, other forms of compensation have also been increasing at a rate faster than inflation, economic growth, etc.

[9]Leonard (2000), as well as Bianco and Lavelle (2000), Lear (2000), Martin (2000), and Lyons (1999), document that CEO turnover has gotten higher and CEO tenure shorter in recent years.

these factors will continue to drive executive compensation higher. The riskiness of executive compensation, that is, pay for performance, also seems to be a permanent fixture, although as discussed next, corporations may take steps to reduce that riskiness. If they do so, that could reduce the level of compensation. Similarly, the risk of turnover, although it may not increase, seems to be permanent, as greater expectations are being placed on the board of directors by shareholders. The major uncertainty is future performance, in particular, future stock price performance. Consider two scenarios, the first being that the bull market, which took a pause in 2000, resumes its upward climb, the second being the market becomes stagnant or even declines.

1. Bull Market Resumes

The market decline during 2000 should have convinced most executives that stock compensation is not riskless. Still, if the market should resume its climb, executives will continue to demand increasing amounts of stock compensation. Rising dilution, however (see discussion in Chapter 6), as well as the increased proxy statement disclosure requirements, and developments in accounting for stock-based compensation have convinced many, if not most, shareholders that stock-based compensation is costly. In addition, academics and politicians have come to realize that stock compensation is not the panacea they once imagined it to be. For example, Reingold and Grover (1999) reported on a study that found returns to shareholders in companies with the highest overhang, which is potential dilution associated with stock options, was lower than that of firms with medium or low overhang. Thus, there will be resistance, in many quarters, to increases in the level of stock compensation, and in fact, there may be resistance to stock compensation continuing at the same level. However, a bull market, and a share-the-wealth mentality, make it more likely the level of stock and overall compensation can be maintained, or even increased, than is likely in a down or stagnant market.

2. Market Becomes Stagnant or Declines

> When the market is up, executives all want equity," said James A. Hatch, an executive vice president at Compensation Resource Group, a pay adviser. "When the market is down, they all say, 'The market has nothing to do with the performance of this company.' "[10]

During 2000 all major stock indexes showed losses. The NASDAQ composite index dropped 39.3%, the Standard & Poors 500 Index 10.1%, and the Dow Jones Industrial Index 6.2% (Ip 2001). Former highfliers Priceline.com and eToys dropped 97 and 99%, respectively.

[10]Leonhardt (2000b), p. 12.

As noted throughout this book, stock compensation makes up a large and increasing portion of the executive compensation package. For example, Table 2.4 shows that in 2000, a mean (median) of 42% (42%) of the value of the compensation package consists of stock option grants, with an additional 5% (zero) coming from stock grants. What should a corporation do after a steep fall in its share price that results in options being out of the money? Simon and Dugan (2001) reported that "at 40% of the companies that issued stock options in 1999, those options were underwater in January" (p. C1). Should those corporations stop granting stock-based compensation? Should they shift from stock options to stock grants?

One could take the view that the compensation package as designed is optimal, and continue to include stock in the package. To maintain the incentives intended to result from the grant of options, which are now far out of the money, and hence, have little incentive and retentive effect for executives, the corporation would have to grant new options and/or reprice existing options, at the new lower price. Repricing options is less palatable than it was just a few years ago for a couple of reasons. First of all, it is politically unpopular with shareholders, whose shares are not repriced.[11] For example, the State of Wisconsin Investment Board introduced the following resolution, which would require shareholder of any future repricings, at the General Datacomm Industries 1999 annual meeting.

> "WHEREAS, the General DataComm Industries, Inc. (GDC) board has supported the adoption of numerous incentive compensation plans over the years, regardless of company or stock performance; and
>
> "WHEREAS, during the previous several years, the company has granted options for millions of GDC shares leading to an unacceptable level of potential dilution; and
>
> WHEREAS, notwithstanding high dilution and poor company performance over the past 3 years, GDC continues to retain a policy that outstanding options can be repriced to a lower exercise price at such time as the board shall determine;
>
> NOW THEREFORE, BE IT RESOLVED:
>
> PURSUANT TO THE AUTHORITY OF SHAREHOLDERS TO CHANGE BYLAWS, THE FOLLOWING BYLAW SHALL BE ADDED TO THE BYLAWS OF GENERAL DATACOMM INDUSTRIES, INC.: OPTION REPRICING. THE COMPANY SHALL NOT REPRICE ANY STOCK OPTIONS ALREADY ISSUED AND OUTSTANDING TO A LOWER STRIKE PRICE AT ANY TIME DURING THE TERM OF SUCH OPTION, WITHOUT THE PRIOR APPROVAL OF SHAREHOLDERS.
>
> SUPPORTING STATEMENT
>
> Stock option plans have been used for many years by corporate management as incentives for attracting and retaining qualified employees. Shareholders generally support the use of reasonable levels of incentive compensation to provide a competitive employment environment. However, excessive reliance on such plans is unfair to existing shareholders.

[11] While shareholders are not insulated from losses, sometimes employees are. Simon and Bryan-Low (2001) and Schroeder and Weil (2001) report that some companies, whose prices had declined, were "wiping out" prior stock option transactions that had occurred at higher prices.

Certain companies have continued to expand the use of such plans to the point where existing shareholders face serious potential dilution. As of July 31, 1998, GDC had options granted or available for grant to employees of over 4,936,688 shares, representing potential dilution of over 22%. This level of potential dilution and the trend toward even higher grants should not be supported.

GDC has a history of repricing "underwater-options". In May, June and July, 1997, the Company repriced 863,400 options with exercise prices as high as $15.50 down to a low of $6.75. GDC again repriced another 93,900 options in June, July and August, 1998 from as high as $15.88 to a low of $3.94 per share. GDC feels it can restart the clock on any number of options at anytime without regard for shareholder concerns. We are concerned about further repricings if GDC stock price continues to drop and have asked that the Company disclose any additional repricings it may engage in prior to the meeting. We urge management to raise the stock price, not lower the exercise price.

We believe GDC has been irresponsible in its use of incentive compensation, since options are authorized, issued and can be repriced without regard to performance. While we support the concept of incentive compensation, the above program is unjustified and inequitable to existing shareholders. Notwithstanding repeated requests, the company has refused to adopt a policy against repricing of "underwater-options". The above resolution will help ensure a measure of fairness to the use of incentive compensation at GDC."[12]

The proposal passed by a vote of 5,755,519 for, versus 4,947,119 against, with 195,563 abstained.[13] Second, the Financial Accounting Standards Board has now imposed the requirement that companies recognize an expense for options repriced. Under Financial Accounting Standard Board Interpretation No. 44: Accounting for Certain Transactions Involving Stock Compensation, any time a company cancels options and reissues new one within 6 months, the transaction would be considered a repricing and would result in earnings charges over the remaining life of the option. However, if the company cancels options and waits at least 6 months to issue new ones, there is no charge. Leonhardt (2001) reported that companies such as Sprint, Ariba, Lante, RealNetworks, and Pumatech have all taken advantage of this loophole to avoid the earnings charge. While avoiding the spirit of the FASB ruling, this maneuver is perfectly legal. More troubling however is the effect of the transaction on incentives. Consider the following paragraph from the 8-K filed by Sprint with the Securities and Exchange Commission on October 17, 2000.

On October 17, 2000, Sprint Corporation announced that its Board of Directors had approved a proposal to offer employees a choice to cancel certain stock options granted to them in 2000 in exchange for new options to purchase an equal number of the same class of shares. The new options will be granted six months and one day from the date the old options are cancelled. The exercise price of the new options will be the market price on the grant date.

Given the exercise price will be the market price on the grant date, which is 6 months and one day later, executives do not have the incentive to increase the

---

[12]General Datacomm Industries Proxy Statement filed with the Securities and Exchange Commission, January 15, 1999, p. 13.

[13]General Datacomm Industries Form 10-Q filed with the Securities and Exchange Commission, May 17, 1999, p. 23.

share price between the date of cancellation and the future date of grant (Brown 2001). More to the point, they have the incentive to make the price as low as possible on the future grant date so that their options will be worth more. That is, the lower the grant date market price, the lower the exercise price, and the greater the value of the option. Executives can do this in part by delaying the release of good news and accelerating the release of bad news. Yermack (1997), Aboody and Kasznik (2000), and Callaghan et al. (2000) found that the timing of stock option awards and stock option repricings are consistent with such behavior. For the record, Sprint's share price on October 17th 2000 was $23.19 and its price on May 18th 2001 was $20.90.

Taking the political and incentive aspects into consideration, unless the corporation is constrained in terms of its ability to grant new options, it should grant new options (immediately) rather than reprice existing ones. Further, the corporation should consider granting a larger than average number of options, as it is likely that a large part of the executive's option portfolio will be out of the money.[14] In addition, corporations should resort to more frequent grants to both minimize risk and maintain compensation now that the market is no longer increasing.[15] However, the corporation must be careful because, as noted in Chapter 6, executives can benefit from fluctuations in a corporations' shares even if the long-term trend is flat. In those situations, the executive, but not the shareholders, will benefit. To control for this possibility, the corporation should consider issuing indexed options despite the ensuing accounting charge. In a declining market, an executive may also be more willing to accept indexed options, rather than depend on an uncertain repricing, as the downward adjustment in stock price is automatic, if the index to which it is tied decreases.

An alternative view is that the optimal compensation package should contain more cash and/or stock grants to compensate for the loss in value of existing stock options and decrease in desirability of future stock options. Although this may be optimal, there are some who take a more cynical view:

> A look back at history would suggest that even in a slow or bear market, executives always manage to get theirs. When the market doesn't cooperate, the rules simply change. In the 1970s, for example, a prolonged bear market made options worthless. So companies switched over to bonus plans based on the achievement of cash-based internal goals and restricted stock; although those shares can't immediately be sold, unlike options they retain their value even if they fall below their grant price.[16]

Osterland (2001) reported "consultants confirm that renegotiated employment contracts and pay packages being offered to new hires involve a large cash element"

---

[14]Some companies have already taken this step. Osterland (2001) reported that "after its stock had plunged by 40 percent, Microsoft doubled its option grants to 34,000 full-time employees to make up for the underwater options issued in 1999" (p. 38).

[15]Osterland (2001) reported that Cisco systems is "considering stepping up the frequency of its grants to a quarterly or monthly basis" (p. 38).

[16]Reingold and Grover (1999), p. 73.

(p. 39). Among the companies taking this approach are Amazon.com, which in 2000 increased the magnitude of the signing bonuses it paid to its new executives, and paid, for the first time, cash bonuses other than signing bonuses, to four of its top executives (all but CEO Jeff Bezos).[17] Similarly, Condon (2001) reported that Globix gave Marc Bell, its Chief Executive Officer, $6 million of restricted stock, the first time it had granted restricted stock, after its stock price dropped by 95%!

Although executives will always look for ways to increase their compensation or maintain it at the current level, shareholders and their representatives on the board of directors may not be willing to acquiesce, especially in a declining market. In a declining market, large absolute amounts of CEO compensation cannot be justified as a small percentage of the increase in shareholder wealth (see Table 10.9). In fact, while in an up market, compensation amounts to a sharing of the gains, in a declining market, compensation, especially stock grants, can viewed as a transfer of ownership from shareholders to executives. Furthermore, in a declining market, the marginal product of an executive will be perceived to be lower.

Overall, the expectation is that in a declining market compensation should decrease, and we should see a change in the composition of the executive compensation package away from stock and toward cash. The shift towards cash can be explained by at least two reasons. First, in a declining market the perceived riskiness of stock compensation increases, so executives require a larger amount of stock to substitute for a given level of cash compensation. Thus, from the corporate point of view the relative costliness of stock-to-cash compensation increases, and in equilibrium the corporation itself will elect to replace stock with cash. Second, as noted above, in a declining market the amount shareholders and directors are willing to pay decreases. In equilibrium, the only way executives would be willing to accept a lower level of compensation is to reduce the risk of that compensation.

III. CONCLUSIONS

Predicting the future level and composition of the executive compensation package is wrought with uncertainty. An uncertainty caused by an unpredictable stock market, political environment, and tax system. Still some educated guesses can be made. The market gyrations of the past year have convinced many, if not most, executives that stock-based compensation is risky. Similarly, the events of the past decade, increasing dilution, revamped disclosure requirements, and revised accounting treatment have convinced most executives, as well as investors, politicians, and regulators that stock-based compensation is costly. Combined with the fact that executives value stock-based compensation at amounts lower than that publicized in proxy statements and the popular press, we should see a shift from stock to cash compensation.

---

[17]Amazon.com proxy statement filed with the Securities and Exchange Commission, April 13, 2001, p. 11.

This shift, because it reduces the risk of the executive, may reduce the overall level of compensation. That is, it may reduce the cost to the firm and the amount disclosed to shareholders, although it may actually increase the value of the compensation package to the executive. However, as noted above, this effect will be countered by an increased demand for executives worldwide, as well as the upward drift in executive compensation caused by the use of surveys.

Glossary

Academic research the hypothesizing, gathering, analyzing, and interpretation of information that is done by educators.

Agency costs the costs that arise because of the separation of the ownership from the management of the corporation.

Agent individual who performs services for compensation on behalf of one or more other individuals, collectively known as the "principal."

Annuity a series of payments of equal amount, usually made at fixed intervals.

Asset economic resources owned by a company.

Arm's length transaction transaction occurring between unrelated parties who are looking out for their own interests.

At-the-money option when the exercise price of an option is equal to the current market price.

Audit committee a group within a company's board of directors, to oversee and provide a check on the company's financial controls. Their duties include the hiring and supervision of the CPA firm engaged to conduct an audit.

Beta a measure of the extent to which the returns on a given stock move in tandem with the stock market. Also known as systematic risk.

Big bath when a company is having a "bad" financial year and takes additional accounting charges to increase the company's loss in that year.

Bonus form of compensation conditioned upon individual, group, or firm performance.

Black–Scholes option pricing model model developed by Fisher Black and Myron Scholes to value stock options.

Blockholder large shareholder.

Board of directors a group of individuals elected by shareholders to represent their interests.

Bond a long-term promissory note issued by a business or governmental unit.

Cafeteria plan compensation plan under which employees may choose among a menu of taxable and nontaxable fringe benefits and taxable salary.

Capital markets financial markets for stocks and long-term debt (can be both public or private).

Capital expenditures costs incurred to acquire a long-lived asset.

Capital gain gain realized on the sale of a capital asset (as defined by the Internal Revenue Code). For individual's, capital gains, if held for more than one year, are taxed at favorable (that is, lower) rates.

Capital stock transferable units of ownership in a company.

Cash flow the corporation's change in cash, based on its operating, investing, and financing activities.

CEO chief executive officer.

Chairman of the board director selected by his or her peers to lead the board.

Class hegemony theory theory which argues that executives share a common bond and that through boards composed primarily of CEOs, executives are able to pursue their own goals and interests.

Common stock a basic type of capital stock that possesses the rights of ownership, including the right to elect the corporation's directors.

Compensation all forms of financial payments and/or tangible services and benefits employees receive as part of an employment relationship.

Compensation committee a subcommittee of the Board of Directors responsible for setting executive compensation.

Compensation package the different forms of remuneration that are included in an employee's compensation.

Compliance costs costs associated with drawing up benefit plans to meet regulations, for example, the requirements of the Internal Revenue Code.

Conditional compensation compensation dependent on individual, group, or corporate performance.

Consumer price index measure of the average change over time in the prices paid by consumers for a market basket of goods and services.

Compensation contract an agreement that provides specific details of the executive's employment with the corporation.

Corporate governance laws, regulations, and customs affecting the control of the corporation, including, but not limited to the hiring, firing, and compensating of executives.

Deduction a subtraction in the calculation of taxable income.

Deferred compensation compensation earned in the current period that an employee agrees to receive, and the employer agrees to pay, in a future period.

Deferred compensation plan plan that allows, encourages, and/or mandates that executives defer portions of their salary and/or bonuses.

Defined benefit plan pension plan that provides employees with promised payments after retirement based upon predetermined benefit formulas.

Defined contribution plan pension plan under which the employer makes contributions to an employee's retirement account without specifying payments the employee received in retirement.

Depreciation the allocation of the cost of a tangible asset to expense in the periods in which benefits are received from the asset.

Dilution reduction in percentage ownership of existing shareholders associated with the increase in the number of shares outstanding over time. Major cost of stock option and stock grant programs.

Diversification reduction in risk achieved by the distribution of investments.

Dividends distribution of resources made by a corporation to its stockholders.

Dollar amount formulas defined benefit pension formula where the benefits are based on a dollar amount for each year of service.

Earning per share   net income divided by the weighted-average number of common shares outstanding during the year.

Efficiency wage   theory, that suggests that employees are paid a premium to provide them with the incentive to exert effort to avoid being fired, hence to increase productivity and reduce employee turnover.

Efficient market   a market in which prices rapidly reflect all information concerning the security.

Employee   individual who performs services for compensation under the direction and control of the employer.

Employee retirement income security Act (ERISA)   federal law that sets the provisions and standards for defined benefit and defined contribution pension plans.

Equity-based compensation   compensation whose value varies with the company's share price.

Event study   a research method that uses market reaction to a public disclosure of an action or event to infer the affect of the action on firm value.

Executives   the top managers of a corporation.

Exercise price   the price at which an option allows the holder to purchase shares of stock.

Expenses   decreases in the company's assets associated with its profit-directed activities.

Explicit contract   formal written contract between two parties.

External equity   the comparison of one's compensation to that of peers outside the corporation. That is, a comparison of compensation with peers in similar jobs, but in different organizations.

Fiduciary   person entrusted to oversee the investment of another, with the responsibility to make decisions in accordance with those individuals interests.

Figurehead theory   theory, that suggests that CEO should not be paid based upon operating results, but rather for his or her role as leader or political figurehead.

Financial Accounting Standards Board (FASB)   a private-sector organization that is in charge of determining generally accepted accounting principles in the United States.

Financial *keiretsu*   groups of firms, common in Japan, organized around their major lender and holding a large amount of cross-shareholdings.

Firm   generic name for business organization. Firms include sole proprietorships, partnerships, and corporations.

Fixed compensation   compensation that does not vary with firm performance.

Fixed costs   costs that do not vary with output.

Fringe benefits   usually a noncash item received by an employee as additional compensation.

Generally Accepted Accounting Principles (GAAP)   set of accounting methods required by the Securities and Exchange Commission (SEC) and the Financial Accounting Standards Board (FASB) for financial reporting.

Golden handcuffs   monetary incentive that the executive will receive only if they remain with the corporation for a specified period of time.

Golden parachute   large payments made to a departing executive of a company, usually made after the corporation is acquired.

Gray directors   directors who are not employed by the corporation, but have a relationship with it or its executives.

Hedging   strategy of taking offsetting positions to minimize risks.

Horizon the amount of time a person expects to spend in a particular job.

Horizontal equity refers to equity within a level of the organization.

Human capital the value of an individual's skills and abilities.

Human capital theory theory that posits that the value of the executive, and hence, his or her compensation, is based upon his or her accumulated knowledge and skills.

Implicit contract promises and shared understandings that are not expressed in a formal written contract between two parties

Inelastic the demand for the product or service is constant regardless of price.

In-the-money option an option where the exercise price is less than the current market price (an option that has a positive intrinsic value).

Income statement an activity statement that subtracts from the corporation's revenue those expenses that have generated the revenues, the result is a net income or a net loss.

Independent directors individuals (directors) whose primary employment is not with the corporation.

Indexed options options whose exercise price is adjusted for market and/or industrywide movements. Also known as market-adjusted options.

Inside directors those individuals (directors) who are employed full time with that corporation.

Interlocking directorate when a director is an executive of another corporation, upon whose board this CEO serves.

Internal equity refers to equity within the organization and encompasses both vertical and horizontal equity.

Internal revenue code (IRC) the foundation of all U.S. Federal tax law, containing all the tax laws enacted by Congress. Contains provisions addressing income taxes, estate and gift taxes, employment taxes, alcohol and tobacco taxes, and other excise taxes.

Intrinsic value of an option the excess of the current market price of a share of stock over the exercise price of the option at a point in time.

Liabilities debts or obligations, which will require the future expenditure of assets.

Liquidity a company's ability to meet its continuing obligations.

Managerialism theory theory that suggests that the separation of ownership and control gives executives and top managers the power to increase the level and reduce the risk of their compensation.

Marginal benefit incremental benefits associated with an action.

Marginal cost the additional costs associated with an action.

Marginal product the additional output associated with the employment of one additional resource unit, with other factors held constant.

Marginal productivity theory theory that suggests that in equilibrium, the executive should receive as compensation his or her value to the corporation.

Market-adjusted option options whose exercise price is adjusted for market and/or industrywide movements. Also known as indexed options.

Market share a company's percentage of total sales within its industry.

Megagrants large grants of options or shares.

Merger the combination of two or more business entities to form a single entity.

Net income the excess of revenue earned over expenses in a given period.

Noncompete agreements contract that prohibits an employee from working for other potential employers.

Nonqualified deferred compensation plans deferred compensation plan that does not meet Internal Revenue Code requirements for favorable tax treatment.

Nonqualified options options that do not meet Internal Revenue Code requirements for favorable tax treatment.

Operating cycle the period of time it takes a company to convert its inventory into cash.

Opportunity cost value of a resource in its next best alternative use.

Option-pricing model calculates the value of a stock option, normally incorporating the price of the underlying share, exercise price, risk, dividend yield, and time to expiration.

Ordinary income any income that is not a capital gain (or loss).

Out-of-the-money option options whose exercise price exceeds the current market price. (an option that has no intrinsic value). Also known as an underwater option.

Outside directors those individuals (directors) where the corporation is not their primary employer.

Pensions deferred compensation that provides income to an employee after retirement from the corporation.

Pension back loading a way of structuring a pension plan so that benefits paid from it increase with the individual's tenure with the firm.

Performance-based compensation compensation paid based on performance of the individual, group, or corporation.

Performance-vested options options whose exercisability depends upon future performance.

Political costs costs imposed by the government's ability to tax and regulate.

Premium options options issued with an exercise price exceeding the current market price at the time of grant.

Present value the amount that an investor would pay today for the right to receive a future cash flow.

Principal one who employs another to act on his or her behalf subject to his or her general control and authority.

Prospect theory theory of executive compensation that focuses on the executive's loss aversion, and the need to overcome that aversion.

Proxy a document giving one person the authority to act for another person (usually the power to vote shares of common stock).

Proxy statement statement given to stockholders prior to a stockholders' meeting.

Qualified options options that meet Internal Revenue Code requirements for favorable tax treatment. As a result, the employee will be able to defer taxation upon exercise, and if certain holding requirements are met, will pay taxes at the lower capital gains rate. Also see *Tax-qualified options.*

Qualified deferred compensation plan- deferred compensation plan that meets Internal Revenue Code requirements for favorable tax treatment. As a result the employer will be able to claim a tax deduction when the plan is funded, while the employee will be able to defer taxation until receipt of the compensation.

Rabbi trust trust established for the benefit of the participant by an employer, which the employer cannot touch, but creditors of the employer can. Allows a corporation to fund deferred compensation without the deferred compensation becoming taxable to the employee.

Reload options/replacement options options that allow the executive to pay the exercise price with previously owned shares and then receive new options to replace those used to pay the exercise price.

Repurchase program program whereby a corporation buys back its own shares, sometimes to mitigate the dilutive impact of employee compensation programs.

Repricing options either decreasing or increasing the exercise price of options that the executive already holds.

Restricted stock stock that has certain limitations.

Return on assets operating income expressed as a percentage of average total assets.

Return on equity net income expressed as a percentage of average total stockholders equity.

Revenue the dollar amount of goods and services charged to customers for these goods and services given by a company.

Risk the uncertainty regarding an outcome.

Risk averse the assumed preference of an individual for less risk.

Risk premium the difference between the return generated on a given risky item and risk less one.

Salary fixed contractual amount of compensation that does not explicitly vary with performance.

Securities and Exchange Commission (SEC) governmental organization that has the legal authority to set accounting principles and financial reporting requirements for publicly held corporations in the United States. Also regulates U.S. securities markets.

Severance package benefits executive receives when leaving a company.

Shareholder owner of capital stock in a corporation.

Share price the amount someone would pay to purchase one share of capital stock in a corporation.

Social comparison theory theory by which board members use their own pay as a reference point when setting pay of executives

Stock appreciation rights form of compensation whereby the corporation pays the executive, in cash and/or shares, the difference between the current market price and the exercise price of the stock appreciation rights.

Stock based compensation stock options and stock grants given to employees of the corporation.

Stock grants transfer of shares from the corporation to the individual, normally an employee, in exchange for services rendered.

Stock options allows their holder to purchase one or more shares of stock at a fixed "exercise" price over a fixed period of time.

Stock units compensation plan whose ultimate value is limited to the corporation's stock price.

Supplemental executive retirement plans additional pension plans and/or agreements designed for executive officers.

Systematic risk a measure of the extent to which the returns on a given stock move in tandem with the stock market. Also known as Beta.

Tax-qualified options options that meet IRS requirements for preferential tax treatment. As a result, the employee will be able to defer taxation upon exercise, and if certain holding requirements are met, will pay taxes at the lower capital gains rate. Also see *qualified options.*

Terminal earnings formulas   pension whereby benefits are based on average earnings during a specified number of years, at the end of a worker's career.

Time value of an option   the value attached to the potential increase in the stock price over the life of the option.

Tournament theory   theory that suggests that executive compensation is set to provide incentives, not to the executives themselves, but rather to their subordinates, so that those subordinates will strive for promotion to the executive ranks.

Treasury bond   a U.S. government security with a maturity of more than 10 years that pays interest periodically.

Unsystematic risk   movement of company's stock price not caused by market movements.

Underwater options   when the exercise price of an option is greater than the current market price. Also known as an out-of-the-money option.

Vertical equity   refers to equity in compensation across levels of the organization.

Vesting period   amount of time that must pass before an employee has unconditional right to pension, to exercise his or her options, or to sell restricted shares of stock.

References

Abdel-Khalik, A. Rashad. 1988. Incentives for accruing costs and efficiency in regulated monopolies subject to ROE constraint. *Journal of Accounting Research* 26 (Supplement): 144–174.

Aboody, David, and Ron Kasznik. 2000. CEO stock option awards and the timing of corporate voluntary disclosures. *Journal of Accounting & Economics* 29 (1): 73–100.

Abowd, John M. 1990. Does performance based managerial compensation affect corporate performance? *Industrial and Labor Relations Review* 43(3): 52–73.

Agarwal, Naresh C. 1981. Determinants of executive compensation. *Industrial Relations* 20 (Winter): 36–46.

Aggarwal, A., and G. Mandelker. 1987. Managerial incentives and corporate investment and financing decisions. *Journal of Finance* 42(September): 823–837.

Aggarwal, Rajesh, and Andrew A. Samwick. 1999. The other side of the tradeoff: The impact of risk on executive compensation. *Journal of Political Economy* 107(1): 65–105.

Allen, M. P. 1981. Power and privilege in the large corporation: Corporate control and managerial compensation. *American Journal of Sociology* 86: 1112–1123.

Antle, Rick, and Abbie Smith. 1985. Measuring executive compensation: Methods and an application. *Journal of Accounting Research* 23: 296–325.

Antle, Rick, and Abbie Smith. 1986. An empirical investigation of the telative performance evaluation of corporate executives. *Journal of Accounting Research* 24: 1–39.

Baber, William R., Surya N. Janakiraman, and Sok-Hyon Kang. 1996. Investment opportunities and the structure of executive compensation. *Journal of Accounting and Economics* 21(3): 297–318.

Bailey, J. 1999. Where it hurts: An accounting scandal endangers big payout For a retired CEO—Waste Management's board withholds $40 million from Buntrock, others—Alma Mater loses $3 million. *Wall Street Journal* (May 19) p. A1.

Baker, George, Robert Gibbons, and Kevin J. Murphy. 1994. Subjective performance measures in optimal incentive contracts. *The Quarterly Journal of Economics* 109(4): 1125–1156.

Baker, George P., Michael C. Jensen, and Kevin J. Murphy. 1988. Compensation and Incentives: Practice vs. Theory. *Journal of Finance* 43 (3) : 593–616.

Baker, John C. 1977. Are corporate executives overpaid? *Harvard Business Review* 55(4): 51–56.

Baker, John C. 1978. Are executives overpaid? Readers respond. *Harvard Business Review* 56(4): 54–66.

Balsam, Steven. 2001. Long-term firm responses to tax law changes involving the deductibility of executive compensation. Working Paper, Temple University, Philadelphia, PA.

Balsam, Steven. 1998. Discretionary accounting choices and CEO compensation. *Contemporary Accounting Research* 15(3): 229–252.

Balsam, Steven. 1994. Extending the method of accounting for stock appreciation rights to employee stock options. *Accounting Horizons* 8(4): 52–60.

Balsam, Steven. 1995. The Effect of the Tax Reform Act of 1986 on the composition of the executive compensation package. *Advances in Taxation* 7:1–24.

Balsam, Steven. 1993. Treatment of executive compensation. *Pennsylvania CPA Journal.*

Balsam, Steven, Eli Bartov, and Carol Marquardt. 2000a. Accruals management, investor sophistication, and equity valuation: Evidence from 10-Q filings. Working Paper, Temple and New York Universities.

Balsam, Steven, Haim Mozes, and Harry A. Newman. 2000b. Reporting of stock option grant information under FASB 123. Working Paper, Temple and Fordham Universities.

Balsam, Steven, Robert Halperin, and Haim A. Mozes. 1997. Tax costs and nontax benefits: The case of incentive stock options. *Journal of the American Taxation Association* 19(2): 19–37.

Balsam, Steven, and Wonsun Paek. 2001. Insider holding requirements, stock options and stock appreciation rights. *Journal of Accounting, Auditing and Finance* 16(3): 227–248.

Balsam, Steven, and David Ryan. 1996. Response to tax law changes involving the deductibility of executive compensation: A model explaining behavior. *Journal of the American Taxation Association* 18 (supplement): 1–12.

Bank, D. 1999. Microsoft to increase pay, stock options as demand for skilled workers grows. *Wall Street Journal* (May 10).

Banker, Rajiv D., Seok-Young Lee, Gordon Potter, and Dhinu Srinivasan. 1999. An empirical analysis of continuing improvements following the implementation of a performance-based compensation plan. Working paper, University of Pittsburgh, Pennsylvania.

Beatty, Randolph P., and Edward J. Zajac. 1994. Managerial incentives, monitoring and risk bearing: A study of executive compensation, ownership, and board structure in initial public offerings. *Administrative Science Quarterly* 39: 313–335.

Berle, A. A., and G. C. Means. 1932. *The modern corporation and private property.* New York: Commerce Clearing House.

Bertrand, Marianne, and Sendhil Mullainathan. 2000. Agents with and without principals. *The American Economic Review* 90 (2): 203–208.

Bhagat, Sanjai, Dennis C. Carey, and Charles M. Elson. 1998. Director ownership, corporate performance, and management turnover. Working paper, University of Colorado at Boulder, Spencer Stuart, and Stetson University College of Law.

Bianco, Anthony, and Louis Lavelle. 2000. The CEO trap. *Business Week* December 11: 86–92.

Bizjak, John M., James A. Brickley, and Jeffrey L. Coles. 1993. Stock-based incentive compensation and investment behavior. *Journal of Accounting and Economics* 16: 349–372.

Blackhurst, Chris. 1995. The sorry saga of share options. *Management Today,* November: 66–69.

Boschen, John F., and Kimberly J. Smith. 1995. You can pay me now and you can pay me later: The dynamic response of executive compensation to firm performance. *Journal of Business* 68(4): 577–608.

Brady, Diane. 2000. Who does Linda Wachner answer to? *Business Week,* August 7: 37.

Bremner, Brian 1999. The stock-option option comes to Japan. *Business Week,* April 19: 39.

Brickley, James A., Sanjai Bhagat, and Ronald C. Lease. 1985. The impact of long-range managerial compensation plans on shareholder wealth. *Journal of Accounting and Economics* 7(1–3): 115–130.

Brickley, James A., James S. Linck, and Jeffrey L. Coles. 1999. What happens to CEOs after they retire? New evidence on career concerns, horizon problems, and CEO incentives. *Journal of Financial Economics* 52: 341–377.

Browing, E. S. 2000. Despite stock slump, Wall Street binges on pay and perks. *The Wall Street Journal,* September 18: A1.

Brown, Clifton. 2000. GOLF; Nike deal for Woods said to be the richest. *The New York Times,* September 15: D4.

Brown, Larry. 1999. Managerial behavior and the bias in analysts' earnings forecasts. Working paper, Georgia State University

Brown, Ken. 2000. Now, some hope for their stock to tank. *The Wall Street Journal* June 4: C1.

Brubaker, Harold. 2000. Genesis offers stock for worthless options. *Philadelphia Inquirer,* March 12, P E1.

Bryan, Stephen, Lee-Seok Hwang, April Klein, and Steven Lilien. 2000. Compensation of outside directors: An empirical analysis of economic determinants. Working paper, Wake Forest University, Baruch College, and New York Universities.

Bryan, Stephen, Lee-Seok Hwang, and Steven Lilien. 1999. The change in operating and regulatory environment and the CEO compensation-performance sensitivity: An empirical analysis of electric utilities. Working paper, Baruch College.

Buckman, Rebecca. 2000. Microsoft uses stock options to lift morale, *Wall Street Journal,* April 26, p a3.

Burgstahler, D., and I. Dichev. 1997. Earnings management to avoid earnings decreases and losses. *Journal of Accounting and Economics,* 24:99–126.

Burgstahler, D., and M. Eames. 1998. Management of earnings and analysts' forecasts. Working paper, University of Washington, Seattle.

Bushman, Robert M., Raffi J. Indjejikian, and Abbie Smith. 1996. CEO compensation: The role of individual performance evaluation. *Journal of Accounting and Economics* 21(2): 161–193.

Business Week. 2000. The best and worst corporate boards. January 24, p. 142.

Byrd, John W., Marilyn F. Johnson, and Susan L. Porter. 1998. Discretion in financial reporting: The voluntary disclosure of compensation peer groups in proxy statement performance graphs. *Contemporary Accounting Research* 15(1): 25–52.

Byrne, John A. 1996. And you thought CEOs were overpaid. *Business Week,* August 26: 34.

California Public Employees Retirement System. 1998. *Corporate Governance Core Principles & Guidelines: The United States,* April 13. Sacramento, CA. California Public Employees Retirement System.

Callaghan, Sandra Renfro, P. Jane Saly, and Chandra Subramaniam. 2000. The timing of option repricing. Working paper, Texas Christian and St. Thomas Universities.

Campbell, Cynthia J., and Charles E. Wasley. 1999. Stock-based incentive contracts and managerial performance: The case of Ralston Purina Company. *Journal of Financial Economics* 51: 195–217.

Carlton, Jim. 2000. Dot-com executives depart for pre-IPO start-ups. *Wall Street Journal,* April 27, p. B6.

Carpenter, Jennifer N., and Barbara Remmers. 1998. Stock price performance following insider option exercise. Working Paper, New York University.

Carpenter, Jennifer N., and David Yermack. 1999. Introduction: Executive compensation and shareholder value. In *Executive compensation and shareholder value: Theory and evidence,* Jennifer Carpenter and David Yermack, editors.

Chauvin, Kevin W., and Catherine Shenoy. 2001. Stock price decreases prior to executive stock option grants. *Journal of Corporate Finance* 7: 53–76.

Clarke, Robert N., Martin J. Conyon, and Simon I. Peck. 1998. Corporate governance and directors' remuneration: Views from the top. *Business Strategy Review* 9(4): 21–30.

Cohen, Adam. 2000. Are lawyers running America? *Time,* July 17, 22–25.

Compensation Resource Group. 2000. Executive benefits: A survey of current trends.

Condon, Bernard. 2001. Share scare. *Forbes,* May 14, 146–148.

Conyon, Martin J., and Kevin J. Murphy. 2000. The prince and the pauper? CEO pay in the US and UK. *The Economic Journal* 110: F640–F671.

Conyon, Martin J., and Simon I. Peck. 1998. Board control, remuneration committees, and top management compensation. *Academy of Management Journal* 41(2): 146–157.

Conyon, Martin J., and Joachim Schwalbach. 1999. Corporate governance, executive pay and performance in Europe. In *Executive compensation and shareholder value: Theory and evidence,* Jennifer Carpenter and David Yermack, editors.

Conwell, Alan. 2001. Overseas, salaries are kept hush-hush. *New York Times,* April 1, Section 3, p. 7.

Core, John E., and Wayne Guay. 2000. Stock option plans for non-executive employees. Working Paper, University of Pennsylvania.

Core, John E., and David F. Larcker. 2000. Performance consequences of mandatory increases in CEO stock ownership. Working Paper, University of Pennsylvania.

Core, John E., Robert W. Holthausen, and David F. Larcker. 1999. Corporate governance, chief executive officer compensation, and firm performance. *Journal of Financial Economics* 51:371–406.

Coughlin, Anne T., and Ronald M. Schmidt. 1985. Executive compensation, management turnover, and firm performance: An empirical investigation. *Journal of Accounting and Economics* 7: 44–66.

Cowherd, Douglas M., and David I. Levine. 1992. Product quality and pay equity between lower-level employees and top management: An investigation of distributive justice theory. *Administrative Science Quarterly* 37: 302–320.

Cragg, Michael I., and I. J. Dyck. 2000. Executive pay and UK privatization: The demise of "one country, two systems." *Journal of Business Research* 47: 3–18.

Cross, P. 1977. Not can but will college teaching be improved? *New Directions for Higher Education* 17: 1–15.

Crystal, Graef. 1991. *In search of excess: The overcompensation of the American executive.* New York : W.W. Norton & Company.

Daily, Catherine M., Jonathan L. Johnson, Alan E. Ellstrand, and Dan R. Dalton. 1998. Compensation committee composition as a determinant of CEO compensation. *Academy of Management Journal* 41: 209–220.

David, Parthiban, Rahul Kochhar, and Edward Levitas. 1998. The effect of institutional investors on the level and mix of CEO compensation. *Academy of Management Journal* 41: 200–208.

DeAngelo, Harry, and Linda DeAngelo. 1991. Union negotiations and corporate policy: A study of labor concessions in the domestic steel industry during the 1980s. *Journal of Financial Economics* 30(1), 3–44.

Dechow, Patricia M., and Richard G. Sloan. 1991. Executive incentives and the horizon problem: An empirical investigation. *Journal of Accounting and Economics* 14(1): 51–90.

Defusco, Richard A., Robert R. Johnson, and Thomas S. Zorn. 1990. The effect of executive stock option plans on stockholders and bondholders. *Journal of Finance* 45(2): 617–627.

Degeorge, F., J. Patel, and R. Zeckhauser. 1999. Earnings management to exceed thresholds. *Journal of Business* 72: 1–33.

Denis, David J., Diane K. Denis, and Atulya Sarin. 1997. Ownership structure and top executive turnover. *Journal of Financial Economics* 45: 193–221.

Du Pree, David. 2000. NBA salaries. *USA Today,* December 8: 25C.

Dyl, E. A. 1988. Corporate control and management compensation. *Managerial and Decision Economics* 9: 21–25.

The Economist. 1997. Exercised. August 2: 59–60.

Ely, Kirsten. 1991. Interindustry differences in the relation between executive compensation and firm performance variables. *Journal of Accounting Research* 29, 37–58.

Ewing, Jack, Stephen Baker, William Echikson, and Kerry Capell. 1999. Eager Europeans press their noses to the glass. *Business Week,* April 19: 40.

Ezzamel, Mahmoud, and Robert Watson. 1998. Market comparison earnings and the bidding-up of executive cash compensation: Evidence from the United Kingdom. *Academy of Management Journal* 41(2): 221–231.

Ezzell, John R., and James A. Miles. 1995. Bank CEO pay-performance relations and the effects of deregulation. *Journal of Business* 68 (2): 231–256.

Fama, Eugene F. 1980. Agency problems and the theory of the firm. *Journal of Political Economy* 88: 288–307.

Fama, Eugene F., and Michael C. Jensen. 1983. Separation of ownership and control. *Journal of Law and Economics* 26 (2): 301–325.

Fairclough, Gordon. 2000. Philip Morris to pay special bonuses to executives, citing an "unusual year." *Wall Street Journal,* March 14, A22.

Fenn, George W., and Nellie Liang. 1999. Corporate payout policy and managerial stock incentives. Working Paper, Federal Reserve, Washington, DC.

Ferris, Stephen, Murali Jagannathan, and Adam C. Pritchard. 1999. Monitoring by directors with multiple board Appointments: Corporate performance and the incidence of fraud." Working Paper, University of Missouri Department of Finance and University of Michigan Law School.

Fierman, Jaclyn. 1990. The people who set the CEO's pay. *Fortune,* March 12: 58–61.

Finkelstein, Sydney, and Brian K. Boyd. 1998. How much does the CEO matter? The role of managerial discretion in the setting of CEO compensation. *Academy of Management Journal* 41(2): 170–199.

Flint, Joe. 2000. NBC will retain "Friends" in Lineup. Cast accepts deal. *Wall Street Journal* May 15:B16.

Foster, Taylor W., Paul R. Koogler, and Don Vickrey. 1991. Valuation of executive stock options and the FASB proposal. *The Accounting Review,* July: 595–610.

Freedman, Michael. 2001. Judgment day. *Forbes,* May 14: 132.

Gaver, Jennifer J., and Kenneth M. Gaver. 1993. Additional evidence on the association between the investment opportunity set and corporate financing, dividend and compensation policies. *Journal of Accounting and Economics* 16(1–3): 125–160.

Gaver, Jennifer J., and Kenneth M. Gaver. 1995. Compensation policy and the investment opportunity set. *Financial Management* 24(1): 19–32

Gaver, Jennifer J., Kenneth M. Gaver, and Jeffrey Austin. 1995. Additional evidence on bonus plans and income management. *Journal of Accounting and Economics* 19(1): 3–28.

Gaver, Jennifer J., Kenneth M. Gaver, and George P. Battistel. 1992. The stock market reaction to performance plan adoptions. *The Accounting Review* 67(1): 172–182.

Gaul, Gilbert M., and Frank Fitzpatrick. 2000. Coaches in the big time can break the bank. *Philadelphia Inquirer,* September 11:A1.

Gibbons, Robert, and Kevin J. Murphy. 1990. Relative performance evaluation for chief executive officers. *Industrial and Labor Relations Review* 43(3): 30–51.

Gibbons, Robert, and Kevin J. Murphy. 1992. Optimal incentive contracts in the presence of career concerns: Theory and evidence. *Journal of Political Economy* 100(3): 468–505.

Gilles, Paul L. 1999. Alternatives for stock options. *HR Magazine* January: 40–48.

Gomez-Mejia, Luis R. 1994. Executive compensation: A reassessment and a future research agenda. *Research in personnel and human resources management.* 12: 161–222.

Gomez-Mejia, L. R., H. Tosi, and T. Hinkin. 1987. Managerial control, performance, and executive compensation. *Academy of Management Journal* 30: 51–70.

Goyal, Vidhan K., and Chul W. Park. 2000. Board leadership structure and CEO turnover. Working Paper, Hong Kong University of Science and Technology.

Guay, Wayne R. 1999. The sensitivity of CEO wealth to equity risk: An analysis of the magnitude and determinants. *Journal of Financial Economics* 53(1): 43–71.

Hall, Brian J., and Jeffrey B. Liebman. 1998. Are CEOs really paid like bureaucrats? *The Quarterly Journal of Economics* 113: 653–691.

Hall, Brian J., and Kevin J. Murphy. 2000. Optimal exercise prices for executive stock options. *American Economic Review* 90(2): 209–214.

Hallinan, Joseph T. 2000a. Wendt gave up $20 million to take Conseco's CEO Post. *Wall Street Journal,* July 12, C16.

Hallinan, Joseph T. 2000b. Conseco removes two directors who failed to pay back loans. *Wall Street Journal,* December 13: B10.

Hallock, Kevin F. 1998. Layoffs, top executive pay, and firm performance. *The American Economic Review* 88(4): 711–723.

Hallock, Kevin F. 1997. Reciprocally interlocking boards of directors and executive compensation. *Journal of Financial and Quantitative Analysis* 32: 331–344.

Hambly, Bob. 2000. *Time,* April 24, 25.

Hambrick, Donald C., and Eric Abrahamson. 1995. Assessing managerial discretion across industries: A multimethod approach. *Academy of Management Journal* 38 (5): 1427–1441.

Hambrick, Donald C., and Eric M. Jackson. 2000. Outside directors with a stake: The linchpin in corporate governance. *California Management Review* 42 (4): 108–127.

Hartzell, Jay C., and Laura T. Starks. 2000. Institutional investors and executive compensation. Working Paper, New York University and University of Texas at Austin.

Hayes, Rachel M., and Scott Schaefer. 1999. How much are differences in managerial ability worth? *Journal of Accounting and Economics* 27 (2): 125–148.

Hayes, Rachel M., and Scott Schaefer. 2000. Implicit contracts and the explanatory power of top executive compensation for future performance. *Rand Journal of Economics* 31 (2): 273–293.

Healy, Paul. 1985. The effect of bonus schemes on accounting decisions. *Journal of Accounting and Economics* 7: 85–107.

Hebner, Kevin J., and Takao Kato. 1997. Insider trading and executive compensation: Evidence from the U.S. and Japan. *International Review of Economics and Finance* 6(3): 223–237.

Himmelberg, Charles P., Glenn R. Hubbard, and Darius Palia. 1999. Understanding the determinants of managerial ownership and the link between ownership and performance. *Journal of Financial Economics* 53(3), September: 353–384.

Holmes, Stanley. 1999. Boeing gives lots of extras to make sure Mulally stays—His deal stands out among execs. *The Seattle Times,* March 19, A1.

Holthausen, Robert, David Larcker, and Richard Sloan (1995). Annual bonus schemes and the manipulation of earnings. *Journal of Accounting and Economics* 19(1): 29–74.

Horn, Patricia. 2000. Loose change. *The Philadelphia Inquirer,* October 22: E1,E6.

Huddart, Steven. 1994. Employee stock options; *Journal of Accounting & Economics* 18(2): 207–231.

Huddart, Steven, and Mark Lang. 2000. Information distribution within firms: Evidence from stock option exercises. Working Paper, Pennsylvania State University.

Ip, Greg. 2001. Year of living dangerously. *The Wall Street Journal,* January 2: R1, R6.

Ip, Greg. 2001b. Floor show: If Big Board specialists are an anachronism, they're a profitable one. *The Wall Street Journal,* March 12: A1.

Ittner, Christopher D., David F. Larcker, and Madhav V. Rajan. 1997. The choice of performance measures in annual bonus contracts. *The Accounting Review* 72, 231–255.

Jensen, Michael J. 1993. Presidential address: The modern industrial revolution, exit and the failure of internal control systems. *Journal of Finance* 48: 831–880.

Jensen, Michael, J., and William H. Meckling. 1976. Theory of the firm: Managerial behavior, agency costs and ownership structure. *Journal of Financial Economics* 3, 305–360.

Jensen, Michael J., and Kevin J. Murphy. 1990a. Performance pay and top-management incentives. *Journal of Political Economy* 98 (2): 225–64.

Jensen, Michael, and Kevin J. Murphy. 1990b. CEO incentives: It's not *how much,* but *how. Harvard Business Review,* May/June, 68(3): 138–149.

Johnson, Alan. 1999. Should options reward absolute or relative shareholder returns? *Compensation and Benefits Review* 31(1): 38–43.

Johnson, Marilyn F., Susan Porter, and Margaret B. Shackell. 1997. Stakeholder pressure and the structure of executive compensation. Working Paper, University of Michigan and University of Texas at Austin.

Johnson, Shane A., and Yisong S. Tian. 2000. The value and incentive effects of nontraditional executive stock option plans. *Journal of Financial Economics* 57(1): 3–34.

Johnston, David Cay. 1999. Computer associates to appeal ruling on 3 executives' stock. *The New York Times,* November 11: C8.

Jones, Sally M. 2001. Principles of taxation for business and investment planning. *McGraw-Hill Higher Education.*

Kadlec, Daniel. 2001. Time bomb: 401(k)s stuffed with employer stock are a national calamity. Here's how to fix it. *Time,* March 5: 84.

Kaplan, Steven N. 1999. Top executive incentives in Germany, Japan and the USA: A comparison. In *Executive compensation and shareholder value: Theory and evidence,* Jennifer Carpenter and David Yermack, editors.

Kaplan, Steven N. 1994. Top executive rewards and firm performance: A comparison of Japan and the United States. *Journal of Political Economy* 102(3): 510–546.

Kato, Takao. 1997. Chief executive compensation and corporate groups in Japan: New evidence from micro data. *International Journal of Industrial Organization* 15: 455–467.

Kay, Ira T. 1998. *CEO pay and shareholder value: Helping the U.S. win the global economic war.* Boca Raton, FL: London: St. Lucie Press.

Kinney, Michael, and Robert Trezevant. 1996. Smoothing, big baths, and special items. Working Paper, Texas A & M and University of Southern California.

Klein, Frederick C. 2000. Tennis's glam girl seeks a bit of substance. *The Wall Street Journal,* May 30: A24.

Kole, Stacey R. 1997. The complexity of compensation contracts. *Journal of Financial Economics* 41: 79–104.

Kotlikoff, Laurence J., and David A. Wise. 1989. The wage carrot and the pension stick. Kalamazoo, MI: W.E. Upjohn Institute for Employment Research.

Koudsi, Suzanne. 2000. Why CEOs are paid so much to beat it. *Fortune,* May 29: 34–35.

Kraft, Kornelius, and Antonia Niederprum. 1999. Determinants of managerial compensation with risk-averse agents and dispersed ownership of the firm. *Journal of Economic Behavior & Organization* 40: 17–27.

Kraus, David. 1980. Executive pay: Ripe for reform? *Harvard Business Review* 58(5): 36–48.

Kroll, Luisa. 1998. Warning: Capitalism is contagious. *Forbes,* May 18: 220–221.

Kumar, Raman, and R. Sopariwala. 1992. The effect of long-term performance plans on stock prices and accounting numbers. *Journal of Financial and Quantitative Analysis* 27: 561–573.

Lambert, Richard A., William N. Lanen, and David F. Larcker, 1989. Executive stock option plans and corporate dividend policy. *Journal of Financial and Quantitative Analysis* 24: 409–425.

Lambert, Richard A., and David F. Larcker. 1987. An analysis of the use of accounting and market measures of performance in executive compensation contracts. *Journal of Accounting Research* 25, Supplement, 85–121.

Lambert, Richard A., David F. Larcker, and Robert E. Verrecchia. 1991. Portfolio considerations in valuing executive compensation. *Journal of Accounting Research* 29 (Spring): 129–149.

Lambert, Richard A., David F. Larcker, and Keith Weigelt. 1993. The structure of organizational incentives. *Administrative Science Quarterly* 38: 438–461.

Larcker, David F. 1983. The association between performance plan adoption and corporate capital investment. *Journal of Accounting and Economics* 5: 3–30.

Lavelle, Louis. 2000. CEO pay: The more things change . . . *Business Week,* October 16: 106,108.

Lazear, Edward P., and Sherwin Rosen. 1981. Rank-order tournaments as optimum labor contracts. *Journal of Political Economy* 89(5): 841–864.

Lear, Robert W. 2000. Fire the CEO! *Chief Executive* 153: 12.

Leggett, Karby. 2000. Small investors rail against China. *The Wall Street Journal,* December 28: p C1, C10.

Leonard, Bill. 2000. CEO's length of tenure is becoming quite short-lived. *HR Magazine* 45(5): 20.

Leonard, Jonathan S. 1990. Executive pay and firm performance, *Industrial and Labor Relations Review* 43(3): 13–30.

Leonhardt, David. 2000a. Report on executive pay: Will today's huge rewards devour tomorrow's earnings? *New York Times,* April 2, Section 3, p. 1.

Leonhardt, David. 2000b. Report on executive pay: Order of compensation universe reflects pull of new economy. *New York Times,* April 2, Section 3, p. 1.

Leonhardt, David. 2001. The letter, if not the spirit, on options pricing. *New York Times,* April 1, Section 3, p. 8.

Lewellen, Wilbur G., and B. Huntsman. 1972. Managerial pay and corporate performance. *American Economic Review* 60: 710–720.

Lewellen, Wilbur G., Claudio Loderer, and Kenneth Martin. 1987. Executive compensation and executive incentive problems. An empirical analysis, *Journal of Accounting and Economics* 9, 287–310.

Lippman, John. 2001. Creative differences: Battle over residuals could set the stage for a Hollywood strike. *The Wall Street Journal,* March 28: A1.

Loderer, Claudio, and Kenneth Martin. 1997. Executive stock ownership and performance: Tracking faint traces. *Journal of Financial Economics* (August): 223–255.

Lorsch, Jay L., and Elizabeth M. MacIver. 1989. *Pawns or potentates? The reality of America's corporate boards.* Cambridge, MA: Harvard Business School Press.

Lublin, Joann S. 1998. Major Disney investor scraps proposal calling for greater board independence. *The Wall Street Journal,* Dec. 4.

Lublin, Joann S. 1996. Sunbeam's chief picks holder activist and close friend as outside director. *The Wall Street Journal,* September 26: B9.

Lublin, Joann S., and L. Scism. 1999. Stock options at firms irk some investors. *The Wall Street Journal,* January 12: C1–4.

Lublin, Joann S., Matt Murray, and Rick Brooks. 2000. Home Depot nabs GE's Nardelli as CEO. *The Wall Street Journal,* December 6: A3.

Lyons, Dennis B. K. 1999. CEO casualties: A battlefield report. *Directors and Boards* 23(4): 43–45.

Mace, Myles L. 1971. *Directors: Myth and reality.* Cambridge, MA: Harvard Business School Press.

Main, Brian. 1999. The rise and fall of executive share options in Britain. In *Executive compensation and shareholder value: Theory and evidence.* Jennifer Carpenter and David Yermack, editors.

Main, Brian, Charles A. O'Reilly, and James Wade. 1995. The CEO, the board of directors and executive compensation: Economic and psychological perspectives. *Industrial and Corporate Change* 4: 293–332.

Mallette, Paul, R. Dennis Middlemist, and Willie E. Hopkins. 1995. Social, political, and economic determinants of chief executive compensation. *Journal of Managerial Issues* 7(3): 253–276.

Martin, Justin. 2000. CEOs in danger. *Chief Executive* 160: 22–28.

Masson, Robert T. 1971. Executive motivations, earnings, and consequent equity performance. *Journal of Political Economy* 79: 1278–1292.

Matsunaga, Steven R. 1995. The effects of financial reporting costs on the use of employee stock options. *The Accounting Review* 70(1): 1–26.

Matsunaga, Steve, Terry Shevlin, and D. Shores. 1992. Disqualifying dispositions of incentive stock options: Tax benefits versus financial reporting costs. *Journal of Accounting Research* 30 (Supplement): 37–68.

Mayers, David, Anil Shivdasani, and Clifford W. Smith, Jr. 1997. Board composition and corporate control: Evidence from the insurance industry. *Journal of Business* 70 (1): 33–62.

McKay, Betsy. 2000. Coke CEO to tie pay to diversity goals, create post on promotion of minorities. *Wall Street Journal,* March 10, A3.

McQuiston, John T. 1995. Lilco chairman declines a much-criticized increase in his $580,000 salary. *New York Times,* February 24, B6.

Mehran, Hamid. 1995. Executive compensation structure, ownership, and firm performance. *Journal of Financial Economics* 38: 163–184.

Menn, Joseph. 2000 Apple's reward to Jobs in options may be most ever. *Philadelphia Inquirer,* January 23, E3.

Meulbroek, Lisa K. 2000. The efficiency of equity-linked compensation: Understanding the full cost of awarding executive stock options. Working Paper, Harvard University, Cambridge, MA.

Meyer, Harvey. 2000. Boards take on the heavy lifting. *Journal of Business Strategy* July/August: 18–23.

Miller, M. H., and M. S. Scholes. 1982. Executive compensation, taxes and incentives. In Sharpe, W., and C. Cootner (Eds.), Financial economics: Essays in honor of Paul Cootner. Englewood Cliffs, NJ: Prentice-Hall: 179–201.

Mishra, Chandra S., David H. Gobeli, and Don O. May. 2000. The effectiveness of long-term accounting-based incentive plans. *Journal of Managerial Issues* 12(1): 48–60.

Mishra, Chandra S., Daniel L. McConaughy, and David H. Gobeli. 2000. Effectiveness of CEO pay-for-performance. *Review of Financial Economics* 9: 1–13.

Mollenkamp, Carrick. 2000. Retiring First Union Chairman cuts deal for $1.8 million a year plus his pension. *The Wall Street Journal* November 15: A10.

Morck, Randall, Andre Shleifer, and Robert Vishney. 1988. Management ownership and market valuation: An empirical analysis. *Journal of Financial Economics* 20: 293–315.

Morgan, Angela G., and Annette B. Poulsen. 2000. Linking pay to performance—Compensation proposals in the S&P 500. Working Paper, Clemson University and the University of Georgia.

Morgenson, Gretchen. 1998. Stock options are not a free lunch. *Forbes* 10: 212–217.

Moskowitz, Gary. 1998. Incentive alignment or cooptation? Outside director compensation at large publicly-traded U.S. firms. Working Paper.

Murphy, Kevin. J. 1985. Corporate performance and management remuneration: An empirical analysis. *Journal of Accounting and Economics* 7: 11–42.

Murphy, Kevin J. 1999. Executive compensation. *Handbook of labor economics 3,* Orley Ashenfelter and David Card (Editors). North Holland: Elsevier, 2485–2525.

Murphy, Kevin J. 1998. Executive compensation. Working Paper. University of Southern California, Los Angeles.

Murphy, Kevin J. 1995. Politics, economics, and executive compensation. *University of Cincinnati Law Review* 63: 713–746.

Murphy, Kevin J. 1996. Reporting choice and the 1992 proxy disclosure rules. *Journal of Accounting Auditing and Finance* 11(3): Summer, pp. 497–515.

Murphy, Kevin J., Andrei Shleifer, and Robert W. Vishny. 1991. The allocation of talent. *Quarterly Journal of Economics* 106(2): 503–530.

Murphy, Kevin J., and Jerold L. Zimmerman. 1993. Financial performance surrounding CEO turnover. *Journal of Accounting and Economics* 16: 273–317.

Murray, Matt. 2001. Critical mass: As huge companies keep growing, CEOs struggle to keep pace. *The Wall Street Journal* February 8: A1.

National Association of Corporate Directors. 2000. *1999–2000 Director Compensation Survey.* Washington, DC: National Association of Corporate Directors.

Newman, Harry A., and Haim A. Mozes. 1999. Does the composition of the compensation committee influence CEO compensation practices? *Financial Management* 28:3, Autumn, pp. 41–53.

Ofek, Eli, and David Yermack. 2000. Taking stock: Equity-based compensation and the evolution of managerial ownership. *The Journal of Finance,* June: 1367–1384.

Olney, Buster. 2000. Clemens's new deal is most unusual, *New York Times,* August 12: D3.

O'Reilly, Charles A., Brian G. Main, and Graef S. Crystal. 1988. CEO compensation as tournament and social comparison: A tale of two theories. *Administrative Science Quarterly* 33: 257–274.

O'Reilly, Charles A., James Wade, and Tim Pollock. 1996. Overpaid CEOs and underpaid managers: Equity and executive compensation. Working Paper, Stanford University.

Orr, Deborah, and Nigel Holloway. 1999. Earning more and hiding it. *Forbes,* May 17.

Orwall, Bruce. 1998. Disney holders use annual meeting to protest lack of independent board. *The Wall Street Journal,* February 25, p. 1.

Orwall, Bruce, and Joanne S. Lublin. 2000. Calpers to withhold votes for 2 directors paid fees by Disney. February 9, B10.

Orwall, Bruce, and Joanne S. Lublin. 1997. The plutocracy: If a company prospers, should its directors behave by the book?—Disney's Eisner shoots back at critics who say board isn't truly independent—"A Study in What Works." *The Wall Street Journal* (Feb 24), p. A1.

Osterland, Andrew. 2001. Keeping options afloat. *CFO* March: 37–40.

Palia, Darius. 2000. The impact of regulation on CEO labor markets. *RAND Journal of Economics* 31(1) Spring: 165–179.

Parade Magazine 2001. What people earn. February 25: 1–14.

Patton, Arch. 1985. Those million-dollar-a-year executives. *Harvard Business Review* 63(1): 56–62.

Pfeffer, Jeffrey, and Nancy Langton. 1993. The effect of wage dispersion on satisfaction, productivity, and working collaboratively: Evidence from college and university faculty. *Administrative Science Quarterly* 38: 382–407.

Pfeffer, Jeffrey, and Alison Davis-Blake. 1992. Salary dispersion, location in the salary distribution, and turnover among college administrators. *Industrial and Labor Relations Review* 45(4): 753–763.

Pfeffer, Jeffrey. 1972. Size and composition of corporate boards of directors. *Administrative Science Quarterly* 17: 218–228.

Philadelphia Inquirer. 2000. Sports in brief: Lakers extend O'Neal's deal for 3 years. October 15: C3.

Porac, Joseph F., James B. Wade, and Timothy G. Pollock. 1999. Industry categories and the politics of comparable firm in CEO compensation. *Administrative Science Quarterly* 44: 112–144.

Pourciau, Susan. 1993. Earnings management and nonroutine executive changes. *Journal of Accounting and Economics* 16: 317–336.

Prendergast, Canice. 1999. The provision of incentives in firms. *Journal of Economic Literature* 37: 7–63.

Pulliam, Susan. 2000. New Dot-Com mantra: "Just pay me in cash, please." *The Wall Street Journal,* November 28: C1.

Pulliam, Susan, and Scott Thurm. 2000. What goes up: For some executives the Internet dream has a deep downside. *The Wall Street Journal,* October 20:A1, A6.

Puri, Shaifali. 1997. The GM–VW battle: Blood feud. *Fortune,* April 14: 90–102.

Rappaport, Alfred. 1999. New thinking on how to link executive pay with performance, *Harvard Business Review* 77(2): 91–101.

Ratnesar, Romesh. 2000. Get rich quick! Europe's executives are finally following the lead of their U.S. counterparts and making a bundle on stock-option bonuses. *Time,* May 8: B7–8.

Reingold, Jennifer. 2000. An options plan your CEO hates, *Business Week,* February 28: 82–87.

Reingold, Jennifer, and Ronald Grover. 1999. Executive pay: The numbers are staggering, but so is the performance of American business. So how closely are they linked? *Business Week,* April 19: 72–74.

Reingold, Jennifer, and Fred Jespersen. 2000. Executive pay: It continues to explode—and options alone are creating paper billionaires. *Business Week,* April 17: 100–112.

Rickey, Carrie. 2001. Why we love Julia: Film's $20 million woman, poised to pocket an Oscar tonight, has it all—plus vulnerability and spunk. We love vulnerability and spunk. *The Philadelphia Inquirer,* March 25: H1.

Rose, Nancy L., and Chatherine Wolfram. 2000. Has the "million-dollar cap" affected CEO pay? *The American Economic Review* 90(2): 197–202.

Rose, Robert. 1998. Call to action: Labor has discovered the perfect issue for galvanizing workings: CEO pay. *The Wall Street Journal,* April 9: R8.

Rosen, Sherwin. 1986. Prizes and incentives in elimination tournaments. *The American Economic Review* 76(4): 701–715.

Rouse, Robert W., and Douglas N. Barton. 1993. Stock compensation accounting: Employee stock options might be today's most controversial accounting issue. *Journal of Accountancy* (June): 67–70.

Schellhardt, Timothy D. 1994. Passing of perks: Company cars, country-club memberships, executive dining rooms. Where have all the goodies gone? *The Wall Street Journal,* April 18: R4.

Scholes, Myron S., and Mark A. Wolfson. 1992. *Taxes and business strategy: A planning approach.* Englewood Cliffs, NJ: Prentice Hall.

Schroeder, Michael, and Ruth Simon. 2001.Tech firms object, as SEC gets tougher on their practice of repricing options. *The Wall Street Journal,* February 7: C1.

Schroeder, Michael, and Jonathan Weil. 2001. Firms must disclose effect of accords rescinding stock purchases, SEC says. *The Wall Street Journal,* February 2: C15.

Selz, Michael. 1996. Big companies heed investors' call for cutting outside directors' benefits. *The Wall Street Journal,* January 10:B2.

Sessa, Danielle, and Laura Saunders Egodigwe. 1999. Incentive plans can fuel insider buying. *The Wall Street Journal,* January 13: C1.

Shivdasani, Anil, and David Yermack. 1999. CEO involvement in the selection of new board members: An empirical analysis. *Journal of Finance,* 54(5): 1829–1853.

Silverman, Rachel Emma. 2000a. The jungle: What's news in recruitment and pay. *The Wall Street Journal,* August 1: B12.

Silverman, Rachel Emma. 2000b. The jungle: What's news in recruitment and pay. *The Wall Street Journal,* October 31: B18.

Simon, Ruth, and Cassell Bryan-Low. 2001. Unlike most investors, some insiders can cancel unprofitable stock purchases. *The Wall Street Journal,* February 15: C1.

Simon, Ruth, and Ianthe Jeanne Dugan. 2001. Options overdose: Use of stock options spins out of control. Now a backlash brews. *The Wall Street Journal,* June 4: C1.

Sridharan, Uma V. 1996. CEO influence and executive compensation. *The Financial Review* 31(1): 51–66.

Sloan, Richard. 1993. Accounting earnings and top executive compensation. *Journal of Accounting and Economics* 16, 55–100.

Smith, Clifford W., and Ross L. Watts. 1992. The investment opportunity set and corporate financing, dividend, and compensation policies. *Journal of Financial Economics* 32(3): 263–292.

Smith, Randall. 2000. Citigroup chief Weill's pay package rose 37% to $14.1 million last year. *Wall Street Journal,* March 8: A4.

Stodghill, Ron, Christina Del Valle, Greg Sandler, and Lois Therrien. 1992. United they stand. *Business Week,* October 19: 40–41.

Straus, Gary. 1999. Sweet exit deals get sweeter: Today's executives hit pay dirt when their golden parachutes open. *USA Today,* April 1: 1B.

Straus, Gary. 2000. Shareholder wants to oust Tyson Foods' board: CalPers questions accountability, compensation. *USA Today* January 10: 1B.

Sullivan, Robert. 2000/2001. Big bucks and baseball: The idea of overpaying for an athlete's services didn't start with A-Rod, and it won't end with him. *Time,* December 25/January 1: 144.

Swartz, Steve. 1986. How embarassing! Bear Stearns officials wallow in a windfall—Concern says its bonus plan has provided executives with "exorbitant" sums. *The Wall Street Journal,* August 26.

Swartz, Steve. 1987. Bear Stearns aides, despite pay cuts, can grin and bear it—Six executives at concern outearned all others at major public firms. *Wall Street Journal,* August 18.

Taussig, F. W., and W. S. Barker. 1925. American corporations and their executives: A statistical inquiry. *The Quarterly Journal of Economics,* November: 1–51.

Teachers Insurance and Annuity Association—College Retirement Equities Fund. 2000. *Corporate governance: TIAA-CREF's policy statement on corporate governance.* New York: Teachers Insurance and Annuity Association—College Retirement Equities Fund.

Tehranian, Hassan, and James F. Waegelein. 1985. Market reaction to short-term executive compensation plan adoption. *Journal of Accounting and Economics* 7(1–3): 131–144.

Tejada, Carlos. 1997. Longtime Tandy director quits board, says he was punished for faulting CEO. *Wall Street Journal,* January 16: B9.

Thomas, Randall S., and Kenneth J. Martin. 1999. The effect of shareholder proposals on executive compensation. *University of Cincinnati Law Review,* 67: 1021–1081.

Thurm, Scott. 2001. No-exit strategies: Their outlook bright, fiber-optics firms put job-hoppers on notice. *The Wall Street Journal,* February 6: A1.

Tosi, Henry, Steve Werner, Jeffrey P. Katz, and Luis R. Gomez-Mejia. 2000. How much does performance matter? A meta-analysis of CEO pay studies. *Journal of Management* 26(2): 301–339.

Towers, Perrin. 1999. Worldwide total remuneration.

Toyne, Michael F., James A. Millar, and Bruce L. Dixon. 2000. The relation between CEO control and the risk of CEO compensation. *Journal of Corporate Finance* 6: 291–306.

Unger, Harlow. 1984. Life at the top is too rich, U.S. critics say. *Industrial Management* 8(6): 14.

Ungson, Gerardo Rivera, and Richard M. Steers. 1984. Motivation and politics in executive compensation. *Academy of Management Review* 9(2): 313–323.

Wade, James, Charles A. O'Reilly, and Ike Chandratat. 1990. Golden parachutes: CEOs and the exercise of social influence. *Administrative Science Quarterly* 35: 587–603.

Wall Street Journal. 1999. Chairman and CEO of U.S. air decline their cash bonuses. May 20)

Wall Street Journal. 2000a. J.C. Penney Co. CEO's salary is raised 73%, but bonus is cut by 93%. April 17: B13.

Wall Street Journal. 2000b. Retired Kodak CEO received $4.9 million in pay in 1999. March 14, A8.

Wall Street Journal. 2000c, Big pay for directors of small companies comes to light in a new study. March 9, A1.

Wall Street Journal. 2000d. Retiring plans, January 25, B14.

Wall Street Journal. 2000e. Law firm hits $1 billion mark. July 5:B1.

Wall Street Journal. 2000f. CEO's deal to trade his salary for stock begins to pay off big, September 13: B6.

Walsh, James P. 1989. Doing a deal: Merger and acquisition negotiations and their impact upon target company top management turnover. *Strategic Management Journal* 10: 307–322.

Walsh, James P. 1988. Top management turnover following mergers and acquisitions. *Strategic Management Journal* 9(2): 173–183.

Warner, Jerold B., Ross L. Watts, and Karen H. Wruck. 1988. Stock prices and top management changes. *Journal of Financial Economics* 20: 461–492.

Watts, Ross L., and Jerold L. Zimmerman. 1986. *Positive accounting theory,* Englewood Cliffs, NJ: Prentice Hall.

Weisbach, Michael S. 1988. Outside directors and CEO turnover. *Journal of Financial Economics* 20:431–460.

Welles, Edward O. 1998. Motherhood, apple pie & stock options. *Inc.* February: 84–91.

Westphal, James J., and Edward S. Zajac. 1994. Substance and symbolism in CEO's long-term incentive plans. *Administrative Science Quarterly* 39: 367–390.

White, Lourdes Ferreira. 1996. Executive compensation and dividend policy. *Journal of Corporate Finance* 2: 335–358.

Whitford, David. 1999. Consultants chase the Internet express: What the departure of Andersen Consulting's chief really means. *Fortune,* October 25: 44.

Williams, Melissa A., Andrew K. Prevost, and Ramesh P. Rao. 2000. Institutional shareholder proposals and the impact on top-management compensation. Working Paper, Georgia State University, Cordia University, and Texas Tech University.

Williams, Monci Jo. 1985. Why chief executives' pay keeps rising. *Fortune* April 1: 66–76.

Wiseman, Robert M. and Luis R. Gomez-Mejia. 1998. A behavioral agency model of managerial risk taking. *Academy of Management Review* 23(1): 133–153.

Woodruff, David. 2001. Europe, a latecomer, embraces options. *The Wall Street Journal* May 15: A18.

Yeo, Gillian H. H., Sheng-Syan Chen, Kim Wai Ho, and Cheng-few Lee. 1999. Effects of executive share option plans on shareholder wealth and firm performance: The Singapore evidence. *The Financial Review* 34: 1–20.

Yermack, David. 1995. Do corporations award CEO stock options effectively? *Journal of Financial Economics* 39 (October-November): 237–269.

Yermack, David. 1996. Higher market valuation of companies with a small board of directors. *Journal of Financial Economics* 40: 185–211.

Yermack, David. 1997. Good timing: CEO stock option awards and company news announcements. *The Journal of Finance* 52 (2): 449–476.

Zajac, Edward J., and James D. Westphal. 1995. Accounting for the explanations of CEO compensation: Substance and symbolism. *Administrative Science Quarterly* 40: 283–308.

Zhou, Xianming. 1999. CEO pay, firm size, and corporate performance: Evidence from Canada, Working Paper, University of Sydney.

Zuckerman, Gregory, Randall Smith, and Ianthe Dugan. 2000. Steinberg has seen rich payoff. *Wall Street Journal* August 16: C1.

Zuckerman, Laurence. 1999. Boeing bets faith and money on jetliner executive. *New York Times,* March 19, C4.

Zuckerman, Sam. 2000. CalPERS protests B of A chief's huge pay: State pension system has say in bank board. *The San Francisco Chronicle,* April 12, A1.

Index